# The Outpatient Treatment of Eating Disorders

# The Outpatient Treatment of Eating Disorders

A Guide for Therapists, Dietitians, and Physicians

James E. Mitchell, M.D., Editor

University of Minnesota Press
Minneapolis • London

Published by the University of Minnesota Press
111 Third Avenue South, Suite 290
Minneapolis, MN 55401-2520
http://www.upress.umn.edu

Library of Congress Cataloging-in-Publication Data

The outpatient treatment of eating disorders : a guide for therapists, dietitians, and physicians / James E. Mitchell, editor.
      p.    ; cm.
   Includes bibliographical references and index.
   ISBN 0-8166-3718-0 (HC : alk. paper)
   1. Eating disorders—Treatment.   2. Ambulatory medical care.
3. Cognitive therapy.
   [DNLM: 1. Eating Disorders—therapy. WM 175 094 2001]
   I.   Mitchell, James E. (James Edward), 1947–
   RC552.E18  093  2001
   616.85'2606—dc21                                    2001001831

Printed in the United States of America on acid-free paper

The University of Minnesota is an equal-opportunity educator and employer.


12 11 10 09 08 07 06 05 04 03 02 01   10 9 8 7 6 5 4 3 2 1

# Contents

# Preface

This book was designed to provide clinical practitioners who work with eating disorder patients with a concise yet scholarly review of the recent literature on anorexia nervosa, bulimia nervosa, and binge eating disorder, and also a more in-depth, detailed treatment approach emphasizing the outpatient management of patients with these disorders.

A logical question to ask is, "Why another book on eating disorders?" Many excellent books have been published over the past decade. We wrote this book to provide a comprehensive model based on cognitive-behavioral techniques that includes information on the roles of the various health care providers involved, including psychiatrists, nonpsychiatric physicians, psychologists and other psychotherapists, dietitians, and exercise physiologists.

We apply the information in the treatment chapters to specific case vignettes, which we hope provide a broad integrative approach to these "patients." The treatment chapters refer to the same three "patients": a woman with anorexia nervosa, a woman with bulimia nervosa, and a man with binge eating disorder. Obviously, this approach is not meant to imply that patients with these disorders can all be treated in the same way. As we know, the clinical variability among patients with eating disorders is dramatic both in terms of their presentation and in terms of their needs in treatment. We offer these vignettes as templates to be modified in clinical practice.

All of us who work in this field know that the treatment of eating disorders is changing rapidly. Developments over the past decade have been substantial, and one can anticipate continued progress. Therefore, readers of this text are encouraged to keep abreast of the most recent

developments, which will supplement and at times replace the recommendations offered here.

James E. Mitchell, M.D.
Fargo, North Dakota

# Part I

# Overview of Eating Disorders

# Introduction

# Literature Overview

Part I of this book is an overview of literature on eating disorders. In chapters 1, 2, and 3, we succinctly review the literature on anorexia nervosa, bulimia nervosa, and binge eating disorder, and in chapter 4, the literature on eating disorders not otherwise specified. This material will be of most utility to those practitioners who have come to the field of eating disorders recently. Clinicians who are experienced in working with this patient population will probably already know much of this work, although some of the more recent findings summarized may be of interest.

In considering this literature it is important to remember that many patients being seen in clinics—in some series the majority of patients—do not meet formal criteria for an eating disorder and are so-called subthreshold or atypical cases and are classified as eating disorders not otherwise specified. Therefore, these patients should not be thought of as simply a "fringe" group of atypical patients but as a group that encompasses a variety of eating disorder problems. Whether any of these groupings will be given individual diagnoses remains unclear, but it is reasonable to assume that this might eventually be the case.

In reading this literature the reader is encouraged to remember that this material is in a distilled form. Those who are interested in a deeper understanding of these disorders are encouraged to read other texts that focus in greater detail on the individual illnesses discussed.

Chapter 1

# Anorexia Nervosa

*Melissa Pederson Mussell, James E. Mitchell, and Roslyn B. Binford*

Although descriptions of anorexia nervosa have been well documented since the sixteenth century (see Silverman, 1995), the term *anorexia* was first used by Sir William Gull (1874) in a manuscript presenting case descriptions of four women exhibiting significantly low body weight. The derivation of the term *anorexia* is Greek for "loss of appetite." It is important to note, however, that individuals with anorexia nervosa do not experience a loss of desire to eat, but rather a fear of eating that promotes excessive dieting and subsequent weight loss. Within the past few decades, attitudinal disturbance regarding weight and shape has emerged as a central feature of the disorder, which has been referred to as a "relentless pursuit of thinness" (Bruch, 1966, p. 555), "weight phobia" (Crisp, 1967, p. 5), and "morbid fear of becoming fat" (Russell, 1970, p. 134).

This aspect of the disorder is reflected in the DSM-IV (APA, 1994), which indicates that individuals with anorexia nervosa exhibit "an intense fear of gaining weight or becoming fat, even though underweight" (p. 544). In fact, individuals with anorexia nervosa often experience panic as a result of minimal weight gain, which may actually represent normal weight fluctuation. Additional DSM-IV criteria include refusal to maintain what would be expected to be a minimally normal (e.g., at least 85%) body weight, or for younger individuals, to refuse to achieve an expected weight gain. Furthermore, individuals with anorexia nervosa exhibit at least one of the following symptoms: attitudinal disturbance regarding weight and shape, self-evaluation "unduly influence(d)" by body weight and shape, or denial of the seriousness of maintaining a low body weight. The final DSM-IV criterion for anorexia nervosa is amenorrhea, operationalized as an absence of menstrual periods for at least three consecutive months.

5

## Associated Features and Differential Diagnosis

The presence of binge eating and vomiting among some individuals with anorexia nervosa has been recognized for some time (e.g., Bliss & Branch, 1960), and is found in approximately 40% to 45% of individuals seeking treatment for anorexia nervosa (Hsu, 1988). In 1979, Russell used the term *bulimia nervosa* to describe a clinical syndrome involving binge eating and purging behaviors among women, some of whom were low weight. With the third revision of DSM (DSM-III-R; APA, 1987) the syndrome of bulimia nervosa was distinguished from anorexia nervosa, although both diagnoses could be given to an individual. Currently, according to the DSM-IV (APA, 1994), the primary distinction between the disorders is based on body weight.

Subtypes of anorexia nervosa are now identified as binge eating/purging type versus restricting type. The binge eating/purging type has been associated with less favorable treatment outcome (see review by Steinhausen, Rauss-Mason, & Seidel, 1991), increased impulsivity (DaCosta & Halmi, 1992; Garner, Garfinkel, & O'Shaughnessy, 1985) and increased comorbid psychopathology (Garner, Garner, & Rosen, 1993). Cluster B (i.e., borderline, histrionic, antisocial, narcissistic) personality disorders have been associated with the binge eating/purging subtypes of anorexia nervosa, whereas restricting subtypes have been more closely associated with Cluster C (i.e., obsessive-compulsive, avoidant, and dependent) personality disorders (see Vitousek & Manke, 1994). It is important to note that over time individuals may move between categories, which is exemplified by the observation that many individuals with restricting anorexia nervosa develop normal-weight eating pathology (Bruch, 1985; Crisp, Hsu, Harding, & Hartshorn, 1980; Hsu, 1988), and many normal-weight bulimic women have a history of anorexia nervosa (Russell, 1979). Furthermore, follow-up studies suggest that over time some individuals with bulimia nervosa eventually develop anorexia nervosa (see Keel & Mitchell, 1997). Therefore, considerable overlap between these categories exists, and the distinction between the two disorders at times may be blurred.

Individuals with anorexia nervosa commonly engage in other food-related activities, such as preparing (without eating) elaborate meals and chewing gum excessively. Some of those with anorexia nervosa engage in exercise daily to the point of exhaustion (e.g., using a stair-stepping machine for two hours after lifting weights for an hour and completing a 90-minute high-impact aerobic class).

With regard to differential diagnosis, it is important to note that the attitudinal disturbance about eating and weight or shape is what distinguishes anorexia nervosa from other forms of psychologically related malnutrition (i.e., depression or "hysteria"). Interestingly, there is some question as to whether weight phobia should be included as a core feature of anorexia nervosa, given that it did not occur as a primary reason for refusing food until the 1930s (see Hsu & Lee, 1995), which may be explained in part by sociocultural issues.

## Epidemiology

Prevalence rates of anorexia nervosa have been reported to range from 0.10% to 1.0%, with partial-syndrome anorexia nervosa being even more common (see Walters & Kendler, 1995). The public perception that anorexia nervosa has become an epidemic may be best explained by increased public awareness of the presence and seriousness of the disorder rather than by increasing incidence (Fombonne, 1995; Lucas, 1992). The overwhelming majority of individuals with anorexia nervosa who come to the attention of treatment providers are girls and women, although approximately 5% to 10% are males (see Anderson, 1990; Hsu, 1990).

## Course

Although reports of anorexia nervosa in children have been documented (Jacobs & Isaacs, 1986; Lask & Bryant-Waugh, 1992), the onset of the disorder usually occurs around puberty (see Hindler, Crisp, McGuigan, & Joughin, 1994; Hsu, 1990). Onset of the disorder involves the development of behaviors that at first may appear to be normative for female adolescents, such as dieting and increased focus on appearance. Often not until weight loss becomes pronounced do family members or concerned others recognize the potential gravity of the situation for the young individual. Due to the seriousness of the consequences of prolonged starvation, expeditious intervention is indicated when signs of anorexia nervosa are present.

Much has been learned about the effects of human starvation and emaciation from research conducted during World War II by Keys, Brozek, Henschel, Mickelsen, & Taylor (1950) regarding malnutrition of healthy male research volunteers. Based on research it is now understood that many of the symptoms manifested by individuals with anorexia nervosa may be attributed directly to the effects of starvation. Such symptoms include increased interest in and preoccupation with food; isolation and loss of social interest; decreased alertness, motivation, or sexual interest; and mood changes including depression, irritability, and apathy. Unfortunately, to cope with many of these symptoms, individuals with anorexia nervosa often increase the intensity of anorectic behaviors (e.g., fasting, intense exercising), without appreciating consequent adverse reciprocal effects. A further complication is that most individuals with anorexia nervosa deny that anything is wrong in the early months or years of the disorder (Noordenbos, 1992).

These behaviors are primarily egosyntonic in nature and, once established, become firmly entrenched and resistant to change (Bruch, 1982; Vitousek, Watson, & Wilson, 1998). For this reason, early intervention is highly recommended. Results of intermediate outcome studies (conducted roughly 4 to 12 years following identification of the disorder) indicate that approximately 50% of patients recover (i.e., resume a healthy weight status and menstrual functioning), 25% remain in various stages of illness, and 25% continue to meet full diagnostic criteria (Burns & Crisp, 1984; Hall, Slim, Hawker, & Salmond, 1984; Hsu, Crisp, & Harding, 1979; Morgan, Purgold, & Welbourne, 1983; Morgan & Russell, 1975; Tolstrup et al., 1985).

Unfortunately, results of long-term follow-up studies indicate that many remain chronically ill (see review by Pike, 1998; Ratnasuriya, Eisler, Szmukler, & Russell, 1989; Theander, 1985). Many individuals with a history of anorexia nervosa continue to be underweight and amenorrheic, and to struggle with comorbid psychopathology and difficulties with psychosocial adjustment (see review by Pike, 1998). Particularly concerning is the alarmingly elevated mortality rate of this disorder, estimated to be as high as 20% at long-term follow-up (Steinhausen & Glanville, 1983; Theander, 1985), most commonly due to starvation and suicide (Hsu, 1988). A review of multiple studies on this topic reported a crude mortality rate of 5.9%, which exceeds the rate for female psychiatric inpatients (Sullivan, 1995). This rate highlights the importance of early, swift intervention that is based on an understanding of the multiple factors involved in development and maintenance of anorexia nervosa.

## Etiology and Maintenance

The factors involved in the development and maintenance of anorexia nervosa may best be conceptualized as multidimensional, involving sociocultural, personality, developmental, familial, and biological factors.

### Sociocultural Factors

Current societal standards that place inordinate value on thinness are pervasive. Body image dissatisfaction among women has become so common it has been referred to as "normative discontent" (Rodin, Silberstein, & Striegel-Moore, 1985; Striegel-Moore, Silberstein, & Rodin, 1986).

Individuals, especially females, receive societal reinforcement for dieting and losing weight. Those who achieve an unusually thin physique often receive praise for their beauty and self-control. In reviewing trends of cultural standards of weight for women, Wiseman, Gray, Mosimann, and Ahren (1992) indicated that most women who might be considered physically "ideal" would meet the DSM-IV low body weight criteria for anorexia nervosa. From this perspective, anorexia nervosa may be viewed as a "culturally syntonic" disorder (Garner & Bemis, 1985). Despite the substantial societal pressure for thinness to which most women in Western societies are exposed, given the rarity of anorexia nervosa, sociocultural factors alone cannot account for the development of this disorder.

*Personality Factors*

Individuals with anorexia nervosa may be particularly attuned to cultural messages about weight and shape. Being teased about one's weight has been identified as an antecedent for the development of an eating disorder (see Hsu, 1990). According to Garner and Bemis (1985), individuals with anorexia nervosa are distinguished by a personal domain comprised primarily of weight-related self-schemata; weight is used as a frame of reference for self-evaluation as a means of coping with other feelings of inadequacy. Given that individuals with anorexia nervosa often struggle with feelings of inadequacy and low self-esteem (Bruch, 1973), dieting and weight loss may be viewed as vehicles to obtain confidence based on attractiveness.

Bruch (1973) suggested that premorbid personality traits are implicated in the development of anorexia nervosa, which she described as a "desperate struggle for a self-respecting identity" (p. 250). She concluded that in addition to a delusional disturbance in body image and concept, individuals with anorexia nervosa also have difficulty identifying and describing internal states (i.e., alexithymia) and a sense of personal inadequacy. Although they may outwardly appear confident, competent, and often highly accomplished, inwardly, individuals with this disorder usually suffer from pervasive feelings of ineffectiveness (Bruch, 1961, 1973, 1982; Garner, Olmsted, Polivy, & Garfinkel, 1984) and low self-esteem (Hsu, Crisp, & Harding, 1979). Within the interpersonal sphere, individuals with anorexia nervosa often are described as introverted (Strober, 1985), shy (Vitousek & Manke, 1994), and distrustful (Garner et al., 1984). Other personality features associated with anorexia nervosa include risk avoidance, emotional restraint, and conformity (Casper, 1990).

Individuals with anorexia nervosa tend to be perfectionistic (Bastiani, Rao, Weltzin, & Kaye, 1995; Vitousek & Manke, 1994) and obsessional (Strober, 1985). Although they evidence average or above average intellectual abilities (Bemis, 1978; Hamscher, Halmi, & Benton, 1981), their thinking is often characterized as concrete and rigid, replete with cognitive distortions (Garfinkel & Garner, 1982; Garner & Bemis, 1985; Toner, Garfinkel, & Garner, 1987). Dichotomous or "all-or-none" thinking (Garfinkel, 1985) is particularly salient among this population. Such "black-and-white" thinking leads to a variety of cognitive fallacies or faulty conclusions (e.g., all foods containing fat are "bad"; if one's weight deviates by a pound, one is "fat," etc.).

Dichotomous thinking contributes to the increased anxiety these individuals experience regarding eating and weight gain. However, this aversive conditioning also serves an adaptive function of helping to maintain dietary restraint (Garner & Bemis, 1985). Consequent weight loss, which is viewed as an "accomplishment," serves as positive reinforcement of weight loss, by eliciting a sense of mastery, self-control, and competence (Garner & Bemis, 1985).

### Developmental Factors

A strong developmental component is suggested given that eating disorders usually develop during adolescence (Hsu, 1990). The psychopathology that develops as part of anorexia nervosa is often consistent with the individual's personality style, which is exacerbated by difficulties encountered during adolescence. The developmental period of adolescence involves multiple demands that require individuals to interact socially and to function more autonomously from their families. Individuals with shy and avoidant temperaments may find the tasks involved in individuating from the family to be particularly threatening. Unfortunately, the anorectic behavior serves to perpetuate and heighten feelings of isolation and obsessionality.

Physical development is also often experienced as distressing, as girls become more attuned to societal messages about the importance of obtaining an ideal body while they also contend with deposition of fat during puberty. Crisp (1965, 1967, 1980) contends that individuals with anorexia nervosa are afraid of being normal weight and exhibit a "psychobiological regression from adolescence," which he describes as an adaptive psychological coping mechanism stemming from the demands associated with psychosexual maturity. Such demands include issues related to sexuality, separation from family, interpersonal relationship conflicts, and performance expectations (Crisp, 1965, 1980; Kalucy, 1978; Lacey, 1983; Palmer, 1979). Reduction of food intake serves as a means of inhibiting fat deposition and menstruation.

As discussed by Johnson, Sansone, and Chewning (1996), because the teen years are associated with "lofty idealism and pursuit of asceticism," food deprivation may also be viewed by the adolescent as a desirable form of self-denial and purity, which can (temporarily) counter feelings of self-doubt. Food restriction and weight loss may also serve as a means of enhancing self-esteem through what may be experienced as an achievement in comparison with female peers and other women.

It is worthy of note that upon weight restoration, personality features such as introversion and obsessionality diminish for some individuals with anorexia nervosa (Strober, 1985). This finding suggests an important reminder that some of the personality features associated with anorexia nervosa may be consequences of prolonged starvation rather than etiological precipitants.

*Familial Factors*

The role of the family among individuals with anorexia nervosa has been recognized for many years. The probable genetic contribution to the development of anorexia nervosa also has received recent support (Walters & Kendler, 1995). Individuals who develop anorexia nervosa are sometimes described as having been a "perfect child" within the family. Consequently, parents often are surprised and genuinely confused when they realize that their child has this disorder. Families of individuals with anorexia nervosa often are characterized as being middle to upper class, financially successful, and concerned about maintaining outward appearances, including issues regarding physical appearance and fitness (Yager, 1982). Bruch (1970) described the families of young individuals with anorexia nervosa as attending well to the child's physical needs and highly valuing their child, yet overprotective and overconcerned. Such families were found to have exceedingly high expectations of obedience and performance, and to limit areas of psychological growth for the child, such as self-expression or autonomy (Bruch, 1970). She reported that many individuals with anorexia nervosa experience "themselves as acting only in response to demands coming from other people in situations, and not as doing things because they want to" (Bruch, 1973, p. 254). Minuchin, Rosman, and Baker (1978) characterized families of those with anorexia nervosa as being enmeshed, overprotective, rigid, and deficient in abilities to resolve conflicts. Such families exhibit a strong investment in maintaining an emotional status quo; issues that could threaten the status quo are dealt with using indirect communication, such that conflict is diffused but not resolved. This overprotectiveness and intrusiveness are believed to impair development of autonomy for the child.

In light of these family characteristics, refusal of adequate food intake may be viewed as an assertive act (Johnson, Sansone, & Chewning, 1996). However, physical problems resulting from prolonged starvation may require extensive intervention, may interfere with the individual's ability to develop a more independent lifestyle, and may serve to increase the degree of overenmeshment and overprotectiveness (Johnson et al., 1996).

Given the multidimensional nature of the development and maintenance of this disorder, treatment interventions may be most effective when encompassing approaches that are responsive to the societal, personality, developmental, familial, and biological aspects of anorexia nervosa.

## Treatment

Treatment of anorexia nervosa often requires a multidisciplinary approach, involving medical management, nutritional intervention, hospitalization, and individual and family psychotherapy. Although anorexia nervosa has been the subject of clinical interest and investigation for several decades, the research literature for treatment of this condition is relatively modest, for several reasons. First, because treatment of anorexia nervosa requires a multitude of interventions, trials that can control adequately for several treatment interventions are difficult to design and execute. Second, because anorexia nervosa is a relatively rare condition, researchers have difficulty obtaining access to sufficient numbers of patients to conduct randomized trials. Third, given that a common clinical characteristic of anorexia nervosa is denial about the seriousness of the problem, many such individuals are reluctant to participate in treatment in general, including treatment studies. Fourth, the initial treatment for many patients with anorexia nervosa includes inpatient hospitalization; third-party reimbursement to finance this treatment often precludes participation in randomized trials with inpatient psychiatric patients. These reasons help to explain why the treatment literature on anorexia nervosa is not as well developed as one might assume, given the notoriety of this illness and the substantial duration of time it has been studied. The following sections will review the research findings on two treatment strategies for which empirical evidence has accrued: pharmacotherapy and psychotherapy. These and other intervention strategies will be addressed in greater detail in subsequent chapters.

*Pharmacotherapy*

Several different classes of psychopharmacological agents have been studied to treat anorexia nervosa. The earliest reported drug trial, conducted using historical controls, involved use of the antipsychotic chlorpromazine. This study suggested that anorexia nervosa patients treated with chlorpromazine gained weight more quickly than historical controls. However, although the use of historical controls was common at the time (Dally, Oppenheim, & Sargant, 1958; Dally & Sargant, 1960; Dally & Sargant, 1966), this methodology is not considered adequate by current standards; therefore, in retrospect these findings are difficult to interpret. Two subsequent randomized trials using the antipsychotic drugs Pimozide (Vandereycken & Pierloot, 1982; marketed in the United States for Tourette's syndrome) and sulpiride (Vandereycken, 1984; not marketed in the United States) evidenced negative outcomes. Although it is reasonable to conclude that there is a paucity of empirical literature suggesting efficacy for antipsychotics in this population, such drugs continue to be used by experienced clinicians in rare situations with treatment-resistant patients. The newer atypical neuroleptics, with more favorable side-effect profiles, are usually administered at low dosages. However, clinical practice behooves infrequent use of any class of antipsychotic medication for anorexia nervosa.

Following isolated case reports, a randomized trial of lithium carbonate in anorexia nervosa was replicated by Gross, Ebert, and Fadden in 1981. Although the results suggested some statistical advantage at certain time points, overall the benefit was deemed not to be of clinical significance. Furthermore, the authors were cautionary in their discussion, pointing out the limitations and potential problems in using this drug with low-weight anorectic patients, given their cardiovascular status and their fluid and electrolyte problems. Therefore, lithium is used rarely, if ever, in this population.

Given the comorbidity of affective symptoms in anorexia nervosa, a logical type of drug to consider is antidepressant medication. Only three clinical trials have examined the efficacy of tricyclic antidepressants in anorexia nervosa patients. An early trial by Crisp, Lacey, and Crutchfield (1987) using clomipramine at 50 mg per day yielded negative findings. This conservative dosing was justified given concerns about the side effects of this drug in this population, but may have been subtherapeutic. Two other trials using amitriptyline found different results. A trial by Biederman, Herzog, Rivinus, & Herper (1985) using a lower mean dosage (160 mg) was also negative. The only tricyclic anorexia nervosa trial to detect positive findings was by Halmi, Eckert, LaDu, and Cohen (1986); it used a higher mean dosage (175 mg), which showed benefit for the drug in terms of a clinical index based on rate of weight gain. It is important to note, however, that tricyclic compounds are not well tolerated by these patients, who are already frequently bothered by constipation and hypertension, and are very sensitive to sedation.

With the advent of the newer antidepressants, in particular the selective serotonin reuptake inhibitors (SSRIs), has come renewed interest in antidepressant use in this population. Although initially there was some concern that SSRIs might engender weight loss among anorexia nervosa patients, clinical experience has suggested that these drugs seem to have the opposite effect: they seem to reduce obsessionality, improve mood, and attenuate hunger, which result in some anorexia nervosa patients being less afraid of eating and more likely to gain weight.

Much of the anorexia nervosa research on SSRIs has involved outpatient maintenance and relapse prevention strategies, reflecting a methodological shift in the anorexia nervosa antidepressant literature away from acute treatment strategies. Several open label studies appeared first (Gwirtsman, Guze, Barry, Yager, & Gainsley, 1990; Kaye, Weltzin, Hsu, & Bulik, 1991). The first randomized study to be reported, by Kaye et al. (1991), suggested a statistically and clinically significant advantage of fluoxetine over placebo in preventing relapse in weight-restored patients with anorexia nervosa who were also receiving outpatient therapy; this study has generated considerable enthusiasm for the use of this class of drugs. However, a second study, by Strober, Freeman, DeAntonio, Lampert, & Diamond (1997), utilizing historical controls with patients who received more intensive psychotherapy whether or not they received pharmacotherapy, failed to demonstrate an advantage for the active drug. Of interest, and of theoretical importance, the SSRIs appear to be ineffective in very low-weight anorexia nervosa patients (Attia, Haiman, Walsh, & Flater, 1998), although further work needs to be done in this area to conclusively rule out their efficacy. Currently, a multicenter study examining the utility of fluoxetine versus cognitive-behavioral therapy (CBT) versus the combination of these treatments in relapse prevention in patients with anorexia nervosa is under way at the University of Minnesota, Stanford University, Cornell University, and the Neuropsychiatric Research Institute in North Dakota. Given the evidence of persistent obsessive/compulsive symptoms and frequent mood disturbance in many patients with anorexia nervosa and the high relapse rate among these patients, strong consideration should be given to the use of SSRIs in this population.

Cyproheptadine, a drug usually not considered part of the psychiatric armamentarium, has been known for some time to induce appetite and weight gain, and for this reason was used in several trials in anorexia nervosa patients. Two preliminary studies (Goldberg, Halmi, Eckert, Casper, & Davis, 1979; Vigersky & Loriaux, 1977) failed to demonstrate benefit for this drug. In contrast, a third study (Halmi et al., 1986), utilizing higher dosages (32 mg daily targeted dose) of the drug, did evidence improvement with respect to rate of weight gain and mood. Despite this positive finding, cyproheptadine is used in this population infrequently.

Because of the appetite-enhancing effects noted with marijuana usage, one study examined the utility of the active compound delta 9-tetrahydrocannabinol in the treatment of anorexia nervosa, with diazepam serving as an active control (Gross et al., 1983). The results suggested poor tolerance of this medication by anorexia nervosa patients and lack of therapeutic benefit.

Gastric peristaltic agents are sometimes used clinically with these patients, particularly early in the course of refeeding when delayed gastric emptying can make refeeding problematic. There have been two randomized trials, and in neither study was there advantage for the active drug (Stacher et al., 1993; Szmukler, Young, Miller, Lichtenstein, & Binns, 1995). However, all patients in both studies also received intensive psychotherapy, which may have attenuated any medication effect. Moreover, the negative results may be attributed to the small sample size in both studies. Further research in this area appears indicated.

A trial of zinc therapy suggested benefit in terms of rate of weight gain (target of 10% gain in BMI) in an inpatient sample (Birmingham, Goldner, & Bakan, 1994). This strategy, based on the observation of hypozincemia in some anorexia nervosa patients and the association between impaired taste and decreased zinc levels, is of interest but has not widely influenced practice.

In summary, although a number of medications have been investigated, the current medication of choice is an SSRI. Given the complexity and seriousness of this disorder, however, treatment with psychological interventions is imperative.

*Psychotherapy*

Although theoretical literature and clinical wisdom clearly indicate that psychotherapeutic approaches remain the cornerstone of the treatment of anorexia nervosa, little systematic research has been done in this area. The general recommendation is that such approaches initially need to be supportive and directive, given that patients frequently have difficulty meaningfully involving themselves in psychotherapy when they are at a critically low weight, which is partly attributed to cognitive impairment due to malnourishment. As weight gain progresses, a gradual shift to a more insight-oriented approach may be employed.

One study that has generated a great deal of interest and controversy (Crisp et al., 1991; Gowers, Norton, Halek, & Crisp, 1994) compared the utility of a standard inpatient treatment program to an outpatient individual plus family therapy format, an outpatient group treatment with a separate group for patients, and an evaluation-only control group. The results failed to demonstrate any advantage for the more intensive inpatient treatment.

Researchers at the Maudsley in London have reported a series of studies examining the role of family therapy and family counseling in anorexia nervosa patients (Eisler et al., 1997; Hodes, Dare, Dodge, & Eisler, 1999; Hodes, Eisler, & Dare, 1991; Russell, Szmukler, Dare, & Eisler, 1987; Szmukler, Berkowitz, Eisler, Leff, & Dare, 1987). Their first study (Russell, 1987) examined the utility of family versus individual psychotherapy in weight-restored anorexia nervosa patients post-hospital. Interestingly, the results suggested an age-specific effect: younger patients having a shorter duration of the disorder clearly profited from the family therapy approach more than the individual therapy protocol, whereas the converse was true for those over age 18 with a longer duration of illness. A second study (Szmukler et al., 1987) focusing on adult patients compared individual, family, and psychodynamic individual therapy approaches. Results favored family counseling. A third study (Eisler et al., 1997) compared family counseling wherein patients were seen with their parents to a family counseling approach where patients' parents were seen separately. The latter approach tended to be more supportive and informative, and suppressed conflict in these families. Families were classified as having low or high levels of expressed emotion (EE), a negative communication pattern characterized by the patient's family becoming emotionally overinvolved, yet excessively critical to the identified patient. Families with low EE did about equally well in both treatments, while those with high levels of EE clearly did better in the approach where the parents were seen separately, suggesting that direct family involvement in such families may not be as efficacious, and a more psychoeducational approach working with the parents separately may be preferable.

Overall, this literature suggests that certain patients, particularly adolescents, may benefit from family involvement. However, in families with a high degree of expressed emotion, the involvement may best be accomplished not with family therapy per se, but with the implementation of a counseling and psychoeducational approach, seeing the patient and the parents separately. This family-based approach is described in a recently published treatment manual (Lock, le Grange, Agras, & Dare, 2001), which also is being used in ongoing studies at Stanford University.

Twenty-two anorexia nervosa patients participated in a study using a random assignment design (Robin, Siegel, Koepke, Move, & Tice, 1994; Robin, Siegel, & Moyert, 1994) comparing behavioral family systems therapy to an ego-oriented individual therapy that did not involve the patients' respective families. Both conditions positively affected communication patterns and parent-adolescent conflict, raising questions as to whether the family needs to be seen as a unit.

Treasure and colleagues (1995) reported a random assignment study of anorexia nervosa participants who received either cognitive analytic treatment or educational behavioral treatment. No differences in most outcome parameters were noted, although those receiving the cognitive analytic treatment reported greater subjective improvement.

Although cognitive-behavioral therapy (CBT) has been advocated as a treatment for anorexia nervosa, it has been insufficiently studied (Fairburn, Shafran, & Cooper, 1999; Wilson, 1999). Researchers have advocated for the special treatment needs of children with anorexia nervosa, despite a lack of empirical data on the treatment of this population (Robin, Gilroy, & Dennis, 1998). Another theme that has emerged in the treatment literature in anorexia nervosa is that highly structured, coercive inpatient environments that focus strictly on food intake and weight gain, and which tend to use punishment as a component treatment paradigm, do not work as well and clearly are not as accepted by patients, compared to programs that more heavily emphasize flexibility, support, and encouragement.

## Conditions

Despite the fact that anorexia nervosa has been recognized as a serious medical and psychological disorder for a number of decades, the controlled treatment literature in patients with anorexia nervosa remains quite limited, with few firm findings to guide treatment decisions. Clearly, this is an area where considerable research is warranted, and given the impediments of sample size and site-specific effects, multicenter studies are needed. Single case designs and qualitative methods may also be useful in furthering our understanding of the intricacies of beneficial treatments.

Given the profound medical, psychological, and social consequences associated with anorexia nervosa, the importance of early intervention cannot be overstated. Hospitalization is often required, as in the case of weight loss posing a serious medical risk, failure to achieve weight restoration on an outpatient basis, or suicidality. It is important to be aware that successful treatment of anorexia nervosa may require long-term psychotherapy, addressing multiple aspects of the disorder. Whereas early interventions may need to focus on weight restoration, fears of food, and concerns about weight and shape, issues related to self-esteem, perfectionism, possible abuse, and family dynamics are important to address. For younger individuals struggling with anorexia nervosa, family therapy is particularly recommended.

As mentioned earlier, appropriate treatment often requires the involvement of professionals from several disciplines, including physicians, psychologists, social workers, and dietitians. A team approach is recommended in which professionals coordinate services to assist the patient in optimizing treatment outcome. Given the seriousness and complexity of the disorder, assisting someone in overcoming anorexia nervosa is often a challenging and taxing endeavor. It is highly advisable, therefore, that treating professionals obtain specialized training and participate in ongoing supervision and consultation.

## References

American Psychiatric Association. (1987). *Diagnostic and statistical manual of mental disorders* (3rd ed , rev.). Washington, DC: Author.

American Psychiatric Association. (1994). *Diagnostic and statistical manual of mental disorders* (4th ed.). Washington, DC: Author.

Anderson, A. E. (1990). Diagnosis and treatment of males with eating disorders. In A. E. Anderson (Ed.), *Males with eating disorders* (pp. 133–162). New York: Brunner/Mazel.

Attia, E., Haiman, C., Walsh, T., & Flater, S. R. (1998). Does fluoxetine augment the inpatient treatment of anorexia nervosa? *American Journal of Psychiatry, 155,* 548–551.

Bastiani, A. M., Rao, R., Weltzin, T., & Kaye, W. H. (1995). Perfectionism in anorexia nervosa. *International Journal of Eating Disorders, 17,* 147–152.

Bemis, K. M. (1978). Current approaches to the etiology and treatment of anorexia nervosa. *Psychological Bulletin, 85,* 593–617.

Biederman, J., Herzog, D. B., Rivinus, T. M., & Herper, J. D. (1985). Amitriptyline in the treatment of anorexia nervosa: A double-blind, placebo-controlled study. *Journal of Clinical Psychopharmacology, 5,* 10–16.

Birmingham, C. L., Goldner, E. M., & Bakan, R. (1994). Controlled trial of zinc supplementation in anorexia nervosa. *International Journal of Eating Disorders, 15,* 251–255.

Bliss, E., & Branch, C. H. H. (Eds.). (1960). *Anorexia nervosa: Its history, psychology, and biology.* New York: Hoeber.

Bruch, H. (1961). Family transactions in eating disorders. *Comprehensive Psychiatry, 12,* 238–248.

Bruch, H. (1966). Anorexia nervosa and its differential diagnosis. *Journal of Nervous and Mental Disease, 141,* 555–566.

Bruch, H. (1970). Family background in eating disorders. In E. J. Anthony & C. Koupemik (Eds.), *The child in his family.* New York: Wiley.

Bruch, H. (1973). *Eating disorders: Obesity, anorexia nervosa, and the person within.* New York: Basic Books.

Bruch, H. (1982). Anorexia nervosa: Therapy and theory. *American Journal of Psychiatry, 139,* 1531–1538.

Bruch, H. (1985). Four decades of eating disorders. In D. M. Garner & P. E. Garfinkel (Eds.), *Handbook of psychotherapy for anorexia nervosa and bulimia* (pp. 7–18). New York: Guilford Press.

Burns, T., & Crisp, A. H. (1984). Outcome of anorexia nervosa in males. *British Journal of Psychiatry, 145,* 319–325.

Casper, R. (1990). Personality features of women with good outcome from restricting anorexia. *Psychosomatic Medicine, 52,* 156–170.

Crisp, A. H. (1965). Clinical and therapeutic aspects of anorexia nervosa: A study of 30 cases. *Journal of Psychosomatic Research, 9,* 67–78.

Crisp, A. H. (1967). Anorexia nervosa. *Hospital Medicine, 1,* 713–718.

Crisp, A. H. (Ed.). (1980). *Anorexia nervosa: Let me be.* London: Balliere Tindall.

Crisp, A. H., Hsu, L. K. G., Harding, B., & Hartshorn, J. (1980). Clinical features in anorexia nervosa. *Journal of Psychosomatic Research, 24,* 179–191.

Crisp, A. H., Lacey, J. H., & Crutchfield, M. (1987). Clomipramine and "drive" in people with anorexia nervosa: An inpatient study. *British Journal of Psychiatry, 150,* 355–358.

Crisp, A. H., Norton, K., Gowers, S., Halek, C., Bowyer, C., Yeldham, D., Levett, G., & Bhat, A. (1991). A controlled study of the effect of therapies among adolescent and family psychopathology in anorexia nervosa. *British Journal of Psychiatry, 159,* 325–333.

DaCosta, M., & Halmi, K. A. (1992). Classifications of anorexia nervosa: Question of subtypes. *International Journal of Eating Disorders, 4,* 305–313.

Dally, P. J., Oppenheim, G. B., & Sargant, W. (1958). Anorexia nervosa. *British Medical Journal,* 633–634.

Dally, P. J., & Sargant, W. (1960). A new treatment of anorexia nervosa. *British Medical Journal,* 1770–1773.

Dally, P. J., & Sargant, W. (1966). Treatment and outcome of anorexia nervosa. *British Medical Journal, 2,* 793–795.

Eisler, I., Dare, C., Russell, G. F., Szmukler, G., le Grange, D., & Dodge, E. (1997). Family and individual therapy in anorexia nervosa. A 5-year follow-up. *Archives of General Psychiatry, 54,* 1025–1030.

Fairburn, C. G., Shafran, R., & Cooper, Z. (1999). A cognitive behavioral theory of anorexia nervosa. *Behavioral Research and Therapy, 37,* 1–13.

Fombonne, E. (1995). Anorexia nervosa: No evidence of an increase. *British Journal of Psychiatry, 166,* 462–471.

Garfinkel, P. E. (1985). The treatment of anorexia nervosa in Toronto. *Journal of Psychiatric Research, 19,* 405–411.

Garfinkel, P. E., & Garner, D. M. (1982). *Anorexia nervosa: A multidimensional perspective.* New York: Brunner/Mazel.

Garner, D. M., & Bemis, K. M. (1985). Cognitive therapy for anorexia nervosa. In D. M. Garner and P. E. Garfinkel (Eds.), *Handbook of psychotherapy for anorexia and bulimia* (pp. 107–146). New York: Guilford Press.

Garner, D. M., Garfinkel, P. E., & O'Shaughnessy, M. (1985). The validity of the distinction between bulimia with and without anorexia nervosa. *American Journal of Psychiatry, 142,* 581–587.

Garner, D. M., Garner, M. V., & Rosen, L. W. (1993). Anorexia nervosa "restricters" who purge: Implications for subtyping anorexia nervosa. *International Journal of Eating Disorders, 18,* 171–185.

Garner, D. M., Olmsted, M. P., Polivy, J., & Garfinkel, P. E. (1984). Comparison between weight-preoccupied women and anorexia nervosa. *Psychosomatic Medicine, 46,* 255–266.

Goldberg, S. C., Halmi, K. A., Eckert, E. D., Casper, R. C., & Davis, J. M. (1979). Cyproheptadine in anorexia nervosa. *American Journal of Psychiatry, 134,* 67–70.

Gowers, S., Norton, K., Halek, C., & Crisp, A. H. (1994). Outcome of outpatient psychotherapy in a random allocation treatment study of anorexia nervosa. *International Journal of Eating Disorders, 15,* 165–177.

Gross, H. A., Ebert, M. H., & Faden, V. B. (1981). A double-blind controlled study of lithium carbonate in primary anorexia nervosa. *Journal of Clinical Psychopharmacology, 1,* 376–381.

Gross, H. A., Ebert, M. H., Faden, V. B., Goldberg, S. C., Kaye, W. J., Caine, E. D., Hawks, R., & Zinberg, N. (1983). A double-blind trial of delta-9-tetrahydrocannabinol in primary anorexia nervosa. *Journal of Clinical Psychopharmacology, 3,* 165–171.

Gull, W. W. (1874). Anorexia nervosa (apepsia hysterica, anorexia hysterica). *Transactions of the Clinical Society of London, 7,* 22–28.

Gwirtsman, H. E., Guze, B. H., Barry, H., Yager, J., & Gainsley, B. (1990). Fluoxetine treatment of anorexia nervosa: An open clinical trial. *Journal of Clinical Psychiatry, 51,* 378–382.

Hall, A., Slim, E., Hawker, F., & Salmond, C. (1984). Anorexia nervosa: Long-term outcome in 50 female patients. *British Journal of Psychiatry, 145,* 407–413.

Halmi, K. A., Eckert, E., LaDu, T. J., & Cohen, J. (1986). Anorexia nervosa: Treatment efficacy of cyproheptadine and amitriptyline. *Archives of General Psychiatry, 43,* 177–181.

Hamscher, K., Halmi, K., & Benton, A. (1981). Prediction of outcome in anorexia nervosa from neuropsychological status. *Psychiatry Research, 4,* 79–88.

Hindler, C. G., Crisp, A. H., McGuigan, S., & Joughin, N. (1994). Anorexia nervosa: Change over time in age of onset, presentation and duration of illness. *Psychological Medicine, 24,* 719–729.

Hodes, M., Dare, C., Dodge, E., & Eisler, I. (1999). The assessment of expressed emotion in a standardized family interview. *Journal of Child Psychology & Psychiatry, 40,* 617–625.

Hodes, M., Eisler, I., & Dare, C. (1991). Family therapy for anorexia nervosa in adolescence: A review. *Journal of the Royal Society of Medicine, 84,* 359–362 .

Hsu, L. K. (1988). The outcome of anorexia nervosa: A reappraisal. *Psychological Medicine, 18,* 807–812.

Hsu, L. K. (1990). *Eating disorders.* New York: Guilford Press.

Hsu, L. K., Crisp, A. H., & Harding, B. (1979). Outcome of anorexia nervosa. *Lancet, 13,* 61–65.

Hsu, L. K., & Lee, S. (1995). Is weight phobia always necessary for a diagnosis of anorexia nervosa? *American Journal of Psychiatry, 150,* 1466–1471.

Jacobs, B. W., & Issacs, S. (1986). Pre-pubertal anorexia nervosa: A retrospective controlled study. *Journal of Child Psychology and Psychiatry and Allied Disciplines, 27,* 237–250.

Johnson, C. L., Sansone, R. A., & Chewning, M. (1996). Good reasons why young women would develop anorexia nervosa: The adaptive context. *National Eating Disorders Organization Newsletter, 30,* 1–4.

Kalucy, R. S. (1978). An approach to the therapy of anorexia nervosa. *Journal of Adolescence, 10,* 197–228.

Kaye, W. H. (1996, November). *The use of fluoxetine to prevent relapse in anorexia nervosa.* Paper presented at the annual meeting of the Eating Disorders Research Society, Pittsburgh, PA.

Kaye, W. H., Weltzin, T. E., Hsu, L. K. G., & Bulik, C. C. (1991). An open trial of fluoxetine in patients with anorexia nervosa. *Journal of Clinical Psychiatry, 52,* 464–471.

Keel, P. K., & Mitchell, J. E. (1997). Outcome in bulimia nervosa. *American Journal of Psychiatry, 154,* 313–321.

Keys, A., Brozek, J., Henschel, A., Mickelsen, O., & Taylor, H. L. (1950). *The biology of human starvation.* Minneapolis: University of Minnesota Press.

Lacey, J. H. (1983). The patient's attitude to food. In M. H. Lessof (Ed.), *Clinical reactions to food* (pp. 35–58). New York: Wiley.

Lacey, J. H., & Crisp, A. H. (1980). Hunger, food intake and weight: The impact of clomipramine on a refeeding anorexia nervosa population. *Postgraduate Medical Journal, 56,* 79–85.

Lask, B., & Bryant-Waugh, R. (1992). Early-onset anorexia nervosa and related eating disorders. *Journal of Child Psychology and Psychiatry and Allied Disciplines, 33,* 281–300.

Lock, J., le Grange, D., Agras, W. S., & Dare, C. (2001). *Treatment manual of anorexia nervosa: A family-based approach.* New York: Guilford.

Lucas, A. R. (1992). The eating disorder "epidemic": More apparent than real? *Pediatric Annals, 21,* 746–751.

Minuchin, S., Rosman, B. L., & Baker, L. (1978). *Psychosomatic families: Anorexia nervosa in context.* Cambridge: Harvard University Press.

Morgan, H. G., Purgold, J., & Welbourne, J. (1983). Management and outcome in anorexia nervosa: A standardized prognosis study. *British Journal of Psychiatry, 143,* 282–287.

Morgan, H. G., & Russell, G. F. M. (1975). Value of family background and clinical features as predictors of long-term outcome in anorexia nervosa: Four-year follow-up study of 41 patients. *Psychological Medicine, 5,* 355–371.

Noordenbos, G. (1992). Important factors in the process of recovery according to patients with anorexia nervosa. In W. Herzog, H. C. Deter, & W. Vandereycken (Eds.), *The course of eating disorders: Long-term follow-up studies of anorexia and bulimia nervosa* (pp. 304–322). New York: Springer-Verlag.

Palmer, R. L. (1979). The dietary chaos syndrome: A useful new term? *British Journal of Medical Psychology, 52,* 187–190.

Pike, K. M. (1998). Long-term course of anorexia nervosa: Response, relapse, remission, and recovery. *Clinical Psychology Review, 18,* 447–475.

Ratnasuriya, R. H., Eisler, I., Szmukler, G. I., & Russell, G. F. M. (1989). Outcome and prognostic factors after 20 years of anorexia nervosa. *Annals of the New York Academy of Sciences, 575,* 567–568.

Robin, A. L., Gilroy, M., & Dennis, A. B. (1998). Treatment of eating disorders in children and adolescents. *Clinical Psychology Review, 18,* 421–446.

Robin, A. L., Siegel, P. T., Koepke, T., Move, A. W., & Tice, S. (1994). Family therapy versus individual therapy for adolescent females with anorexia nervosa. *Journal of Developmental and Behavioral Pediatrics, 15,* 109–116.

Robin, A. L., Siegel, P. T., & Moyert, A. (1994). Family versus individual therapy for anorexia: Impact on family conflict. *International Journal of Eating Disorders, 17,* 313–322.

Rodin, J., Silberstein, L. R., & Striegel-Moore, R. H. (1985). Women and weight: A normative discontent. In T. B. Sonderegger (Ed.), *Nebraska Symposium on Motivation: Psychology and gender* (pp. 267–307). Lincoln: University of Nebraska Press.

Russell, G. F. M. (1970). Anorexia nervosa: Its identity as an illness and its treatment. In J. H. Price (Ed.), *Modern trends in psychological medicine: Vol. 2* (pp. 131–164). London: Butterworths.

Russell, G. (1979). Bulimia nervosa: An ominous variant of anorexia nervosa. *Psychological Medicine, 9,* 429–448.

Russell, G. F., Szmukler, G. I., Dare, C., & Eisler, I. (1987). An evaluation of family therapy in anorexia nervosa and bulimia nervosa. *Archives of General Psychiatry, 44,* 1047–1056.

Silverman, J. A. (1995). History of anorexia nervosa. In K. D. Brownell & C. G. Fairburn (Eds.), *Eating disorders and obesity: A comprehensive handbook* (pp. 141–144). New York: Guilford Press.

Stacher, G., Abatz-Wenzel, T. A., Wiesnagroteki, S., Bergman, H., Schneidner, C., & Gaupmann, G. (1993). Gastric emptying, body weight and symptoms in primary anorexia nervosa. *British Journal of Psychiatry, 162,* 398–402.

Steinhausen, H. C., & Glanville, K. (1983). Follow-up studies of anorexia nervosa: A review of research findings. *Psychological Medicine, 13,* 239–249.

Steinhausen, H. C., Rauss-Mason, C., & Seidel, R. (1991). Follow-up studies of anorexia nervosa: A review of four decades of outcome research. *Psychological Medicine, 21,* 447–454.

Striegel-Moore, R., Silberstein, L. R., & Rodin, J. (1986). Toward an understanding of risk factors for bulimia. *American Psychologist, 41,* 246–263.

Strober, M. (1985). Personality factors in anorexia nervosa. *Pediatrician: International Journal of Child and Adolescent Health, 12,* 134–138.

Strober, M., Freeman, R., DeAntonio, M., Lampert, C., & Diamond, J. (1997). Does adjunctive fluoxetine influence the post-hospital course of restrictor type anorexia nervosa? A 24-month prospective, longitudinal follow-up and comparison with historical controls. *Psychopharmacology Bulletin, 33,* 425–431.

Sullivan, P. F. (1995). Mortality in anorexia nervosa. *American Journal of Psychiatry, 152,* 1073–1074.

Szmukler, G. I., Berkowitz, R., Eisler, I., Leff, J., & Dare, C. (1987). Expressed emotion in individual and family settings: A comparative study. *British Journal of Psychiatry, 151,* 174–178.

Szmukler, G. I., Young, G. P., Miller, G., Lichtenstein, M., & Binns, D. S. (1995). A controlled trial of cisapride in anorexia nervosa. *International Journal of Eating Disorders, 17,* 347–367.

Theander, S. (1985). Outcome and prognosis in anorexia nervosa and bulimia: Some results of previous investigations, compared with those of a Swedish long-term study. *Journal of Psychiatric Research, 19,* 493–508.

Tolstrup, K., Brinch, M., Isager, T., Nielsen, S., Nystrup, J., Severin, B., & Olesen, N. S. (1985). Long-term outcome of 151 cases of anorexia nervosa: The Copenhagen anorexia nervosa follow-up study. *Acta Psychiatrica Scandinavia, 71,* 380–387.

Toner, B. B., Garfinkel, P. E., & Garner, D. M. (1987). Cognitive style of patients with bulimic and diet-restricting anorexia nervosa. *American Journal of Psychiatry, 144,* 510–512.

Treasure, J., Todd, G., Brolly, M., Tiller, J., Nehmed, A., & Denman, F. (1995). A pilot study of a randomized trial of cognitive analytic therapy versus educational behavioral therapy for adult anorexia nervosa. *Behavioral Research Therapy, 33,* 363–367.

Vandereycken, W. (1984). Neuroleptics in the short-term treatment of anorexia nervosa: A double-blind placebo-controlled study with sulpiride. *British Journal of Psychiatry, 144,* 288–292.

Vandereycken, W., & Pierloot, R. (1982). Pimozide combined with behavior therapy in the short-term treatment of anorexia nervosa: A double-blind placebo-controlled cross-over study. *Acta Psychiatrica Scandinavia, 66,* 445–450.

Vigersky, R. A., & Loriaux, D. L. (1977). The effect of cyproheptadine in anorexia nervosa: A double-blind trial. In R. A. Vigersky (Ed.), *Anorexia nervosa.* New York: Raven Press.

Vitousek, K., & Manke, F. (1994). Personality variables and disorders in anorexia nervosa and bulimia nervosa. *Journal of Abnormal Psychology, 103,* 137–147.

Vitousek, K., Watson, S., & Wilson, G. T. (1998). Enhancing motivation for change in treatment-resistant eating disorders. *Clinical Psychology Review, 18,* 391–420.

Walters, E. E., & Kendler, K. S. (1995). Anorexia nervosa and anorexia-like syndromes in a population-based female twin sample. *American Journal of Psychiatry, 152,* 64–71.

Wilson, G. T. (1999). Cognitive behavior therapy for eating disorders: Progress and problems. *Behavior Research Therapy, 37,* S79-S95.

Wiseman, C. V., Gray, J. J., Mosimann, J. E., & Ahren, A. H. (1992). Cultural expectations of thinness in women: An update. *International Journal of Eating Disorders, 11,* 85–89.

Yager, J. (1982). Family issues in the pathogenesis of anorexia nervosa. *Psychosomatic Medicine, 44,* 43–60.

Chapter 2

# Bulimia Nervosa

*Scott Crow and James E. Mitchell*

Although variously noted as a clinical syndrome for much of the twentieth century, bulimia nervosa was first recognized as a common, distinct diagnostic entity in a classical paper by Russell published in *Psychological Medicine* in 1979, at which time the term *bulimia nervosa* was first applied. This paper followed a period of several years during which eating disorder researchers and clinicians had focused on the treatment of anorexia nervosa, and the term *eating disorders*—suggesting several distinct types—was not yet in widespread use. However, "variants" of anorexia nervosa started to be seen commonly, and in many clinics came to predominate (Casper, Eckert, Halmi, Goldberg, & Davis, 1980; Garfinkel, Moldofsky, & Garner, 1980). It was noted that many of these patients had the same weight preoccupation as was seen among those with anorexia nervosa, but they were not at such a low weight, and some were at normal weight or above normal weight.

### Diagnosis

Several of the patients Russell described in his original paper would in retrospect be classified as having the binge/purge subtype of anorexia nervosa. However, the paper clearly underscored many of the comorbid psychopathological problems seen in bulimic patients, including substance abuse and depression, and also noted the variability in the symptoms. Our group at the University of Minnesota published a description of a series of normal-weight bulimia nervosa subjects in 1981 (Pyle, Mitchell, & Eckert, 1981). This work stressed the observation that the weight difference distinguished these patients from those with anorexia nervosa. In a historical context, then, bulimia nervosa has really been the focus of study for about 20 years. Therefore, much of the literature in this area is still descriptive, and most of the treatment literature has not progressed much beyond the first and second generation of studies, wherein certain treatments have been shown to have some degree of effectiveness, and then have been shown to have superior, equal, or inferior effectiveness compared to other treatments on certain variables.

In considering this syndrome it is worthwhile also to review the evolution of the criteria. Russell originally stressed the importance of body image disturbance among these patients, and following his model, in the United Kingdom researchers tended to differentiate between "bulimia nervosa" wherein the core psychopathology of anorexia nervosa was also present, and normal-weight bulimia, where it was lacking (1979). The DSM-III criteria, which were introduced in 1980, shortly after the syndrome was described, reflected an American point of view, and given the paucity of information available at that time, served well to delineate the syndrome in a useful way clinically and as a stimulus for research in the area. When the revision of the DSM-III was introduced in 1987, bulimia took on a new form, renamed bulimia nervosa, and offered something of a synthesis of the British and American approaches. Also, the criteria were tightened up considerably. According to the DSM-III-R system, patients could receive both the diagnosis of bulimia nervosa and anorexia nervosa, a practice that tended to underscore the importance of diagnosing both disorders, but that often failed to work in practice since physicians tended to record only one Axis I diagnosis. Frequently this resulted in anorexia nervosa being diagnosed but the presence or absence of bulimic symptoms not being coded. Because of this omission, in the DSM-IV, introduced in 1994, anorexia nervosa was subtyped to restrictor and bulimic groups. Bulimia nervosa criteria were also improved in two ways: (1) the binge eating criteria were tightened up in terms of language, and (2) although strong consideration was given to restricting bulimia nervosa to purging type (vomiting, laxatives, and/or diuretics), in the end the committee elected to include both purging and non-purging subgroups (Garfinkel et al., 1996). Both were included despite the fact that the non-purging subgroup had not really been studied adequately, and such patients had usually been excluded from clinical trials; however, it was thought that including both subgroups would stimulate research on both categories and allow physicians to diagnose the same spectrum of eating disorders as they had in DSM-III-R. Also, the body image disturbance criterion was modified to better reflect our current understanding of the disturbance as it is manifested in patients with bulimia nervosa.

The DSM-IV criteria for bulimia nervosa are as follows:

A.  Recurrent episodes of binge eating. An episode of binge eating is characterized by both of the following:
    (1) eating, in a discrete period of time (e.g., within any 2-hour period) an amount of food that is definitely larger than most people would eat during a similar period of time and under similar circumstances
    (2) a sense of lack of control over eating during the episode (e.g., a feeling that one cannot stop eating or control what or how much one is eating)
B.  Recurrent inappropriate compensatory behavior in order to prevent weight gain, such as self-induced vomiting; misuse of laxatives, diuretics, enemas, or other medications; fasting; or excessive exercise.
C.  The binge eating and inappropriate compensatory behaviors both occur, on average, at least twice a week for 3 months.
D.  Self-evaluation is unduly influenced by body shape and weight.
E.  The disturbance does not occur exclusively during episodes of Anorexia Nervosa.

*Specify type:*

Purging Type: during the current episode of Bulimia Nervosa, the person has regularly engaged in self-induced vomiting or the misuse of laxatives, diuretics, or enemas.

Non-purging Type: during the current episode of Bulimia Nervosa, the person has used other inappropriate compensatory behaviors, such as fasting or excessive exercise, but has not regularly engaged in self-induced vomiting or the misuse of laxatives, diuretics, or enemas.

These are the criteria that we will be using for the next few years, and their evolution shows progress (Walsh & Kahn, 1997). However, obvious potential problems remain. Many patients coming for treatment in eating disorders clinics do not satisfy criteria for anorexia nervosa or bulimia nervosa, and must be classified as having an eating disorder not otherwise specified (EDNOS) (Ash & Piazza, 1995). Also we must consider binge eating disorder, which was not included as a separate diagnosis in DSM-IV, but as a disorder for further study in the appendix, an example of EDNOS. Although binge eating is described in a fashion identical to that in bulimia nervosa, there is some evidence to suggest that binge eating in the two disorders may actually be both qualitatively and quantitatively different (Mitchell et al., 1999), yet the boundaries are not clear. Another problem concerns the issue of the "compensatory" behaviors. For vomiting and laxative abuse, the purging behavior is quite clearly compensatory in many cases. However, in considering non-purging compensatory behavior, such as excessive exercise and fasting, the definitions are less clear. For example, let us assume a patient indicates that after binge eating, she attenuates her food intake the next day. This might be considered a compensatory behavior, but is not really substantially different from someone who binge eats and then restricts her caloric intake as a weight control technique. Operationally the two phenomenon may be identical, although such patients might receive different diagnoses. Functionally, however, we find that binge eating disorder is far more likely to be diagnosed in people who are overweight, and bulimic symptoms with compensatory behaviors including purging behavior are less commonly seen in overweight individuals. Therefore, some of the boundaries remain difficult to draw. One thing is perfectly clear, however, and that is that there is a large subgroup of bulimia nervosa individuals who binge eat on a regular basis, frequently several times a day, and follow this behavior by compensatory purging behavior such as vomiting and/or laxative abuse. This pattern accounts for the vast majority of patients in the clinical trials of bulimia nervosa reported to date and represents a substantial group of the patients seen in most eating disorder clinics.

This discussion raises another interesting problem that surfaces when we discuss eating disorders. We label what we consider to be pathological behaviors, yet we do not adequately define exactly what their non-pathologic equivalent would be. For example, we can say that an individual with bulimia nervosa has abnormal (e.g., binge-eating) behavior, but what is normal? Is the eating behavior of a typical adolescent, who may eat excessive fat and low amounts of protein, who consumes much "fast-food" and frequently misses one or two meals a day, followed by overeating at other times, "normal"? Such problems are difficult to sort out and are certainly beyond the scope of this text. It is important to remember, however, that the term *eating disorders* may label discrete, to some extent, homogeneous subgroups, but that outside of these subgroups are many other individuals, some of whom may need help and many of whom may be distressed by their behavior, who do not satisfy criteria for any specific eating disorder. Therefore, it is important that we not take the current diagnostic categories as the final answer to the problem but instead as a systematic attempt that will at some point be remodeled.

Bulimia nervosa may be best conceptualized as a behavioral disorder, in the sense that it can develop in at least two separate contexts: as a symptom in patients with other forms of primary psychopathology, such as major depressive disorder, or as a discrete problem in individuals who develop bulimia nervosa on a cultural basis, often in the context of unnecessary dieting during adolescence. Therefore, a unitary concept of the disorder may not be optimal. The disorder can have a variable age of onset (mean age 18) and variable course, and markedly variable prognosis. Some individuals apparently experience a waxing and waning of their symptoms over time, and some recover as they grow older without any intervention whatsoever. The long-term (mean 11.5 years) outcome suggests that many do recover, with or without treatment, but that approximately 30% continue to at least sporadically binge eat and/or purge (Keel, Mitchell, Miller, Davis, & Crow, 1999).

### Risk Factors

The two variables that have been often cited concerning eating disorders in general, and in this case bulimia nervosa, are culture and gender: bulimia nervosa tends to occur in Westernized, industrialized societies where there is an abundance of food and where a high valence is placed on slimness as a model of attractiveness for women. Eating disorders occurring in other contexts are very rare. Also of particular interest, as minorities are assimilated into the mainstream culture and obtain higher socioeconomic status, they also tend to develop higher rates of eating disorders. Therefore, it is useful to think about bulimia nervosa as at least partially determined by cultural variables.

Gender is also extremely important (Casper, 1998b). We know that only 5% to 10% of cases of eating disorders (anorexia nervosa and bulimia nervosa) occur in males (Andersen, 1990; Andersen & Holman, 1997; Herzog, Newman, & Warsaw, 1991). This has held true over time and across geographic areas. While it is important not to minimize the problem among males, the high preponderance in girls and women strongly speaks to the need to consider what factors in societies like our own seem to preordain that certain girls and young women develop eating disorders, in this case bulimia nervosa. Although it is difficult to prove, there is a widespread consensus that the high valence placed on slimness as a model of attractiveness for women is involved (DiNicola, 1990; Dolan, 1991; Striegel-Moore, Silberstein, & Rodin, 1986). This "thinness" model is well accepted by females by the time they enter puberty, a time when their bodies are changing in ways that many of them find disconcerting or even frightening (wider hips, increased fat distribution, increased weight, etc.). We know that this is the time of life when they are most vulnerable to the development of these disorders, and etiologic models of bulimia nervosa must address this observation. Of interest, considerable research suggests that childhood sexual abuse may be a risk factor for the development of bulimia nervosa (Wonderlich, Brewerton, Jocic, Dansky, & Abbott, 1997).

## Demography

As stated previously, bulimia nervosa is primarily a disorder of women, and usually develops in adolescence or young adulthood, occurring in 1% to 2% of girls and women at risk (Drewnowski, Hopkins, & Kessler, 1988; Fairburn and Beglin, 1990; Kurtzman, Yager, Landsverk, Wiesmeier, & Bordurka, 1989; Shotte & Stunkard, 1989; Striegel-Moore, Silberstein, Frensch, & Rodin, 1989). The prevalence rates in various minorities remain controversial (Crago, Shisslak, & Estes, 1996). All socioeconomic groups are represented, and there is some suggestion of overrepresentation from lower socioeconomic groups (Gard & Freeman, 1996). The relative rarity with which this disorder develops earlier in life suggests that there are factors operational in this particular age group that determine a high likelihood for the disorder, and this has led many investigators to focus on the developmental tasks for girls and women of late adolescence and early adulthood in seeking to understand how the disorder evolves.

The mean age of onset of illness for this disorder is around 18, with limited variability, although the disorder can develop in childhood (Sokol, Steinberg, & Zerbe, 1998; Steiner & Lock, 1998). This leads one to speculate about the role of age in onset (Mitchell, Hatsukami, Pyle, & Eckert, 1985). A classical pattern of onset would be that a young woman who has been dieting off and on (probably unnecessarily) much of adolescence, who also has a certain amount of body dissatisfaction, and who then in the context of dieting, with the superimposed stressors of her changing roles from a high school student to a member of the workforce, or to college, develops periods of breakthrough binge eating (Howard & Porzelius, 1999; Story, French, Resnick, & Blum, 1995). To compensate for the excess caloric intake, she begins to self-induce vomiting or to use laxatives. Of interest, a subgroup of patients with bulimia nervosa, probably a fairly small subgroup, appear to develop binge eating outside of the context of dieting, and this finding suggests that some other factor may mediate their abnormal eating behavior. At any rate, regardless of the exact mechanism of onset, the average patient with bulimia nervosa is symptomatic with this disorder for four to six years before seeking treatment (Mitchell, Soll, Eckert, Pyle, & Hatsukami, 1989). This observation has not changed for several years and suggests that many patients do not seek help for the disturbed eating per se, but instead because of the development of adverse psychosocial sequelae, or medical complication, or because of the development of comorbid psychopathology. In the early 1980s this disorder was little known and rarely discussed, and the behaviors involved were often considered offensive to practitioners. Because of these circumstances, many patients thought that what they were doing was very unusual and very unacceptable, and they were reticent to talk about it. However, that picture has gradually changed over the past 15 years, and now bulimia nervosa is a commonly discussed phenomenon. Despite this change, there does not appear to have been a shortened duration of symptoms prior to seeking treatment. Indeed, we know that many patients with this illness will first see general physicians with abdominal complaints, or psychiatrists with complaints of depression or anxiety, and not mention the eating disorder (Batal, Johnson, Lehman, Steel, & Mehler, 1998).

The epidemiology of bulimia nervosa became a focus of research shortly after the disorder was first recognized as a distinct phenomenon. As in delineating the epidemiology of any disorder that clusters in certain populations, the first studies were cross-sectional surveys, focusing on female high school and college students (Fairburn & Beglin, 1990). Subsequently surveys of specialized populations such as graduate schools, family practice clinics, women in the work setting, and even "suburban shoppers" have been reported in the literature. More recently population-based surveys have been reported. These results suggest the pattern of the disorder clustering in older adolescent and young adult females. It is important to note that these studies also show that many of the individual features of the disorder, such as the binge eating, appear to be quite common in adolescents, at least if self-defined, with 50% to 70% of women and a surprisingly high percentage of men reporting such symptoms in various surveys. However, when stricter criteria are used, such as requiring binge eating coupled with self-induced vomiting or laxative abuse at a minimum frequency of two times a week for three months (operationally the DSM-IV purging type of bulimia nervosa), the prevalence rates drop to around 1% to 2% of high school and college-age women, making bulimia nervosa a very common disorder but nowhere near the "epidemic" that was occasionally mentioned in the early literature (Fairburn & Beglin, 1990). Increasingly other samples are being surveyed for eating disorders, including groups from third-world countries, and these studies suggest clearly that in any population wherein the upper socioeconomic strata are adopting Western styles and ideals, eating disorders are problematic and often becoming more so.

## Longitudinal Course

The clinical course and outcome of bulimia nervosa over time have only recently begun to be studied in protocols with large samples (Vaz, 1998). Beginning with the report by Abraham in 1983, various long-term follow-up studies have been reported, but most have been fairly modest in duration, at most three to five years, and the rates of recovery in these surveys are also highly variable, with complete abstinence rates from bulimic symptoms at follow-up ranging anywhere from 13% to 87% depending on various factors including the nature of the treatment received at baseline, and the duration to follow-up (Keel & Mitchell, 1997).

The largest, carefully designed study, still in progress, is one being conducted by Herzog and colleagues at Massachusetts General Hospital, which now is surveying subjects beyond five years (Herzog, Keller, & Lavori, 1988). This study suggests a highly variable course for bulimia nervosa, and that treatment, which is not systematically applied as part of the study, can exert a positive influence on outcome. However, this and other studies also must be interpreted as showing that many of these patients do remain symptomatic despite exposure to some form of therapy. Most studies also suggest, at least in the short run, low mortality rates compared to anorexia nervosa, wherein the mortality remains significant. This observation underscores that many of the medical complications associated with anorexia nervosa are attributable to the starvation rather than the abnormal eating behavior per se, a finding compatible with the knowledge of human starvation gained from other studies.

One study of relapse in bulimia nervosa suggests that most relapses, if they occur after treatment, occur in the first six months after leaving therapy.

There is also some data to suggest that for a subgroup of bulimic patients, symptoms are seasonally linked, with exacerbation during the winter months (Blouin et al., 1992; Lam, Goldner, & Grewal, 1996; Levitan, Kaplan, & Rockert, 1996).

### Bulimic Behavior

#### Binge Eating

The central diagnostic feature of bulimia nervosa is the binge eating episodes (Wiseman, Harris, & Halmi, 1998). Although that feature might sound straightforward, on reflection it becomes clear that it is difficult to define a binge eating episode, and the concept remains open to interpretation by both clinicians and patients. Fairburn and Cooper (1993) attempted to circumvent this problem at least in part by differentiating "subjective" from "objective" binges, the latter involving the intake of at least 1,000 kilocalories of food. While this differentiation is useful, it does not solve all the problems. It suffices to say that most binge eating behavior involves the consumption of an amount of food that most people would consider inappropriate to consume in a given period of time, at least in front of others. Many patients describe binge eating as being characterized by a sense of lack of control, and when discussing binge eating behavior, many emphasize the fact that it is quite different from their normal eating, wherein one tastes and chews the food, and is very much subjectively aware of the eating experience. The term *stuffing syndrome* was suggested for bulimia nervosa at one point, and this term seems descriptive of the binge eating episodes related by many patients, but again there is a high amount of heterogeneity.

Most studies show a great deal of variability in the amount of food consumed during subjective binge eating episodes (Mitchell, Crow, Peterson, Wonderlich, & Crosby, 1998). When large amounts are consumed, certainly above 1,000 kilocalories or more, the intake is likely to be that of a bulimic rather than a control subject. In one study reported in our clinic the mean amount of kilocalories consumed during a binge eating episode was 3,415. Taken together, these studies do suggest that most binge eating episodes are far in excess of what one would consider a normal or a large meal. Then again, it is important to remember that some patients actually describe eating very little while binge eating and seem to be referring more to the type of the food (a forbidden food) or the sense of lack of control rather than the amount of food eaten per se. This characteristic is typical of binge eating in anorexia nervosa patients.

*Vomiting*

The primary compensatory behavior for patients with bulimia nervosa is self-induced vomiting, and in most reported studies the frequency of this behavior is actually somewhat higher than the number of binge eating episodes. It is not uncommon for patients to punctuate binge eating episodes with vomiting intermittently. The classical sequence is for an individual to self-induce vomiting after binge eating as a way of "getting rid" of the food, and for many this may become a highly ritualized compulsive behavior, with certain foods eaten in sequence, followed by certain rituals in the bathroom in preparation for the vomiting behavior. Some patients report that they need to stimulate the vomiting reflex by using a finger or some mechanical device such as a toothbrush. Many, however, particularly those who have been vomiting for years, report that it is relatively easy to vomit simply by standing over the toilet and bending forward. Electrolyte abnormalities may help to identify bulimic patients who vomit (Crow, Salisbury, Crosby, & Mitchell, 1997).

*Laxative Abuse*

The second most common compensatory behavior is laxative abuse (Mitchell & Boutacoff, 1986). This problem appears to be increasing in prevalence. Laxative abuse involves the ingestion of large amounts of a stimulant-type laxative in an effort to induce abrupt, watery diarrhea and a sense of weight loss (Mitchell & Boutacoff, 1986; Mitchell, Bouta-coff, Hatsukami, Pyle, & Eckert, 1986). Although several types of laxatives may be used experimentally by patients, in the final analysis, most of these patients end up using laxatives that cause rapid evacuation of the colon. These are usually laxatives that contain senna or cascara sagrada, or some other substance that irritates the colon. The most common over-the-counter laxatives that are abused are Correctol® and Ex-lax®. The most common pattern is for an individual with an eating disorder to start by taking one or two pills, but later to develop tolerance and increase the number gradually. Not uncommonly several dozen laxatives will be needed to produce diarrhea eventually. The diarrhea results in a prompt weight loss if one gets on the scale. What is lost, however, is primarily fluid and electrolytes from the lower bowel. Most of the ingested food that was binge eaten is still in the upper gastrointestinal tract being absorbed (Bo-linn, Santa Ana, Morawski, & Fordtran, 1983). Studies have shown that very little of the ingested food is actually lost through laxative abuse. The sense of weight loss, however, is very reinforcing to the patient. The weight loss is followed by a return of the weight the following day. The body, sensing the loss of the fluid and the attendant volume contraction, activates the renin-aldosterone system and retains fluid as a way of reestablishing fluid homeostasis. This response then results in reflex weight gain, and the need to take the laxatives again.

Analogous to the problem of using laxatives is the abuse of diuretics by patients with this illness (Mitchell, Pomeroy, Seppala, & Huber, 1988). The pathophysiology of this behavior is similar to that seen with laxative abuse, except the fluid loss occurs through the kidney rather than the bowel. Most patients who experiment with diuretics use over-the-counter diuretics such as Aquaban®, which are not very potent, and many times not very reinforcing. However, a small percentage of patients with eating disorders gravitate toward the use of highly potent prescription diuretics, such as Lasix®. Use of these can result in the loss of large amounts of fluid and accompanying weight loss, which can cause significant medical complications analogous to the problems with laxatives. Research has shown that diuretic abuse is a problem among some women in its own right, and studies have shown that if one surveys individuals who are using diuretics inappropriately, one finds a higher than expected rate of eating disorders.

## Diet Pills

Diet pills are used by some patients with eating disorders but generally only transiently (Pomeroy, Mitchell, Seim, & Seppala, 1988). This is particularly true of over-the-counter diet pills that contain phenylpropanolamine and, if taken as directed by the package, result in a total intake of 75 mg a day, the maximum permitted by the FDA for over-the-counter usage. There have been reports of adverse medical complications such as hypertension and stroke occurring in association with phenylpropanolamine usage.

## Excessive Exercise

Excessive exercise is a difficult behavior to define and to quantify (Brewerton, Stellefson, Hibbs, Hodges, & Cochrane, 1995). There is a subgroup of patients with bulimia nervosa who exercise specifically in response to binge eating. Others engage in this behavior excessively (such as hundreds of sit-ups) to modify abdominal fat distribution, ignoring other exercises that would engender cardiovascular fitness. Therefore, the assessment must include the type, the amount, and the reasons for the exercise. Although excessive exercise is often a focus of concern, in reality many patients are not exercising at all, and a healthy exercise program may aid them in their efforts to maintain a normal body weight.

## Fasting

The usual definition of fasting is a 24-hour period without eating. Many patients with bulimia nervosa frequently skip meals, particularly breakfast and often lunch, which is fasting under a broader definition. Whether the problem is fasting for 24 hours or skipping meals, the importance of instituting a regular meal pattern with three balanced meals each day plus snacks cannot be overemphasized in treatment.

## Chewing and Spitting Out Food

In an early report, Fairburn and Cooper (1982) reported that 13 of 35 patients chewed and spit out food, and several reported doing this on a regular basis. In our report of 275 patients with bulimia, 65.4% reported having engaged in this behavior, although we did not obtain data on frequency (Mitchell, Pyle, Hatsukami, & Eckert, 1988). Occasionally one encounters such patients, although usually this is an infrequent behavior.

## Rumination

Fairburn and Cooper reported that 7 of 35 patients engaged in this behavior, with 4 ruminating on a daily basis. We more recently reported a certain series of ruminators; some developed the behavior in the context of an eating disorder, and others pursued the behavior independently. This phenomenon has been little studied but is frequent enough that patients should be asked about it routinely when being interviewed about their eating disorder.

Other less frequent behaviors, such as the misuse of enemas and the use of Ipecac®, should also be inquired about on a routine basis. Ipecac® abuse is particularly worrisome, and the clinician should couple the inquiry with basic education about the risks involved (Friedman, 1984). The emetine alkaloid in Ipecac® has been found to be associated with the development of myopathy, including cardiomyopathy, particularly when subjects ingest more than a gram of the emetine alkaloid. A few cases of Ipecac® abuse and myopathy have been reported; there are also a few case reports suggestive of death from cardiomyopathy in patients misusing Ipecac®.

## Comorbidity

Many patients with bulimia nervosa present with one or more other Axis I or Axis II forms of comorbid psychopathology. This area, dealt with only superficially in this chapter, will be a major focus in some of the treatment chapters. There are three major forms of comorbidity that have been studied intensively.

## Depression

Depression is by far the form of comorbidity most often encountered in patients with bulimia nervosa (Casper, 1998a; Hudson, Pope, Yurgelun-Todd, Jonas, & Frankenburg, 1987; Zanarini et al., 1990). From 40% to 80% of patients presenting with bulimia nervosa in described samples have a lifetime history of major depressive disorder, with 30% to 60%

meeting criteria for current major depressive disorder, and an additional subgroup meeting criteria for dysthymia or cyclothymia. However, the rate of bipolar affective disorder appears to be low.

This comorbidity has been a source of considerable debate relative to the relationship to eating disorders. Some patients with bulimia nervosa appear to develop the eating disorder in the context of an ongoing problem with major depression, while others, perhaps at the other end of the spectrum, appear to develop depression in the context of an ongoing problem with bulimia nervosa, perhaps owing to the medical and psychological consequences of the disorder. In others it is difficult to separate out the temporal relationship between the two conditions. Some authors have speculated that bulimia nervosa might actually represent a form of affective disorder, and indeed there is some evidence to support this in a subgroup of patients. However, the relationship is often far more complex, as is true when we examine comorbidity in general. The DSM system directs clinicians to choose multiple diagnostic categories for patients. However, it would be naive to assume that they are purely independent phenomena. Nonetheless, such is the current system, and the comorbidity with depression is a major complicating variable in planning treatment strategy.

### Alcohol/Drug Abuse

Russell in his original 1979 description noted that some of his patients had problems with alcohol and drug abuse, and indeed various series reports at the time have documented high rates. In the original report of 275 women evaluated for bulimia nervosa reported from Minnesota, 30.4% gave a history of problems with alcohol, and 18% had been in alcohol/drug abuse treatment, a figure that may be somewhat inflated by the high rate of substance abuse treatment in Minnesota compared to other parts of the country. More recently, studies have shown familial relationships between bulimia nervosa and alcohol/substance abuse. Several studies focusing on women undergoing substance abuse treatment have also found higher than expected rates of eating disorders.

### Personality Disorder

The relationship between bulimia nervosa and personality disorders or traits, including those detailed in the DSM-IV system, remains quite controversial, as will be discussed in chapter 8 (Gartner, Marcus, Halmi, & Loranger, 1989; Wonderlich & Mitchell, 1991; Yager, Landsverk, Edelstein, & Hyler, 1989). In summary, there is considerable evidence that certain forms of Axis II psychopathology, particularly Cluster-B problems, appear to be more common in patients with bulimia nervosa than in age- and sex-matched controls, and perhaps compared to some other forms of psychopathology. Impulsivity seems to characterize many of these individuals (Kaye, Bastiani, & Moss, 1995). Beyond this observation, the situation becomes complex, as will be reviewed in chapter 8.

## Psychobiology

Recently considerable research has focused on attempts to delineate possible underlying psychobiological factors that predispose to, or develop in, the context of bulimia nervosa (Walsh & Devlin, 1998). This literature is becoming increasingly rich, partly owing to the fact that the underlying biological systems that control appetite and satiety are being elucidated by basic scientists, and increasingly clinical researchers are attempting to translate these changes into meaningful work with humans. Much of this work has not progressed to the point where it can be used clinically for treatment purposes, and is, therefore, not directly relevant to this text. However, we will review some of this literature so as to keep the reader abreast of developments in the field, and to point out that these data lend considerable support for certain types of treatment interventions.

Many of the neurobiological systems known to be involved in appetite are now being studied in individuals with bulimia nervosa. These include the traditional biogenic amines, such as serotonin and norepinephrine, some of the peptide systems, such as pancreatic polypeptide groups (peptide NPY and PYY), and cholecystokinin (CCK), an important putative satiety peptide.

Much of the recent research in this area has focused on serotonin (Wolfe, Metzger, & Jimerson, 1997), which is known to produce effects opposite of those of norepinephrine on food intake, resulting in a reduction in feeding, in particular a preferential reduction in carbohydrate intake, in animals. Research has demonstrated that serotonin agonists reduce food consumption, with a relative sparing of protein intake. Synthesis of brain serotonin is known to be enhanced by eating calorie-rich, low-protein foods, while eating high-protein foods inhibits serotonin synthesis, since many of the amino acids in high-protein foods compete with tryptophan (the precursor of serotonin) for uptake into the central nervous system. Various authors have hypothesized that bulimic behaviors may result from hypofunctioning within serotonergic systems. Further evidence for this hypothesis comes from the observation that various disorders characterized by impulsivity have been found to be characterized by low levels of serotonin metabolites in the cerebrospinal fluid, particularly 5 hydroxyindoleacetic acid (5-HIAA), from the high rate of depression in patients with bulimia nervosa, a disorder that at times has been linked to low levels of serotonin, and from their response to serotonin reuptake inhibitors (Mayer & Walsh, 1998; Stunkard, 1997).

There are many ways to assess serotonin activity. Various observations using these approaches have suggested that serotonin regulation may indeed be abnormal in this patient group. This includes evidence of enhanced prolactin response to the serotonin precursor L-tryptophan, or the serotonin post-synaptic receptor agonist m-chlorophenylpiprazine (m-CCP), suggesting underlying endogenous hypofunctioning of the system. Also, Kaye and Weltzin (1991) have found that bulimic subjects who terminate binge eating episodes when they still have access to food generally tend to have low levels of tryptophan compared to other large neutral amino acids in serum. Binge eating increases this ratio, suggesting that increased tryptophan may be getting into the central nervous system and resulting in increased serotonin synthesis.

Relative to peptidergic transmission, abstinent bulimic patients (compared to patients who remain symptomatic) have high levels of PYY. PYY is a member of the pancreatic polypeptide family that is known to be a very potent stimulator of feeding and has been referred to by Morley as the "bulimic" peptide because of its strong feeding induction properties. The fact that this peptide is elevated in cerebrospinal fluid in abstinent bulimics suggests that there may be a strong biological drive for them to overeat, a drive that may be reversed somewhat during periods of active illness, suggesting a possible underlying trait diathesis or at least an underlying abnormality that tends to increase the risk of relapse.

Another peptide that has been intensively investigated for its satiety effects is CCK, a peptide that exists in various molecular forms both in the periphery and the central nervous system. This peptide binds to vagal afferents when released from the gut mucosal cells in the small intestine. It appears to be a potent satiety signal in various infrahuman species and in humans, although the peripheral mediation of CCK effects appears to be via the vagal system only in some species. Geraciori and Liddle (1988) showed that CCK response to a test meal was markedly attenuated in patients with bulimia nervosa before treatment but improved with treatment with antidepressants. Lydiard et al. (1993), studying the octapeptide of CCK in human cerebrospinal fluid, again found low levels in bulimia subjects compared to normal controls.

Opiates and opiate antagonists have also been evaluated in patients with bulimia nervosa because of the observation that various opioid peptides appear to stimulate feeding in animals. Recent work suggests that opiates may increase the hedonic or reward value of food or other reinforcing substance, since opiates seem to preferentially stimulate intake of foods when animals are bred for such a preference. Stress-induced feeding in animals has been shown to be attenuated by the administration of opiate antagonists, and some studies in humans suggest that the admission of short-acting opiate antagonists will reduce bulimic behavior in patients with bulimia nervosa. Studies using long-acting orally active antagonists, such as naltrexone, are reviewed in the chapter on psychopharmacology (chapter 7).

There is also evidence of changes in gastric capacity in bulimic patients. Geliebter et al. (1992) have shown a significantly enlarged gastric capacity in these patients, which may promote binge eating.

## Treatment

Shortly after the initial description of bulimia nervosa by Russell in 1979, a variety of controlled studies were initiated examining potential treatments for bulimia nervosa. Two general approaches have been used: psychotherapy and pharmacotherapy. At this point more than 20 controlled studies of each of these forms of treatment have been conducted, and many different drugs and techniques have been examined. Pharmacotherapy and psychotherapies have also been compared directly, and their potential additive effects have been examined. We will review the studies of both psychotherapy and pharmacotherapy for bulimia nervosa, examine the comparative efficacy of these treatments, and discuss the role of combined treatments for bulimia nervosa.

### Psychotherapeutic Treatment

More than 20 studies have examined the use of psychotherapy for bulimia nervosa using a control or comparison group, and these are summarized in Table 2.1. Both individual and group treatments were tried, alone and in combination, and at least one study compared group with individual therapy (Freeman, Barry, Dunkeld-Turnbull, & Henderson, 1988). The great majority of these trials involved short-term, structured psychotherapies. The duration of the trials ranged between 6 and 24 weeks, but most commonly was between 12 and 16 weeks. A number of

Table 2.1. Controlled Psychotherapy Studies of Bulimia Nervosa

| Investigators (year) | Group vs. individual | Treatment | Sample size | % completers | Outcome % reduction in binge eating | % abstinent at termination |
|---|---|---|---|---|---|---|
| Lacey, 1983 | Individual + group | Individual + group | 30 | 100 | 95 | 80 |
| Connors et al., 1984 | Group | Psychoeducation | 26 | 77 | 70 | 13 |
| Yates & Sambrailo, 1984 | Group | CBT + BT | 24 | 67 | | 13 |
| | | CBT | | | | 0 |
| Kirkley et al., 1985 | Group | CBT | 14 | 93 | 64 | 97 |
| | | Nondirective | 14 | | | 64 |
| Ordman & Kirschenbaum, 1985 | Individual | Full | 10 | 100 | | 20 |
| | | Brief | 10 | 100 | | 20 |
| Lee & Rush, 1986 | Group | CBT | 15 | 73 | 70 | 29 |
| Wolchik et al., 1986 | Individual + group | Psychoeducation | 13 | 85 | 58 | 0 |
| Wilson et al., 1986 | Group | Cognitive restructuring +ERP | 9 | 85 | 82 | 71 |
| | | Cognitive restructuring | 8 | 67 | 51 | 33 |
| Fairburn et al., 1986 | Individual | CBT | 12 | 92 | 87 | 27 |
| | | Short-term focal | 12 | 92 | 82 | 36 |
| Laessle et al., 1987 | Group | BT | 8 | 100 | | 38 |
| Leitenberg et al., 1988 | Group | CBT + ERP (ss) | 13 | 92 | 67[a] | 42 |
| | | CBT + ERP (ms) | 13 | 85 | 73[b] | 36 |
| | | CBT | 12 | 100 | 40 | 8 |
| Freeman et al., 1988 | Individual + group | Individual CBT | 32 | 66 | 70 | |
| | | Individual BT | 30 | 83 | 87 | |
| | | Group | 30 | 63 | 87 | |

| Study | Format | Treatment | | | | |
|---|---|---|---|---|---|---|
| Agras et al., 1989 | Individual | Self-monitor | 19 | 86 | 63[c] | 24 |
| | | CBT | 22 | 99 | 95 | 56 |
| | | CBT + ERP | 17 | 94 | 52 | 31 |
| Mitchell et al., 1990 | Group | CBT + placebo | 34 | 85 | 89 | 43 |
| | | CBT + imipramine | 52 | 75 | 92 | 56 |
| | | Imipramine | 54 | 67 | 49 | 16 |
| Fairburn et al., 1991 | Individual | CBT | 25 | 84 | 96.7 | 71 |
| | | IPT | 25 | 88 | 98.0 | 62 |
| | | BT | 25 | 76 | 91.3 | 62 |
| Fichter et al., 1991 | | Fluoxetine + BT | 20 | 100 | 46.7 | |
| | | Placebo + BT | 20 | 100 | 25.4 | |
| Wilson et al., 1991 | Individual | CBT + ERP | 11 | 82 | 78 | 54.6 |
| | | CBT | 11 | 73 | 75 | 63.6 |
| Laessle et al., 1991 | Group | Nutrition management | 27 | 81 | 70 | 50 |
| | | Stress management | 28 | 93 | 70 | 27 |
| Garner et al., 1993 | Individual | Psychodynamic | 30 | 83 | 69 | 40 |
| | | CBT | 50 | 83 | 73 | 11 |
| Agras et al., 1992 | Individual | Desipramine 16 wks | 12 | | -12.7 | 35 |
| | | Desipramine 24 wks | 12 | | 44.1 | 42 |
| | | CBT + desipramine 16 wks | 12 | 83 | 57.3 | 65 |
| | | CBT + desipramine 24 wks | 12 | | 59.2 | 70 |
| | | CBT | 12 | | 71.3 | 55 |
| Mitchell et al., 1993 | Group | CBT | 33 | 88 | 76.7 | 69.7 |
| | | High emphasis on abstinence/high intensity | | | | |
| | | High/low | 41 | 88 | 73.2 | 73.2 |
| | | Low/high | 35 | 86 | 70.6 | 70.6 |
| | | Low/low | 34 | 82 | 32.4 | 32.4 |

Table 2.1. *Continued*

| Investigators (year) | Group vs. individual | Treatment | Sample size | % completers | Outcome | |
|---|---|---|---|---|---|---|
| | | | | | % reduction in binge eating | % abstinent at termination |
| Thackwray et al., 1993 | Individual | Self-monitoring | 47 | 82 | 82 | 69 |
| | | Behavioral | | | 100 | 100 |
| | | CBT | | | 89 | 92 |
| Goldbloom et al., 1997 | Individual | Fluoxetine | 23 | | 52 | 17 |
| | | CBT | 24 | | 73 | 43 |
| | | Fluoxetine + CBT | 29 | | 86 | 27 |
| Walsh et al., 1997 | Individual | CBT + medication | 120 | | 93 | 50 |
| | | CBT + placebo | | 66 | 77 | 19 |
| | | SPT + medication | | | 60 | 18 |
| | | SPT + placebo | | | 51 | 12 |
| | | Medication | | | 85 | 25 |
| Agras et al., 2000 | Individual | CBT | 110 | 72 | | 29 |
| | | IPT | 110 | 76 | | 66 |

*Note:* CBT = cognitive behavioral therapy; BT = behavioral therapy; ERP = exposure and response prevention; ss = single site; ms = multiple sites; IPT = interpersonal psychotherapy; SPT = supportive therapy. Adapted from Peterson, C. P., & Mitchell, J. E., Cognitive behavior therapy, in C. O. Gabbard (Ed.), *Treatment of psychiatric disorders* (2d ed.) (Washington, DC: APA Press, 1995).
[a]multiple sites; [b]single site; [c]reduction in vomiting.

therapeutic techniques were examined, but the most commonly used approach was cognitive-behavioral therapy (CBT).

Generally, CBT yielded the highest abstinence rates and greatest decrements in binge eating and purging of any of the studied treatments. It appears to be effective both in group and individual formats. Several investigations attempted to add exposure and response prevention, with mixed results. Dismantling studies, comparing CBT with behavioral therapy, have generally found CBT to be superior.

One recent major development is the finding that interpersonal psychotherapy (IPT) also leads to substantial improvement in bulimic symptoms, at times approaching that seen with CBT. This finding is particularly striking in that IPT, as delivered in these trials, seeks to avoid food- and weight-related issues, focusing only on the interpersonal domain. Also of note is that a delayed improvement, or "sleeper effect," appears to occur in the years that follow cessation of IPT (Fairburn, Jones, Peveler, Hope, & O'Connor, 1993).

Other forms of psychotherapy have also been examined, including focal (Fairburn, Kirk, O'Connor, & Cooper, 1986), supportive-expressive (Garner et al., 1993), stress management (Laessle et al., 1991), nondirective (Kirkley, Schneider, Agras, & Bachman, 1985), and supportive (Walsh et al., 1997). Generally, these treatments have yielded lower response rates than those seen with CBT (which usually has been used as a comparison condition in the same studies), the exception being interpersonal psychotherapy, which appears to be equally effective (Agras, Walsh, Fairburn, Wilson, & Kraemer, 2000).

Essentially all of these studies employed patient self-monitoring. Generally, self-monitoring has been included not only to provide outcome data, but also because it offers significant therapeutic benefits in its own right (Agras, Schneider, Arnow, Raeburn, & Telch, 1989). Some form of nutritional intervention also occurred in most of these trials, and nutritional approaches used alone received some support (Laessle, Waadt, & Pirke, 1987).

### Psychopharmacologic Treatment

Many psychotropic medications have been studied for the treatment of bulimia nervosa; most of this research has focused on the use of antidepressants. Early trials were prompted by hypotheses about the etiology of bulimia nervosa. First, Green and Rau in 1974 tried phenytoin after hypothesizing that bulimic behaviors were a variant of a seizure disorder. Later, antidepressants were used, relating in part to the hypothesis that bulimia nervosa represented a form of affective disorder. Neither of these hypotheses is currently thought to be correct, but they provided the stimulus for a large body of research on the pharmacologic treatment of this illness.

Table 2.2 summarizes the blinded placebo controlled trials of antidepressants for the treatment of bulimia nervosa. Only two of these trials, Mitchell and Groat (1984) and Sabine, Yonace, Farrington, Barratt, & Wakeling (1983), have failed to support the efficacy of these medications for bulimia nervosa. The main outcome measures were bulimic behaviors, either binge eating or vomiting or both. Although issues about body shape and weight are of great clinical significance, these variables have received little attention. Eight studies have examined whether pharmacotherapy can change body image disturbance, and the results are evenly split: Fichter et al. (1991), Fluoxetine Bulimia Nervosa Collaborative Study Group (FBNCSG) (1992), Hsu, Clement, Santhouse, & Ju (1991), and Walsh, Hadigan, Devlin, Gladis, & Roose (1991) support an effect; and Barlow, Blouin, Blouin, & Perez (1988), Goldstein et al. (1995), Mitchell et al. (1990), and Pope, Hudson, Jonas, & Yurgelun-Todd (1985) had negative results.

These medication studies ranged in duration from 6 to 16 weeks, with most lasting around 8 weeks. Some studies of antidepressants excluded depressed subjects, while others did not, and interestingly, it appears that response to antidepressants is independent of mood status.

A few specific comments pertinent to various trials should be made. First, in the direct comparison of fluoxetine in a standard antidepressant dose of 20 mg versus 60 mg per day, 60 mg per day was more effective. Second, it is notable that buproprion was effective when compared to placebo, but 5.7% of subjects in that study had generalized tonic clonic seizures. For this reason, bulimia nervosa is considered to be a contraindication for the use of buproprion. Finally, the MAO inhibitor phenelzine has been shown in a report by Walsh et al. (1988) to be effective for bulimia nervosa. Because of the necessity of dietary limitations to avoid tyramine reactions, the MAO inhibitors are relatively rarely used in this patient population, but in Walsh et al.'s study no problems with dietary indiscretions or tyramine reactions were noted.

The appropriate duration for antidepressant treatment for bulimia nervosa is not known. However, in the study involving desipramine conducted by Agras et al. (1992), treatment for 24 weeks was more effective than treatment for 16 weeks, suggesting that longer periods are more appropriate. A naturalistic follow-up study (Pope et al., 1985) suggested

Table 2.2.   Controlled Antidepressant Studies of Bulimia Nervosa

| Investigators (year) | Sample size | Treatment (dosage) | Outcome | |
|---|---|---|---|---|
| | | | % reduction in binge eating | % abstinent at termination |
| Pope et al., 1983 | 36 | Imipramine (≤ 200 mg) | | 0 |
| Sabine et al., 1983 | 19 | Mianserin (60 mg) | | |
| Mitchell & Groat, 1984 | 32 | Amitriptyline (150 mg) | 72 | 19 |
| Hughes et al., 1986 | 22 | Desipramine (200 mg) | 91 | 68 |
| Agras et al., 1987 | 22 | Imipramine (x = 167 mg) | 72 | 30 |
| Horne et al., 1988 | 81 | Buproprion (≤ 450 mg) | 67 | 30 |
| Barlow et al., 1988 | 24 | Desipramine (10 mg) | 4 | |
| Blouin et al., 1988 | 10 | Desipramine (150 mg) | 45* | |
| Kennedy et al., 1988 | 18 | Isocarboxaizid (60 mg) | | 33 |
| Walsh et al., 1988 | 50 | Phenelzine (60–90 mg) | 64 | 35 |
| Pope et al., 1989 | 42 | Trazodone (≤ 400 mg) | 31 | 10 |
| Fichter et al., 1991 | 40 | Fluoxetine (60 mg) | | |
| FBNCSG, 1992 | 387 | Fluoxetine (20 mg, 60 mg) | 67 | |
| Kennedy et al., 1993 | 36 | Brofaromine (≤ 200 mg) | 62 | |
| Goldstein et al., 1995 | 398 | Fluoxetine (60 mg) | 50 | |

*Vomiting frequency

that the long-term pharmacologic treatment of these patients frequently involves trials of multiple medications; in that study, only 25% of subjects received a single medication during the study period. One study attempted to examine the course of longer-term treatment, but high relapse rates during maintenance treatment made interpretation of a planned discontinuation phase difficult (Walsh et al., 1991).

One study to date has examined pharmacotherapy for relapse prevention in bulimia nervosa (Fichter, Krüger, Rief, Halland, & Doehne, 1996). Recently treated patients in remission were randomized to fluvoxamine or placebo for 3 weeks in the hospital followed by 12 more weeks after inpatient treatment. Fluvoxamine was found to be superior to placebo on several measures.

These findings naturally lead one to ask whether using antidepressants in sequence can improve outcome. A recent study by Walsh and colleagues (1997) utilized a sequence of desipramine for 8 weeks, followed by fluoxetine for nonresponders. Notably, the rates of abstinence and reduction in binge eating (29% and 69% respectively) were higher than those commonly seen in single drug trials, suggesting that sequential use may be a useful strategy.

Finally, the time course for improvement with pharmacologic treatment of bulimia nervosa has not been fully described, but it appears that improvement may occur more quickly for bulimia nervosa than for depression, at least with fluoxetine. In one study examining this question, most of those subjects who eventually would benefit from fluoxetine had done so within the first two weeks of treatment (FBNCSG, 1992).

In addition to the antidepressants, a wide variety of other medications have been tried for bulimia nervosa, including opiate antagonists (Alger, Schwalberg, Bigaouette, Michalek, & Howard, 1991; Igoin-Apfelbaum & Apfelbaum, 1987; Mitchell, Christenson, et al., 1989; Mitchell, Laine, Morley, & Levine, 1986), lithium (Hsu, Clement, Santhouse, & Ju, 1991), fenfluramine (Blouin et al., 1988; Russell, Checkley, Feldman, & Eisler, 1988), L-tryptophan (Krahn & Mitchell, 1985), and anticonvulsants (Wermuth, Davis, Hollister, & Stunkard, 1977). For the most part, these studies have been negative, although fenfluramine (in one study) appeared to be effective.

### Combination Treatment

Five studies have examined the combination of pharmacotherapy and psychotherapy for the outpatient treatment of bulimia nervosa. Two studies found additive effects on measures of eating pathology for combined treatment, while two others did not. One additional small trial did find efficacy for combining CBT plus desipramine; however, initial subject numbers were relatively low, and dropout rates were high (Leitenberg et al., 1994). Finally, an inpatient trial combining fluoxetine with CBT did not support improved efficacy with combined treatment. Any potential added benefit from fluoxetine may have been obscured by the use of (presumably more intensive) inpatient treatment.

Taken in combination, these studies have led many investigators to conclude that combining pharmacotherapy with psychotherapy provides more benefit than either treatment alone.

### Conclusions

Both psychotherapy and pharmacotherapy have been shown to be effective for bulimia nervosa. Cognitive-behavioral therapy, which appears effective both in group and individual settings, is often thought to be "the gold standard" of treatment for this illness, as it provides higher response rates and has been more widely studied than other available treatments. Similarly, interpersonal therapy has received increasing support. Antidepressants are the major pharmacologic treatment for this illness at this time, yielding results that, although beneficial, fall short of those seen with psychotherapeutic treatment. The strategy of using antidepressants sequentially may improve response rates. Finally, recent work combining these treatment modalities suggests that combination therapies do provide better results than either therapy alone.

## References

Abraham, S. F., Mira, M., & Llewellyn-Jones, D. (1983). Bulimia: A study of outcome. *International Journal of Eating Disorders, 2,* 175–180.

Agras, W. S., Dorian, B., Kirkley, B. G., Arnow, B., & Bachman, J. (1987). Imipramine in the study of bulimia: A double-blind, controlled study. *International Journal of Eating Disorders, 6,* 29–38.

Agras, W. S., Rossiter, E. M., Arnow, B., Schneider, J. A., Telch, C. F., Raeburn, S. D., Bruce, B., Perl, M., & Koran, L. M. (1992). Pharmacologic and cognitive-behavioral treatment for bulimia nervosa: A controlled clinical comparison. *American Journal of Psychiatry, 149,* 82–87.

Agras, W. S., Schneider, J. A., Arnow, B., Raeburn, S. D., & Telch, C. F. (1989). Cognitive behavioral and response prevention treatments for bulimia nervosa. *Journal of Consulting and Clinical Psychology, 57,* 215–221.

Agras, W. S., Walsh, B. T., Fairburn, C. G., Wilson, G. T., & Kraemer, H. C. (2000). Multicenter comparison of cognitive-behavioral therapy and interpersonal therapy for bulimia nervosa. *Archives of General Psychiatry, 57,* 459–468.

Alger, S. A., Schwalberg, M. D., Bigaouette, J. M., Michalek, A. V., & Howard, L. J. (1991). Effect of a tricyclic antidepressant and opiate antagonist on binge-eating behavior in normal-weight bulimic and obese, binge-eating subjects. *American Journal of Clinical Nutrition, 53,* 865–871.

Andersen, A. E. (Ed.). (1990). *Males with eating disorders.* New York: Bruner/Mazel.

Andersen, A. E., & Holman, J. E. (1997). Males with eating disorders: Challenges for treatment and research. *Psychopharmacological Bulletin, 33,* 391–397.

Ash, J. B., & Piazza, E. (1995). Changing symptomatology in eating disorders. *International Journal of Eating Disorders, 18,* 27–38.

Barlow, J., Blouin, J., Blouin, A., & Perez, E. (1988). Treatment of bulimia with desipramine: A double-blind, crossover study. *Canadian Journal of Psychiatry, 33,* 129–133.

Batal, H., Johnson, M., Lehman, D., Steele, A., & Mehler, P. S. (1998). Bulimia: A primary care approach. *Journal of Women's Health, 7,* 211–220.

Blouin, A., Blouin, J., Aubin, P., Carter, J., Goldstein, C., Boyer, H., & Perez, E. (1992). Seasonal patterns of bulimia nervosa. *American Journal of Psychiatry, 149,* 73–81.

Blouin, A. G., Blouin, J. H., Perez, E. L., Bushnik, T., Zuro, C., & Mulder, E. (1988). Treatment of bulimia with fenfluramine and desipramine. *Journal of Clinical Psychopharmacology, 8,* 261–269.

Bo-linn, G., Santa Ana, C., Morawski, S., & Fordtran, J. S. (1983). Purging and calorie absorption in bulimic patients and normal women. *Annals of Internal Medicine, 99,* 14–17.

Brewerton, T. D., Stellefson, E. J., Hibbs, N., Hodges, E. L., & Cochrane, C. E. (1995). Comparison of eating disorder patients with and without compulsive exercising. *International Journal of Eating Disorders, 17,* 413–416.

Casper, R. C. (1998a). Depression and eating disorders. *Depression and Anxiety, 8,* 96–104.

Casper, R. C. (1998b). Recognizing eating disorders in women. *Psychopharmacological Bulletin, 34,* 267–269.

Casper, R. C., Eckert, E. D., Halmi, K. A., Goldberg, S. C., & Davis, J. M. (1980). Bulimia: Its incidence and clinical importance in patients with anorexia nervosa. *Archives of General Psychiatry, 37,* 1030–1035.

Connors, M. E., Johnson, C. L., & Stuckey, M. K. (1984). Treatment of bulimia with brief psychoeducational group therapy. *American Journal of Psychiatry, 141,* 1512–1516.

Crago, M., Shisslak, C. M., & Estes, L. S. (1996). Eating disturbances among American minority groups: A review. *International Journal of Eating Disorders, 19,* 239–248.

Crow, S. J., Salisbury, J. J., Crosby, R. D., & Mitchell, J. E. (1997). Serum electrolytes as markers of vomiting in bulimia nervosa. *International Journal of Eating Disorders, 21,* 95–98.

DiNicola, V. F. (1990). Anorexia multiforme: Self-starvation in historical and cultural context. *Transcultural Psychiatry Research Review, 27,* 247–286.

Dolan, B. (1991). Cross-cultural aspects of anorexia nervosa and bulimia: A review. *International Journal of Eating Disorders, 10,* 67–80.

Drewnowski, A., Hopkins, S. A., & Kessler, R. C. (1988). The prevalence of bulimia nervosa in the U.S. college student population. *American Journal of Public Health, 78,* 1322–1325.

Fairburn, C. G. (1983). Bulimia: Its epidemiology and management. In A. J. Stunkard & E. Steller (Eds.), *Eating and its disorders.* New York: Raven Press.

Fairburn, C. G., & Beglin, S. J. (1990). Studies of the epidemiology of bulimia nervosa. *American Journal of Psychiatry, 147,* 401–408.

Fairburn, C. G., & Cooper, P. J. (1982). Self-induced vomiting and bulimia nervosa—an undetected problem. *British Medical Journal, 284,* 1153–1155.

Fairburn, C. G., & Cooper, Z. (1993). The Eating Disorders Examination (12th ed.). In C. G. Fairburn and G. T. Wilson (Eds.), *Binge eating: Nature, assessment, and treatment* (pp. 317–360). New York: Guilford Press.

Fairburn, C. G., Jones, R., Peveler, R. C., Hope, R. A., & O'Connor, M. (1993). Psychotherapy and bulimia nervosa: Longer-term effects of interpersonal psychotherapy, behavior therapy, and cognitive behavior therapy. *Archives of General Psychiatry, 50,* 419–428.

Fairburn, C. G., Jones, R. T., Peveler, R. C., Carr, S. J., Solomon, R. A., O'Connor, M. E., Burran, J., & Hope, R. A. (1991). Three psychological treatments for bulimia nervosa. *Archives of General Psychiatry, 48,* 463–469.

Fairburn, C. G., Kirk, J., O'Connor, M., & Cooper, P. J. (1986). A comparison of two psychological treatments for bulimia nervosa. *Behavior Research and Therapy, 24,* 629–643.

Fichter, M. M., Krüger, R., Rief, W., Halland, R., & Doehne, J. (1996). Fluvoxamine in prevention of relapse in bulimia nervosa: Effects on eating-specific psychopathology. *Journal of Clinical Psychopharmacology, 16,* 9–18.

Fichter, M. M., Leibl, K., Rief, W., Brunner, E., Schmidt-Auberger, S., & Engel, R. R. (1991). Fluoxetine versus placebo: A double-blind study with bulimic inpatients undergoing intensive psychotherapy. *Pharmacopsychiatry, 24,* 1–7.

Fluoxetine Bulimia Nervosa Collaborative Study Group. (1992). Fluoxetine in the treatment of bulimia nervosa. *Archives of General Psychiatry, 49,* 139–147.

Freeman, C. P. L., Barry, F., Dunkeld-Turnbull, J., & Henderson, A. (1988). Controlled trial of psychotherapy for bulimia nervosa. *British Medical Journal, 296,* 521–525.

Friedman, E. J. (1984). Death from ipecac intoxication in a patient with anorexia nervosa. *American Journal of Psychiatry, 141,* 702–703.

Gard, M. C. E., & Freeman, C. P. (1996). The dismantling of a myth: A review of eating disorders and socioeconomic status. *International Journal of Eating Disorders, 20,* 1–12.

Garfinkel, P. E., Lin, E., Goering, P., Spegg, C., Goldbloom, D. S., Kennedy, S., Kaplan, A. S., & Woodside, D. B. (1996). Purging and non-purging forms of bulimia nervosa in a community sample. *International Journal of Eating Disorders, 20,* 231–238.

Garfinkel, P. E., Moldofsky, H., & Garner, D. M. (1980). The heterogeneity of anorexia nervosa: Bulimia as a distinct subgroup. *Archives of General Psychiatry, 37,* 1036–1040.

Garner, D. M., Rockert, W., Davis, R., Garner, M. V., Olmsted, M. P., & Engle, M. (1993). Comparison of cognitive-behavioral and supportive-expressive therapy for bulimia nervosa. *American Journal of Psychiatry, 150,* 37–46.

Gartner, A. F., Marcus, R. N., Halmi, K., & Loranger, A. W. (1989). DSM-III-R personality disorders in patients with eating disorders. *American Journal of Psychiatry, 146,* 1585–1591.

Geliebter, A., Melton, P. M., McCray, R. S., Gallagher, D. R., Gage, D., & Hashim, S. A. (1992). Gastric capacity, gastric emptying and test-meal intake in normal and bulimic women. *American Journal of Clinical Nutrition, 56,* 656–661.

Geraciori, T. D., & Liddle, R. A. (1988). Impaired cholecystokinin secretion in bulimia nervosa. *New England Journal of Medicine, 319,* 683–688.

Goldbloom, D. S, Olmsted, M., Davis, R., Clews, J., Heinmaa, M., Rockert, W., & Shaw, B. (1997). A randomized controlled trial of fluoxetine and cognitive behavioral therapy for bulimia nervosa: Short-term outcome. *Behavior Research and Therapy, 35,* 803–811.

Goldstein, D. J., Wilson, M. G., Thompson, V. L., Porvin, J. H., Rampey, A. H., & Fluoxetine Bulimia Nervosa Research Group. (1995). Long-term fluoxetine treatment of bulimia nervosa. *British Journal of Psychiatry, 166,* 660–666.

Green, R. S., & Rau, J. H. (1974). Treatment of compulsive eating disturbances with anticonvulsant medications. *American Journal of Psychiatry, 131,* 428–432.

Herzog, D. B., Keller, M. B., & Lavori, P. W. (1988). Outcome in anorexia nervosa and bulimia nervosa: A review of the literature. *Journal of Nervous and Mental Disorders, 176,* 131–143.

Herzog, D. B., Newman, K. L., & Warsaw, M. (1991). Body image dissatisfaction in homosexual and heterosexual males. *Journal of Nervous and Mental Disorders, 179,* 356–359.

Horne, R. L., Ferguson, J. M., Pope, H. G., Hudson, J., Lineberry, C. G., Ascher, J., & Caro, A. (1988). Treatment of bulimia with buproprion: A multicenter, controlled trial. *Journal of Clinical Psychiatry, 42,* 262–266.

Howard, C. E., & Porzelius, L. K. (1999). The role of dieting in binge eating disorder: Etiology and treatment implications. *Clinical Psychology Review, 19,* 25–44.

Hsu, L. K. G., Clement, L., Santhouse, R., & Ju, E. S. (1991). Treatment of bulimia nervosa with lithium carbonate: A controlled study. *Journal of Nervous Mental Disorders, 179,* 351–355.

Hudson, J. I., Pope, H. G., Jr., Yurgelun-Todd, D., Jonas, J. M., & Frankenburg, F. R. (1987). A controlled study of lifetime prevalence of affective and other psychiatric disorders in bulimic outpatients. *American Journal of Psychiatry, 144,* 1283–1287.

Hughes, P. L., Wells, L. A., Cunningham, C. J., & Ilstrup, D. M. (1986). Treating bulimia with desipramine. *Archives of General Psychiatry, 43,* 182–186.

Igoin-Apfelbaum, L., & Apfelbaum, M. (1987). Naltrexone and bulimic symptoms [Letter]. *Lancet, 2* (8567), 1087–1088.

Kaye, W. H., Bastiani, A. M., & Moss, H. (1995). Cognitive style of patients with anorexia nervosa and bulimia nervosa. *International Journal of Eating Disorders, 18,* 287–290.

Kaye, W. H., & Weltzin, T. E. (1991). Neurochemistry of bulimia nervosa. *Journal of Clinical Psychiatry, 52 (Suppl.),* 21–28.

Keel, P. K., & Mitchell, J. E. (1997). Outcome in bulimia nervosa. *American Journal of Psychiatry, 154,* 313–321.

Keel, P. K., Mitchell, J. E., Miller, K. B., Davis, T. L., & Crow, S. J. (1999). Long-term outcome of bulimia nervosa. *Archives of General Psychiatry, 56,* 63–69.

Kennedy, S. H., Goldbloom, D. S., Ralevski, E., D'Souza, J. D., & Lofchy, J. (1993). Is there a role for selective monoamine oxidase inhibitor therapy in bulimia nervosa? A placebo-controlled trial of brofaromine. *Journal of Clinical Psychopharmacology, 13,* 415–422.

Kennedy, S. H., Piran, N., & Warsh, J. J. (1988). A trial of isocarboxazid in the treatment of bulimia nervosa. *Journal of Clinical Psychopharmacology, 8,* 391–396.

Kirkley, B. G., Schneider, J. A., Agras, W. S., & Bachman, J. A. (1985). Comparison of two group treatments for bulimia. *Journal of Consulting and Clinical Psychology, 53,* 43–48.

Krahn, D., & Mitchell, J. E. (1985). Use of L-tryptophan in treating bulimia [Letter]. *American Journal of Psychiatry, 142,* 1130.

Kurtzman, F. D., Yager, J., Landsverk, J., Wiesmeier, E., & Bordurka, D. C. (1989). Eating disorders among select female student populations at UCLA. *Journal of the American Dietetic Association, 89,* 45–53.

Lacey, J. H. (1983). An outpatient treatment program for bulimia nervosa. *International Journal of Eating Disorders, 286,* 1609–1613.

Laessle, R. G., Beumont, P. J. V., Butow, P., Lennerts, W., O'Connor, M., Pirke, K. M., Touyz, S. W., & Waadt., S. (1991). A comparison of nutritional management with stress management in the treatment of bulimia nervosa. *British Journal of Psychiatry, 159,* 250–261.

Laessle, R. G., Waadt, S., & Pirke, K. M. (1987). A structured, behaviorally oriented group treatment for bulimia nervosa. *Psychotherapy and Psychosomatics, 48,* 141–145.

Lam, R. W., Goldner, E. M., & Grewal, A. (1996). Seasonality of symptoms in anorexia and bulimia nervosa. *International Journal of Eating Disorders, 19,* 35–44.

Lee, N. F., & Rush, A. J. (1986). Cognitive-behavioral group therapy for bulimia. *International Journal of Eating Disorders, 5,* 599–615.

Leitenberg, H., Rosen, J. C., Gross, J., Nudelman, S., & Vara, L. S. (1988). Exposure plus response-prevention treatment of bulimia nervosa. *Journal of Consulting and Clinical Psychology, 56,* 535–541.

Leitenberg, H., Rosen, J. C., Wolf, J., Vara, L. S., Detser, M. J., & Srebnik, D. (1994). Comparison of cognitive-behavior therapy and desipramine in the treatment of bulimia nervosa. *Behavioral Research Therapy, 32,* 37–45.

Levitan, R. D., Kaplan, A. S., & Rockert, W. (1996). Characterization of the "seasonal" bulimic patient. *International Journal of Eating Disorders, 19,* 187–192.

Lydiard, R. B., Brewerton, T. D., Fossey, M. D., Laraia, M. T., Stuart, G., Beinfeld, M. C., & Ballenger, J. C. (1993). CSF cholecyctokinin octapeptide in patients with bulimia nervosa and normal comparison controls. *American Journal of Psychiatry, 150,* 1099–1101.

Mayer, L. E., & Walsh, B. T. (1998). The use of selective serotonin reuptake inhibitors in eating disorders. *Journal of Clinical Psychiatry, 59,* 28–34.

Mitchell, J. E., & Boutacoff, M. A. (1986). Laxative abuse complicating bulimia: Medical and treatment implications. *International Journal of Eating Disorders, 5,* 325–334.

Mitchell, J. E., Boutacoff, L. I., Hatsukami, D., Pyle, R. L., & Eckert, E. D. (1986). Brief communication: Laxative abuse as a variant of bulimia. *Journal of Nervous and Mental Disorders, 174,* 174–176.

Mitchell, J. E., Christenson, G., Jennings, J., Huber, M., Thomas, B., Pomeroy, C., & Morley, J. (1989). A placebo-controlled, double-blind crossover study of naltrexone hydrochloride in patients with normal weight bulimia. *Journal of Clinical Psychopharmacology, 9,* 94–97.

Mitchell, J. E., Crow, S., Peterson, C. B., Wonderlich, S. A., & Crosby, R. D. (1998). Feeding laboratory studies in patients with eating disorders: A review. *International Journal of Eating Disorders, 24,* 115–124.

Mitchell, J. E., & Groat, R. (1984). A placebo-controlled, double-blind trial of amitriptyline in bulimia. *Journal of Clinical Psychopharmacology, 4,* 1186–1193.

Mitchell, J. E., Hatsukami, D., Pyle, R., & Eckert, E. D. (1985). Characteristics of 275 patients with bulimia. *American Journal of Psychiatry, 142,* 482–485.

Mitchell, J. E., Laine, D. E., Morley, J. E., & Levine, A. S. (1986). Naloxone but not CCK-8 may attenuate binge-eating behavior in patients with the bulimia syndrome. *Biological Psychiatry, 21,* 1399–1406.

Mitchell, J. E., Mussell, M. P., Peterson, C. B., Crow, S. J., Wonderlich, S., Crosby, R., Davis, T., & Weller, C. (1999). Hedonics of binge eating in women with bulimia nervosa and binge eating disorder. *International Journal of Eating Disorders, 26,* 165–170.

Mitchell, J. E., Pomeroy, C., Seppala, M., & Huber, M. (1988). Pseudo-Bartter's syndrome, diuretic abuse, idiopathic edema and eating disorders. *International Journal of Eating Disorders, 7,* 225–237.

Mitchell, J. E., Pyle, R. L., Eckert, E. D., Hatsukami, D., Pomeroy, C., & Zimmerman, R. (1990). A comparison study of antidepressants and structured intensive group psychotherapy in the treatment of bulimia nervosa. *Archives of General Psychiatry, 47,* 149–157.

Mitchell, J. E., Pyle, R. L., Hatsukami, D., & Eckert, E. D. (1988). Chewing and spitting out food as a symptom of bulimia. *Psychosomatics, 29,* 81–84.

Mitchell, J. E., Pyle, R. L., Pomeroy, C., Zollman, M., Crosby, R., Seim, H., Eckert, E. D., & Zimmerman, R. (1993). Cognitive behavioral group psychotherapy for bulimia nervosa: The importance of logistical variables. *International Journal of Eating Disorders, 14,* 277–288.

Mitchell, J. E., Soll, E., Eckert, E. D., Pyle, R. L., & Hatsukami, D. (1989). The changing population of bulimia nervosa patients in a university eating disorders program. *Hospital and Community Psychiatry, 40,* 1188–1189.

Ordman, A. M., & Kirschenbaum, D. S. (1985). Cognitive behavioral therapy for bulimia: An initial outcome study. *Journal of Consulting and Clinical Psychology, 53,* 305–313.

Pomeroy, C., Mitchell, J. E., Seim, H. C., & Seppala, M. (1988). Prescription diuretic abuse as a symptom of bulimia nervosa. *Journal of Family Practice, 27,* 493–496.

Pope, H. G., Hudson, J. I., Jonas, J. M., & Yurgelun-Todd, D. (1983). Bulimia treated with imipramine: A double-blind, placebo-controlled study. *American Journal of Psychiatry, 140,* 554–558.

Pope, H. G., Hudson, J. I., Jonas, J. M., & Yurgelun-Todd, D. (1985). Antidepressant treatment of bulimia: A two-year follow-up study. *Journal of Clinical Psychopharmacology, 5,* 320–327.

Pope, H. G., Keck, P. E., McElroy, S. L., & Hudson, J. I. (1989). A placebo-controlled study of trazodone in bulimia nervosa. *Journal of Clinical Psychopharmacology, 9,* 254–259.

Pyle, R. L., Mitchell, J. E., & Eckert, E. D. (1981). Bulimia: A report of 34 cases. *Journal of Clinical Psychiatry, 42,* 60–64.

Russell, G. (1979). Bulimia nervosa: An ominous variant of anorexia nervosa. *Psychological Medicine, 9,* 429–448.

Russell, G. F. M., Checkley, S. A., Feldman, J., & Eisler, J. (1988). A controlled trial of *d* -fenfluramine in bulimia nervosa. *Clinical Neuropharmacology, 11,* S146-S159.

Sabine, E. J., Yonace, A., Farrington, A. J., Barratt, K. H., & Wakeling, A. (1983). Bulimia nervosa: A placebo-controlled double-blind therapeutic trial of mianserin. *British Journal of Clinical Pharmacology, 15,* S195–S202.

Shotte, D. E., & Stunkard, A. J. (1989). Bulimia vs. bulimic behaviors on a college campus. *Journal of the American Medical Association, 258,* 1213–1215.

Sokol, M. S., Steinberg, D., & Zerbe, K. J. (1998). Childhood eating disorders. *Current Opinion in Pediatrics, 10,* 369–377.

Steiner, H., & Lock, J. (1998). Anorexia nervosa and bulimia nervosa in children and adolescents: A review of the past 10 years. *Journal of the American Academy of Child and Adolescent Psychiatry, 37,* 352–359.

Story, M., French, S. A., Resnick, M. D., & Blum, R. W. (1995). Ethnic/racial and socioeconomic differences in dieting behaviors and body image perceptions in adolescents. *International Journal of Eating Disorders, 18,* 173–179.

Striegel-Moore, R. H., Silberstein, L. R., Frensch, P., & Rodin, J. (1989). A prospective study of disordered eating among college students. *International Journal of Eating Disorders, 8,* 499–509.

Striegel-Moore, R. H., Silberstein, L. R., & Rodin, J. (1986). Toward an understanding of risk factors for bulimia. *American Psychologist, 41,* 246–263.

Stunkard, A. (1997). Eating disorders: The last 25 years. *Appetite, 29,* 181–190.

Thackwray, D. E., Smith, M. C., Bodfish, J. W., & Meyers, A. W. (1993). A comparison of behavioral and cognitive behavioral interventions for bulimia nervosa. *Journal of Consulting and Clinical Psychology, 61,* 639–645.

Vaz, E. J. (1998). Outcome of bulimia nervosa: Prognostic indicators. *Journal of Psychosomatic Research, 45,* 391–400.

Walsh, B. T. (1991). Psychopharmacologic treatment of bulimia nervosa. *Journal of Clinical Psychiatry, 52,* S34-S38.

Walsh, B. T., & Devlin, M. J. (1998). Eating disorders: Progress and problems. *Science, 280,* 1387–1390.

Walsh, B. T., Gladis, M., Roose, S. P., Stewart, J. W., Stetner, F., & Glassman, A. H. (1988). Phenelzine vs. placebo in 50 patients with bulimia. *Archives of General Psychiatry, 45,* 471–475.

Walsh, B. T., Hadigan, C. M., Devlin, M. J., Gladis, M., & Roose, S. P. (1991). Long-term outcome of antidepressant treatment for bulimia nervosa. *American Journal of Psychiatry, 148,* 1206–1212.

Walsh, B. T., & Kahn, C. B. (1997). Diagnostic criteria for eating disorders: Current concerns and future directions. *Psychopharmacological Bulletin, 33,* 369–372.

Walsh, B. T., Wilson, G. T., Loeb, K. L., Devlin, M. J., Pike, K. M., Roose, S. P., Fleiss, J., & Waternaux, C. (1997). Medication and psychotherapy in the treatment of bulimia nervosa. *American Journal of Psychiatry, 154,* 523–531.

Wermuth, B. M., Davis, K. L., Hollister, L. E., & Stunkard, A. J. (1977). Phenytoin treatment of the binge eating syndrome. *American Journal of Psychiatry, 134,* 1249–1253.

Wilson, G. T., Eldredge, K. L., Smith, D., & Niles, B. (1991). Cognitive-behavioral treatment with and without response prevention for bulimia. *Behavior Research and Therapy, 29,* 575–583.

Wilson, G. T., Rossiter, E., Kleifeld, E. I., & Lindholm, L. (1986). Cognitive behavioral treatment of bulimia nervosa: A controlled evaluation. *Behavioral Research and Therapy, 24,* 227–238.

Wiseman, C. V., Harris, W. A., & Halmi, K. A. (1998). Eating disorders. *Medical Clinics of North American, 82,* 145–159.

Wolchik, S. A., Weiss, L., & Katzman, M. A. (1986). An empirically validated, short-term psychoeducational group treatment program for bulimia. *International Journal of Eating Disorders, 5,* 21–34.

Wolfe, B. E., Metzger, E., & Jimerson, D. C. (1997). Research update on serotonin function in bulimia nervosa and anorexia nervosa. *Psychopharmacological Bulletin, 33,* 345–365.

Wonderlich, S. A., Brewerton, T. D., Jocic, Z., Dansky, B., & Abbott, D. W. (1997). Relationship of childhood sexual abuse and eating disorders. *Journal of the American Academy of Child and Adolescent Psychiatry, 36,* 1107–1115.

Wonderlich, S. A., & Mitchell, J. E. (1991). Eating disorders and personality disorder. In J. Yager, H. E. Gwirtsman, and C. K. Edelstein (Eds.), *Special problems in managing eating disorders.* Washington, DC: American Psychiatric Press.

Yager, J., Landsverk, J., Edelstein, C. K., & Hyler, S. E. (1989). Screening for Axis II personality disorders in women with bulimic eating disorders. *Psychosomatics, 30,* 255–262.

Yates, A. J., & Sambrailo, F. (1984). Bulimia nervosa: A descriptive and therapeutic study. *Behavioral Research and Therapy, 5,* 505–517.

Zanarini, M. C., Frankenburg, F. R., Pope, H. G., Jr., Yurgelun-Todd, D., & Cicchetti, C. J. (1990). Axis II comorbidity of normal weight bulimia. *Comprehensive Psychiatry, 31,* 20–24.

Chapter 3

# Binge Eating Disorder

*Martina de Zwaan and James E. Mitchell*

A large number of individuals in the general population report serious overeating or binge eating but do not engage in compensatory behaviors, such as vomiting. This binge eating is frequently associated with marked distress. This group of individuals is identified in the DSM-IV as having binge eating disorder, a diagnosis included in the appendix as a disorder for further study, and as an example of eating disorders not otherwise specified (EDNOS). Although there was a considerable debate as to whether to include this diagnosis in the DSM-IV text as a full diagnostic grouping, it was finally decided to include it in the appendix to stimulate further research in the area, and indeed much research has appeared since the concept was first elucidated (Devlin, Walsh, Spitzer, & Hasin, 1992; Spitzer et al., 1991; Yanovski, 1993).

Readers should keep in mind that although it is not required for the diagnosis, many individuals with binge eating disorder are overweight, and the relationship between binge eating disorder and obesity is an intriguing one, as we will discuss.

Binge eating was first systematically described among the obese in the American literature in the early 1950s. In 1951, Hamburger described a type of hyperphagia among obese patients characterized by "compulsive craving for food, especially candy, ice cream, and other sweets, which is frequently uncontrollable." In 1959, Stunkard in his classic paper "Eating Patterns and Obesity" described binge eating as a distinct subtype, characterized the eating binge as having an "orgiastic quality," and noted that "enormous amounts of food are consumed in relatively short periods." He also noted that binge eating was "frequently related to a specific precipitating event, and is regularly followed by severe discomfort and self-condemnation." Kornhaber in 1970 described the "stuffing syndrome"

59

among the obese, characterized by hyperphagia, emotional withdrawal, and clinical depression. Although this phenomenon has been recognized for a relatively long period of time among the obese, it has only recently been the focus of research attention.

## Associated Features and Differential Diagnosis

Relative to the diagnostic criteria, binge eating in binge eating disorder is described identically as binge eating in bulimia nervosa. Both require eating an unusually large amount of food and a sense of loss of control. However, our understanding and definition of binge eating remain problematic, and the boundaries of this phenomenon remain unclear, although the Eating Disorder Examination developed by Cooper and Fairburn (1987) represents an attempt to differentiate between subjective and objective binge eating as a way to address this problem. Binge eating disorder criteria also require a frequency of two binge eating days a week over the previous six months. Days per week rather than episodes per week (as is used in the bulimia nervosa criteria) was selected because of the lack of purging behavior, which seems to make it easier for patients with bulimia nervosa to recall discrete episodes. Also, Marcus, Smith, Santelli, & Kaye (1992) have reported that 25% of binge eating episodes in obese binge eaters last at least an entire day, suggesting a great deal of variability in this phenomenon. The binge episodes of overweight individuals are generally not as large and may differ in other important ways from the bingeing described by patients with bulimia nervosa (Brody, Walsh, & Devlin, 1994). If these episodes are different, the single definition of a binge episode for both disorders, as currently proposed in DSM-IV, may not fit clinical reality (Gladis, Wadden, Foster, Vogt, & Wingate, 1998).

As mentioned, distress is required for the diagnosis of binge eating, including unpleasant feelings during and after the episode, as well as concerns about the long-term effects on body weight and shape and the accompanying problems with self-esteem. The inclusion of this criterion was meant to minimize "false positives," and in the first multisite field trial (Spitzer et al., 1992), it was noted that to not include this criterion would have markedly increased the prevalence of binge eating disorder (by 10% in a weight-control sample, and by more than 100% in community samples). However, "marked distress" is difficult to define, and it is possible that including this criterion actually lends to identification of individuals with high levels of distress in general. This issue requires further study.

Some investigators have argued that binge eating disorder is still an unproven category, and that there is not enough evidence in predicting prognosis, treatment selection, or outcome to identify this diagnostic group. However, the increasing number of studies on binge eating disorder that have provided information on clinical features, eating and weight histories, course, and response to treatment suggest that it was a reasonable decision to include the criteria in the DSM-IV. Furthermore, it would be unrealistic to expect that a new diagnosis should only be recognized after there is definitive evidence about treatment, a criterion that would eliminate various other well-recognized illnesses.

**Epidemiology**

In research predating the DSM-IV, and in subsequent work using the proposed binge eating disorder guidelines or more recently the DSM-IV, investigators have relied on various methodologies for identifying binge eating syndromes, including the Binge Eating Scale (Gormally, Black, Daston, & Rardin, 1982) and the Binge Scale (Hawkins & Clement, 1980). Others have employed qualitative definitions, such as self-reported subjective overeating. However, regardless of the definition or assessment method used, the results of epidemiologic studies suggest that a significant minority (18–46%) of those in weight-control programs will present with significant binge eating problems without satisfying criteria for bulimia nervosa, making binge eating disorder a very common disorder.

In support of this high prevalence figure, two large multisite field trials were reported, both coordinated by Spitzer (Spitzer et al., 1992; Spitzer et al., 1993), using a self-administered questionnaire, the Questionnaire on Eating and Weight Patterns (QEWP).

The first multisite field trial involved 1,084 subjects who were screened using the QEWP. The disorder was quite common among subjects attending weight-loss programs (30%) but was relatively rare in the general population, with only 2% meeting full criteria. Interestingly, half of the binge eating disorder subjects in the community were obese (BMI > 27.5), but only 5% of the obese subjects in the community sample met binge eating disorder criteria. Among those in community samples who indicated that they had attended a weight-loss treatment program in the prior week, the frequency was 11.3%. Binge eating disorder was most common in an Overeaters Anonymous sample, with a prevalence of 71.2%.

The second multisite study involved 2,727 subjects. Very similar rates were found using the QEWP: 29% of patients in weight-loss treatment,

4.6% of subjects in the community sample, and 2.6% of college students met the criteria. In this study, the prevalence of bulimia nervosa was 0.5% in the community sample, and 1.2% in the college student sample, a figure similar to other prevalence studies of bulimia nervosa, supporting the validity of the results regarding the QEWP used in these studies. Also, there is evidence of modest but encouraging agreement (Kappa = .57) between self-report and structured interview (de Zwaan et al., 1993), although it may be less reliable in a sample with a low prevalence of such disorders, such as a community sample.

Subsequently, Bruce & Agras (1992) reported a cross-sectional investigation of the prevalence of binge eating disorder in a randomly sampled community-based population of 455 females. In this sample, 1.8% met criteria for DSM-III-R non-purging bulimia nervosa, and 3.8% met all criteria for binge eating disorder with the binge eating frequency criterion of twice a week. In the subgroup of overweight individuals, the prevalence was higher, at 8%. Subsequently, several additional studies on the prevalence of binge eating disorder and subthreshold binge eating disorder in different subject groups have been published, finding prevalence similar to the obese but with considerable variability depending on the population surveyed (Adami, Gandolofo, Bauer, & Scopinaro, 1995; Brody et al., 1994; French, Jeffery, Sherwood, & Neumark-Sztainer, 1999; Grissett & Fitzgibbon, 1996; Ho, Nichaman, Taylor, Lee, & Foreyt, 1995; Kinzl, Traweger, Trefalt, Mangweth, & Biebl, 1999; Kuehnel & Wadden, 1994; Powers, Perez, Boyd, & Rosemurgy, 1999; Stunkard, Berkowitz, Wadden, et al., 1996; Wilson, Nonas, & Rosenblum, 1993; Yanovski, Nelson, Dubbert, & Spitzer, 1993).

## Course

The course of binge eating disorder appears to be chronic (Spitzer et al., 1993), and prolonged periods of abstinence from binge eating appear to be rare. Available data (Raymond, Mussell, Mitchell, Crosby, & de Zwaan, 1995) do not suggest that binge eating disorder is a less severe form of bulimia nervosa. In one series, only two binge eating disorder subjects had ever engaged in purging behavior at a frequency high enough to meet criteria for past bulimia nervosa, and the binge eating disorder group reported a significantly earlier age of onset of binge eating than the bulimia nervosa group (14.3 vs. 19.8 years).

Using food diaries, obese binge eaters report fewer binge eating episodes compared with the frequencies commonly reported among bulimia nervosa subjects, with rates in binge eating disorder subjects of 3.5

to 10 per week (Alger, Schwalberg, Bigaouette, Michalek, & Howard, 1991; de Zwaan et al., 1994; Goldfein, Walsh, LaChaussee, Kissileff, & Devlin, 1993; McCann & Agras, 1990; Rossiter, Agras, Telch, & Bruce, 1992; Telch, Agras, Rossiter, Wilfley, & Kenardy, 1990). There is no evidence that obese subjects with binge eating disorder are more prone to the medical complications of obesity, if one controls for weight. However, binge eating does correlate with severity of obesity in some studies (Telch, Agras, & Rossiter, 1988), which suggests that binge eating disorder subjects overall may be at particular risk for developing medical complications.

### Etiology and Maintenance

*Risk Factors*

Fairburn et al. (1998) compared putative risk factors proceeding the onset of binge eating disorder in 52 women with binge eating disorder, 104 without an eating disorder, 102 with other psychiatric disorders, and 102 with bulimia nervosa. Binge eating disorder appears to be associated with exposure to risk factors for psychiatric disorders and for obesity (e.g., childhood obesity, critical comments by family about shape, weight, or eating). Compared with bulimia nervosa, however, the risk factors for binge eating disorder are weaker. Even vulnerability to obesity seems to be more pronounced in bulimia nervosa.

*Dietary Restraint*

There is no evidence that in obese patients binge eating is a result of dietary restraint. Unlike patients with bulimia nervosa, binge eating disorder subjects report greater energy intake than obese controls not only on days during which they report binges, but also on days during which they feel their eating is under control. Binge eating disorder subjects usually show no relationship between feeling hungry and bingeing. In addition, dietary restriction (e.g., weight loss treatment) does not worsen binge eating among binge eating disorder patients, nor does it result in binge eating among those who report little difficulty with binge eating (Yanovski & Sebring, 1994). Consequently, disinhibition rather than dietary restraint seems to precipitate binge eating in the obese.

*Metabolism*

A few studies have directly investigated physiological differences between obese individuals with or without binge eating and/or binge eating disorder. In the available studies there is no evidence of differences in blood pressure, resting metabolic rate, resting energy expenditure, body fat distribution, percent body fat, or serum levels such as glucose, insulin, lipids, and thyroid between obese binge eaters and non–binge eaters matched for weight and height. However, Wing, Marcus, Epstein, Blair, & Burton (1989) did find an association between binge eating severity as assessed with the Binge Eating Scale and glycemic control in obese patients with Type II diabetes. Interestingly, the lack of difference in the amount and distribution of fat is somewhat surprising, given the hypothesis that weight cycling may be more common among binge eating disorder than non–binge eating disorder obese subjects, and that this might increase body fat, particularly in the upper body (Brownell, 1988). One study (Fichter, Quadflieg, & Brandl, 1993) found that 22.4% of obese binge eating disorder subjects had had amenorrhea for at least three months at the time of admission. This percentage decreased to 12.3% at discharge, and to 8.3% at three-year follow-up, when the eating behavior of many of these patients was much improved.

Two independent research groups have suggested that pain threshold may be elevated in bulimia nervosa subjects compared to controls (Faris et al., 1992), and recently Raymond, de Zwaan, et al. (1995) demonstrated similar elevations in obese subjects with binge eating disorder. This finding was specific to pain thresholds, since tactile thresholds did not differ. Taken together, these data suggest some abnormality in reporting or in physiological processing of painful stimuli in patients with binge eating symptoms, be they patients with bulimia nervosa or binge eating disorder.

### Food Selection

Yanovski et al. (1992) and Goldfein et al. (1993) have studied eating behavior in obese subjects with and without binge eating disorder in laboratory settings. Both groups demonstrated that obese binge eaters consume significantly more energy both in normal meal conditions and in binge eating meal conditions, and eat for longer periods of time compared to non–binge eating controls. Binge eating disorder subjects also tended to consume a greater percentage of energy as fat and a lesser percentage of energy as protein.

### Eating-Related and General Psychopathology

Overall, binge eating disorder seems to be more common in overweight women than men, at a ratio of approximately 3 to 2 (Spitzer et al., 1992). However, LaPorte (1992) found that 29% of women and 22% of men were binge eaters among 96 obese subjects participating in a very-low-calorie diet (VLCD) program. With few exceptions (Bruce & Agras, 1992), most studies have found that obese subjects with binge eating disorder are significantly younger than non–binge eating disorder obese subjects, especially when presenting for treatment (de Zwaan, Nutzinger, & Schönbeck, 1992). Compared to purging bulimic patients, however, obese binge eaters appear to be significantly older. Men with binge eating disorder did not differ from women with binge eating disorder. Men who experience problems with recurrent binge eating do not differ from female binge eaters on a wide range of indices of body image concerns, dieting behavior, and associated psychological distress (Striegel-Moore, Wilson, Wilfley, Elder, & Brownell, 1998). Very few studies have included men or racial minorities, and we know surprisingly little about binge eating disorder in these large segments of the population.

Studies have tended to find either a positive correlation between binge eating severity and weight (Hawkins and Clement, 1980; Kolotkin, Revis, Kirkley, & Janick, 1987; Lowe and Caputo, 1991; Marcus, Wing, & Lamparski, 1985; Spitzer et al., 1992; Spitzer et al., 1993; Telch et al., 1988) or no significant correlation between degree of obesity and binge eating (Keefe, Wyshogrood, Weinberger, & Agras, 1984; LaPorte, 1992; Wadden, Foster, Letizia, & Wilk, 1993; Wilson et al., 1993; Wing et al., 1989; Yanovski & Sebring, 1994). Interestingly, there are no reports of a negative correlation. There is also evidence that binge eating obese have an earlier age of onset of obesity than non–binge eating obese and that they start dieting at an earlier age (see, for example, Kuehnel & Wadden, 1994; and Mussell et al., 1995). Few studies have examined the specific chronology of the onset of binge eating, dieting, binge eating disorder, and obesity. There is some evidence, however, that among a sizable subgroup of individuals, binge eating develops before the onset of dietary restraint or purposeful weight loss (Mussell et al., 1995; Spitzer et al., 1993; Spurrell, Wilfley, Tanofsky, & Brownell, 1997; Wilson et al., 1993). In addition, in the group that does report dieting first, restriction of food intake appears to occur on average nearly 10 years before the onset of binge eating. Both of these sources of information raise questions about the hypothesis that dieting causes binge eating in obese subjects not meeting criteria for bulimia nervosa, for at least a sizable subgroup of these individuals.

Several well-validated, self-rating questionnaires assessing eating behavior and attitudes and cognitions toward weight and shape have been shown to successfully distinguish between binge eating and non–binge eating obese. It must be noted that several of these differences may arise directly from the diagnostic criteria, since by definition patients with binge eating disorder have higher scores on scales measuring binge eating, loss of control, and distress.

A tendency toward disinhibition of control over eating, and a higher susceptibility to hunger (on the Three-Factor Eating Questionnaire [TFEQ], Stunkard & Messick, 1985) have been shown consistently to correlate strongly with binge eating among the obese. Using a different assessment instrument, the Eating Self-Efficacy Scale, Kuehnel and Wadden (1994) found that binge eating disorder subjects were more likely to report overeating in response to negative affect and in social situations than non–binge eaters. The third subscale of the TFEQ, which measures the extent of cognitive restraint of eating, as well as similar scales of the Eating Disorder Examination (EDE), have shown either no correlation or even a negative correlation with binge eating, in the available literature. In addition, studies have found an increase in cognitive restraint after weight-loss treatment (Fichter et al., 1993) as well as successful treatment focusing on binge eating (McCann & Agras, 1990). Possibly these scales measure "flexible control" that is not necessarily maladaptive or correlated with rigid cognitions about dieting that has been shown to positively correlate with binge eating (Gormally et al., 1982; Marcus, Wing, & Hopkins, 1988; Marcus, Wing, & Lamparski, 1985). There are also data using the Eating Disorders Inventory (EDI) (Garner, Olmsted, & Polivy, 1983) or the EDI-2 in obese subjects, although the validity of the EDI in this group is yet to be established. Results in obese patients generally demonstrate that binge eaters exhibit more eating-related psychopathology on most subscales than non–binge eating obese (de Zwaan et al., 1994; Fichter et al., 1993; Hawkins & Clement, 1980; Kuehnel & Wadden, 1994; Lowe & Caputo, 1991).

The results on body image and body dissatisfaction are controversial, and the results appear to depend at least in part on the instrument used. Overall, the results indicate that obese binge eaters may have a somewhat higher tendency to report more body dissatisfaction than non–binge eating obese, and may be more likely to judge their self-worth in terms of their weight and shape (de Zwaan et al., 1992; de Zwaan et al., 1994; Hawkins & Clement, 1980; Marcus, Wing, & Hopkins, 1988; Williamson, Prather, & McKenzie, 1989). Compared with bulimic subjects, obese binge eaters appear to have either comparable or less body dissatisfaction (Garner et al., 1983; Marcus et al., 1992). Finally, the available results indicate that women who describe themselves as relatively more impulsive and less controlled are more likely to engage in periodic binge eating than women who describe themselves as less impulsive and more reflective (de Zwaan et al., 1994).

Relative to general psychopathology, most investigators have found higher levels of general psychiatric symptomatology in obese patients with binge eating than those without binge eating (Fichter et al., 1993; Kirkley, Kolotkin, Hernandez, & Gallagher, 1992; Kolotkin et al., 1987; Marcus, Wing, Ewing, Kern, Gooding, et al., 1990; Marcus et al., 1988; Schlundt et al., 1991; Specker, de Zwaan, Raymond, & Mitchell, 1994; Spitzer et al., 1993; Telch & Agras, 1994; Yanovski et al., 1993) (Table 3.1), but significantly lower levels when compared to bulimic subjects (Fichter et al., 1993; Spitzer et al., 1993). In particular, in most of the available work there appears to be a positive relationship between the presence of binge eating and depressive symptomatology, as well as a lifetime history of affective disorders (Hudson et al., 1988; LaPorte, 1992; Marcus et al., 1988; Spitzer et al., 1993; Wing et al., 1989; Yanovski et al., 1993). Also, female binge eaters appear to have significantly higher levels of both state and trait anxiety then their non–binge eating counterparts, although such differences have not been found among male binge eaters. In comparison to normal-weight purging bulimia nervosa subjects, results suggest a somewhat mixed picture, with some studies finding higher rates of psychopathology among bulimia nervosa than binge eating disorder subjects, and others finding similar levels of psychopathology (Fichter et al., 1993; Hudson et al., 1988; McCann, Rossiter, King, & Agras, 1991; Raymond, Mussell, et al., 1995). In one study, prevalence rates of personality disorders did not differ between overweight bulimic subjects, normal-weight bulimic subjects, and a sample of obese patients in a weight-loss program, but the rates were significantly different when these three clinical groups were compared to normal-weight controls in a community sample of obese (Prather & Williamson, 1988).

## Treatment

As indicated in the chapter on binge eating disorder, several studies have documented that binge eating is common among the obese, especially among obese women seeking treatment for weight reduction. However, few controlled studies have been conducted investigating treatments for this subgroup of obese individuals. Treatment should target eating behavior and associated psychopathology, weight, and psychiatric symptomatology (Wilfley & Cohen, 1997). There have been three types of treatment studies: those focusing on weight loss, those targeting the binge

Table 3.1. Treatment Studies Focusing on Weight Loss in Obese Binge Eaters

| Authors (year) | Diagnosis | N* | Treatment approach | Setting | Duration of treatment/ follow-up (wks/mos) | Outcome (weight, binge eating) |
|---|---|---|---|---|---|---|
| Wilson, 1976 | – | 5 | BT | Open | – | Stress management, assertiveness training > weight control |
| Gormally et al., 1982 | BES (6 items) | 40 | Group BT | Open | 16/7 | Weight loss B > NB<br>Weight regain B > NB |
| Keefe et al., 1984 | DSM-III bulimia (all or all but 1 criteria) (B)<br>No bulimia (NB) | 23<br><br><br>31 | Group CBT | Open | 9/6 | Weight loss B < NB<br>Difference remained significant at 6 mos |
| Marcus et al., 1988 | BES ≥ 27 (B)<br>BES 17 (NB) | 26<br>30 | Standard BT vs. Modified BT (group) | Randomized | 10/12 | Weight loss B = NB and BT = modified BT<br>Drop-out rate higher in B<br>More rapid weight regain in B<br>Weight regain B = NB at 1 year |
| Marcus, Wing, Ewing, Kern, McDermott, et al., 1990 | BES > 29 (B)<br>BES < 17 (NB) | 11<br>10 | Fluoxetine + BT vs. Placebo + BT | Double-blind | 52/3–6 | Weight loss B = NB and fluoxetine + BT significant > placebo + BT in B and NB<br>Rapid weight regain after fluoxetine stopped |
| de Zwaan et al., 1992 | Overeating loss of control (B)<br>No overeating + loss of control (NB) | 15<br><br>29 | Fluvoxamine +CBT Placebo + CBT<br>Fluvoxamine + NC Placebo + NC (group) | Double-blind | 18/12 | Weight loss B + NB, CBT = NC, and fluvoxamine = placebo. Weight regain during follow-up B not significantly > NB |

| Study | Diagnostic criteria | N | Treatment | Design | Duration | Results |
|---|---|---|---|---|---|---|
| Wadden et al., 1992 | DSM-III-R bulimia nervosa (non-purging) (B) Overeaters No overeating | 29 26 18 | Very-low-calorie diet + BT | Open | 26/12 | Weight loss B = overeaters = no overeating; Weight regain B = overeaters = no overeating (B = 7; overeaters = 6 pts.) |
| LaPorte, 1992 | BES ≥ 27 (B) BES ≤ 14 (NB) | 25 24 | Very-low-calorie diet + BT | Open | 10/– | Weight loss B = NB; Drop-out rate B not significantly > NB (32% vs. 17%) |
| Telch & Agras, 1993 | DSM-III-R | 12 | Very-low-calorie diet + BT | Open | 52/3 | Weight loss B = NB; Drop-out rate B = NB; Fasting: binge eating decreased in B; Refeeding: binge eating increased in B and NB; Follow-up (3 mo: weight regain B = NB); 15% of NB met criteria for B; 39% of B no longer met criteria for B |
| Yanovski et al., 1994 | DSM-IV BED, BES > 25 No BED, BES < 17 | 19 17 | Very-low-calorie diet + BT | Open | 26/12 | Weight loss BED = no BED; Non-significant reduction of binge days in BED |
| Brody et al., 1994 | DSM-IV BED No BED | 13 54 | Diet meal program | Open | 16/ | Weight regain BED = no BED at 1 yr; Attrition, lapses, early regain BED > no BED; Weight loss BED = no BED; Drop-outs BED = no BED (42% vs. 53%) |

Table 3.1. *Continued*

| Authors (year) | Diagnosis | N* | Treatment approach | Setting | Duration of treatment/ follow-up (wks/mos) | Outcome (weight, binge eating) |
|---|---|---|---|---|---|---|
| Porzelius et al., 1995 | BES < 17 (NB) BES 17–27 (moderate B) BES > 27 (severe B) | 46 | Standard BWLT vs. OBET | Randomized | 15/12 | Weight loss BWLT significantly > OBET for moderate B<br>Weight loss OBET > BWLT for severe B<br>Weight loss BWLT = OBET for NB<br>12 mos: Weight loss OBET > BWLT for severe B sustained reduction in binge eating in both treatment groups |
| Gladis, Wadden, Vogt, et al., 1998 | DSM-IV BED Subthreshold BED Episodic overeating No overeating | 12 18 16 50 | BT + diet + exercise | Open | 48/12 | Weight loss BED significantly > no BED<br>Weight regain BED = no BED at 1 yr<br>Drop-outs BED = no BED |
| Goodrick et al., 1998 | BES > 20 | 185 | Diet treatment Nondiet treatment Waiting-list control | Randomized | 72/– | Weight loss was poor; diet treatment = nondiet treatment = waiting-list control<br>Reduction BES diet treatment = nondiet treatment significantly > waiting-list control |

*Note:* *completers; BT = behavior therapy; BES = Binge Eating Scale; B = binge eaters; NB = non-binge eaters; CBT = cognitive-behavioral therapy; NC = nutritional counseling.
BED = binge eating disorder; BWLT = behavior weight loss treatment; OBET = obese binge eating treatment.

eating behavior and related psychopathology rather than weight, and those targeting both. We will briefly review each of these types of studies.

### Behavioral and Cognitive-Behavioral Treatment

Several studies have looked at the relationship between binge eating and weight loss. Gormally et al. (1982) found that persons who reported serious and frequent eating binges lost the most weight in a behavioral group treatment. The same was true for those who had lost the most in past dietary attempts. However, the authors also reported that these same patients gained the most weight during follow-up. They concluded that these patients might be used to rigid diets and are therefore more able to achieve rapid weight loss, but that this rigid control of eating might be difficult to maintain. A similar conclusion had been made four years earlier by Wilson (1976), who described the treatment of six obese binge eaters. He stated that in his experience assertiveness training, interpersonal skills, and stress management rather than weight loss should be addressed in such patients. However, an opposite result was obtained by Keefe et al. (1984) in a retrospective evaluation of a sample of 44 obese women carried out after completion of a cognitive-behavioral treatment (CBT) for obesity. They found that binge eaters meeting DSM-III criteria for bulimia lost significantly less weight than non–binge eaters (4.2 ± 5.3 and 9.7 ± 10.8 lbs, respectively). This difference remained significant at 6-month follow-up, although both groups lost additional weight (6.7 ± 8.8 and 12.1 ± 8.1 lbs, respectively).

Marcus et al. (1988) examined a standard and a modified behavioral treatment (BT). There were no significant differences in the amount of weight lost between binge eating and non–binge eating subjects at the end of the 10-week treatment or at the end of the 1-year follow-up period. Even though binge status did not predict weight loss, binge eating problems were associated with dropping out of treatment. Overall, the long-term results were poor, emphasizing once again that effective programs need to focus on weight-loss maintenance strategies and long-term treatment approaches (Björvell & Rössner, 1992).

In a study by Porzelius, Houston, Smith, Arfken, & Fisher (1995) women with no, moderate, or severe binge eating were treated with either a standard behavior weight-loss treatment (BWLT) or a weight-loss treatment modified to better address binge eating problems (OBET). The authors reported that moderate binge eating obese lost more weight in the standard BWLT than in the modified weight-loss treatment targeting binge eating, whereas severe binge eating obese lost more weight in the modified treatment. These women even continued to lose weight from post-treatment to 1-year follow-up. Binge eating severity was significantly reduced at post-treatment and follow-up regardless of the treatment condition.

Non-dieting therapeutic approaches have been developed for the treatment of obesity based on the belief that restrictive dieting may be associated with eating-related and general psychopathology. Goodrick, Poston, Kimball, Reeves, & Foreyt (1998) compared a behavioral diet treatment with a non-diet treatment in 219 obese patients with a Binge Eating Scale score of more than 20. Neither behavioral diet treatment nor non-diet treatment was successful in producing short- or long-term weight loss. However, both treatments resulted in a sustained reduction in binge eating severity compared to a waiting-list control group.

Gladis, Wadden, Vogt, et al. (1998) conducted a 48-week trial of structured diet combined with exercise and behavior therapy. At the end of treatment, participants with binge eating disorder lost more weight than participants without binge eating disorder. At follow-up, all subjects regained an average of 46% of the weight they had lost.

### Drug Treatment with or without Behavioral or Cognitive-Behavioral Therapy

Marcus, Wing, Ewing, Kern, McDermott, et al. (1990) conducted another weight loss study comparing 60 mg of fluoxetine to placebo over 54 weeks of behavioral treatment. Again, there was no significant difference in the amount of weight lost between binge eating and non–binge eating subjects. In general, fluoxetine-treated patients lost significantly more weight (mean = −13.9 kg) than patients treated with placebo, who even gained an average of 0.6 kg. Approximately 90% of the weight was lost during the first 5 months of the trial. The authors suggested that that result might represent a lack of drug compliance over time, the lack of behavior therapy during the second half of the year, or even an attenuation of the weight-loss effect of fluoxetine over time. Three to 6 months after treatment completion, the fluoxetine patients reported a rapid weight regain of 5.4 ± 4.9 kg, whereas the placebo patients gained 0.3 ± 2.7 kg.

De Zwaan et al. (1992) did not find a differential outcome following short-term treatment (18 weeks) or long-term outcome (1 year) for binge eating obese subjects in a placebo-controlled study for weight reduction using 100 mg of fluvoxamine plus CBT or fluvoxamine plus nutritional counseling. The respective weight loss was 6.1 ± 4.7 kg for the binge eaters, and 5.6 ± 3.7 kg for the non–binge eaters.

*Very-Low-Calorie Diets*

The overall response of obese binge eaters and non–binge eating obese to very-low-calorie diet (VLCD) programs did not differ (LaPorte, 1992; Wadden, Foster, & Letizia, 1992; Yanovski, Gormally, Leser, Gwirtsman, & Yanovski, 1994). Telch and Agras (1993) reported that patients with binge eating successfully lost weight and actually reduced binge eating frequency. Brody et al. (1994) found no difference between binge eating disorder and non–binge eating disorder subjects in the rate of premature drop-out (42% vs. 53%, respectively) or in mean weight loss (11.7 ± 10.9 and 8 ± 6.4 lbs, respectively) in a 16-week diet program. Yanovski et al. (1994) compared 21 binge eating disorder patients meeting DSM-IV criteria with 17 non–binge eating disorder patients undergoing an 800 kcal/day modified fast for 12 weeks followed by refeeding and stabilization. Overall, the two groups did not differ in mean weight loss at the end of treatment, and in mean weight regain at the end of a 12-month follow-up. However, dietary restriction did not worsen severity of binge eating in either binge eating disorder or non–binge eating disorder patients. In fact, at 3-month follow-up, frequency and severity of binge eating had improved slightly in binge eating disorder patients and had remained the same in non–binge eating disorder patients.

Comparable results were obtained by Wadden et al. (1992), who did not find a significant difference in weight change during a similar VLCD program and a 1-year follow-up between binge eating subjects meeting DSM-III-R criteria for non-purging bulimia nervosa (n = 29), episodic overeating subjects who denied a feeling of loss of control while overeating (n = 26), and non–binge eating subjects (n = 180). LaPorte (1992) reported preliminary results of the first 10 weeks of supplemented fasting in a VLCD treatment study. He, too, found no significant differences between binge eating (n = 25) and non–binge eating subjects (n = 24) on measures of weight loss (18.7 kg and 20.2 kg, respectively), adherence to the diet, or drop-out rate. However, there was a trend toward greater attrition in the binge eating group (32% versus 17%).

Wadden, Foster, and Letizia (1994) compared the weight losses of 49 women randomly assigned to a 52-week behavioral program combined with either moderated (BDD) or severe (VLCD) caloric restriction. VLCD subjects lost significantly more weight than the BDD subjects through week 26, at which time mean losses were 21.5 and 11.9 kg, respectively. VLCD subjects, however, regained weight during the next 26 weeks of weekly therapy and during the 26-week weight maintenance program that provided biweekly meetings. Mean weight losses at the end of the maintenance program were 10.9 and 12.2 kg, respectively. Reports of binge eating declined in both groups.

In summary, treatment studies to date focusing on weight reduction do not show a significant differential outcome in weight loss between binge eating and non–binge eating obese individuals, regardless of the approach employed (CBT, VLCD, pharmacotherapy, and combined psycho- and pharmacotherapy). Consequently, there does not appear to be any reason to exclude such individuals from weight-loss treatment programs on this basis.

Results on attrition rates are inconsistent, but there seems to be enough evidence that binge status does not increase the risk for early drop-out. One study even found that binge status predicted retention in a 6-month weight loss program among 156 obese women (Ho et al., 1995).

In addition, adherence to a diet can even provide abstinence from binge eating. It may be possible to directly treat the obesity without first treating the binge eating problem. The evidence to date raises doubts about the need for specialized treatments for obese binge eaters such as to eliminate binge eating first and address weight concerns later. In fact, it could be argued that standard behavioral and dietary interventions are sufficiently able to address all of the treatment needs of this group.

Studies focusing on binge eating and related psychopathology have usually applied treatment approaches that have been found useful for patients with purging bulimia nervosa. Researchers have written CBT treatment manuals that have been modified specifically from the treatment of bulimia nervosa to the treatment of binge eating disorder (Fairburn, 1995; Telch et al., 1990). On average, subjects were gaining weight during CBT adapted for binge eating disorder. Consequently, binge eating disorder manuals were changed to address weight-control issues.

### Cognitive-Behavioral Treatment

CBT treatment studies for binge eating generally have not addressed weight reduction. Patients are usually given the rationale that suppression of binge eating is necessary before long-term weight loss can occur. The main behavioral strategies used are self-monitoring of eating behavior, stimulus control, the development of alternative responses to stresses, the consumption of regular meals without omitting "forbidden" food, goal setting, self-reinforcement, problem solving, and cognitive restructuring. Special emphasis is laid on relapse prevention by anticipating high-risk situations. The results of a study by Telch et al. (1990) suggested a

Table 3.2. Treatment Studies Focusing on Eating Behavior in (Obese) Binge Eaters

| Authors (Year) | Diagnosis | N* | Treatment approach | Setting | Duration of treatment/follow-up (wks/mos) | Outcome (weight, binge eating) |
|---|---|---|---|---|---|---|
| Telch et al., 1990 | DSM-III-R BN (non-purging) | 44 | Group CBT vs. Waiting-list control | Randomized | 10/2.5 | CBT significantly > waiting-list control in reducing binge eating (94% vs. 9%) Abstinence rate 79% vs. 0% Reduction of binge eating for CBT still 69% at 2.5 mos follow-up No weight loss in either group |
| McCann & Agras, 1990 | DSM-III-R BN (non-purging) | 23 | Desipramine vs. placebo | Double-blind | 12/1 | Desipramine significantly > placebo in reducing binge eating (63% vs. +16%) Abstinence rate 60% vs. 15% Rapid relapse after despipramine stopped Weight loss desipramine = placebo |
| Alger et al., 1991 | BES > 25, overweight, 2 episodes w/(B) DSM-III-R BN | 33 22 | Imipramine vs. Naltrexone vs. Placebo | Double-blind | 8/– | Imipramine = naltrexone = placebo and B = BN in reducing binge eating (imipramine 73%, naltrexone 48%, placebo 50%) Imipramine significantly > placebo in B and naltrexone significantly > placebo in BN in reducing binge duration Weight loss not significant B = BN, imipramine = naltrexone = placebo |

Table 3.2. *Continued*

| Authors (Year) | Diagnosis | N* | Treatment approach | Setting | Duration of treatment/follow-up (wks/mos) | Outcome (weight, binge eating) |
|---|---|---|---|---|---|---|
| Wilfley et al., 1993 | DSM-III-R BN (non-purging) | 48 | Group CBT vs. group IPT vs. waiting-list control | Randomized | 16/12 | CBT, IPT significantly > waiting-list control in reducing binge eating (CBT 48%, IPT 71%, waiting-list control 10%) Abstinence rates: CBT 28%, IPT 44%, waiting-list control 0% 1 yr: Binge eating still below baseline levels Reduction in binge eating CBT 55%, IPT 50% |
| Smith et al., 1992 | Obese binge eaters (EDE) | 8 | Group CBT | Open | 16/– | Abstinence rate CBT 46%, IPT 40%, weight gain 2 kg Reduction binge eating days 81% Abstinence rate 50% (28 days) and 75% (7 days); no weight change |
| Fichter et al., 1993, 1998 | DSM-IV BED | 68 | Anti-diet + BT (inpatients) | Open | 77d[a]/36 | Tx: Significant reduction of binge eating 3 yrs: Reduction maintained; no weight gain 6 yrs: 79% no DSM-IV eating disorder; slight weight increase; BMI > 30: 38.2% |
| Gardiner et al., 1993 | DSM-III-R atypical eating disorders (non-vomiters) | 5 | Fluvoxamine | Open | 8/– | Significant reduction of binge eating Significant weight loss |
| Prats et al., 1994 (abstract) | BED | 9 | Paroxetine | Open | 16/– | Significant reduction of binge eating |

| | | | | |
|---|---|---|---|---|
| Stunkard, Berkowitz, Tanrikut, et al., 1996 | DSM-IV BED | 24 | *d-*Fenfluramine vs. placebo | Double-blind | 8/4 | Fenfluramine significantly > placebo in reducing binge eating; remission 80%[b] vs. 33% Rapid relapse after fenfluramine stopped No weight loss in either group |
| Hudson et al., 1998 | DSM-IV BED | 67 | Fluvoxamine vs. placebo | Double-blind | 9/– | Fluvoxamine significantly > placebo in reducing binge eating (median 75% vs. 42%) Weight loss fluvoxamine significantly > placebo |

*Note:* *completers; CBT = cognitive-behavioral therapy; BN = bulimia nervosa; B = binge eaters; BED = binge eating disorder; IPT = interpersonal psychotherapy; EDE = Eating Disorder Examination
[a]mean duration of inpatient treatment; [b]of patients with adequate serum levels

positive effect for a manual-based CBT in patients with non-purging DSM-III-R bulimia nervosa, most of whom were overweight. Ten weekly 90-minute sessions of CBT were significantly superior to a waiting-list control. At a 10-week follow-up, however, several patients lapsed from post-treatment levels, although the authors emphasized that binge eating remained improved compared to baseline levels (69% reduction). Forty-six percent of the CBT subjects who reported abstinence from binge eating at post-treatment remained abstinent at 20 weeks.

A similar result was obtained in a study by Smith, Marcus, & Kaye (1992), who conducted a 16-week CBT group in an open design in eight patients, with an 81% reduction of binge days, and a 75% 7-day remission rate. After expanding the post-treatment assessment period from 1 week to 1 month using the EDE, however, the abstinence rate was reduced to 50%.

Fichter, Quadflieg, & Gnutzmann (1998) and Fichter et al. (1993) applied an "anti-diet" approach to 68 obese inpatients with binge eating disorder, focusing on perception, emotional expression, social skills, and eating behavior. This inpatient treatment extended over 76.7 ± 40 days, and follow-up data are available for 63 patients 3 years and 6 years after discharge. The disturbed eating behavior as well as general psychopathology improved significantly in obese binge eaters and remained stable during follow-up. The mean reduction in BMI was 3 kg/m², with maximum weight loss achieved 3 months after discharge. However, patients had regained most of the weight by the 3-year follow-up.

In a pilot study, cue exposure was compared with self-control in the treatment of bulimic patients, many of whom were obese (6 vs. 6 patients) (Jansen, Broekmate, & Heymans, 1992). Cue exposure is the prolonged exposure to stimuli known to predict the urge to eat in a given individual. Subsequent prevention of food intake is supposed to extinguish this urge. The authors reported that all patients treated with cue exposure were abstinent directly after treatment and during a 1-year follow-up, whereas self-control techniques (basically the avoidance of binge-related cues) led to abstinence in only 33% of the subjects.

*Interpersonal Psychotherapy*

Wilfley et al. (1993) compared two different psychotherapeutic approaches—CBT (n = 18) and interpersonal psychotherapy (IPT) (n = 18)—with a waiting-list control group (n = 20) in nonpurging bulimics. IPT focuses on interpersonal and social difficulties and their effect on mood. Both treatment conditions resulted in significant improvement in reducing binge eating while the waiting list did not. At the end of treatment the CBT group had reduced binge eating frequency by 48% (28% abstinent), and the IPT group by 71% (44% abstinent), while the reduction in the waiting-list group was minimal (10%, 0% abstinent). The positive results were generally maintained at a 6-month and 1-year follow-up.

*Drug Treatment*

Imipramine and desipramine are the best-studied tricyclic drugs in the treatment of normal-weight and overweight subjects with binge eating problems. In general, these studies show a significant superiority for imipramine and desipramine over placebo in the reduction of binge eating frequency. McCann and Agras (1990) found a striking superiority for desipramine 100–300 mg/day over placebo in subjects with non-purging bulimia nervosa. The patients who received desipramine reduced their frequency of binge eating days by 63%. The authors suggested that the primary action of desipramine on binge eating was through appetite suppression. The results were most likely not due to the antidepressant action of desipramine, since the participants had low scores on measures of depression. After discontinuation of the drug, binge eating frequency rapidly increased.

There has been recent interest in the use of serotonin reuptake inhibitors (SSRIs) in the treatment of binge eating, since they have been shown to enhance satiety. Because many antidepressants increase the turnover of serotonin, these drugs may reduce binge eating, if binge eating is conceptualized as driven by the need to modify levels of brain serotonin. Two small open-label trials suggest that SSRIs such as paroxetine (Prats, Diez-Quevedo, Avila, & Planell, 1994) and fluvoxamine (Gardiner, Freeman, Jesinger, & Collins, 1993) may be effective for patients with binge eating disorder. In a recent study, Hudson et al. (1998) reported the results of a double-blind, placebo-controlled study with fluvoxamine in 85 outpatients with binge eating disorder according to DSM-IV criteria. The dosage used ranged from 50 to 300 mg with a mean dose at endpoint of 260 mg. After a 9-week treatment period, fluvoxamine was associated with a significantly greater reduction in the frequency of binge eating (median 75%) compared with placebo (median 42%). In addition, fluvoxamine-treated patients lost some weight (median 1.0 lbs), whereas placebo-treated patients gained weight (median 1.9 lbs).

The appetite suppressant *d*-fenfluramine has been extensively used in the treatment of obesity. Stunkard, Berkowitz, Tanrikut, et al. (1996)

reported the results of an 8-week, double-blind, placebo-controlled clinical trial of $d$-fenfluramine 30 mg/day with 24 obese women with DSM-IV binge eating disorder. The drug significantly reduced the frequency of binge eating. Eighty percent of the patients with $d$-fenfluramine who had adequate blood levels (10 out of 12) stopped binge eating completely compared to only 33% in the placebo group. There was no weight loss in either group, which led the authors to conclude that the drug's action in suppressing binge eating may be independent of its action in reducing weight.

Like the serotonergic system, the endogenous opioid peptide system appears to be important in the control of feeding behavior, in particular stress-induced feeding. Selective opiate antagonists including naloxone, naltrexone, and nalmefene have proven to have robust short-term effects in reducing food consumption (de Zwaan & Mitchell, 1992). These observations have led to the hypothesis that opioid antagonists might decrease eating and/or stress-induced overeating. However, in clinical practice opioid antagonists have not proven to be effective. Alger et al. (1991) compared both imipramine 150–200 mg and naltrexone 100–150 mg to placebo in obese binge eaters and in purging bulimic subjects. Interestingly, after 6 weeks of double-blind drug administration, the two active treatment conditions and the placebo condition did not produce different results. Obese binge eaters on naltrexone reduced their binge eating by 48 ± 21%, those on imipramine by 73 ± 15.6%, and those on placebo by 50 ± 20%. The same respective values for bulimic subjects were 30 ± 25%, 26 ± 17.5%, and 30 ± 16%. According to the authors, this lack of difference was due to an extremely strong placebo effect.

In summary, the findings of studies focusing on binge eating and related psychopathology rather than weight loss suggest that a similar mechanism may drive the binge eating in patients with purging bulimia nervosa and obese binge eating individuals who do not engage in purging behavior, and that similar treatments may be useful with both groups in reducing binge eating behavior and improving psychological impairment, at least in the short-term. Treatment studies of binge eating disorder have adapted their treatments from those developed for bulimia nervosa, and results have indicated similar outcomes.

The prevalence of binge eating increases with increasing levels of obesity. Consequently, this subgroup of obese are among those at highest risk for medical complications of obesity. Given the fact that reduction of binge eating frequency will result in only modest weight loss, if any, in subjects who have already become obese, combining treatments for binge eating with treatment of obesity may be useful. Even small weight losses, such as 5% to 10% of body weight, can produce impressive medical benefits.

Studies addressing the effectiveness of combined treatment targeting both the patients' eating disorder as well as their obesity are beginning to appear. Agras et al. (1994) examined the potential efficacy of a sequential treatment for binge eating and weight loss among obese binge eaters. They compared the effects of weight-loss treatment, cognitive-behavioral treatment, and desipramine on binge eating and weight in a three-group additive design involving 108 obese subjects with binge eating disorder. Thirty-seven subjects were allocated to a 9-month behavioral weight-loss therapy (BWLT), 36 subjects to a 3-month CBT followed by BWLT for 6 months, and 36 subjects to the combination treatment with desipramine (mean daily dose 285 mg) added for the last 6 months. A follow-up assessment was held 3 months post-treatment. BWLT was significantly superior to CBT during the first 3 months of treatment in inducing weight loss, and CBT was significantly superior to BWLT in reducing binge eating, but these advantages were lost at the end of the 9-month treatment phase. Adding desipramine increased weight loss and reduced disinhibition. Abstinence from binge eating at 3 months was related to more successful weight loss. At the 3-month post-treatment follow-up, the CBT/BWLT-desipramine group had lost significantly more weight than the CBT/BWLT group but not than the BWLT-only group. All groups demonstrated a significant relapse in the frequency of binge eating.

Marcus, Wing, & Fairburn (1995) compared CBT and BWLT both delivered in individual psychotherapy. The comparison of CBT and BWLT in 115 overweight women with binge eating disorder showed that both CBT and traditional BWLT for obesity led to improvements in binge eating, but only BWLT produced weight loss. Devlin (1996) reported a series of 12 patients who were treated with CBT over 4 to 7 months. In addition they were offered a trial of the stimulant appetite suppressant phentermine combined with a serotonergic agent (fenfluramine or fluoxetine). Nine of the 11 patients who completed the open-label trial stopped binge eating. They lost an average of 19.1 lbs. Because of severe adverse events, these appetite suppressants are no longer marketed in the United States.

In 1995, Agras et al. reported a subsequent treatment post-group CBT for binge eating disorder. Fifty overweight individuals were randomly allocated to either 12 weeks of group CBT or an assessment-only control

Table 3.3. Treatment Studies Focusing on Weight and Eating Behavior in (Obese) Binge Eaters

| Authors (Year) | Diagnosis | N* | Treatment approach | Setting | Duration of treatment/follow-up (wks/mos) | Outcome (weight, binge eating) |
|---|---|---|---|---|---|---|
| Agras et al., 1994 | DSM-IV BED | 84 | BWLT vs. G-CBT + BWLT vs. G-CBT + BWLT + desipramine | Sequential Randomized | 36/3 | 12 wks: G-CBT significantly > BWLT in reducing binge eating (67% vs. 44%); weight loss BWLT significantly > G-CBT (2 kg vs. +0.7 kg) 36 wks: BWLT = CBT + BWLT = CBT + BWLT + desipramine; abstinence rates of 19 vs. 37 vs. 41%; weight loss 3.7 vs. 1.6 vs. 6.0 kg 3-mos follow-up: BWLT = CBT + BWLT + desipramine = CBT + BWLT; abstinence rates of 14 vs. 28 vs. 32%; BWLT = CBT + BWLT + desipramine > CBT + BWLT regarding weight loss since baseline 4.2 vs. 4.8 vs. 0 kg |
| Agras et al., 1995 | DSM-IV BED | 42 | G-CBT + BWLT or G-CBT + G-IPT vs. waiting-list control | Sequential Randomized (waiting-list control) | 24/– | Active treatment significantly > waiting-list control in reducing binge eating (77% vs. 22%) and in weight loss (–0.6 vs. –4.1 kg) Abstinence rate after G-CBT 55% BWLT following CBT: 4.1 kg. Weight loss, and binge eating remained low IPT following CBT: no subsequent decrease in binge eating or weight |
| Marcus et al., 1995 (abstract) | DSM-IV BED | 115 | BWLT vs. CBT (individual) Waiting-list control | Randomized | 24/12 | Weight loss BWLT > CBT (BWLT 21.6 lbs) BWLT = CBT significantly > waiting-list control in reducing binge eating 12 mos: BWLT weight regain of 8.5 lbs. |

| Study | Diagnosis | N | Treatment | Design | | Results |
|---|---|---|---|---|---|---|
| Devlin, 1996 (abstract) | DSM-IV BED | 11 | CBT + phentermine + fenfluramine or CBT + phentermine + fluoxetine | Open | 16–32/2 | Abstinence rate 81.8% (9 of 11) Weight loss 19.1+/– 20.8 lbs. |
| De Zwaan et al., 1996 (abstract) | DSM-IV BED / No BED | 71 / 83 | VLCD + G-CBT vs. VLCD (no G-CBT) | Randomized | 26/12 | Weight loss BED significantly > no BED VLCD + CBT = VLCD in reducing binge eating (60% vs. 81%) Abstinence rates: 58% vs. 74% 12 mos: Weight regain BED significantly > no BED binge eating frequency VLCD = VLCD + CBT |
| Levine et al., 1996 | DSM-IV BED | 77 | Exercise component to BED treatment vs. Delayed treatment control | Randomized | 24/– | BED treatment significantly > control in reducing binge eating Abstinence rate BED treatment 81.4% Abstinent subjects increased their exercise frequency significantly > nonabstinent subjects |
| Eldredge et al., 1997 | DSM-IV BED | 37 | G-CBT + BWLT or G-CBT-extended G-CBT vs. waiting-list control | Sequential Randomized (waiting-list control) | 24/– | Abstinence rate G-CBT 50% and with extended CBT additional 6 of 14 to a total abstinence rate of 66.7% No weight change in G-CBT and waiting-list control |
| Agras et al., 1997 | DSM-IV BED | 75 | G-CBT + BWLT | Follow-up study combining 3 treatment studies | 36/12 | Reduction of binge eating 64% Abstinence rate 33% Weight loss of abstinent subjects 4 kg Weight gain of those who continued binge eating 3.6 kg |

*Note:* *completers; BED = binge eating disorder; BWLT = behavioral weight-loss treatment; G-CBT = group cognitive-behavioral therapy for binge eating; G-IPT = group interpersonal psychotherapy; VLCD = very-low-calorie diet group. Those who achieved abstinence with CBT subsequently were treated in a behavioral weight loss program (BWLT), while those who were not abstinent were referred for group IPT. After 12 weeks of group CBT, 55% of the patients abstained from binge eating. Of note, those CBT subjects referred for weight loss did not experience an increase of binge eating during subsequent weight-loss treatment, and had a mean weight loss of 4.1 kg. Also of importance, those treated with IPT following CBT did not demonstrate any subsequent decrease in binge eating behavior or in weight.

In a similar study by Eldredge et al. (1997), individuals with binge eating disorder who failed to stop binge eating after an initial 12-week CBT intervention received 12 additional sessions of CBT for binge eating. Those who achieved abstinence with CBT subsequently were treated in a behavioral weight-loss program (BWLT). Fifty percent of treated participants improved with the initial 12-week course of CBT. The extension of CBT led to further abstinence from binge eating in 6 of 14 subjects. Treated subjects reduced the frequency of their binge eating by 68.2% after 12 weeks, while waiting-list subjects decreased their binge eating by 19.8%. The results suggest that—as opposed to subsequent IPT—an extended course of CBT will likely maximize the number of potential responders to treatment.

Agras, Telch, Arnow, Eldredge, & Marnell (1997) reported the results of a 1-year post-treatment follow-up of patients with binge eating disorder treated with group CBT followed by weight-loss treatment (BWLT). The patients had participated in three controlled studies conducted by this research group. Binge eating was reduced by 64%, and 33% were abstinent. Twenty-six percent of those abstinent had relapsed, whereas 25% of those who were not abstinent after CBT were abstinent after 1 year. As a whole, participants regained the weight lost during treatment. Those who stopped binge eating during CBT maintained a weight loss of 4 kg; those who continued to binge gained 3.6 kg. Stopping binge eating appears to be critical to sustained weight loss in binge eating disorder.

Levine, Marcus, and Moulton (1996) reported the results of a 24-week treatment program for binge eating disorder including an exercise component in the form of a regular walking program. At the end of the treatment, 81.4% were abstinent from binge eating. Women who were abstinent increased their weekly exercise frequency and increased their overall caloric expenditure as opposed to the women who continued to binge eat. The increase in physical activity was associated with improvements in binge eating. Abstinent women reported significantly greater increases in their overall level of physical activity and their frequency of exercise. However, exercise was not related to changes in weight.

Recently, de Zwaan, Mitchell, Mussell, & Crosby (1996) conducted a study evaluating the efficacy of CBT focusing on binge eating behavior coupled with a VLCD in patients with binge eating disorder. Since the period of transition from modified fasting to resumption of a food-based diet may be a time of particular difficulty for individuals with binge eating disorder, the CBT component was offered during the last third of the 26-week treatment phase. One hundred and fifty-four females (83 non–binge eating disorder, 71 binge eating disorder) completed the 26-week program. All subjects attended a behaviorally oriented group weekly during the entire treatment protocol. In addition, one half of the binge eating disorder subjects also received 10 CBT group sessions for binge eating, which started after 2 weeks of refeeding. The active treatment phase was followed by a 1-year follow-up period. On average, the patients lost 17% (SD 7.8) of their initial body weight during the VLCD and maintained an average weight loss of 6.4% (SD 9.8) of initial body weight during follow-up, one-third of the patients in each group regained all the weight or more, and one-third maintained a weight loss of more than 10%. Binge eating disorder patients lost significantly more weight during treatment and regained significantly more weight during follow-up. In the short-term the VLCD with or without CBT appeared to be successful in suppressing high-frequency binge eating (reduction of 60% and 81%, respectively). At the 1-year follow-up, 41.7% of the binge eating disorder patients receiving CBT, and 37.1% of the binge eating disorder patients not receiving CBT continued to meet criteria for binge eating disorder. In summary, the combination of a VLCD with a CBT component did not improve the short- and long-term results with regard to weight loss and binge eating frequency in obese binge eating subjects.

In summary, treatment outcome must focus at a minimum on the binge eating characterizing this disorder, on weight changes, and preferably also on changes in comorbid psychopathology.

## Self-Help

In bulimia nervosa a substantial proportion of patients can be helped by cognitive-behavioral self-help manuals, a treatment that can be applied more generally, for example, in the primary care setting (Carter & Fairburn, 1995). The compliance with guided self-help in conjunction with

Table 3.4. Self-Help for Binge Eating Disorder

| Authors (Year) | Diagnosis | N* | Treatment approach | Setting | Duration of treatment/follow-up (wks/mos) | Outcome (weight, binge eating) |
|---|---|---|---|---|---|---|
| Wells et al., 1997 | DSM-IV binge eating disorder | 7 | Self-help book[#] Telephone-guided | Open | 12/– | Marked reduction in binge frequency Abstinence rate 42.9% No weight change |
| Carter & Fairburn, 1998 | DSM-IV binge eating disorder | 72 | Self-help book[#] Therapist-led vs. Partial self-help vs. Structured self-help vs. Waiting-list control | Groups Randomized | 8/– | Therapist-led = partial self-help = structured self-help significantly > waiting-list control in reducing binge frequency and hours of binge eating Abstinence rates: therapist-led = 18.8%; partial self-help = 36.8%; structured self-help = 53.3%; waiting-list control = 0% |

*Note:* *completers; [#]*Overcoming binge eating* (Fairburn, 1995).

**Psychotherapy**

1. CBT and IPT are successful in reducing binge eating frequency in the short-term.
2. Many subjects resume binge eating after completion of treatment.
3. In obese subjects with binge eating disorder, reduction of binge eating through short-term psychotherapy results in only modest weight loss, if any.
4. Individuals who stop binge eating during CBT lose more weight than those who do not.
5. Binge eating disorder subjects who stop binge eating during CBT are usually successful in maintaining their weight.

**Antidepressant Medication**

1. Pharmacotherapy is successful in reducing binge eating frequency in the short-term.
2. Withdrawal of drug treatment is frequently followed by immediate relapse.
3. Medication does not add to the effectiveness of CBT in reducing binge eating.
4. However, antidepressant medication may enhance weight loss beyond the effects of CBT.

**Weight-Loss Treatment**

1. In weight-reduction treatments, the amount of weight lost does not differ between binge eating obese and non–binge eating obese. Obese binge eating subjects have been found to respond to weight-loss programs similarly to non–binge eating subjects.
2. There are studies showing greater attrition and faster weight regain in binge eating disorder subjects than in non–binge eating disorder subjects. However, most studies on the use of weight-loss programs found that binge eating did not affect weight regain, adherence to the diet, or attrition. There is even evidence for lower attrition rates in binge eating subjects.
3. Weight-loss treatment is able to significantly reduce binge eating frequency.

**General**

1. Most studies used a group format.
2. Most subjects were treated as outpatients.

Figure 3.1. Summary of results of treatment approaches for obese binge eating disorder subjects.

a limited amount of external guidance from a nonspecialist therapist is usually better than self-help only. Self-help programs can be brief, inexpensive, nonstigmatizing, and potentially empowering (Garvin, Striegel-Moore, & Wells, 1998). Although psychotherapy has been found to be beneficial in reducing binge eating symptoms, this type of intervention is costly in the treatment of eating disorders and may be unnecessarily intensive for some individuals with binge eating disorder. In addition, it is unlikely that there will ever be sufficient specialist resources to deal with the large number of cases that exist.

There are now results from studies of self-help in patients with binge eating disorder using various modes of service delivery, for example, group format with videotapes (Peterson et al., 1998), in person on a one-to-one basis (Carter & Fairburn, 1998), and even by telephone (Wells, Garvin, Dohm, & Striegel-Moore, 1997). The results show a marked reduction in binge eating frequency as well as improvement in secondary outcome measures. Abstinence rates of 40% to 50% could be achieved after 8 to 12 weeks of working with a self-help manual or book (Fairburn, 1995). In one study (Carter & Fairburn, 1998) this result could be maintained over a 6-month follow-up period.

## References

Adami, G. F., Gandolfo, P., Bauer, B., & Scopinaro, N. (1995). Binge eating in massively obese patients undergoing bariatric surgery. *International Journal of Eating Disorders, 17,* 45–50.

Agras, W. S., Telch, C. F., Arnow, B., Eldredge, K., Detzer, M. J., Henderson, J., & Marnell, M. (1995). Does interpersonal therapy help patients with binge eating disorder who fail to respond to cognitive-behavioral therapy? *Journal of Consulting and Clinical Psychology, 63,* 356–360.

Agras, W. S., Telch, C. F., Arnow, B., Eldredge, K., & Marnell, M. (1997). One-year follow-up of cognitive-behavioral therapy for obese individuals with binge eating disorder. *Journal of Consulting and Clinical Psychology, 65,* 343–347.

Agras, W. S., Telch, C. F., Arnow, B., Eldredge, K., Wilfley, D. E., Raeburn, S. D., Henderson, J., & Marnell, M. (1994). Weight loss, cognitive-behavioral, and desipramine treatments in binge eating disorder. An additive design. *Behavior Therapy, 25,* 225–238.

Alger, S. A., Schwalberg, M. D., Bigaouette, J. M., Michalek, A. V., & Howard, L. J. (1991). Effect of a tricyclic antidepressant and opiate antagonist on binge-eating behavior in normal-weight bulimic and obese, binge-eating subjects. *American Journal of Clinical Nutrition, 53,* 865–871.

American Psychiatric Association. (1987). *Diagnostic and statistical manual of mental disorders* (3rd ed., rev.). Washington, DC: Author.

American Psychiatric Association. (1994). Diagnostic and statistical manual of mental disorders (4th ed.). Washington, DC: Author.

Björvell, H., & Rössner, S. (1992). A ten-year follow-up of weight change in severely obese subjects treated in a combined behavioural modification program. *International Journal of Obesity, 16,* 623–625.

Brody, M. L., Walsh, B. T., & Devlin, M. J. (1994). Binge eating disorder: Reliability and validity of a new diagnostic category. *Journal of Consulting and Clinical Psychology, 62,* 381–386.

Brownell, K. D. (1988). The yo-yo trap. *American Health, 3,* 78–84.

Bruce, B., & Agras, W. S. (1992). Binge eating in females: A population-based investigation. *International Journal of Eating Disorders, 12,* 365–373.

Carter, J. C., & Fairburn, C. G. (1995). Treating binge eating problems in primary care. *Addictive Behaviors, 20,* 765–772.

Carter, J. C., & Fairburn, C. G. (1998). Cognitive-behavioral self-help for binge eating disorder: A controlled effectiveness study. *Journal of Consulting and Clinical Psychology, 66,* 616–623.

Cooper, Z., & Fairburn, C. (1987). The eating disorder examination: A semi-structured interview for the assessment of the specific psychopathology of eating disorders. *International Journal of Eating Disorders, 6,* 1–8.

Devlin, M. J. (1996, April). *Treatment of binge eating disorder with psychotherapy and medication.* Poster presented at the Seventh International Conference on Eating Disorders, New York.

Devlin, M. J., Walsh, B. T., Spitzer, R. L., & Hasin, D. (1992). Is there another binge eating disorder? A review of the literature on overeating in the absence of bulimia nervosa. *International Journal of Eating Disorders, 11,* 333–340.

de Zwaan, M., & Mitchell, J. E. (1992). Opioid antagonists and feeding in humans: A review of the literature. *Journal of Clinical Pharmacology, 32,* 1060–1072.

de Zwaan, M., Mitchell, J. E., Mussell, M. P., & Crosby, R. D. (1996, November). *Does CBT improve treatment outcome in obese binge eaters participating in a very-low-calorie diet treatment?* Paper presented at the Second Meeting of the Eating Disorders Research Society, Pittsburgh.

de Zwaan, M., Mitchell, J. E., Seim, H. C., Specker, S. M., Pyle, R. L., Crosby, R. B., & Raymond, N. C. (1994). Eating related and general psychopathology in obese females with binge eating disorder (BED). *International Journal of Eating Disorders, 15,* 43–52.

de Zwaan, M., Mitchell, J. E., Specker, S. M., Pyle, R. L., Mussell, M. P., & Seim, H. C. (1993). Diagnosing binge eating disorder: Level of agreement between self-report and expert rating. *International Journal of Eating Disorders, 14,* 289–295.

de Zwaan, M., Nutzinger, D. O., & Schönbeck, G. (1992). Binge eating in overweight females. *Comprehensive Psychiatry, 33,* 256–261.

Eldredge, K. L., Agras, W. S., Arnow, B., Telch, C. F., Bell, S., Castonguay, L. G., & Marnell, M. (1997). The effects of extending cognitive-behavioral therapy for binge eating disorder among initial treatment nonresponders. *International Journal of Eating Disorders, 21,* 347–352.

Fairburn, C. G. (1995). *Overcoming binge eating.* New York: Guilford Press.

Fairburn, C. G., Doll, H. A., Welch, S. L., Hay, P. J., Davies, B. A., & O'Connor, M. E. (1998). Risk factors for binge eating disorder. A community-based, case-control study. *Archives of General Psychiatry, 55,* 425–432.

Faris, P. L., Raymond, N. C., de Zwaan, M., Howard, L. A., Eckert, E. D., & Mitchell, J. E. (1992). Evidence for vagal involvement in bulimia nervosa: Alterations in both satiety and nociception. *Biological Psychiatry, 32,* 462–466.

Fichter, M. M., Quadflieg, N., & Brandl, B. (1993). Recurrent overeating: An empirical comparison of binge eating disorder, bulimia nervosa, and obesity. *International Journal of Eating Disorders, 14,* 1–16.

Fichter, M., Quadflieg, N., & Gnutzmann, A. (1998). Binge eating disorder: Treatment outcome over a 6-year course. *Journal of Psychosomatic Research, 44,* 385–405.

French, S. A., Jeffery, R. W., Sherwood, N. E., & Neumark-Sztainer, D. (1999). Prevalence and correlates of binge eating in a nonclinical sample of women enrolled in a weight gain prevention program. *International Journal of Obesity, 23,* 576–585.

Gardiner, H. M., Freeman, C. P. L., Jesinger, D. K., & Collins, S. A. (1993). Fluvoxamine: An open pilot study in moderately obese female patients suffering from atypical eating disorders and episodes of bingeing. *International Journal of Obesity, 17,* 301–305.

Garner, D. M., Olmsted, M. P., & Polivy, J. (1983). Development and validation of a multi-dimensional Eating Disorder Inventory for anorexia nervosa and bulimia. *International Journal of Eating Disorders, 2,* 15–34.

Garvin, V., Striegel-Moore, R. H., & Wells, A. M. (1998). Participant reactions to a cognitive-behavioral guided self-help program for binge eating: Developing criteria for program evaluation. *Journal of Psychosomatic Research, 44,* 407–412.

Gladis, M. M., Wadden, T. A., Foster, G. D., Vogt, R. A., & Wingate, B. J. (1998). A comparison of two approaches to the assessment of binge eating in obesity. *International Journal of Eating Disorders, 23,* 17–26.

Gladis, M. M., Wadden, T. A., Vogt, R., Foster, G., Kuehnel, R. H., & Bartlett, S. J. (1998). Behavioral treatment of obese binge eaters: Do they need different care? *Journal of Psychosomatic Research, 44,* 375–384.

Goldfein, J. A., Walsh, B. T., LaChaussee, J. L., Kissileff, H. R., & Devlin, M. J. (1993). Eating behavior in binge eating disorder. *International Journal of Eating Disorders, 14,* 427–431.

Goodrick, C. K., Poston, W. S. C., Kimball, K. T., Reeves, R. S., & Foreyt, J. P. (1998). Nondieting versus dieting treatment for overweight binge-eating women. *Journal of Consulting and Clinical Psychology, 66,* 363–368.

Gormally, J., Black, S., Daston, S., & Rardin, D. (1982). The assessment of binge eating severity among obese persons. *Addictive Behaviors, 7,* 47–55.

Grissett, N. I., & Fitzgibbon, M. L. (1996). The clinical significance of binge eating in an obese population: Support for BED and questions regarding its criteria. *Addictive Behaviors, 21,* 57–66.

Hamburger, W. H. (1951). Emotional aspects of obesity. *Medical Clinics of North America, 35,* 483–499.

Hawkins, R. C., & Clement, P. F. (1980). Development and construct validation of a self-report measure of binge eating tendencies. *Addictive Behaviors, 5,* 219–226.

Ho, K. S. I., Nichaman, M. Z., Taylor, W. C., Lee, E. S., & Foreyt, J. P. (1995). Binge eating disorder, retention, and dropout in an adult obesity program. *International Journal of Eating Disorders, 18,* 291–294.

Hudson, J. I., McElroy, S. L., Raymond, N. C., Crow, S., Keck, P. E., Carter, W. P., Mitchell, J. E., Strakowski, S. M., Pope, H. G., Coleman, B., & Jonas, J. M. (1998). Fluvoxamine in the treatment of binge eating disorder. *American Journal of Psychiatry, 155,* 1756–1762.

Hudson, J. I., Pope, H. G., Wurtman, J., Yurgelun-Todd, D., Mark, S., & Rosenthal, N. E. (1988). Bulimia in obese individuals: Relationship to normal-weight bulimia. *Journal of Nervous and Mental Disorders, 176,* 144–152.

Jansen, A., Broekmate, J., & Heymans, M. (1992). Cue-exposure vs. self-control in the treatment of binge eating: A pilot study. *Behavior Research and Therapy, 30,* 235–241.

Keefe, P. H., Wyshogrood, D., Weinberger, E., & Agras, W. S. (1984). Binge eating and outcome of behavioral treatment of obesity: A preliminary report. *Behavior Research and Therapy, 22,* 319–321.

Kinzl, J. F., Traweger, C., Trefalt, E., Mangweth, B., & Biebl, W. (1999). Binge eating disorder in females: A population-based investigation. *International Journal of Eating Disorders, 25,* 287–292.

Kirkley, B. G., Kolotkin, R. L., Hernandez, J. T., & Gallagher, P. N. (1992). A comparison of binge-purgers, obese binge eaters, and obese nonbinge eaters on the MMPI. *International Journal of Eating Disorders, 12,* 221–228.

Kolotkin, R. L., Revis, E. S., Kirkley, B. G., & Janick, L. (1987). Binge eating in obesity: Associated MMPI characteristics. *Journal of Consulting and Clinical Psychology, 55,* 872–876.

Kornhaber, A. (1970). The stuffing syndrome. *Psychosomatics, 11,* 580–584.

Kuehnel, R. H., & Wadden, T. A. (1994). Binge eating disorder, weight cycling, and psychopathology. *International Journal of Eating Disorders, 15,* 321–329.

LaPorte, D. J. (1992). Treatment response in obese binge eaters: Preliminary results using a very-low-calorie diet (VLCD) and behavior therapy. *Addictive Behaviors, 17,* 247–257.

Levine, M. D., Marcus, M. D., & Moulton, P. (1996). Exercise in the treatment of binge eating disorder. *International Journal of Eating Disorders, 19,* 171–177.

Lowe, M. R., & Caputo, G. C. (1991). Binge eating in obesity: Toward the specification of predictors. *International Journal of Eating Disorders, 10,* 49–55.

Marcus, M. D., Smith, D., Santelli, R., & Kaye, W. (1992). Characterization of eating disordered behavior in obese binge eaters. *International Journal of Eating Disorders, 12,* 249–255.

Marcus, M. D., Wing, R. R., Ewing, L., Kern, E., Gooding, W., & McDermott, M. (1990). Psychiatric disorders among obese binge eaters. *International Journal of Eating Disorders, 9,* 69–77.

Marcus, M. D., Wing, R. R., Ewing, L., Kern, E., McDermott, M., & Gooding, W. (1990). A double-blind, placebo-controlled trial of fluoxetine plus behavior modification in the treatment of obese binge-eaters and non–binge-eaters. *American Journal of Psychiatry, 147,* 876–881.

Marcus, M. D., Wing, R. R., & Fairburn, C. G. (1995). Cognitive treatment of binge eating versus behavioral weight control in the treatment of binge eating disorder. *Annals of Behavioral Medicine, 17,* S090.

Marcus, M. D., Wing, R. R., & Hopkins, J. (1988). Obese binge eaters: Affect, cognitions, and response to behavioral weight control. *Journal of Consulting and Clinical Psychology, 56,* 433–439.

Marcus, M. D., Wing, R. R., & Lamparski, D. M. (1985). Binge eating and dietary restraint in obese patients. *Addictive Behaviors, 10,* 163–168.

McCann, U. D., & Agras, W. S. (1990). Successful treatment of non-purging bulimia nervosa with desipramine: A double-blind, placebo-controlled study. *American Journal of Psychiatry, 147,* 1509–1513.

McCann, U. D., Rossiter, E. M., King, R. J., & Agras, W. S. (1991). Nonpurging bulimia: A distinct subtype of bulimia nervosa. *International Journal of Eating Disorders, 10,* 679–687.

Mussell, M., Mitchell, J., Weller, C., Raymond, N., Crow, S., & Crosby, R. (1995). Onset of binge eating, dieting, obesity, and mood disorders among subjects seeking treatment for binge eating disorder. *International Journal of Eating Disorders, 4,* 395–400.

Peterson, C. B., Mitchell, J. E., Engbloom, S., Nugent, S., Mussell, M. P., & Miller, J. P. (1998). Group cognitive-behavioral treatment of binge eating disorder: A comparison of therapist-led versus self-help formats. *International Journal of Eating Disorders, 24,* 125–136.

Porzelius, L. K., Houston, C., Smith, M., Arfken, C., & Fisher, E. (1995). Comparison of a standard behavioral weight loss treatment and a binge eating weight loss treatment. *Behavior Therapy, 26,* 119–134.

Powers, P. S., Perez, A., Boyd, F., & Rosemurgy, A. (1999). Eating pathology before and after bariatric surgery: A prospective study. *International Journal of Eating Disorders, 25,* 293–300.

Prather, R. C., & Williamson, D. A. (1988). Psychopathology associated with bulimia, binge eating, and obesity. *International Journal of Eating Disorders, 7,* 177–184.

Prats, M., Diez-Quevedo, C., Avila, C., & Planell, L. S. (1994, April). *Paroxetine treatment for bulimia nervosa and binge eating disorder.* Paper presented at the Sixth International Conference on Eating Disorders, New York, Abstract 308.

Raymond, N. C., de Zwaan, M., Faris, P. L., Nugent, S. M., Ackard, D. M., Crosby, R. D., & Mitchell, J. E. (1995). Pain thresholds in obese binge eating disorder subjects. *Biological Psychiatry, 37,* 202–204.

Raymond, N., Mussell, M., Mitchell, J. E., Crosby, R., & de Zwaan, M. (1995). An age-matched comparison of subjects with binge eating disorder and bulimia nervosa. *International Journal of Eating Disorders, 18,* 135–143.

Rossiter, E. M., Agras, W. S., Telch, C. F., & Bruce, B. (1992). The eating patterns of non-purging bulimic subjects. *International Journal of Eating Disorders, 11,* 111–120.

Schlundt, D. G., Taylor, D., Hill, J. O., Sbrocco, T., Pope-Cordle, J., Kasser, T., & Arnold, D. (1991). A behavioral taxonomy of obese female participants in a weight-loss program. *American Journal of Clinical Nutrition, 53,* 1151–1158.

Smith, D. E., Marcus, M. D., & Kaye, W. (1992). Cognitive-behavioral treatment of obese binge eaters. *International Journal of Eating Disorders, 12,* 257–262.

Specker, S., de Zwaan, M., Raymond, N., & Mitchell, J. (1994). Psychopathology in subgroups of obese women with and without binge eating disorder. *Comprehensive Psychiatry, 35,* 185–190.

Spitzer, R. L., Devlin, M. J., Walsh, B. T., Hasin, D., Wing, R., Marcus, M. D., Stunkard, A., Wadden, T., Yanovski S., Agras, S., Mitchell, J., & Nonas, C. (1991). Binge eating disorder: To be or not to be in DSM-IV. *International Journal of Eating Disorders, 10,* 627–629.

Spitzer, R. L., Devlin, M. J., Walsh, B. T., Hasin, D., Wing, R., Marcus, M. D., Stunkard, A., Wadden, T., Yanovski S., Agras, S., Mitchell, J., & Nonas, C. (1992). Binge eating disorder: A multisite field trial of the diagnostic criteria. *International Journal of Eating Disorders, 11,* 191–203.

Spitzer, R. L., Yanovski, S., Wadden, T., Wing, R., Marcus, M. D., Stunkard, A., Devlin, M., Mitchell, J., Hasin, D., & Horne, R. L. (1993). Binge eating disorder: Its further validation in a multisite study. *International Journal of Eating Disorders, 13,* 137–153.

Spurrell, E. B., Wilfley, D. E., Tanofsky, M. B., & Brownell, K. D. (1997). Age of onset for binge eating: Are there different pathways to binge eating? *International Journal of Eating Disorders, 21,* 55–65.

Striegel-Moore, R. H., Wilson, G. T., Wilfley, D. E., Elder, K. A., & Brownell, K. D. (1998). Binge eating in an obese community sample. *International Journal of Eating Disorders, 23,* 27–37.

Stunkard, A. J. (1959). Eating patterns and obesity. *Psychiatry Quarterly, 33,* 284–92.

Stunkard, A., Berkowitz, R., Tanrikut, C., Reiss, E., & Young, L. (1996). *d*-Fenfluramine treatment of binge eating disorder. *American Journal of Psychiatry, 153,* 1455–1459.

Stunkard, A., Berkowitz, R., Wadden, T., Tanrikut, C., Reiss, E., & Young, L. (1996). Binge eating disorder and the night eating syndrome. *International Journal of Obesity and Related Metabolic Disorders, 20,* 1–6.

Stunkard, A. J., & Messick S. (1985). The Three-factor Eating Questionnaire to measure dietary restraint, disinhibition and hunger. *Journal of Psychosomatic Research, 29,* 71–83.

Telch, C. F., & Agras, W. S. (1993). The effects of a very-low-calorie diet on binge eating. *Behavior Therapy, 24,* 177–193.

Telch, C. F., & Agras, W. S. (1994). Obesity, binge eating, and psycho-pathology: Are they related? *International Journal of Eating Disorders, 15,* 53–61.

Telch, C. F., Agras, W. S., & Rossiter, E. M. (1988). Binge eating increases with increasing adiposity. *International Journal of Eating Disorders, 7,* 115–119.

Telch, C. F., Agras, W. S., Rossiter, E. M., Wilfley, D., & Kenardy, J. (1990). Group cognitive-behavioral treatment for the nonpurging bulimic: An initial evaluation. *Journal of Consulting and Clinical Psychology, 58,* 629–635.

Wadden, T. A., Foster, G. D., & Letizia, K. A. (1992). Response of obese binge eaters to treatment by behavioral therapy combined with very-low-calorie diet. *Journal of Consulting and Clinical Psychology, 60,* 808–811.

Wadden, T. A., Foster, G. D., & Letizia, K. A. (1994). One-year behavioral treatment of obesity: Comparison of moderate and severe caloric restriction and the effects of weight maintenance therapy. *Journal of Consulting and Clinical Psychology, 62,* 165–171.

Wadden, T. A., Foster, G. D., Letizia, K. A., & Wilk, J. E. (1993). Metabolic, anthropometric, and psychological characteristics of obese binge eaters. *International Journal of Eating Disorders, 14,* 17–25.

Wells, A. M., Garvin, V., Dohm, F. A., & Striegel-Moore, R. H. (1997). Telephone-based guided self-help for binge eating disorder: A feasibility study. *International Journal of Eating Disorders, 21,* 341–346.

Wilfley, D. E., Agras, W. S., Telch, C. F., Rossiter, E. M., Schneider, J. A., Golomb Cole, A., Sifford, L., & Raeburn, S. D. (1993). Group cognitive-behavioral therapy and group interpersonal psychotherapy for the nonpurging bulimic individual: A controlled comparison. *Journal of Consulting and Clinical Psychology, 61,* 296–305.

Wilfley, D. E., & Cohen, L. R. (1997). Psychological treatment of bulimia nervosa and binge eating disorder. *Psychopharmacology Bulletin, 33,* 437–454.

Williamson, D. A., Prather, R. C., & McKenzie, S. J. (1989). Behavioral assessment procedures can differentiate bulimia nervosa, compulsive overeaters, obese and normal subjects. *Behavior Assessment, 12,* 239–252.

Wilson, G. T. (1976). Obesity, binge eating, and behavior therapy: Some clinical observations. *Behavior Therapy, 7,* 700–701.

Wilson, G. T., Nonas, C. A., & Rosenblum, G. D. (1993). Assessment of binge eating in obese patients. *International Journal of Eating Disorders, 13,* 25–33.

Wing, R. R., Marcus, M. D., Epstein, L. H., Blair, E. H., & Burton, L. R. (1989). Binge eating in obese patients with Type II diabetes. *International Journal of Eating Disorders, 8,* 671–679.

Yanovski, S. (1993). Binge eating disorder: Current knowledge and future directions. *Obesity Research, 1,* 306–324.

Yanovski, S. Z., Gormally, J. F., Leser, M. S., Gwirtsman, H. E., & Yanovski, J. A. (1994). Binge eating disorder affects outcome of comprehensive very-low-calorie diet treatment. *Obesity Research, 2,* 205–212.

Yanovski, S. Z., Leet, M., Yanovski, J. A., Flood, M., Gold, P. W., Kissileff, H. R., & Walsh, B. T. (1992). Food selection and intake of obese women with binge eating disorder. *American Journal of Clinical Nutrition, 56,* 975–980.

Yanovski, S. Z., Nelson, J. E., Dubbert, B. K., & Spitzer, R. L. (1993). Association of binge eating disorder and psychiatric comorbidity in obese subjects. *American Journal of Psychiatry, 150,* 1472–1479.

Yanovski, S. Z., & Sebring, N. G. (1994). Recorded food intake of obese women with binge eating disorder before and after weight loss. *International Journal of Eating Disorders, 15,* 135–150.

Chapter 4

# Eating Disorders Not Otherwise Specified

*Pamela K. Keel*

Popular portrayals of eating disorders typically present cases of anorexia nervosa and bulimia nervosa. When eating disorders are mentioned, many people think of Karen Carpenter, or perhaps Lady Diana. However, many individuals who have an eating disorder do not fit the standard profiles. Such cases were previously considered atypical eating disorders (in the DSM-III) and now may receive a diagnosis of Eating Disorders Not Otherwise Specified (EDNOS; APA, 1994 [DSM-IV]). The prevalence of atypical eating disorder diagnoses depends on the population surveyed and on the criteria used, ranging widely from 2.9% among a sample of Scottish psychiatric inpatients (Kutcher, Whitehouse, & Freeman, 1985) to 24% among inpatients on a Child and Adolescent Psychosomatic Unit in Israel (Mitrany, 1992). Among patient samples diagnosed with eating disorders, atypical eating disorders comprise from 6.5% (Ash & Piazza, 1995) to 36% (Mitrany, 1992), with a cumulative percentage across several studies of 16% (Ash & Piazza, 1995; Beumont, Kopec-Schrader, Talbot, & Touyz, 1993; Clinton & Glant, 1992; Hall & Hay, 1991; Mitchell, Pyle, Hatsukami, & Eckert, 1986; and Mitrany, 1992). Thus, EDNOS diagnoses clearly represent a significant portion of patients seeking treatment for an eating disorder and may represent a larger percentage of individuals in the general population with eating problems.

The classification system used to diagnose an eating disorder determines the rates of atypical diagnoses and accounts for much of the variability in the prevalences noted above. Ash and Piazza (1995) retrospectively reviewed charts of 33 consecutive admissions into a children's hospital for eating disorders in the 1970s, 1980s, and 1990s. A main finding of this study was a shift in the distribution of eating disorder diagnoses within these three cohorts. In the 1970s, 100% of admissions met criteria for anorexia nervosa. In the 1980s, 87.1% were diagnosed with anorexia nervosa, 3.1% with bulimia nervosa, and 3.1% with mixed diagnoses of anorexia and bulimia, and 6.5% received a diagnosis of atypical eating disorder. By the 1990s, only 48.4% were diagnosed with anorexia nervosa, 29.0% with bulimia nervosa, 16.1% with mixed anorexia and bulimia nervosa, and 6.5% with atypical eating disorder. Consistent with these figures, average weight at intake increased significantly over the three decades. To some extent, this distribution shift also represents the effect of altering diagnostic criteria as to what is considered an eating disorder. Prior to 1979 and Russell's definition of normal-weight bulimia nervosa, a diagnosis of anorexia nervosa was often considered for individuals who were not underweight but fasted, binged, and purged. The expansion of eating disorder diagnoses has led to increased awareness of disordered eating, greater variations in who qualifies as having an eating disorder, and perhaps increased numbers of individuals who are labeled as eating disordered.

The focus of this chapter is to describe atypical eating disorders within the context of DSM-IV classification. This chapter will provide descriptions and case examples of disordered eating patterns that fall into the category of EDNOS and atypical eating disorders. The following topics will be discussed: atypical eating disorders and eating disorders not otherwise specified, eating disorders that are atypical due to case presentation, unusual eating patterns, and the significance of atypical eating disorders.

## Atypical Eating Disorders and Eating Disorders Not Otherwise Specified

The approach to defining eating disorder diagnoses within the DSM-IV sets two ways in which an individual may fail to meet full diagnostic criteria for an eating disorder: quantitatively or qualitatively. Quantitative failure to meet criteria occurs when an individual has all of the core symptoms and signs of a disorder, yet she fails to meet the criteria for duration, frequency, or severity. Qualitative failure to meet full criteria occurs when an individual meets many criteria, but a core feature of the disorder is absent or replaced by symptoms that are not defined within the eating disorder classification.

### Quantitative EDNOS

Quantitative failure to meet full criteria often occurs when arbitrary limits must be defined for degree of severity, frequency, or duration of behaviors.

For example, in the DSM-IV an individual would receive an EDNOS diagnosis if she met all criteria for anorexia nervosa but her significant weight loss did not fall below 85% of the weight expected for her height and age. Consider the following case:

> Gina is a 19-year-old freshman in college. She is 5'0" and at the beginning of her senior year in high school weighed 150 pounds. During her senior year she lost 45 pounds taking a liquid diet and exercising by running. She maintained her weight at 105 pounds and received many compliments from her friends and family for her willpower. When Gina left for college she felt very confident with her new figure and weight. Shortly into her freshman year, Gina slowly began to gain weight. At 140 pounds, she decided to regain control of her weight and began fasting for extended periods in addition to her running program, which she steadily increased in intensity and duration. When she was seen by a gynecologist at the University Health Services, she had been amenorrheic for five months and weighed 93 pounds. She ate infrequently and when she ate, she avoided eating anything "unhealthy," that is, food Gina perceived to be high in sugar, fat, or salt. Mostly she preferred fruits and raw vegetables. When the gynecologist suggested that Gina increase her food intake, Gina expressed an extreme fear of gaining weight and insisted that she was still too fat and needed to lose more weight.

Although Gina does not weigh below 85% of that expected for her height, she appears to be experiencing anorexia nervosa. If she does not receive treatment for an eating disorder, she may lose more weight and begin to experience medical and greater psychological complications of low weight. Her loss of 47 pounds (from 140 to 93) within a relatively short period of time suggests that she is engaging in extreme and unhealthy behaviors.

Another example of EDNOS in DSM-IV is an individual who meets all criteria of bulimia nervosa without binge eating and inappropriate compensation occurring as often as twice a week for three months. An example follows:

> Amanda is a 25-year-old female who works as the night manager of a fast-food restaurant. Four months ago, Amanda went on a diet in preparation for a vacation in Florida with her boyfriend. Shortly after beginning her diet, Amanda found herself binge eating at work—eating leftover french fries and milk shake mix that would have to be thrown

out. At first she only binge ate once a week, but then she began binge eating more regularly, and she started gaining weight. After her boyfriend commented on her weight, and after she noticed that her clothes were too tight, Amanda resolved to increase her dieting efforts and not to binge at work. She maintained this for two weeks and then had a very large binge eating episode. After everyone else left work, she started eating the leftover fries, moved on to the milk shake mix, then made an entire batch of fries, and continued to eat ice cream and fries until she began to feel physically ill. She went to the bathroom and threw up and felt immediately relieved. That was two months ago. Since then, she has been binge eating and making herself throw up four to eight times a week. She feels she cannot control her eating binges, but she cannot allow herself to "get fat."

Amanda's case is similar to Gina's in that both women appear to be on the verge of developing full eating disorder diagnoses, and both women would probably benefit from treatment before their disorders progress any further. Also, both individuals possess all of the characteristics required for a diagnosis except they do not meet quantitative criteria (i.e., severity, frequency, or duration).

Some women maintain a lower level of disordered eating for a long period of time. For example, it is possible for a woman to binge eat and self-induce vomiting once a week and maintain this behavioral pattern for years. This individual may also receive an EDNOS diagnosis. In this case, providing an EDNOS diagnosis avoids the difficulty of justifying the validity of current quantitative requirements, especially when these requirements have changed and may continue to change over future editions of the DSM. For example, in DSM-III, an individual was required to maintain a weight 20% below that expected to meet criteria for a diagnosis of anorexia nervosa, but no frequency criteria were set for bulimia nervosa. Thus, shifts from DSM-III to DSM-IV have resulted in greater inclusiveness in anorexia nervosa and greater exclusiveness in bulimia nervosa. Providing an EDNOS diagnosis for individuals falling just outside current criteria is partially a recognition of the somewhat arbitrary and perhaps transient nature of such criteria.

### Qualitative EDNOS

A qualitative failure to meet full criteria is an apparent mismatch between the syndrome displayed by an individual and that defined within the DSM. The causes of this mismatch may reflect a syndrome that has yet to be defined. For example, binge eating disorder involves recurrent binge eating in the absence of inappropriate compensatory behavior. In DSM-III, this pattern often met the criteria for bulimia because inappropriate compensation was not required; it was one symptom of many a patient could display in the definition of bulimia. In DSM-III-R, this abnormal behavioral pattern failed to meet criteria for bulimia nervosa because the diagnosis required purging or other inappropriate compensation. In DSM-IV, binge eating disorder is included among examples of EDNOS and is also presented in the appendix as a disorder with defined research criteria.

Another source of disordered eating that is qualitatively distinct from defined eating disorders is a syndrome due to a separate psychiatric or medical illness. For example, an individual may engage in extreme food avoidance resulting in significant weight loss if they are experiencing psychotic delusions that all food is poisonous. Such an individual would be expected to lack any fear of weight gain or feelings of being fat or needing to be thin. In this case, a diagnosis of EDNOS is not appropriate because treatment of the primary disorder should resolve the secondary eating disorder. In some cases an individual may have a psychiatric disorder that contributes to the disordered eating pattern, such as a social phobia; however, sufficient symptoms unrelated to a fear of eating in public must exist to support an EDNOS diagnosis.

An example of EDNOS due to qualitative differences within the DSM-IV is a normal-weight individual who engages in self-induced vomiting or laxative abuse in the absence of binge-eating:

> Cindy is a 29-year-old mother of two children. She is 5'4" and weighs 128 pounds. She does not experience episodes of overeating or feel a loss of control during food consumption. She does, however, abuse laxatives daily. She feels particularly concerned now that she has resorted to stealing laxatives from drugstores because she is very embarrassed by how many she uses. She says she uses them because they make her feel thinner and lighter. She has come to a point where she is unable to have bowel movements without using laxatives. She is afraid that if she does not stop, she will continue to need more and more laxatives and that she will then be unable to obtain laxatives without calling attention to herself or suffering financial problems. She is also obsessed with maintaining her weight and shape.

Cindy's laxative abuse places her at risk for developing medical complications such as electrolyte imbalances. She is also experiencing distress and functional impairment (shoplifting). For these reasons, both diagnosis and treatment are important.

The following case of an individual who regularly engages in the chewing and spitting out of large amounts of food also exemplifies an atypical eating disorder due to qualitative differences:

> Rita is a 44-year-old woman who had been a former patient treated for bulimia nervosa 20 years previously. Her bulimia nervosa began after a period of anorexia nervosa. After treatment, she successfully remained abstinent from vomiting, laxative abuse, and diuretic abuse. Additionally, Rita remained successfully abstinent from drug and alcohol use, both of which she had been dependent on prior to her treatment for bulimia nervosa. Currently, Rita regularly chews and spits out large amounts of food without swallowing. Approximately four times a week, she chews and spits out a package of cookies or a pan of brownies, typically full containers of sweets. Rita chews and spits out food in private because she is embarrassed by this behavior and feels ashamed of the amount of food she wastes. She also exercises five to seven times a week for an hour. Previously, she had exercised every day for two to three hours; however, she came to view this as excessive and reduced her regimen. At 5'9" and 140 pounds, she does not view herself as fat and does not express a particular fear of gaining weight; however, she states emphatically that she would not allow herself to gain 5 pounds. Additionally, she states that she could not refrain from exercising for one week.

Unlike the atypical eating disorders presented previously, these behaviors do not appear to place Rita at a high risk for medical complications nor do they seem to be a precursor to developing a full eating disorder diagnosis. Rather, the behaviors appear to be the remnants of a past eating disorder diagnosis. However, the behaviors are still clinically significant and suggest a pattern of loss of control around food consumption and use of exercise to compensate. Additionally, her behaviors are distressing and expensive. Depending on the degree of social impairment, she may qualify for an EDNOS diagnosis. Conflicts with her husband concerning the amount of food bought and essentially thrown away, or the development of numerous dental caries are examples of impairment as a result of her behaviors that would support providing a diagnosis.

In summary, atypical cases of eating disorders result from quantitative or qualitative failure to meet criteria. Quantitative differences are cases in which frequency, duration, or severity criteria are not met. Because such criteria are often arbitrarily set, an individual may fail to meet the specific cutoff but have a clinically significant disorder. Alternatively, such individuals may simply be in the process of developing full criteria for a specific eating disorder. Qualitative differences are cases in which a core feature is absent or replaced by a variation of the behavior. Qualitatively different eating disorders may represent yet to be defined categories or disorders due to another illness. The following are examples of disordered eating patterns that could receive EDNOS diagnoses within the DSM-IV:

1. For females, all of the criteria for Anorexia Nervosa are met except that the individual has regular menses.
2. All of the criteria for Anorexia Nervosa are met except that, despite significant weight loss, the individual's current weight is in the normal range.
3. All of the criteria for bulimia nervosa are met except that the binge eating and inappropriate compensatory mechanisms occur at a frequency of less than twice a week or for a duration of less than 3 months.
4. The regular use of inappropriate compensatory behaviors by an individual of normal body weight after eating small amounts of food (e.g., self-induced vomiting after the consumption of two cookies).
5. Repeatedly chewing and spitting out, but not swallowing, large amounts of food.
6. Binge-eating disorder: recurrent episodes of binge eating in the absence of the regular use of inappropriate compensatory behaviors characteristic of Bulimia Nervosa (APA, 1994, p. 550).

### Eating Disorders That Are Atypical Due to Case Presentation

Thus far, atypical eating disorders and EDNOS have been treated as synonymous entities. However, some researchers and clinicians regard case presentation as a significant aspect of a diagnosis, especially in terms of understanding the course and outcome of a disorder. Thus, "atypical" eating disorders may also include eating disorders that meet full criteria (i.e., can be diagnosed as anorexia nervosa, bulimia nervosa, or binge eating disorder) but differ significantly from the usual presentation in some aspect thought to be important for understanding the nature and perhaps the cause of the disorder (Andersen, 1977).

Examples of these atypical eating disorders often defy typical demographic patterns. For example, a very early or very late age of onset for anorexia nervosa might represent a syndrome distinct from the typical category:

> Marion is a 30-year-old woman who recently gave birth to her first child. After delivery, Marion became obsessed with losing the weight she had gained during pregnancy. She is 5'5" and had weighed 138 pounds prior to becoming pregnant. She was never particularly concerned about her weight prior to the pregnancy and had no history of emotional problems. She gained 27 pounds during pregnancy and weighed 153 pounds after delivery. She began severely restricting her food intake while insisting upon breast-feeding her child. Currently, Marion weighs 102 pounds and insists that she still needs to lose more weight. She expresses intense fear of gaining weight and for this reason has decided she will have no more children despite initially wanting two or three children. She has not menstruated since conception; however, it is doubtful that she would menstruate at normal weight because she breast-feeds frequently.

Although Marion meets full criteria for anorexia nervosa and would not receive a diagnosis of EDNOS, understanding her disorder may require recognition of the unusual circumstances surrounding its development. Her age of onset is older than that usually displayed by most females with anorexia nervosa. Her seemingly normal psychosocial development prior to pregnancy and then intense reaction to weight gain during pregnancy is also unusual for anorexia nervosa.

The occurrence of anorexia or bulimia nervosa in males is considered by some authors (e.g., Andersen, 1977) to be another example of eating disturbances that meet full criteria but represent a distinct phenomenon. Such authors argue that males are not subjected to similar cultural pressures to be thin and therefore their eating disorders necessarily imply a differential etiology. Such cases may provide insight into the specific triggers that produce eating disorders and help explain why among the many women who diet to lose weight, only a few develop eating disorders. The following example provides an illustration:

> Jeff is a 22-year-old recent college graduate. He is 5'10" and weighs 185 pounds. During college, Jeff participated in wrestling for which he would seasonally work to reduce his weight to below 170 pounds. He was always able to reach that weight, although he occasionally resorted

to the use of laxatives and diuretics to remove unwanted pounds prior to a competition. At the end of each season he typically went through a period of binge eating until he returned to his previous weight. Off-season, Jeff also worked out regularly to build his strength and muscle tone. Currently, Jeff is obsessed with his body fat percentage and calculates the fat grams in everything he eats, trying to eat less than 5 grams of fat a day. Additionally, he spends 3 to 5 hours at the gym every evening after work. His typical workout involves using a stair-stepping machine for 90 minutes, then riding a stationary bicycle for an hour, and following the aerobic workout with 30 to 60 minutes of lifting free weights. Occasionally, he will spend an additional 1 to 2 hours swimming laps. Every evening, on his way home from the gym, he stops by the grocery store, where he will buy several packages of fat-free cookies and family-size frozen packages of pasta and macaroni and cheese. He usually begins eating the cookies in the car and finishes eating the rest of the food once he gets home. Although he knows that he will binge eat when he goes to the grocery store and feels that he is in control of his decision to go to the store, he also feels that once he starts eating, he cannot stop until all of the food is gone.

Jeff meets full criteria for bulimia nervosa, non-purging subtype; however, similar to Marion's case, the unusual circumstances of his disorder may provide unique insight into how voluntary disordered eating patterns can lead to an involuntary eating disorder. Thus, while he would be diagnosed with bulimia nervosa, in research and treatment it may be useful to view him as a case of atypical eating disorder.

A final example of a qualitatively distinct atypical eating disorder might include the following case, in which anorexia nervosa results from the persistence of weight loss that initially resulted from a medical condition:

Monica is a 26-year-old female who is 5'4" and currently weighs 75 pounds. She has not menstruated for seven months. One year ago, Monica was living abroad working for the Peace Corps, building houses in an underdeveloped nation. During this year, she became severely ill, having contracted an intestinal parasite. She went from weighing 125 pounds to 95 pounds. Upon returning to the United States, she was successfully treated for the parasite; however, she continued to lose weight rapidly. A number of months were spent attempting to determine the physical cause of her continued weight loss. After numerous negative tests, Monica was referred to a psychiatrist. Interviews revealed that after passing the parasite in her bowel movements, she became intensely disgusted with the realization she had consumed the parasite in contaminated food or water. Following this realization, she could not bring herself to eat anything that she could not visually inspect for infestation. Thus, she had limited herself to bottled water and clear broths that she boiled for an hour before consuming. She did not perceive herself as being fat; however, she also did not appreciate the dangers of eating so little food and felt that others were exaggerating the risks associated with her continued weight loss. Additionally, she expressed the belief that if she continued to starve herself, she would starve any parasites that might still be within her.

Monica's case lacks an intense fear of weight gain; however, she does seem to misperceive her current weight by failing to realize the severity of her condition. Her case presents possible options of diagnosing her with an atypical eating disorder or an anxiety disorder, potentially obsessive compulsive disorder, or a specific phobia. Because her weight loss is medically significant, she may be best treated as an inpatient on an eating disorders unit, which would probably result in a diagnosis of atypical eating disorder or EDNOS.

In summary, it may be useful to distinguish syndromes that differ significantly in terms of case presentation from what is typically seen, even if the individual satisfies full criteria. The reason for this discrimination is similar to the reasons for discriminating any category of behavior. The differences observed in age of onset, gender, or relation to a physical condition may indicate a distinct etiology, course, and outcome. The presence or absence of such distinctions can only be adequately determined if individuals with differing presentations are set apart from individuals displaying more typical patterns and demographics.

### Unusual Eating Patterns

Much debate surrounds where the lines should be drawn separating "normal" from unusual eating behaviors, and where to separate these from diagnosable eating disorders. Body dissatisfaction, dieting, and binge eating are fairly common phenomena, especially among high school and college-age females (Heatherton, Nichols, Mahamedi, & Keel, 1995; Leon, Fulkerson, Perry, & Cudeck, 1993). Atypical eating behaviors may also be quite common among female adolescents and young adults (Tordjman, Zittoun, Anderson, Flament, & Jeammet, 1994).

The sometimes arbitrary nature of cutoffs for severity or frequency of certain symptoms was discussed earlier in the chapter. The reason for setting limits is not arbitrary, however. The usefulness of any diagnostic system rests on its reliability, that is, the extent to which it can be applied consistently. Prior to the third edition of the DSM, diagnoses were made less reliably because concrete criteria were not set forth. Without cutoffs, individual clinicians and researchers were often left to determine what they individually believed to be clinically significant. If there is no consistency in how things are placed into existing categories, then misplacement will occur frequently, resulting in the lumping of dissimilar syndromes. Misplacement of syndromes defeats the purpose of categorization.

Compared to the other eating disorder diagnoses, EDNOS lacks specific criteria for inclusion and exclusion. Although examples are given within DSM-IV for what behavioral patterns would be considered diagnosable, many more variations of disordered eating patterns are present in the community than are covered in the system. To address this issue, the following guidelines are provided for use when unusual eating patterns appear to qualify for an eating disorder diagnosis and when they fall into the more normative side of the continuum. The DSM-IV provides these general guidelines and examples for the use of Not Otherwise Specified Categories:

- The presentation conforms to the general guidelines for a mental disorder in the diagnostic class, but the symptomatic picture does not meet the criteria for any of the specific disorders. This would occur either when the symptoms are below the diagnostic threshold for one of the specific disorders or when there is an atypical or mixed presentation.
- The presentation conforms to a symptoms pattern that has not been included in the DSM-IV Classification but that causes clinically significant distress or impairment.
- There is uncertainty about etiology (i.e., whether the disorder is due to a general medical condition, is substance induced, or is primary).
- There is insufficient opportunity for complete data collection (e.g., in emergency situations) or inconsistent or contradictory information, but there is enough information to place it within a particular diagnostic class (e.g., the clinician determines that the individual has psychotic symptoms but does not have enough

information to diagnose a specific psychotic disorder). (APA, 1994, p. 4)

If a case presents with unusual eating patterns, such as consuming foods at odd times of the day (for example, only between 10 P.M. and 10 A.M.) or consuming unusual food combinations (such as grapefruit stirred into mashed potatoes with ketchup), but these patterns cause neither significant impairment nor distress to the individual, then they would not qualify for a diagnosis. Similarly, intense exercising in the absence of distress, impairment, or compensation for binge eating would not qualify for an eating disorder diagnosis. Behaviors that occur only sporadically or in isolation from other symptoms of a syndrome should not be diagnosed. For example, an individual who binges once every six months should not receive an eating disorder diagnosis. Similarly, an individual of normal or above normal weight should not receive a diagnosis for anorexia nervosa regardless of how intensely they fear weight gain or perceive themselves to be fat; these particular symptoms are clinically significant because they occur, by definition, in an underweight individual. Similarly, if an individual does not report a feeling of loss of control during episodes of overeating, then they do not meet criteria for binge eating. Although these examples suggest unusual behaviors or thoughts, they do not suggest clear psychopathology.

DSM-IV provides the following statement for the definition of a mental disorder:

> In DSM-IV, each of the mental disorders is conceptualized as a clinically significant behavioral or psychological syndrome or pattern that occurs in an individual and that is associated with present distress (e.g., a painful symptom) or disability (i.e., impairment in one or more important areas of functioning) or with a significantly increased risk of suffering death, pain, disability, or an important loss of freedom. In addition, this syndrome or patterns must not be merely an expectable and culturally sanctioned response to a particular event, for example, the death of a loved one. Whatever its original cause, it must currently be considered a manifestation of a behavioral, psychological, or biological dysfunction in the individual. Neither deviant behavior (e.g., political, religious, or sexual) nor conflicts that are primarily between the individual and society are mental disorders unless the deviance or conflict is a symptom of a dysfunction in the individual, as described above. (APA, 1994, pp. xxi–xxii)

Thus, these requirements are applied in determining whether an individual should receive an atypical eating disorder diagnosis.

In summary, atypical eating disorders hold a somewhat ill-defined place along a continuum of eating behaviors. At the extreme end of this continuum, diagnosable eating disorders are defined by the criteria set forth in DSM-IV (reviewed in previous chapters). Because these definitions are not all-inclusive, EDNOS diagnoses are given when an individual fails to meet full criteria but appears to have a clinically significant eating disorder. The point at which eating patterns should be considered unusual rather than disordered is not perfectly clear. As a guideline, DSM-IV suggests that behavioral patterns result in significant distress, disability, or increased risk to suffer pain, death, disability, or important loss of freedom. Additionally, the patterns cannot be a culturally sanctioned response to an event, nor can they be behaviors that are simply in conflict with cultural norms.

### Conclusions

Disordered eating patterns that result in clinically significant detriment and appear to have an internal source and involuntary manifestation may be considered to fall within the domain of eating disorders regardless of whether they meet full criteria. Notably, atypical eating disorders that represent subclinical forms (e.g., they differ quantitatively) have been found to progress to meet full eating disorder diagnoses in 46% of cases (Herzog, Hopkins, & Burns, 1993). Thus, intervention sooner rather than later is likely to be important. Additionally, such findings suggest that treatments applied to individuals with full eating disorder diagnoses would probably be effective for individuals with EDNOS diagnoses due to quantitative differences.

Whether atypical eating disorders that differ qualitatively also result in full eating disorder diagnoses is unclear. However, some forms of EDNOS appear to be associated with levels of distress and impairment comparable to those associated with full eating disorders (Tobin, Griffing, & Griffing, 1997). Research on atypical eating disorders is sparse because most research is conducted on individuals who meet full DSM criteria for a disorder. The individuals presenting with atypical eating disorders are exactly those individuals excluded from clinically based research and treatment studies. It is important to remember that some qualitatively atypical eating disorders (such as purging in the absence of binge eating at normal weight, and maintained low weight in the absence of weight phobia) present risk for severe medical complications. Thus, effective treatment for these disorders is needed.

Finally, atypical eating disorders of today may represent new eating disorder diagnoses of tomorrow as definitions are further refined to reflect these syndromes as they occur. Recent history provides the best example of this progression within eating disorders. First there was one eating disorder: anorexia nervosa. Then there were two eating disorders: anorexia and bulimia nervosa. Now there are two eating disorders with a third disorder—binge eating disorder—in the process of receiving further refinement. As each disorder has been described and defined, greater attention has been given to the eating patterns displayed by individuals, and recognition of these disorders has increased. Currently the challenge in research is to determine the impact of excluding atypical eating disorders from treatment studies for the effective treatment of individuals with these syndromes.

## References

American Psychiatric Association. (1987). *Diagnostic and statistical manual of mental disorders* (3d ed., rev.). Washington, DC: Author.

American Psychiatric Association. (1994). *Diagnostic and statistical manual of mental disorders* (4th ed.). Washington, DC: Author.

Andersen, A. E. (1977). Atypical anorexia nervosa. In R. A. Vigersky (Ed.), *Anorexia nervosa: A monograph of the National Institute of Child Health and Human Development*. New York: Raven Press.

Ash, J. B., & Piazza, E. (1995). Changing symptomatology in eating disorders. *International Journal of Eating Disorders, 18*, 27–38.

Beumont, P. J. V., Kopec-Schrader, E. M., Talbot, P., & Touyz, S. W. (1993). Measuring the specific psychopathology of eating disorder patients. *Australian and New Zealand Journal of Psychiatry, 27*, 506–511.

Clinton, D. N., & Glant, R. (1992). The eating disorders spectrum of DSM-III-R: Clinical features and psychosocial concomitants of 86 consecutive cases from a Swedish urban catchment area. *Journal of Nervous and Mental Disease, 180*, 244–250.

Hall, A., & Hay, P. J. (1991). Eating disorder patient referrals from a population region 1977–1986. *Psychological Medicine, 21*, 697–701.

Heatherton, T. F., Nichols, P., Mahamedi, F., & Keel, P. K. (1995). Body weight, dieting, and eating disorder symptoms among college students 1982 to 1992. *American Journal of Psychiatry, 152*, 1623–1629.

Herzog, D. B., Hopkins, J. D., & Burns, C. D. (1993). A follow-up study of 33 subdiagnostic eating disordered women. *International Journal of Eating Disorders, 14,* 261–267.

Kutcher, S. P., Whitehouse, A. M., & Freeman, C. P. L. (1985). "Hidden" eating disorders in Scottish psychiatric in patients. *American Journal of Psychiatry, 142,* 1475–1478.

Leon, G. R., Fulkerson, J. A., Perry, C. L., & Cudeck, R. (1993). Personality and behavioral vulnerabilities associated with risk status for eating disorders in adolescent girls. *Journal of Abnormal Psychology, 102,* 438–444.

Mitchell, J. E., Pyle, R. L., Hatsukami, D., & Eckert, E. D. (1986). What are atypical eating disorders? *Psychosomatics, 27,* 21–28.

Mitrany, E. (1992). Atypical eating disorders. *Journal of Adolescent Health, 13,* 400–402.

Tobin, D. L., Griffing, A., & Griffing, S. (1997). An examination of subtype criteria for bulimia nervosa. *International Journal of Eating Disorders, 22,* 179–186.

Tordjman, S., Zittoun, C., Anderson, G. M., Flament, M., & Jeammet, P. (1994). Preliminary study of eating disorders among French female adolescents and young adults. *International Journal of Eating Disorders, 16,* 301–305.

# Part II

# Treatment Techniques and Approaches

# Introduction

# The Team Approach

The treatment of patients with eating disorders usually requires a team approach. This caveat is offered so frequently in the literature that it may be taken for granted, but this observation is of great importance. In particular, the requirement that the management of these patients usually requires several individuals with different areas of expertise markedly limits the availability of adequate treatment resources. The average practitioner, whether a psychiatrist or clinical psychologist working in the community, will not have access to such a team unless she or he is associated with a clinical program through which the other team members can be accessed. By analogy, dietitians working with such patients may find themselves frustrated because of their lack of training in dealing with many aspects of the eating disorder, unless they have access to a team working with this patient group.

In thinking about this team and the roles of the individual team members, it is clear that the inclusion of some types of professionals is required. Others are desirable, and some clearly optional, depending on the individual case. The required members are a physician, a psychotherapist, and a dietitian. Highly desirable members include a social worker, an occupational therapist, and someone knowledgeable about exercise, such as an exercise physiologist or a physical medicine and rehabilitation physician interested in this disorder. Optional professional roles are those that need to be available in given situations, such as a pediatrician or an addiction counselor. We will discuss each of the essential and highly desirable roles.

## The Physician

The main functions of this team member are (1) the physical assessment and medical management of the patient with an eating disorder, and (2) assessment for and management of pharmacotherapy. These tasks are frequently split between two individuals. For example, an internist, family physician, or pediatrician may oversee the physical assessment and management of the patient, while a psychiatrist may assess the patient for pharmacotherapy, and if it is indicated, manage the pharmacotherapy. However, some general physicians who are knowledgeable about and interested in this population can do both tasks, while some psychiatrists who have kept current about the medical management of these patients can fulfill both tasks as well. Whether one or two people are involved does not matter as long as both needs are covered, and if more than one person is involved, communication between them is adequate, since working as part of a team requires clear and frequent communication about the management of the patient.

### The Psychotherapist

This person can be someone from a variety of backgrounds, such as a doctoral-level psychologist, a psychiatrist, or another mental health practitioner who is knowledgeable about psychotherapy and this patient population. Again, more than one person may be employed here (e.g., an individual therapist and a family therapist), but if more than one person is involved, communication is of utmost importance. This person must be knowledgeable about and have skills in the following areas: (1) eating disorders, including diagnostic issues, the behaviors involved, and the associated psychopathology; and (2) the forms of psychotherapy that have been shown to be useful in the treatment of these patients, including a supportive and at times didactic approach for low-weight anorexia nervosa patients, cognitive-behavioral treatment approaches for anorexia nervosa and bulimia nervosa patients, family therapy approaches with those patients for whom it is indicated, and at times couples therapy for older patients with eating disorders when the involvement of the significant other is appropriate. Sometimes this person also needs special expertise in child and adolescent issues for working with earlier onset anorexia nervosa and bulimia nervosa patients.

### Dietitian

Most mental health professionals are not highly knowledgeable about nutrition or nutritional counseling. Unfortunately, many dietitians are not knowledgeable about psychotherapy or eating disorders. Because of these mutual deficiencies, the dietitian usually functions best as a member of the team. If she or he is experienced in working with these patients

and has additional training in psychotherapy techniques, so n
better. However, most dietitians work best as part of the team,
the primary psychotherapist to carry the burden of the psychos
tervention. The nutritional part of the treatment of these patients is essential, however.

## Social Worker, Occupational Therapist

A social worker performing what would be considered more traditional
social work duties such as assisting patients with logistical problems such
as housing and transportation, and an occupational therapist working
with the patient on such issues as cooking and food preparation, shopping, and more general socialization skills, are highly desirable. These two
roles are particularly important in inpatient and day-treatment programs.

## Exercise Therapist

Problems with exercise are abundant in patients with eating disorders.
Such problems range from the development of eating disorders in athletes, to overexercise in some patients with anorexia nervosa, to the lack
of exercise among many bulimic patients and many patients with binge
eating disorder. Therefore, someone knowledgeable about exercise and
exercise physiology can be extremely valuable as a member of the team.

In the chapters ahead we will examine the roles of the different team
members by examining the various elements of treatment. Before beginning, however, the necessity for clear and frequent communication must
be underscored again. The team members should have a mutual sense of
trust and respect and must be alert to the possibility of "splitting" on the
part of the patients or their families. The team must share and present
to their patients and families a coherent conceptual model that they
understand and follow, and must be willing to offer support and encouragement to each other in working with this often difficult patient
population.

# Chapter 5

# Basic Counseling Techniques

*Pamela K. Keel*

Health professionals within different specialties often find themselves interacting with patients in a way that requires or that would benefit from familiarity with techniques basic to counseling. However, basic counseling skills are not typically provided as an aspect of training within each health profession. This chapter will present an overview of basic counseling techniques that are conducive to engendering therapeutic change, and then will provide examples of how these basic techniques can be applied when working with patients who have eating disorders. Emphasis will be placed on difficult treatment issues that commonly emerge.

The following topics are covered: distinguishing the personal from professional relationship in health care, developing a therapeutic alliance, communication skills for effective counseling, interpersonal style in counseling, transference and countertransference, resistance and reluctance, and avoiding common counseling mistakes. This chapter may serve as an introduction to health professionals who are not trained in graduate counseling programs or psychiatric residences but who work frequently with eating disordered patients. For trained counselors, this chapter may serve as a basic review.

## Distinguishing the Personal from Professional Relationship

On the surface, counseling appears to involve some of the basic elements of a friendship, such as listening and providing advice when asked for it. However, counseling is actually distinct from friendships in many aspects, and treating a patient as one would treat a friend will often lead to problems. By its very nature, counseling as a health professional requires a professional and not a personal relationship.

Distinguishing personal from professional relationships can be challenging because patients often share personal problems with their health professional. One obvious distinction is the asymmetrical nature of a professional relationship. First, the counselor must recognize that counseling is focused on the needs of the patient and not the needs of the counselor. Thus, when counselors feel inclined to share something personal about themselves or to provide personal advice to a patient, they must ask themselves, "Why am I doing this?" and "Whose needs would this meet?" If the answer is their own, or if they are unsure, then they must forgo the disclosure or advice. In fact, self-disclosure and personal advice as opposed to information are rarely indicated in a "counseling" relationship.

Sometimes this can be difficult because patients may not understand the importance of boundaries in a professional relationship. Patients may think that they will feel more comfortable if the counselor shares his or her problems or opinions, because then they feel they know the "real person." However, sharing personal material or advice often introduces problems into the therapeutic relationship. First, offering advice can place the patient in the position of feeling that she needs to follow it, and place the counselor at risk for feeling personally affronted when patients do not; alternatively, the patient may feel like a failure or "bad patient" if the advice does not work for her. Second, advice based on the counselor's personal experiences may lead him or her into sharing personal problems and take the focus away from the patient. Third, sharing problems leads the patient to see the relationship as reciprocal, and this places her in the position of feeling the need to help or support the counselor. Once the counselor opens the door into his or her personal life, the focus has shifted away from the needs of the patient; it is difficult, and sometimes impossible, to close this door once it is opened.

A second form of asymmetry in professional relationships is the difference in power between the health professional and the patient. The patient is likely to view the professional as having unique knowledge and skills to help him or her. Patients may weigh the opinions or advice of a health professional more heavily than those of friends. Indeed, the perception of the health professional's expertise facilitates therapeutic change because patients take seriously information provided within the professional relationship. This perception places the health professional in a powerful role; the patient does not have equal power to influence the life of the health professional. Consequently, the professional has a unique responsibility to remain carefully aware of the patient's needs and carefully consider the impact of his or her behaviors on the patient.

In accepting the "expert" role health professionals hold, counselors must recognize the limitations in their ability to understand and/or predict a patient's behavior. Patients sometimes believe that counselors can "read their minds," which can be both reassuring and frightening. It is important for counselors to make clear the limitations of what they offer and also explain that they want to understand the patient but that they will only be able to grasp a portion of what the patient is feeling or experiencing. This admission will help to release the counselor from unrealistic expectations that may be harbored by the patient, the counselor, or both. It will also help to protect the counselor from appearing to be overly patronizing in situations where a patient feels her experience is too unique to be fully shared or comprehended by someone who has not had the same experience (such as a male counselor empathizing with a female patient who has elected to have an abortion). Such a recognition does not make certain topics taboo; it simply gives the counselor permission to be human with the same limitations that we all have in trying to communicate with one another.

A final form of asymmetry that distinguishes a professional from a personal relationship is that the patient will have to put forth the greater proportion of work in attaining her goal of therapeutic change. No matter how much work a counselor does, he or she cannot do everything that is necessary for the patient to make changes. Presenting this asymmetry at the outset can provide a framework for discussing the progress of treatment, especially when a patient feels that she is working hard but making gains slowly. Preparing the patient for the unequal distribution of work and remaining focused on the goal of counseling—the benefit of the patient—can help allay feelings of frustration.

In summary, providing support may be an aspect shared by both counseling and friendships, but in counseling, support is provided in the context of meeting the needs of the patient in an attempt to reach some goal, often a behavioral change for the patient. Mutual self-disclosure is a cornerstone of most close friendships; however, self-disclosure within a counseling relationship must be predominantly one-sided. This is not to say that a health professional may not at times choose to disclose some aspect of his or her personal life, but such disclosure must always be planned carefully for the benefit of the patient, not of the counselor, and must be weighed against the possible costs. Finally, education and discussion are not advice; it must always be clear that in the end decisions about what the patient will do must be made by the patient.

## Overview of Basic Counseling Techniques

### The Therapeutic Alliance

The first challenge in establishing a meaningful counseling relationship is to develop a therapeutic alliance. A basic assumption in this process is that the individual has approached a health professional with the desire for something to change in her life. In the case of eating disorders, this assumption may not be entirely accurate. Among some anorectic patients, treatment may not be their choice. In both anorexia nervosa and bulimia nervosa, patients may be highly ambivalent about changing their eating disordered behavior even if they have sought treatment. Depending on their level of personal insight, they may be distressed and realize that their behaviors make them unhappy and distant from others. However, the fear of becoming "fat" if they relinquish their disordered eating is usually quite strong. Managing and addressing this ambivalence requires skill on the part of the counselor in eliciting from the patient both what she desires and what she fears about recovering from the eating disorder. This process typically involves examining realistically the risks versus the benefits of giving up the eating disorder symptoms.

Much of a patient's fear can be allayed by providing her with a relationship in which she feels safe to communicate with the counselor: the therapeutic alliance. This feeling of safety develops when the health professional sets a context of accepting the patient as a person with inherent worth. Rogers (1951) referred to this process as providing "unconditional positive regard." To develop this context, a health professional begins by communicating a willingness to work with the client. This willingness involves the idea that the health professional will be flexible and adopt aspects of the treatment to match the individual needs of the patient. Additionally, the health professional communicates interest in the client as a person rather than merely as an eating disorder. This approach requires the health professional to consistently communicate acceptance of and caring for patients even when patients do not comply with treatment. This stance does not preclude confrontation but suggests that the inherent worth of the person receiving treatment is acknowledged even when confronting aspects of the individual's behavior that are counterproductive.

With this context in place, the health professional is in a much stronger position to develop with the patient an agreed-on plan with agreed-on goals. The plan and goals will be partially determined by the acceptable standards within the field of eating disorders treatment, but they will also reflect the patient's wishes and abilities. Therapeutic change is predicated on the belief that the person can achieve goals and change; however, a key aspect to this ability is selecting reasonable goals that take into account the patient's environment, competing personal goals, and fears.

In the case of a team treatment approach to eating disorders, the therapeutic alliance hopefully will develop within the context of the team. However, the team approach adds to the challenge of developing this alliance. The most important aspect of this alliance is that it not undermine support for the patient or the activities of other team members. Thus, health professionals within the team must communicate with each other often in order to understand what each is doing and to avoid inconsistencies. For example, one health professional may provide advice to a patient that accidentally contradicts information given by another member of the team. One way to avoid this contradiction is for each professional to provide only information and recommendations within the bounds of his or her role in the team. It is not uncommon for a client to ask one health professional a question, and if they are dissatisfied with the answer, ask another member of the team. When a patient asks a question that a team member wants to answer but realizes may be an instance where the patient is attempting to get a different response than she received from another team member, the team member should respond to the patient by saying he or she would like to think about her question and get input from the other team members before responding. When such a situation arises, it is often best to have the patient return to the team member who initially answered the question for a full explanation of the response. When disagreements among team members arise, they should be handled generally within a team meeting and not played out in front of or through a patient. In certain situations, however, disagreements can be handled in front of a patient to demonstrate mature resolution of such issues.

In summary, the therapeutic alliance forms the basis for sharing information between a patient and a health care professional. To be effective, this alliance should be based on communicating consistent respect for the patient, a willingness to work with the patient as an individual, and interest and caring for the patient as a person. Within a team approach, therapeutic goals should be arrived at with the patient and in agreement with the other team members.

## Communication Style

Much of the establishment of the therapeutic alliance and the development of treatment goals depends on a health professional's style of communication. Understanding the needs of the patient requires listening in a way that elicits information from the patient. Active listening communicates openness and understanding and is often used in counseling to increase information sharing, to elicit feedback on how the patient is reacting to treatment, and to confirm that the counselor understands what the patient is saying.

### Active Listening Skills

Active listening employs regular verbal feedback from the listener. Key aspects of active listening include paraphrasing and reflecting. Paraphrasing involves taking what a patient has said and then putting the statement into the listener's own words. Health professionals can use paraphrasing both to determine if they understand what has been said as well as to demonstrate that they want to understand what a patient has said. Paraphrasing needs to be done at appropriate intervals, however, because paraphrasing too frequently creates a parrot effect in which the patient feels that everything she says is being mindlessly repeated. Ideally, a health professional should paraphrase a key statement that in some way seems to pull issues together into a theme. Such paraphrasing may help a patient to listen to herself more carefully and understand her own feelings more fully. When done appropriately, paraphrasing communicates to the patient that the health professional is listening carefully and grasps what she has said.

Reflecting affect is similar to paraphrasing, but it allows the health professional to communicate his or her perception of what the patient may be feeling. The following is an example of the use of paraphrasing and reflecting affect to further communication between a patient and a health professional:

> PATIENT: My boyfriend is always commenting on what I eat. He makes such a big deal out of it that I just lose my appetite and then don't eat anything at all around him. Later, I lose control, and then I get so angry at myself.
> HEALTH PROFESSIONAL: So you binge after avoiding eating around your boyfriend, and then you feel angry with yourself?

This example shows how a link between events can be restated in such a way that it provides a point for intervention. Additionally, by restating both what happened and how the patient felt about what happened, the health professional has provided an empathetic response. The question regarding anger communicates "Is this correct? Do I have it straight?"

Empathy can be defined as respectful understanding of the feelings and point of view of another person. An empathetic response is communication of this understanding in verbal and nonverbal behavior. Therefore, paraphrasing and reflecting affect convey empathy as long as they are delivered respectfully and relatively accurately. The effectiveness of both paraphrasing and reflecting affect can be enhanced by making statements in a tentative fashion or by direct question. For example, statements can be followed with asking, "Is that right?" or inflecting the voice upward at the end of the sentence to imply a question. These techniques communicate that the paraphrasing is open to revision rather than that the health professional assumes he or she understands the patient's message with complete accuracy. By inviting the patient to give feedback, the health professional may help the patient to refine her original statement in a way that further distills the issue. For example:

PATIENT: I guess I do feel angry, but I think I also feel like a failure that I let him get to me so much.

The health professional may then choose to respond with another paraphrase to communicate that he or she perceives and understands the refinement. Alternatively, simply nodding will communicate this information at times. This back-and-forth exchange of communication can provide a mechanism for patients to learn more about their own point of view and feelings by hearing them reflected by the health professional. Increased self-awareness is often therapeutic in and of itself.

One challenge in providing an empathetic response is to avoid becoming personally involved in the event. It is easy for health professionals to forget that they hear only one side of what happened. The information they receive and their role in helping the patient may lead them to feel frustrated or angry with others whom the patient presents as undermining her therapeutic progress. It is helpful for health professionals to keep in mind that their understanding of the event is incomplete. Additionally, the patient often relies on the health professional to remain relatively neutral. This neutrality does not preclude validating a patient's perceptions and feelings that result from the perception; however, it necessitates focusing on the feelings of the patient rather than the listener's own feelings and reactions. This neutrality also precludes agreement concerning perceptions that the health professional cannot really judge. An insidious form of personal involvement occurs when the patient's experience somehow reminds the health professional of something that is very emotionally evocative for him or her. In the example above, a health professional who recently ended a relationship in which her partner was overcontrolling would need to be careful to avoid overinterpreting the event described by the client. The following is an example of a response that displays emotional overinvolvement:

> PATIENT: My boyfriend is always commenting on what I eat. He makes such a big deal out of it that I just lose my appetite and then don't eat anything at all around him. Later, I lose control, and then I get so angry at myself.
>
> HEALTH PROFESSIONAL: Your boyfriend is being overcontrolling, and you should consider breaking up with him for your own health.

Such an attack on the patient's boyfriend is inappropriate. It may result in her defending him to the health professional and feeling misunderstood. The health professional does not really know if he is too controlling, only that the patient perceives it to be so. Certainly the health professional cannot know if she should end her relationship. Also, her defense of him is likely if her boyfriend provides support and caring, and the health professional suggests eliminating him from her life. Alternatively, the health professional's emotionally overinvolved statement may accidentally trigger feelings of insecurity in the patient concerning her ability to determine whether she is in a healthy relationship.

The reverse of emotional overinvolvement is intellectual detachment. Intellectual detachment sometimes occurs when a health professional is uncomfortable with what a client has shared, and in an attempt to push away the feelings, the health professional avoids responding to what a client has said and how the client is feeling. Such avoidance runs the risk of communicating to the client that what happened was unimportant or that her feelings are invalid. In the same scenario, the following is an example of intellectual detachment:

> PATIENT: My boyfriend is always commenting on what I eat. He makes such a big deal out of it that I just lose my appetite and then don't eat anything at all around him. Later, I lose control, and then I get so angry at myself.
>
> HEALTH PROFESSIONAL: The restraint hypothesis predicts that skipping meals will result in binge eating.

As one can see, all three responses are of approximately equal length, but they clearly will have a differential impact on the client and on the therapeutic alliance.

## Processing Emotional Overinvolvement

The previous section addressed two problems that can result when patients evoke emotional responses in health professionals. If the health professional finds that he or she is experiencing intense anger toward a patient or is dreading working with the patient, he or she may wish to identify the point at which the feelings shifted from being neutral to becoming intense. Such a shift may reflect a transition of therapeutic stance from one of neutrality and caring in a professional manner to one of personal overinvolvement. Alternatively, the health professional may find that something occurred within earlier sessions that he or she did not feel comfortable sharing with the patient, and now those feelings of discomfort have expanded. Such development could indicate that the health professional may benefit from seeking supervision to explore his or her discomfort or that an alternative health professional should work with this patient while he or she considers seeking consultation from a colleague.

Although the descriptions thus far have involved primarily negative feelings that may hinder behavioral change, strongly positive feelings must also be monitored carefully. When health professionals recognize within themselves a strong need to protect or defend a patient, or feel strongly attracted to or feel what they perceive as love for a patient, they should also explore the origin of these feelings in themselves. The very imbalance typical of professional relationships makes this exploration of great importance; strong positive feelings may be an artifact of the treatment role or the health professional's needs. If such issues persist, careful supervision is strongly advised, or the care of the patient may need to be transferred to a different professional.

Sometimes patients attempt to initiate a personal relationship with their health care professional. From the patient's perspective, the health care professional may appear "perfect" and may offer them a sense of acceptance that is both unusual and welcome in the patient's life. When this occurs, it is wise to explain why it is necessary to maintain certain boundaries. This explanation should include that it is inappropriate for the health professional to become personally involved with someone he or she is trying to help because the personal involvement might interfere with his or her ability to be objective. Additionally, an underlying goal of the relationship is to bring the patient to the point where she no longer needs the health professional's help. If a patient becomes personally involved with a health professional, her ambivalence toward improvement may increase because it represents the end of a personal relationship. By maintaining a professional relationship, the health professional increases his or her ability to work within a team approach as a team member, and makes it easier for the patient to share problems because she understands that the health professional will provide acceptance, understanding, and, to the degree to which he or she is capable, objectivity.

As a final note, personal relationships between health professionals and their patients of a romantic or sexual nature, regardless of who initiated that relationship, always represent a violation of professional ethics. In many states, such relationships also represent a legal violation or felony, as determined by licensing board policies or statute.

Team consultation can be helpful if the health professional is experiencing strong feelings toward a patient. If the patient is eliciting certain feelings in one team member, it is possible that she is eliciting those same feelings in other team members. Such communication will help the team members better understand the individual patient and develop a coordinated approach to dealing with these issues. Experiencing such issues with patients from time to time is common among health professionals. A health professional should not view these issues as evidence of a lack of skill or knowledge. However, it is absolutely essential in such cases to obtain outside, more objective consultation.

### Confrontation

Confrontation is sometimes useful and necessary and may be a turning point in therapy. Typically, confrontation arises when treatment is not following the agreed-on course and is thus unlikely to result in the agreed-on goals. The source of the problem may be either clear or unclear. For example, an anorectic patient is claiming to eat all of the food prescribed for her, yet her weight continues to drop, and the health professional suspects that she may be compensating by exercising excessively and perhaps purging. The health professional may decide to engage in confrontation:

HEALTH PROFESSIONAL: You have told me that you are eating all of your food, yet you continue to lose weight. Can you help me understand what is going on?

If the patient does not offer any kind of explanation, further probing may be necessary. When necessary, a health professional should focus on possible reasons for avoiding weight gain, such as fear, rather than the exact methods. For example:

HEALTH PROFESSIONAL: How do you feel about gaining weight?

It becomes easier to engage the patient in deciding what to do to get back on course once the reasons, such as, "No one will love me if I get fat," are revealed and discussed. After a patient is educated about what she needs to do, badgering her about the importance of the prescription or the dangers of her current behavior is likely to push her into a defensive position and unlikely to produce positive change. With many anorectics, however, these issues need to be reinforced, and the importance of weight restoration should not be downplayed.

Occasionally, confrontation needs to occur at a more global level, such as asking a patient if she is ready to change her behaviors. In essence, sometimes the question becomes, "Is getting better worth the work it is going to take?" Among nonsuicidal adult outpatients, the decisions of whether or not to attain and/or maintain a safe weight or to receive treatment are the patient's to make. As with any professional relationship, the patient has to decide if she truly wants the services being offered. Although the health professional may use basic counseling techniques to help allay fears associated with change, the bulk of the work will fall to the patient and, thus, depends on her motivation to change. If a patient is sabotaging her own treatment, and the health professional doubts her commitment after exploring possible reasons why her behavior is at odds with her expressed wishes, it is time to address the problem directly:

HEALTH PROFESSIONAL: I am concerned that we are not doing what we need to do to help you reach your treatment goals. Do you think this is the right time to try to make these changes?

PATIENT: I'm working very hard. It's really hard for me to even come here and get weighed—I stopped weighing myself because of how upset it would make me.

HEALTH PROFESSIONAL: Yes, I understand that being weighed has required a lot of effort, but it is only a small part of what needs to be done to make a difference.

PATIENT: What do you mean?

HEALTH PROFESSIONAL: Well, for example, one of the treatment goals was to eat meals at regular intervals rather than skipping meals.

PATIENT: I have done that. I'm eating much more regularly now.

HEALTH PROFESSIONAL: Perhaps I have misunderstood then. It had sounded to me like you were not eating when you were with your boyfriend.

PATIENT: Well, I can't control that—I've told him that it bothers me when he pays so much attention to what I eat.

HEALTH PROFESSIONAL: It's true that you can't control his behavior, but you can be in control of your response, even though it is often very difficult. I find myself wondering why we have been unable to find a new response to this situation.

PATIENT: Well, what do you want me to do then? Stop seeing my boyfriend?

HEALTH PROFESSIONAL: I would like you to consider whether you feel ready to make the kind of changes we have set for you. My intention is not to be critical of you but for us to work together to come to an understanding of what you want to do.

### Focusing the Wanderer

Some patients tend to wander from one topic to another. Wandering may occur when the health professional is addressing a topic with which the patient is not comfortable. Alternatively, wandering may be a general style on the part of the patient. Although some counselors feel that wandering should be allowed as a form of free association, this technique is rarely used with eating disorder patients, and if persistent, wandering can potentially compromise treatment. First, wandering may make change difficult. If the health professional only hears about concerns in vague terms and then the patient moves to another topic, it is difficult to determine a point of intervention. Second, wandering makes communication difficult. When many different important topics are thrown out but then abandoned for the next topic, the health professional is likely to feel overwhelmed and confused and have a difficult time addressing any, much less all, of the issues presented.

One point to remember is that it is not necessary to address all issues presented within the same session that they are mentioned. It is acceptable to say, "That is an important issue you have raised concerning how you feel about yourself at work, and I would like to get back to that later. But first, could you tell me more about only feeling 'real' when you hurt yourself? Could you give me an example of what you mean?" In general, focusing the wanderer involves reforming concerns from vague concepts to concrete examples and then following through with how to address these concerns. It is difficult to help someone develop a new response to a problem situation when the problem is presented as, "Nobody likes me, everyone just pretends to like me." If wandering seems to occur when a particular topic is introduced, the health professional should employ confrontation to explore the issue, as in the following example:

HEALTH PROFESSIONAL: I've noticed that it seems difficult for you to remain focused on the topic of your drinking habits.

PATIENT: What do you mean?

HEALTH PROFESSIONAL: Often when we begin to talk about alcohol use, it seems to me that you begin another topic. Is there something about this topic that is particularly difficult for you?

In summary, communication style determines the quality of interactions between a health professional and patient. Active listening, including the use of paraphrasing and reflecting affect, encourages patients by demonstrating that the health professional is listening and trying to understand their experiences. Confrontation opens discussion with a patient when an impasse in treatment has been reached. Focusing the wanderer is sometimes necessary to gain entry points for intervention and to explore topics that are difficult for the patient to discuss.

## Interpersonal Style

Although different health professionals tend to have differing interpersonal styles, certain elements have been found to encourage positive communication between professionals and patients. Genuineness and positive, receptive nonverbal behaviors have been found to be particularly important to the development of a positive therapeutic relationship (Maurer & Tindall, 1983).

Genuineness involves a combination of congruence and spontaneity. Congruence requires that the words, actions, and feelings of the health professional are consistent. Congruence is important to avoid confusing a patient about what is meant or thought. To borrow from Lewis Carroll (1866), congruence requires that "[you] say what you mean and mean what you say." Congruence is not present when the patient receives mixed messages:

HEALTH PROFESSIONAL: I feel uncomfortable when I seem to be doing most of the talking in our session. I wonder what you are thinking and feeling and if you are bothered by something.

PATIENT: I guess I'm angry at you because the more I do, the more you expect me to do, and sometimes I just get so overwhelmed—it's like you don't understand how hard this is for me.

HEALTH PROFESSIONAL: The only reason I push you is because I don't want you to get stuck or regress from the progress you've made (*said in an angry tone of voice*).

First, this response by the health professional is primarily a defensive response, indicating that the patient should not be angry with the health professional even though the health professional seemingly invited a discussion of negative feelings. Second, the response violates the assumption that the patient has the capacity within herself to achieve goals of change. Third, the response presents goals as something the health professional is in a position to decide unilaterally, rather than in collaboration with the patient. Finally, the angry tone of voice suggests that the health professional is experiencing stronger feelings than simple concern for maintaining progress. If a health professional is having problems coordinating feelings with how he or she is attempting to work with a client, then the health professional needs to seek supervision to explore these feelings or decide if the particular patient might be better served by another professional. A more appropriate response might be the following:

HEALTH PROFESSIONAL: I can understand how difficult it must be for you to make so many changes. I may not have shared with you how well you have done and how impressed I am with how hard you have worked. I also want to thank you for sharing how you are feeling because your feedback helps me understand your perspective better. Please let me know when you feel we are moving too fast or I am pushing too hard. My intention is to encourage and help you reach your goals. I wonder, though, if this is a pattern where you see others as expecting a great deal from you.

The introduction of a possible interpretation of the patient's frustration is an example of transference, which will be discussed in greater detail later in the chapter; however, the way in which the health professional introduces the interpretation requires spontaneity.

Spontaneity is another aspect of genuineness important to a counseling relationship. A health professional's spontaneity is the ability to express him or herself easily and tactfully. Instead of seeming to "walk on egg shells," a health professional should be able to communicate in a way that is spontaneous and assertive without being blunt or aggressive.

Spontaneity models for the patient interactions that are open and honest without being destructive. Sometimes health professionals think that they should always be accepting of whatever the patient says or does. Acceptance is of the person, however, and the alliance is with that part of the person that wants to recover from the eating disorder. Because of the individual's ambivalence, times will arise when a health professional needs to honestly confront problematic behavior. This should be done in a way that makes the patient feel like she is important and valuable but that the specific behavior is harmful. Most often, this can be accomplished by recalling to the patient that the reason the health professional is drawing her attention to this problem behavior is because he or she cares about her and her welfare and believes in her ability to get better. A failure to honestly address such issues rarely protects the therapeutic alliance; instead, it may lead the patient to feel that the health professional is not being honest with her, and that therefore she should not share her feelings. Alternatively, she may attempt to test limits by continuing to engage in increasingly harmful behavior until she successfully elicits a response. Finally, failure to address unhealthy behaviors may communicate that it is not important for her to change her disordered eating behaviors.

Effective health professionals have an interpersonal style that conveys warmth, safety, and support in nonverbal as well as verbal behaviors. In general, it is important to maintain eye contact as a way of showing interest and attention. Sitting in an open position communicates receptivity. An open position means not crossing one's arms in front of one's chest or using one's hands to cover a part of one's face. Some counselors would argue that crossing one's legs is also a form of closing off; however, it is our opinion that a health professional should look comfortable and natural. It is important to occasionally lean forward as someone is sharing something. It is not enough for a health professional to tell patients that he or she values their feedback when they say they are angry with the health professional. Also important is maintaining an open position with eye contact and a calm pleasant expression. Most people are sensitive to a physical retreat and respond by withdrawing themselves. This mutual withdrawal can effectively cut off communication. Thus, incorporating physical habits that encourage communication and express acceptance into interpersonal style will increase a health professional's effectiveness.

In summary, genuineness and positive, receptive nonverbal behaviors are important in developing an interpersonal style that encourages communication between a health professional and patient. Genuineness is marked by congruence and spontaneity. Positive nonverbal behaviors include eye contact, an open body position, leaning forward occasionally, and a calm pleasant facial expression.

## Application of Basic Counseling Techniques

### Common Treatment Issues

In our presentation of basic counseling techniques we have already touched on a number of difficult treatment issues; however, we have not identified categories of common problems in counseling. This section will discuss the types of problems that most health professionals need to be aware of before beginning a therapeutic relationship. These problems can involve transference, countertransference, and resistance and reluctance. Although these issues are typically a focus of counseling, they may affect health professionals of many specialties. Thus, health professionals may not be in a position to work through or even discuss these issues at length with a patient but will find it helpful to recognize them when they occur. Finally, we present a set of common mistakes in therapy and how to avoid these.

### Transference and Countertransference

The concepts of transference and countertransference were fully elaborated by Freud and colleagues, and although we have not focused on using psychodynamic approaches, these concepts seem to be relevant across many treatment approaches. Transference occurs when a patient responds to a health professional based on prior experiences with another individual. In psychoanalysis, transference was purposefully elicited in order to have the psychic conflict played out within the session with the therapist. For our purposes, transference can be viewed as a tool for understanding a patient's perspective and problems that develop in the therapeutic alliance. The types of transference we will discuss are specific, general, positive, and negative.

Specific transference occurs when patients transfer feelings they have toward another person onto the health professional (e.g., patients respond to the health professional as they would respond to their parent). General transference occurs when patients respond to a health professional according to the health professional's role (e.g., they value his opinion because he is an authority). Positive transference occurs when patients imbue a health professional with positive attributes from a specific or general source (e.g., intelligence, expertise, wisdom), and negative transference occurs when patients imbue a health professional with negative attributes from a specific or general source (e.g., jealousy, nagging, nit-picking, critical, distrusting). For example, a specific negative transference might occur if an anorectic teenager responds to her health professional by saying, "You're always telling me what to do and watching over me; when will you let me be an adult?" when these descriptions may really represent aspects of the patient's relationship with her mother. An example of a positive general transference is if a patient says, "You're so smart, you know the answers to everything," when this response in reality is characteristic of her general acquiescence to authority figures.

Transference can be used to understand the patient's needs. However, it is important that the health professional return the patient to viewing him or her as he or she is rather than as she imagines him or her to be. This action is particularly necessary for the health professional who is the target of a negative transference. It is somewhat more difficult to point out and resolve a positive transference, especially when it is general and seems conducive to treatment. Ultimately, positive transference may also cause problems, especially if the health professional finds that he or she is unable to live up to the exaggerated expectations a patient has for him or her. A way of addressing this follows:

PATIENT: You're so smart, you know the answers to everything.

HEALTH PROFESSIONAL: I appreciate the compliment; however, it is not possible for me to know the answers to everything. Is that very important to you?

PATIENT: Well, I seem to always screw things up so I really look up to someone like you who seems to know everything and always does the right thing.

HEALTH PROFESSIONAL: I make my fair share of mistakes, but why do you think you always screw things up?

It is important for the health professional to improve the balance of the therapeutic alliance by decreasing the perception of his or her perfection and decreasing the patient's perception (by comparison) of being personally flawed. Such a shift will be necessary for the patient to believe in her own ability to make positive changes in her life and recover from her eating disorder. One way the health professional can gently and positively confront this patient's statement is by pointing out that the patient has elected to seek treatment for her eating disorder, an action that is very distinct from "screwing up."

Countertransference, as the name implies, is transference that occurs from the health professional onto the patient. For example, if the health professional finds that a patient reminds him of his younger sister, and finds himself thinking that she is irresponsible and that she constantly blames others, he may be experiencing a specific negative countertransference. Alternatively, if the health professional feels a strong need to protect and care for the patient, he may be experiencing a general positive countertransference based on how he feels about people needing help. Most importantly, a health professional should attempt to determine when and if countertransference is occurring and ensure that it is not compromising the quality of the patient's care.

A team approach can be helpful in working through countertransference problems. If the patient is eliciting these feelings in one team member, it is possible that they are being elicited in other team members as well. Team discussion can help team members recognize what the patient does to trigger these responses and in what way the team member's response goes beyond what the patient is actually doing or saying. If the health professional discovers strong unresolved issues that are interfering with his or her ability to treat a patient, it may be necessary to elicit guidance from another team member or supervision from another experienced professional, to step back from treating the particular patient, and even to consider seeking counseling for the issue (especially if the health professional is likely to be faced with this issue often in treating patients with eating disorders). The basic tenet that treatment is for the benefit of the patient, not the health professional, and that a counseling relationship is professional, not personal, should provide the best guidance through these difficult issues.

### Resistance and Reluctance

Resistance occurs when a patient fails to engage in the process of therapeutic change. Resistance can be open, such as open refusal to follow a treatment suggestion, or subtle, such as recurrent excuses for why something cannot be accomplished, or missing appointments. The techniques most important in addressing resistance are those covered in the section on communication style. Essentially the health professional's job is to explore the sources of resistance. Sources may include benefits of dysfunctional behavior, fear associated with changing behavior, an incomplete commitment to behavior change, and transference issues.

Confronting reasons for maintaining dysfunctional behavior can be difficult because a patient may be most aware of her eating disorder as intrusive and shameful, and not perceive possible benefits. She may realize that she is afraid of what happens if she stops but be unaware of what she gains by continuing. Benefits of dysfunctional behavior may be attention and support. A patient may feel that she is special and important, a feeling that is reinforced by the attention she elicits for her disordered eating behaviors. Thus, positive regard and caring based on the person and not her behavior is crucial in encouraging change. An approach to this issue follows:

HEALTH PROFESSIONAL: Let's develop a list of benefits and costs both for continuing your disordered eating and for discontinuing your disordered eating. Now, since you have an eating disorder, it is easier to know for sure costs and benefits of continuing. Costs and benefits of stopping are things you might expect to experience. So let's start.

PATIENT: Okay, well, if I continue making myself throw up, my teeth will rot out.

HEALTH PROFESSIONAL: That would be a cost of continuing.

PATIENT: If I ate more normally, I wouldn't be embarrassed to eat in public with friends.

HEALTH PROFESSIONAL: That would be a benefit of discontinuing. What about a cost of discontinuing?

PATIENT: Well, if I stop throwing up, I may not be able to stop bingeing, and I may get fat.

HEALTH PROFESSIONAL: You're doing a good job. Now what about a benefit of continuing?

PATIENT: There isn't any benefit of continuing, unless you mean because I make myself throw up, I don't get fat.

HEALTH PROFESSIONAL: Well, we've discussed how making yourself throw up doesn't necessarily keep you from gaining weight, and how people at all sorts of weights binge and purge. What I mean is a benefit that you know you get because of the eating disorder that you may not get if you stopped. Sort of like you know your teeth are eroding because of the self-induced vomiting.

PATIENT: I can't think of anything I get because of my bulimia.

HEALTH PROFESSIONAL: Well, what about treatment?

PATIENT: How is that a benefit?

HEALTH PROFESSIONAL: Many people like treatment because attention feels good even if it's for something bad. Attention tells them that someone cares.

This example demonstrates how a health professional might approach difficult topics in a way that is appropriate for the patient's level of awareness and insight. With some planning, the health professional can set up a dialogue that reveals the logic of the patient's behavior to the patient. Such an exchange of information helps patients understand themselves better rather than making them feel ashamed.

Reluctance occurs when a patient seems to make some attempts to follow through on plans for change but cannot carry them to their end. One source of reluctance is a poor understanding of how change is important or how it will help. For example, a patient with bulimia nervosa may not understand how eating regular meals is going to help her keep from binge eating if she feels the source of the binges is a basic lack of self-control. Another source of reluctance can be a patient's lack of trust in the health professional. One way of potentially addressing the issue of trust is to admit that a patient's decision to engage in treatment is based on what she *perceives* as the benefit versus the risks; ultimately the only way to be certain of the outcome of treatment is to try it. The health professional can also refocus emphasis in the decision process from his or her judgment to the patient's own reasoning abilities. The health professional should encourage the patient to decide whether she should engage in treatment based on what she knows, instead of because the health professional says she should. For example, a patient might reason, "If I do nothing, I probably won't get better. If I try this, I may still not get better, but my chances of getting better are higher than if I don't try anything." Trust develops over time. The health professional can only provide an environment that is conducive to trust.

In summary, categories of treatment issues include transference and countertransference, and resistance and reluctance. Obviously, these issues can and often do occur in combination. Such issues are often central in providing therapy for an eating disordered patient, and familiarity with these concepts across specialties may elucidate why certain aspects of treatment seem or are difficult. This level of understanding among health professionals may save much frustration and time and improve the outcome for the patient.

### Avoiding Common Mistakes in Treatment

When problems arise in treatment, it is possible to unintentionally make them worse. The following discussion summarizes common mistakes in treatment of patients with eating disorders. Accompanying each common mistake is a discussion of what to do instead to improve treatment efficacy.

## Advice Giving, Lecturing, and Arguing

Advice giving, lecturing, and arguing are all indicative of a power struggle occurring within the counseling relationship. It is important to remember that there is no way to win a power struggle, and thus it is best to avoid or disengage from it if it develops. Positive regard requires respect for a patient's ability to make her own decisions, including the decision to continue disordered eating behaviors. When positive regard is present, it is incongruent to suddenly switch gears and start telling a patient what to do and then argue the point. Instead, the health professional should use a communication style based on active listening, and allow the patient to arrive at reasons for and consequences of her behaviors on her own. Typically, patients will value connections they help to discover rather than those handed to them. Additionally, advice giving, lecturing, and arguing place the health professional in the position of seeming to or pretending to "know everything," a position that is quite unrealistic and impossible to maintain. After the issue has been discussed, it is easier and less stressful to acknowledge personal fallibility and to respect the patient's position, even when those positions do not seem reasonable from the perspective of the health professional. To do otherwise implies that the patient does not know what is best for herself.

There are situations, however, particularly in working with low-weight anorectic patients, when conveying respect for the patient's ability to make her own decisions is less important than helping the patient to gain weight. Very low weight can lead to depressed mood and irrational thought processes that make it impossible for the health professional to develop a therapeutic alliance with the anorectic patient. In such cases, weight restoration must be the primary and immediate goal.

## Doing Too Much of the Work

Doing too much of the work reverses the necessary distribution of effort in treatment. If the health professional finds that he or she is talking most of the time and guessing at information that the client should be providing, then he or she should discuss with the client the reasons for her low participation (the early example of positive confrontation demonstrates this). The health professional may discover something that he or she is doing tends to exclude the patient's participation. For example, the health professional may be relying too much on closed questions, questions that require "yes" or "no" responses or questions to which the health professional knows the correct answer. The health professional should then switch to open-ended questions. For example, instead of saying, "Did you eat everything on your plan?" she should try, "How did your meal plan go?" Another way of excluding patient participation is to seem to disapprove of what the patient says or feels. Again, the health professional must be conscious of what he or she says and how he or she says it, and remember the importance of congruence. For example, questions phrased as, "You didn't make yourself vomit, did you?" should be rephrased in a way that is less shaming and more encouraging of communication, such as, "And what happened then?" (said in a calm, pleasant, receptive way).

### Becoming Overtly Frustrated with Noncompliance

Overt frustration with noncompliance, such as sighing, physically withdrawing eye contact, or interrupting when a patient is, in the health professional's opinion, making just another excuse for not participating in treatment, is unlikely to benefit the patient. The health professional should instead attempt to explore the patient's reasons for noncompliance with respect and genuineness. The health professional may need to reinforce the importance of the behavioral change by explaining a point that the patient may not have understood the first time it was discussed. Alternatively, the health professional may need to reinforce the therapeutic alliance and the patient's role in determining the course and goals of treatment. Patients are more successful in achieving therapeutic change when they feel they have helped to formulate the goals rather than when they feel that someone else is telling them what they must do.

### Assuming Too Much Responsibility for a Patient's Behavior

Although it is appropriate to feel pleased when a patient is doing well in treatment, it is important for health professionals to avoid basing their sense of self-worth on a patient's progress. Many things determine the success or failure of a particular patient in treatment, and many are beyond a single health professional's control. If a health professional is becoming overcontrolling, for example, expressing opinions as to whether the patient should stay in a relationship with her boyfriend, then the health professional should consider his or her personal investment in the patient's behavior. The health professional should ask the following questions: Do you judge your effectiveness as a health professional by this individual patient's success in treatment? Do you feel that if you don't help her, no one will? Do you feel that you should be there for all her changes and personal growth? Ultimately, as professionals we must remember that we do not treat people to feel better about ourselves. The goal is the patient's improved health. Other health professionals may provide a better match for the individual patient's needs. Occasionally, a thoughtful referral is the most appropriate form of intervention. Finally, any treatment will end before a patient's personal growth is complete. Personal growth is a lifelong process, and treatment is only a time-limited intervention.

## Acting on Assumptions Rather Than Perceptions

After treating a number of patients with similar problems, commonalities among patients appear, and it is tempting to act on these. Part of this problem may result from countertransference; that is, a patient reminds the health professional of another patient, and out of habit or to be efficient, he or she begins responding to the second patient in the way that worked with the first. The health professional must remember that although this may be his or her 100th patient with an eating disorder, this is the first time he or she has worked with this particular patient, and it is the first time this particular patient has worked with him or her. Thus, each patient and each therapeutic alliance are unique. This is not to say that aspects of treatment do not generalize. In fact, certain treatment approaches—types of medication, meal plans, manual-based treatments—that have been shown empirically to produce good results with eating disordered patients should be tried first because of the evidence that these approaches are most likely to succeed. But decisions based on empirical research are not assumptions. An example of an assumption is a health professional's deciding to use a less effective treatment because a patient reminded him or her of someone for whom the conventional treatment did not work. A second example of an assumption is a health professional's believing that a patient did not complete an agreed-on task because of ambivalence about recovering, because this has often been the case with other patients. It is always important to first explore possible reasons before making assumptions when similarities exist. The health professional should avoid responding too quickly, as if he or she knows what is happening before the patient has time to share her feelings, concerns, or behavioral patterns.

## Allowing Loose Boundaries or Dual Relationships

Much of this chapter has been focused on distinguishing personal from professional relationships, and thus it is obvious that not making this distinction is a common mistake. *Dual relationships* refers to a health professional's having an additional relationship with a patient with whom the health professional has established a therapeutic relationship. It is considered inappropriate and unethical to provide therapy to an individual with whom another relationship exists. For example, a psychologist or psychiatrist is ethically bound to avoid treating his or her car mechanic or investment banker. The greatest issue seen in dual relationships is conflicting motivations. A health professional's primary goal should be to help the patient. Any additional relationship may make treatment difficult or impossible.

It is important to avoid developing a friendship in addition to the therapeutic relationship. Occasionally, patients will invite their health professionals to social engagements. Turning down such invitations may be difficult for health professionals because they may feel like they are rejecting their patients. The health professional should, however, explain that he or she appreciates the invitation but has a policy of not attending social events with patients. He or she may wish to add that the policy exists because it becomes harmful to some patients to socialize with their health professionals, and consistency in such matters is important.

To maintain appropriate boundaries and avoid dual relationships, the health professional should decide at the outset how much personal information he or she will share. This issue should also be discussed and agreed on within the team. Some counselors avoid sharing any personal information other than that directly relevant to treatment (such as their educational background and training that makes them qualified to provide treatment). Other counselors feel that simple demographic information can be provided, including information such as marital status, whether they have children, or religious affiliation. Health professionals should be conscious of whatever level of sharing they choose and why they have chosen it. If they are tempted to exceed this level, they must be alert to the need to examine their motivation.

### Conclusion

Treating individuals with eating disorders is often very challenging for a number of reasons. The ambivalence toward changing disordered eating behaviors sometimes seen among patients requires much skill and patience on the part of the health professional. Because the potential medical complications of eating disorders can be so serious, it is often easy to forget about the person and focus on the behaviors. However, it is the person with whom the health professional must ally himself or herself to produce any form of change. The therapeutic alliance as well as communication and interpersonal style will have great impact on the quality of the treatment. Treatment issues invariably arise and require an even greater commitment to maintaining a professional relationship designed for the benefit of the patient.

Subsequent chapters will discuss the content of treatment. This chapter is meant to guide the context in which treatment occurs. Some of what has been presented assumes a certain approach to treatment and may not be appropriate for individuals who are particularly psychoanalytically or psychodynamically oriented. Such orientations may place less emphasis on unconditional positive regard and paraphrasing and reflecting affect and place more emphasis on uncovering unconscious conflicts within the patient's psyche. Alternatively, some of the positions taken in this chapter may not be acceptable to those who prefer a feminist approach to counseling. Such a position would emphasize the need to reduce power asymmetry in the professional relationship by engaging in greater self-disclosure. We do not propose that our overview of basic counseling techniques is the only valid approach, nor do we claim that this approach is sufficient for therapeutic change. Rather, we hope that this chapter can form a basis for making decisions about how to thoughtfully approach treatment with an eating disordered patient.

### References

Lewis, C. (1866/1986). *Alice's adventures in wonderland.* New York: Golden Books.

Maurer, R. E., & Tindall, J. H. (1983). Effect of postural congruence on clients' perception of counselor empathy. *Journal of Counseling Psychology, 30,* 158–163.

Rogers, C. (1951). *Client-centered therapy.* Boston: Houghton Mifflin.

Chapter 6

# Cognitive-Behavioral Therapy for Eating Disorders

*Carol B. Peterson and James E. Mitchell*

Treatment outcome investigations indicate that among the psychotherapies, cognitive-behavioral therapy (CBT) has the most empirical support
in the treatment of anorexia nervosa, bulimia nervosa, and binge eating
disorder, although the data for anorexia nervosa and binge eating disorder are more modest than for bulimia nervosa (Peterson & Mitchell,
1999; Wilson, Fairburn, & Agras, 1997). The rationale for this therapeutic approach is to target the behavioral and cognitive patterns that cause
and maintain the eating disorder symptoms.

In contrast to other approaches, CBT is symptom focused and does
not typically address underlying psychological issues. It is usually time
limited, follows a standardized treatment manual (e.g., Fairburn, Marcus,
& Wilson, 1993), and has structured or semistructured session content.
The therapist plays an active role in treatment sessions, for example,
offering specific suggestions and reviewing psychoeducational information. CBT emphasizes homework, goal setting, and self-monitoring.

CBT for bulimia nervosa and binge eating disorder can be conducted
using an individual format (Fairburn et al., 1993) or a group format
(Mitchell, Pyle, et al., 1993; Wilfley et al., 1993). There is considerably
less empirical information about conducting CBT with anorexia nervosa
patients, but it has generally been practiced in an individual therapy
format because of the difficulties of working with anorexia nervosa patients in groups. In general, group therapy is appropriate for individuals
with bulimia nervosa and binge eating disorder. The advantages of group
therapy in general have been described by Yalom (1985) and include al-
truism, installation of hope, interpersonal learning, and modeling. Groups
are also more cost-effective than individual therapy (Mitchell, Peterson, &

Agras, 1999). However, some patients may not be well suited for group treatment, including individuals with social phobia and certain types of personality disorders. The logistics of assembling a sufficient number of individuals to conduct a close-ended CBT group can also be difficult in a clinical setting, resulting in an unnecessary delay in treatment for some participants. Therefore, the choice of group versus individual therapy may depend on both patient characteristics and the particular clinical setting.

In general, CBT proceeds in three phases after the introductory sessions. The first phase promotes normalization of eating and weight rehabilitation, usually with behavioral and psychoeducational techniques. The second phase focuses on cognitive restructuring to target maladaptive cognitions related to eating, weight, and shape, and associated problems (e.g., low self-esteem, assertiveness). The final phase emphasizes relapse prevention. Specific techniques included in each phase are outlined below. Although session content tends to follow this sequence, it is necessary at times to focus on cognitive symptoms earlier than the outline suggests, especially if the individual is ambivalent about engaging in treatment.

Throughout CBT, self-monitoring is an essential aspect of treatment. An example of a self-monitoring sheet (modified from Fairburn et

---

**Phase One: Normalization of Weight and Eating**
1. Self-monitoring
2. Psychoeducation (risks of semistarvation, restraint theory)
3. Stimulus control
4. Contingency management
5. Exposure to high-risk foods and situations

**Phase Two: Cognitive and Associated Symptoms**
1. Identifying maladaptive cognitions
2. Cognitive restructuring
3. Addressing underlying beliefs
4. Cues and chains
5. Psychoeducation (body image, assertiveness, stress management)

**Phase Three: Relapse Prevention**
1. Psychoeducation ("lapse" vs. "relapse")
2. Exposure and response prevention
3. Specific plan for lapse and relapse scenarios

---

Figure 6.1. Therapeutic strategies.

al., 1993) is shown in Figure 6.2. In self-monitoring, patients record all food and liquid consumed, and may also record the situation and context as well as accompanying thoughts and feelings, depending on the current focus of therapy. Individuals who engage in binge eating also note all episodes of overeating as well as accompanying purging behaviors. We have found it helpful for individuals with bulimia nervosa and binge eating disorder to code types of binge eating episodes using the Fairburn and Cooper (1993) criteria from the Eating Disorders Examination (EDE). According to this scheme, all binge eating is characterized by feelings of loss of control. However, the amount consumed during these episodes can vary. Unusually large amounts of food (e.g., a gallon of ice cream) accompanied by feelings of loss of control, or "objective" episodes (OBs), are larger than "subjective" binges (SBs), in which the individual believes she or he has overeaten but has not consumed what others would regard as an unusually large amount of food (for example, second helpings at dinner). Coding types of binge eating episodes has the added benefit of helping patients to recognize that the amounts of food they consume during overeating episodes are not necessarily large by other's standards.

## Introducing Patients to CBT

Because of the importance of collaboration between the therapist and patient in CBT, initial sessions should focus on reviewing the rationale for treatment, as well as building therapeutic rapport. Rapport can be especially difficult when working with individuals with anorexia nervosa, who often have difficulty talking freely and are usually reluctant to gain weight. Discussed in detail by Garner and Bemis (1985), and Garner, Vitousek, and Pike (1997), specific strategies to improve rapport include demonstrating a clear knowledge of the disorder, recognizing the adaptive functions of the illness for the patient, and accepting the patient's beliefs as genuine. When discussing the rationale for CBT, some patients express concern that CBT will not address the original "causes" of their eating disorders. We explain that considerable research has documented the efficacy of therapeutic approaches that do not target underlying psychological issues in treatment (see reviews by Agras, 1993; Mitchell, Raymond, & Specker, 1993; Peterson & Mitchell, 1999). It is also helpful to explain that factors that maintain the eating disorder may be different from the original causes, and that CBT may be especially effective in targeting these maintenance factors.

**Case example: Kim**

| Time | Food/liquid consumed | Binge | Purge | Context | Thoughts | Feelings |
|---|---|---|---|---|---|---|
| 8 AM | 1 apple | | | Breakfast at home | "I need to cut back today to lose weight." | Anxious |
| 10 AM | Fat free pretzels (1 handful) | | | Snack between classes | "I shouldn't eat this, but I'm hungry—I'll eat less at lunch." | Irritable |
| Noon | 2 cups salad, no dressing | | | At school with friends | "I'm in control—I have to skip the dressing if I want to lose weight." | Happy |
| 8 PM | 1 order of french fries | SB | Vomit | At work—end of shift | "I can't believe I ate something this high in fat. I have to get rid of it or I won't lose weight." | Sad, anxious |
| 9:30 PM | 1 gallon ice cream, 1/2 bag potato chips | OB | Vomit | Home from work alone; boyfriend supposed to come over but couldn't | "I blew it anyway when I ate those french fries. I'll start over tomorrow." | Disgusted, depressed, anxious, angry |

*Note:* SB = subjective bulimic binge; OB = objective bulimic episode
*Source:* Modified from Fairburn, Marcus, & Wilson, 1993.

Figure 6.2. Self-monitoring form.

Considerable attention should be paid to introducing self-monitoring, especially because the procedure is labor intensive for the patient. We emphasize to the patient that CBT aims to help the individual develop skills to address her or his symptoms independently without the assistance of the therapist, and that self-monitoring facilitates this process by maintaining a focus on symptoms outside of the therapy sessions. Completed self-monitoring forms are crucial to provide material for discussion in sessions, and allow the patient and therapist to examine thoughts and behaviors in detail. In addition, treatment outcome studies have found that self-monitoring alone is beneficial in promoting the reduction of bulimic symptoms (Agras, Schneider, Arnow, Raeburn, & Telch, 1989).

Early sessions can also include a review of the advantages and disadvantages the eating disorder provides to the individual. This procedure serves two purposes. First, it increases motivation and commitment to treatment by emphasizing the advantages of recovery. Second, it identifies potential obstacles to treatment, and allows the patient and therapist to anticipate and plan strategies to address these potential problems. An example of this exercise is shown in Figure 6.3.

## Normalization of Eating and Weight

After the introductory phase, initial sessions generally target specific eating patterns and weight maintenance. Psychoeducation about the effects of semistarvation and a review of the research on these symptoms (Keys, Brozek, Henschel, Mickelsen, & Taylor, 1950) are an essential and crit-

---

**Case example: Jody**

| Reasons to change eating patterns | Reasons not to change eating patterns |
|---|---|
| 1. Parents and friends hassling me about my weight. | 1. Afraid of gaining weight. |
| 2. Spending a lot of time thinking about food. | 2. Don't want to give up exercising. |
| 3. Dizziness. | 3. Too busy—takes too much time to come to appointments. |
| 4. Purging is gross—I'm embarrassed that I do it. | 4. People won't like me as much if I'm fat. |
| 5. They won't let me do school activities like athletics unless I change. | 5. I've worked hard to lose weight—I don't want to ruin it. |

---

Figure 6.3. Reasons for and against recovery.

ical focus for most patients with eating disorders. We also find it useful to provide information about dietary restraint theory (Polivy & Herman, 1985), which indicates that individuals with rigid rules about dietary restriction overeat when disinhibited by the slightest transgression of these rules. Dietary restraint theory illustrates that adherence to rigid dietary rules, for example, assigning dichotomous ("good" vs. "bad") labels to foods, puts one at risk of overeating when "bad" foods are eventually consumed or the dietary rule is "broken" in any way. Information about restraint theory also helps to "set the stage" for cognitive restructuring in later sessions.

Behavioral techniques are useful in modifying specific patterns of eating. We start by introducing the concepts of *stimulus* (or *cue*) and *response*. Stimulus control involves modifying specific cues or triggers of eating disorder symptoms that have become associated with certain behaviors through conditioning. The first step requires identifying cues of symptoms, which can include situational, interpersonal, physiological, and psychological variables. After identifying cues, patients can modify their responses to them and alter the cues themselves. Strategies include avoiding the cue, strengthening cues for desired behaviors, building in a delay in response to the cue, substituting an alternative behavior, and structuring the situation to make engaging in the symptom impossible.

### Case Example: Martin

Martin examined his self-monitoring forms in detail and identified a number of cues associated with binge eating episodes. Cues included driving by certain fast-food restaurants, going to the break room at work where vending machine food was available, and watching television, especially when his wife was not at home. He also realized that he was least likely to engage in binge eating episodes during the evening when he was with other people after dinner.

After identifying these patterns, Martin designated specific strategies to address each cue. He *avoided cues* by driving routes that limited exposure to fast-food establishments. He also avoided the break room and chose to go outside on breaks, where no vending machines are available. At times when the weather made it impossible to go outside, he *prevented the behavior from occurring* by entering the break room without any money, making it impossible to use the vending machines. Although he considered avoiding watching television in the evening, he decided that this activity was important to him. He chose to start watching television in the bedroom instead of the den, because he generally did not eat in the bedroom. He also chose to *substitute an alternative behavior* when watching television by doing a crossword puzzle if he felt the urge to binge. He *built in a pause* by waiting for a five-minute interval at the onset of each urge to binge, during which he would set a timer and wait before engaging in the behavior. To *strengthen healthier behavior* by seeking out positive cues, he planned to eat dinner with friends at least twice a week to reduce the likelihood of binge eating in the evenings when his wife was not at home.

In addition to stimulus control, contingency management is an effective behavioral technique in the treatment of eating disorder symptoms. Contingency management is based on the principle that behavior is maintained by rewarding consequences and eliminated if it is not rewarded or is punished. Like cues, consequences of eating disorder symptoms can be classified by categories, including situational (e.g., avoiding an unpleasant activity), physiological (e.g., reduction of hunger), psychological (e.g., experiencing a sense of accomplishment by losing weight), and interpersonal (e.g., expressed concern from others). Although consequences of eating disorders are both positive and negative, symptoms are often maintained because the reinforcing features are more immediate (e.g., reduction of hunger after binge eating) than the negative consequences (e.g., dental erosion that gradually results from vomiting).

Self-monitoring forms can be reviewed to determine consequences of eating disorder symptoms. Contingency management can be implemented by attempting to eliminate the positive consequences of the eating disorder symptoms and by rewarding nonsymptomatic behaviors. Instituting rewards requires setting realistic goals. It is usually most appropriate to set modest goals at the beginning of treatment to facilitate success and thereby increase self-efficacy. Patients often find it useful to set short-term and long-term goals, with different contingencies for each type. Contingencies are especially useful in facilitating weight gain in underweight patients.

### Case Example: Jody

Although she was somewhat reluctant at first, Jody agreed to set specific goals to attempt to reach her goal weight. She collaborated with her clinician and agreed that 2 pounds per week would be a reasonable amount to meet her goal range of 110 to 120 pounds. She decided that for a long-term goal, she would purchase a leather jacket as a reward for reaching her goal range. At her therapist's suggestion, she also agreed to implement short-term goals to institute more frequent positive reinforcement. She decided that each week that she met her goal range, she would spend $10 on a compact disc, audiotape, or item of jewelry. She chose to put a sticker on her calendar on each day that she followed her meal plan. Finally, her therapist encouraged her to use "mental rewards" as well as tangible ones, by saying encouraging statements to herself upon completing each successful meal (e.g., "Good job, Jody").

Systematic in-vivo exposure can be helpful in targeting avoidance behaviors associated with anorexia nervosa, bulimia nervosa, and binge eating disorder. Because in-vivo exposure exercises are uncomfortable for patients, it is essential to explain the rationale of using these techniques before implementing them. Specifically, patients are educated about the nature of anxiety and the necessity of "waiting it out" in order to change the conditioned response to the anxiety. Palliative techniques can also be used (Garner & Bemis, 1985), including parroting reassuring phrases ("anxiety is uncomfortable, but I can get through this if I can just ride it out"). Teaching relaxation skills in the context of in-vivo exposure can be especially helpful.

Perhaps the most important component of behavioral exposure is constructing the hierarchy of feared or avoided foods and situations. Patients begin by identifying a list of foods and situations that they avoid, or eat only when binge eating and experiencing feelings of loss of control. Items should be identified as specifically as possible, for example, the brand of cookies, time of day, and type of conditions (e.g., alone or with others). The items should then be rated and placed in order, from least feared to most feared. Although some patients are willing to engage in "flooding" by starting with the most difficult item on the hierarchy, most prefer to start with the least feared and move down the list systematically. This approach has the added benefit of building successful experiences and confidence. Exposure procedures can be conducted during or between treatment sessions. It is crucial for the patient to maximize the possibility of success during exposure sessions, for example, consuming a feared food when accompanied by a friend and in a controlled setting.

Exposure and response prevention (ERP) is also an important behavioral technique. ERP requires the individual to expose herself to a "high-risk" stimulus without engaging in the binge eating, purging, or restricting symptom. ERP can be applied in various ways, including having the individual binge eat without self-inducing vomiting (Rosen & Leitenberg, 1985).

### Case Example: Kim

Kim found that eating three meals a day was very effective in reducing the frequency of her binge eating and vomiting episodes. However, her self-monitoring forms indicated that she continued to vomit when not binge eating, especially after eating regular meals that included a variety of foods. She reported that certain foods were associated with fear of weight gain and were most likely to trigger purging episodes. She constructed the following hierarchy of high-risk foods and rated them according to degree of fear:

1. white bread (+2)
2. eggs (+3)
3. broiled chicken (+4)
4. cookies (peanut butter) (+5)
5. salad dressing (not fat free, more than 1 tsp.) (+6)
6. red meat, broiled or grilled (+7)
7. mayonnaise (+8)
8. ice cream (chocolate chip) (+9)

After constructing the hierarchy, Kim and her therapist devised exposure sessions that would maximize her success. Kim decided that eating these foods alone or anywhere near a private bathroom would make refraining from vomiting difficult. It was agreed that exposure sessions would be conducted in public settings and that she should be accompanied by a friend or family member.

The therapist started by explaining the nature of anxiety to Kim: anxiety increases with exposure to a cue (e.g., consumption of a feared food); the person will act in a way to reduce the anxiety (e.g., vomit, leave the situation), and because the anxiety is diminished, the symptom is reinforced. Exposure sessions aim to elicit the anxiety but require the patient to "wait it out" (because the anxiety will eventually diminish) instead of engaging in the symptom. Over time and repeated exposure, the anxiety response will diminish in response to the cue.

Kim decided to start her exposure in her therapy session. She brought the first item on her hierarchy, a piece of white bread, to her session and consumed it at the start of the hour in order to manage the anxiety response with the support of her therapist. As expected, her anxiety rose from a "3" to a "7" almost immediately. Cognitions included "I'm going to gain weight," "I can't keep this down," and "I have to vomit to feel better." Her therapist helped by reminding her of the reassuring phrases Kim had been practicing ("I can do this; the anxiety will get better if I can wait this out").

By the end of the session, her anxiety was reduced to a "4." She was confident that she would not vomit after leaving the session but planned to visit a friend immediately afterwards to ensure that purging would be impossible. She agreed to practice consuming white bread repeatedly in "safe" environments until her anxiety response was minimal before attempting exposure to the next item on her list, eggs.

### Targeting Cognitions

Cognitive restructuring is an essential component of CBT. Early in treatment, the cognitive model can be introduced to patients to illustrate the relationship between thoughts, feelings, and behaviors (see Figure 6.4). Specifically, the role of thoughts in affecting feelings and behaviors should be emphasized. Some patients have difficulty understanding the concept of thoughts or cognitions, and various descriptions can be used to help illustrate this process, including the "inner dialogue or monologue in your head," and "what you're saying to yourself when you think." Using examples in sessions can illustrate the concept of cognitions vividly, for example, asking, "What are your specific thoughts right at this moment?"

Self-monitoring assignments help elucidate specific cognitions. We find it useful to help patients identify their maladaptive cognitions according to specific patterns. These patterns were first described by Beck, Rush, Shaw, & Emery (1979), and have been adapted to eating disorders (Garner & Bemis, 1982, 1985). These patterns include dichotomous thinking (e.g., "Foods are either safe or forbidden"), overgeneralization (e.g., "I made a mistake: I always make mistakes"), minimization (e.g., "I went the whole day without vomiting, but anyone could do that"), emotional reasoning (e.g., "If I feel fat, I must be fat"), catastrophizing (e.g., "I ate an extra helping: this is terrible"), mind reading (e.g., "She just looked over at me: she thinks I look fat in this outfit"), and fortune-telling (e.g., "I ate a piece of cake: I'm definitely going to gain five pounds").

After identifying problematic thoughts, the first step in cognitive restructuring, especially in the beginning of treatment, is to determine whether the cognition is a type of maladaptive thought described above. For example, after identifying a problematic cognition, the patient can

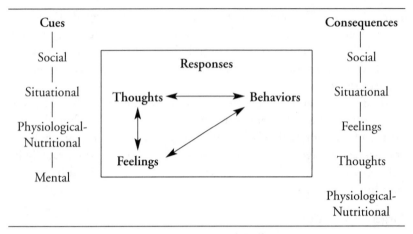

Figure 6.4. Cognitive model of symptoms.

first evaluate whether it is an example of dichotomous thinking, over-generalization, or some other pattern before starting to examine it. Working with the therapist in what Beck et al. (1979) have described as collaborative empiricism, patients can then begin to examine the content of their thoughts objectively. Cognitive restructuring can be conducted in one of two ways: (1) by testing the accuracy of the cognition through experimentation, or (2) by evaluating the validity of the content by questioning it.

To test the accuracy of a thought, the patient can devise an experiment to examine the degree to which the cognition is realistic. For example, Kim believed that eating according to her meal plan would result in immediate weight gain. She agreed to test the accuracy of this cognition by following her meal plan for five days and comparing her weight before and after. She was surprised to find that she did not gain weight, engaged in binge eating less often, and was able to dismiss her belief that eating regular meals results in weight gain.

To examine the validity of the cognition by questioning it, the patient can first evaluate the evidence of the thought by considering what evidence supports it and what evidence refutes it. For example, in examining Jody's belief that people would like her less if she gained weight (see Figure 6.3), the only evidence that she could identify in support of this belief was that she might feel worse about *herself* because dietary restriction was an important source of self-esteem. She was able to identify considerable evidence to refute the thought, including the fact that people had liked her prior to her weight loss, that she had, in fact, lost friends as a result of the eating disorder and the accompanying weight loss, and that body weight was not a determining factor of whether she liked other people. This evidence helped her reevaluate the accuracy of her cognition.

In addition to evaluating evidence, cognitive restructuring involves identifying the implications of the thought, as well as alternative explanations. Jody, for example, evaluated the possibility that some people would not like her as much if she did gain weight (although she found very little evidence to support this belief). In examining the implications, she was able to recognize that if others liked her less as a result of an increase in her body weight, they would be evaluating her worth as a person in terms of her body weight. She decided that anyone who selected a friend based on this criteria was not someone who would be a source of support in her recovery from an eating disorder. As treatment progressed, Jody was also able to identify alternative explanations when examining the thought, "everyone who looks at me thinks I'm getting fat." She was able to consider the possibility that others were not noticing her weight gain, that her friends and family were relieved that she was no longer emaciated, and that those who noticed her weight gain might appreciate that she looked healthier, and not "fat." She also examined the implications of the thought and decided that if others did believe she looked "fat," it meant they approved of the unrealistic ideal of thinness that had contributed to the onset of her eating disorder, a belief she was starting to question in the context of her recovery.

In the early phases of treatment, cognitive restructuring tends to focus on thoughts recorded directly on the self-monitoring forms. As treatment progresses, more attention can be devoted to underlying beliefs or schemas that are revealed in the course of cognitive restructuring (Beck et al., 1979; Garner et al., 1997). Examples of underlying beliefs, which tend to involve implicit assumptions about the self and the environment, include "I must be liked by everyone," "Everything I do must be perfect, or it is worthless," "My needs and urges must be fulfilled immediately," and "It is essential to fulfill others' expectations of me." Cognitions tend to arise in the context of these underlying beliefs. Challenging cognitions can serve as an important step in undermining these beliefs; however, it is often necessary to address underlying beliefs directly as they are identified in session. As described by Burns (1993), examining the costs and benefits of subscribing to self-defeating underlying beliefs can be effective in further objectifying them, challenging them, and restructuring them.

## Attitudes Toward Weight and Shape

As defined by DSM-IV (American Psychiatric Association, 1994), problematic attitudes toward weight and shape are essential components of anorexia nervosa and bulimia nervosa. Specifically, individuals with anorexia nervosa often exhibit body image distortion, in which they misperceive themselves as larger than their actual size, deny the danger of their emaciation, and/or overrely on their weight and shape in their self-evaluation. Individuals with bulimia nervosa, although usually of normal weight, also demonstrate an overreliance on body size and shape in their self-evaluation. Although the criteria for binge eating disorder do not specify a disturbance in body image, research findings have indicated that individuals with binge eating disorder are more disparaging of their weight and shape in comparison to others of comparable size (Mussell et al., 1996). In general, individuals with eating disorders are quite preoccupied with their body shape and weight and report a greater degree of dissatisfaction than individuals without eating disorders (Cash & Brown, 1987). The disturbance in attitudes toward weight and shape, and the fact that these attitudes contribute to and perpetuate maladaptive eating patterns (Fairburn & Garner, 1988) require direct therapeutic attention in the treatment of eating disorders.

Psychoeducation is an important aspect of this type of intervention, starting with a description of body image as a multidimensional phenomenon that incorporates multiple components. These components include visual (e.g., how the body looks in the mirror or the "mind's eye"), spatial (e.g., how the body is experienced in space, for instance, when one is sitting on a bench with others), tactile (e.g., how the body feels when touched), and cognitive (e.g., self-statements about one's body) processes. Although the complexity of body image can be problematic, it also allows for more "pathways" to facilitate improvement. However, it is helpful to explain to individuals with eating disorders that improvements in body image tend to be gradual, often lagging behind improvements in eating patterns (Peterson, 1993).

Because disturbances in body image tend to involve thoughts and attitudes, cognitive restructuring is the primary technique used to address these symptoms. Upon initiating treatment, most individuals with eating disorders believe that the only method to allay their distress about their appearance is to lose weight and change their shape through dietary restriction and exercise. The role of CBT is to introduce the possibility that the thoughts themselves can be altered to improve body image rather than changing one's actual body size.

Specific aspects of body image disturbance are targeted. Compared to individuals without eating disorders, many individuals with anorexia nervosa (Slade & Russell, 1973; Sunday, Halmi, Werdann, & Levey, 1992), bulimia nervosa (Bowden, Touyz, Rodriguez, Hensley, & Beumont, 1989; Powers, Schulman, Gleghorn, & Prange, 1987), and possibly binge eating disorder overestimate their body size, perceiving their body or parts of their body as larger than they actually are. "Emotional reasoning" may contribute to this misperception, with the belief that if one "feels" fat, one must actually *be* fat. Psychoeducation about the distortion of body perception can also be helpful in addressing body image disturbance. Patients can be encouraged to view their body image as a "blind spot" in which they may be unable to perceive themselves accurately (much like someone who is color-blind being unable to differentiate red from green), and can be told that this misperception is an acute symptom of the eating disorder that often improves with normalization of eating and weight (Birtchnell, Lacey, & Harte, 1985; Slade & Russell, 1973).

Because body image is characterized by disparaging thoughts about one's body and its parts, individuals with eating disorders can be instructed to view their attitudes toward their body on a continuum from extremely negative to very positive. The therapeutic goal is to promote more acceptance (or at least neutral feelings) toward hated body parts, and to develop positive feelings toward at least a few parts or aspects of appearance. Patients are often more amenable to treatment when informed that the goal is not to promote a superficial affection for one's appearance, but instead to develop an acceptance and tolerance of weight and shape, with some accompanying positive feelings. Focusing on the *function* of body parts rather than their appearance (e.g., legs are used for walking, dancing) can be helpful in promoting acceptance, as can evaluating one's physical strength and power rather than thinness.

Targeting body image issues usually requires education about the sociocultural factors that contribute to the extreme body dissatisfaction often experienced by individuals with anorexia nervosa, bulimia nervosa, and binge eating disorder. Psychoeducational materials that facilitate this understanding can be useful (Garner, 1997; Rodin, 1992; Wolf, 1991). Specifically, it is essential for individuals with eating disorders to recognize that the ideal of thinness promoted in the current sociocultural context is essentially arbitrary and not "fixed" throughout time. Individuals with eating disorders are often surprised to learn that the ideal for thinness has generally become thinner over the past few decades (Garner,

Garfinkel, Schwartz, & Thompson, 1980), while the average American body weight has actually increased over the same time period (old movies, sculptures, and paintings in art museums help to illustrate the instability of aesthetic ideals and thus to undermine the current overvaluation of thinness as absolute).

Body image issues can be problematic in other ways for individuals with binge eating disorder because they are often overweight and must contend with the social stigma against obesity. Discussing ways to protect oneself psychologically from prejudice and discrimination is important, and especially powerful in a group setting. Identifying examples from other subpopulations that have contended with prejudice successfully can help large-size individuals recognize that criticism from others is a reflection of societal discrimination rather than accurate feedback about self-worth. In addressing these topics, cognitive restructuring that challenges the accuracy of others' criticism can be helpful.

It is important for all individuals with eating disorders to examine fantasies and beliefs they have about weight loss (e.g., that it will lead to changes in interpersonal relationships, jobs and school performance, personality characteristics) and to what degree these are realistic. The role of media images in idealizing thinness and the characteristics associated with it (e.g., self-control, youth, sexuality) should be reviewed. Individuals with eating disorders often realize that they believe that weight loss will "cure" all of their problems. Indeed, some recognize that fantasies about weight loss appear to provide a straightforward "method" to achieve happiness (i.e., by altering weight and shape) and are more appealing than facing the more difficult but necessary steps required to solve interpersonal, academic, or occupational problems.

Many individuals with anorexia nervosa, bulimia nervosa, and binge eating disorder avoid social and other activities because of self-consciousness about weight and shape. This behavior takes on a phobic quality that can cause significant impairment in functioning. Although it is essential for the therapist to express genuine empathy for the degree of distress caused by body image dissatisfaction, use of behavioral exposure exercises to increase the repertoire or frequency of activities can be useful, especially for individuals who have numerous activities they avoid, believing that they cannot engage in them until they have lost weight. Employing a method similar to the exposure exercise described earlier using food hierarchies, individuals with avoidance behaviors secondary to body image disturbance can develop a list of places, situations, and people they avoid, in order from least to most feared. The individual can systematically ex-

Cognitive-Behavioral Therapy    159

pose herself or himself to each scenario on the list, progressing to the next avoided place or person after each is mastered with minimal anxiety upon repeated exposure.

Perhaps the most important aspect of body image requiring therapeutic attention is the evaluation of self-worth based on weight and shape. This underlying belief must be identified and addressed directly, with the goal of broadening criteria used for self-evaluation.

## Case Example: Jody

Jody's self-monitoring forms, including statements like "I will hate myself if I gain weight," "I feel better about myself as a person when I lose weight," and "My self-confidence is ruined if my stomach isn't flat," revealed that her self-evaluation was strongly influenced by her shape and weight. The therapist began by attempting to clarify that her feelings of self-worth were almost exclusively determined by her weight and shape.

The therapist probed further and discovered that the primary determinants of her feelings about herself on a daily basis were the number on the scale when she weighed herself, the flatness of her stomach, and the circumference of her thighs. Jody stated that unless these three criteria were met, she believed that she was worthless. She admitted that although how others perceived her body was important, her own evaluation was most essential in determining her feelings of self-worth (which, she realized, was part of the reason why reassurance from others was only minimally comforting in alleviating her distress about her appearance).

Jody and her therapist spent considerable time in the following sessions clarifying and examining this underlying belief and its implications. Specifically, the therapist sought to understand how and why this belief had become central to her self-concept. They discussed the evidence in favor of and against the notion that one's worth is reflected in weight and shape, including examples of other individuals who Jody valued but who could not meet her own rigid criteria for weight and shape. They reviewed the inconsistency in evaluating others by a different set of expectations than one's self. They discussed the implications if Jody did not meet her self-imposed criteria: what evidence was there that her worth as a person had decreased? The therapist also broadened the questions to ask about self-worth in general: Is there really one "standard," or were Jody's expectations arbitrarily constructed? Can self-worth really be measured or earned?

Finally, they explored the functions of the belief (i.e., that Jody was reassured about her self-worth when she did meet her criteria, that the pursuit of weight loss provided her the illusion of "control") and evaluated whether the benefits of it outweighed the disadvantages. Gradually, although weight and shape remained important influences on her feelings about herself, Jody began to question the validity of using these criteria as sole measures of her self-worth.

Because the process of body image improvement is gradual, patients find it helpful to identify specific strategies they can utilize in the process of developing more self-acceptance in order to minimize their discomfort level. These include the following:

1. Wearing certain clothing (e.g., loose fitting, comfortable fabrics, soothing colors) and avoiding or discarding others (e.g., tight jeans, revealing styles).
2. Avoiding cues that promote the unrealistic sociocultural ideal of thinness (e.g., reading fashion magazines, watching certain television shows or movies).
3. Seeking out situations or people that are more accepting of a wider range of body types (e.g., certain books or periodicals, supportive friends).
4. Engaging in "self-nurturing" activities that promote kindness toward the body through various somatosensory systems (e.g., massage, bubble baths, soothing music, positive visualization).

### Incorporating Behavioral and Cognitive Techniques

After reviewing behavioral and cognitive techniques, the clinician can incorporate these different approaches comprehensively by introducing the concept of "chains." Specifically, eating disorder symptoms are often the result of a long "chain" of stimuli rather than of a single cue or trigger. For this reason, it is important for the patient to identify the origin of the chain and to intervene using behavioral or cognitive techniques as early as possible in the process.

#### Case Example: Martin

Figure 6.5 depicts an example of a chain that Martin identified that had preceded a binge eating episode over the weekend. The chain started with a challenging day at work on Friday, in which he had to meet a deadline under time duress. Because he was busy, he did not have time to eat lunch. He then went out for happy hour with colleagues and ate a

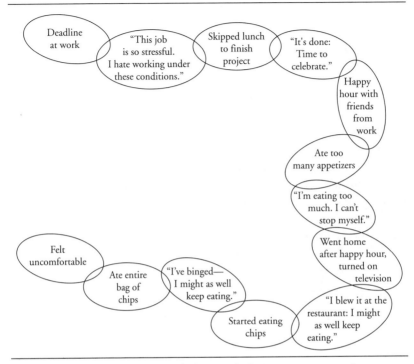

Figure 6.5. Cognitive-behavioral chain: a case example.

large amount of appetizers, accompanied by feelings of loss of control. Martin went home afterwards to watch television and found that his wife was not home. He then had a binge eating episode that lasted through the evening.

In reviewing this chain with his therapist, Martin identified a number of points where he could intervene. The therapist reminded Martin that chains are most easily interrupted earlier in the sequence. Martin realized that while he could not change his work environment, he could modify his cognitions in appraising the stress (e.g., "This deadline is challenging. What can I do to make the work conditions more optimal to meeting my goal?"). Most importantly, he noted that skipping lunch was probably an essential component of the chain of events, and that it was important for him to eat regular meals even under the most difficult circumstances.

Martin recognized that although attending happy hour was somewhat high-risk, it was a decision he did not regret. He noted, however, that planning the types and amounts of foods he would eat ahead of time would have helped eliminate the impulsive decision making that led to overeating. He recognized that he could modify his cognitions about the food he consumed to incorporate more flexibility (e.g., "I ate more appetizers than I wanted, but my meal plan is flexible, and I can accommodate these changes; I am still in control and can stop eating now").

Martin realized that going home might be a cue to binge eat, especially after experiencing a loss of control in the restaurant. He considered other options, including calling home to see if his wife were there and if not, visiting a friend or going to the community center instead. He also recognized that turning on the television was a cue for binge eating and that he could avoid the cue by reading or doing crossword puzzles. He realized that his cognition ("I blew it") was an overgeneralization and considered completing a written cognitive restructuring exercise during similar situations in the future. Finally, Martin agreed that he could have implemented a five-minute pause between the onset of the decision to binge eat and the actual consumption of the food, which might have prevented the episode from occurring.

### Targeting Associated Problems Using CBT

As CBT progresses, the focus of treatment often shifts from direct targeting of eating disorder symptoms to other problems associated with anorexia nervosa, bulimia nervosa, and binge eating disorder, including self-esteem, assertiveness, impulsivity, stress management, and problem solving. Utilizing techniques specifically designed to address these co-occurring problems can be helpful in promoting remission and preventing relapse. The necessity of focusing on these related problems is often revealed in "cues and chains" exercises (e.g., Figure 6.5), when these types of problems are identified as precursors of eating disorder symptoms.

Addressing self-esteem often arises in the context of addressing body image and self-evaluation. Cognitive restructuring specifically focusing on self-esteem issues in addition to body weight and shape is often essential in working with people with eating disorders. As described by McKay and Fanning (1987) and Burns (1993), CBT for self-esteem problems involves evaluating self-statements and underlying beliefs about the self. A self-concept review exercise can be used in which the individual records a number of thoughts about personal strengths and weaknesses in various domains (e.g., appearance, interpersonal, professional). Cognitive restructuring is used to challenge inaccurate language and to provide alternative evidence to promote a more realistic self-appraisal. In addition, personal strengths are identified and emphasized.

CBT does not aim to provide superficial reassurance or false praise. In fact, it is important for individuals to recognize personal weaknesses or aspects of themselves they would like to change. However, CBT helps the individual evaluate these qualities realistically rather than overgeneralizing them as flaws reflecting inherent personal inadequacy.

Cognitive techniques are also useful in addressing stress management, often necessary in the treatment of eating disorders (Cattanach & Rodin, 1988). The importance of the appraisal process in evaluating and adapting to a stressful stimulus is reviewed (Lazarus & Launier, 1978). Patients can reduce stress in two ways: by avoiding the stressor, or by modifying their response to it. Psychoeducational information about time management, prioritization, and proper sleep hygiene can also be useful. Self-monitoring forms provide important clues about stressful stimuli that can be targeted using stress management techniques. Cognitive restructuring can also be used to modify the appraisal of stressors (e.g., challenging statements like, "I can't possibly handle this task").

Related to stress management, problem solving can be effective in reducing eating disorder symptoms. The problems themselves, or the perceived inability to address them, are often cues for maladaptive eating patterns. Problem solving first requires a clear articulation of the problem at hand. Of note, many patients struggle with this preliminary step. The next phase involves generating as many potential solutions as possible, even ones that may not be practical or realistic. Subsequently, each possible solution is evaluated for its feasibility and likely consequences, and a plan of action is determined. Based on an examination of the consequences, the adequacy of the solution is evaluated afterwards, and, if necessary, an alternative solution is applied.

Because many individuals with eating disorders have problematic interpersonal relationships, assertiveness training is a useful component of CBT. Psychoeducation about the differences between assertive, aggressive, and passive communication are reviewed (Butler, 1981). Cognitive restructuring is often useful to address underlying beliefs that may impede assertive expression (e.g., "I should never disagree," "I must avoid conflict at all costs," "It is unacceptable for females to show angry feelings"). Role modeling, behavioral rehearsal, and role playing can facilitate skills during sessions (Schroeder & Black, 1985). Using a method similar to the exposure hierarchies described earlier, patients can devise a list of situations in which it is least to most difficult to communicate assertively. Systematically, each of these situations can be approached and mastered.

## Relapse Prevention

The final phase of treatment is relapse prevention. This process involves a review of the progress made in treatment, with an emphasis on identifying strategies that the patient has found most effective. It is essential that the patient finish treatment with the knowledge that eating disorder symptoms may recur, at least in mild form, in the future. Patients should be informed that the risk of relapse in eating disorders is considerable, and that she or he should remain aware of this possibility even after therapy is complete. Psychoeducation about the difference between a "lapse" and a "relapse" is essential to prevent the abstinence violation effect described by Marlatt and Gordon (1985), in which the individual exaggerates the significance of a minor symptom and escalates the situation into a full relapse. We suggest that patients construct written plans for lapses and relapses, in which they identify early warning signs of relapse (e.g., skipping meals to lose weight, feeling a loss of control when eating regular-size portions, preoccupation with body weight and shape) and outline specific strategies to "get back on track" (e.g., meal planning, completing cognitive restructuring worksheets, seeking social support). An agreement for when and under which conditions the patient should return to treatment should also be devised as part of the relapse plan.

The exposure response prevention procedures described earlier are also important components of relapse prevention. Prior to terminating psychotherapy, the patient should identify foods or situations that are still challenging or are even avoided. After constructing a hierarchy, patients can systematically expose themselves to each item on the list to extinguish the anxiety response. Successful completion of high-risk exposure exercises at the completion of treatment can be helpful in increasing confidence and preventing relapse.

## Conclusions

CBT is a short-term, symptom-focused treatment that addresses thought and behavioral patterns associated with eating disorders. Empirical findings indicate that among psychotherapeutic interventions, CBT has the most evidence in support of its use for individuals with anorexia nervosa, bulimia nervosa, and binge eating disorder. Many strategies can be included in the course of CBT. Earlier sessions usually focus on nutritional rehabilitation and behavioral techniques; later sessions target cognitive and associated problems, along with relapse prevention strategies. Although CBT is a structured approach, it is important for the therapist to be flexible in response to the needs of each patient when applying CBT techniques.

### References

Agras, W. S. (1993). Short-term psychological treatments for binge eating. In C. G. Fairburn & G. T. Wilson (Eds.), *Binge eating: Nature, assessment, and treatment* (pp. 270–286). New York: Guilford Press.

Agras, W. S., Schneider, J. A., Arnow B., Raeburn, S. D., & Telch, C. F. (1989). Cognitive-behavioral and response-prevention treatment for bulimia nervosa. *Journal of Consulting and Clinical Psychology, 57,* 215–221.

American Psychiatric Association. (1994). *Diagnostic and statistical manual of mental disorders* (4th ed.). Washington, DC: Author.

Beck, A. T., Rush, A. J., Shaw, B. F., & Emery, G. (1979). *Cognitive therapy of depression.* New York: Guilford Press.

Birtchnell, S. A., Lacey, J. H., & Harte, A. (1985). Body image distortion in bulimia nervosa. *British Journal of Psychiatry, 147,* 408–412.

Bowden, P. K., Touyz, S. W., Rodriguez, P. J., Hensley, R., & Beumont, P. J. V. (1989). Distorting patient or distorting instrument? Body shape disturbance in patients with anorexia nervosa and bulimia. *British Journal of Psychiatry, 155,* 196–201.

Burns, D. D. (1993). *Ten days to self-esteem.* New York: Quill.

Butler, P. E. (1981). *Self-assertion for women.* San Francisco: Harper & Row.

Cash, T. F., & Brown, T. A. (1987). Body image in anorexia and bulimia nervosa: A review of the literature. *Behavior Modification, 11,* 487–521.

Cattanach, L., & Rodin, J. (1988). Psychosocial components of the stress process in bulimia. *International Journal of Eating Disorders, 7,* 75–88.

Fairburn, C. G., & Cooper, Z. (1993). The Eating Disorders Examination (12th ed.). In C. G. Fairburn & G. T. Wilson (Eds.), *Binge eating: Nature, assessment, and treatment* (pp. 317–360). New York: Guilford Press.

Fairburn, C. G., & Garner, D. M. (1988). Diagnostic criteria for anorexia nervosa and bulimia nervosa: The importance of attitudes to shape and weight. In D. Garner & P. Garfinkel (Eds.), *Diagnostic issues in anorexia nervosa and bulimia nervosa* (pp. 36–55). New York: Brunner/Mazel.

Fairburn, C. G., Marcus, M. D., & Wilson, G. T. (1993). Cognitive-behavioral therapy for binge eating and bulimia nervosa: A comprehensive treatment manual. In C. G. Fairburn & G. T. Wilson (Eds.), *Binge eating: Nature, assessment, and treatment* (pp. 361–404). New York: Guilford Press.

Garner, D. M. (1997). Psychoeducational principles in treatment. In D. M. Garner & P. E. Garfinkel (Eds.), *Handbook of treatment for eating disorders* (2d ed.) (pp. 145–177). New York: Guilford Press.

Garner, D. M., & Bemis, K. M. (1982). Cognitive behavioral approach to anorexia nervosa. *Cognitive Therapy and Research, 6,* 123–155.

Garner, D. M., & Bemis, K. M. (1985). Cognitive therapy for anorexia nervosa. In D. M. Garner & P. E. Garfinkel (Eds.), *Handbook of psychotherapy for anorexia nervosa and bulimia* (pp. 107–146). New York: Guilford Press.

Garner, D. M., Garfinkel, P. E., Schwartz, D., & Thompson, M. (1980). Cultural expectations of thinness in women. *Psychological Reports, 47,* 483–491.

Garner, D. M., Vitousek, K. M., & Pike, K. M. (1997). Cognitive-behavioral therapy for anorexia nervosa. In D. M. Garner & P. E. Garfinkel (Eds.), *Handbook of psychotherapy for anorexia nervosa and bulimia* (pp. 94–144). New York: Guilford Press.

Keys, A., Brozek, J., Henschel, A., Mickelsen, O., & Taylor, H. L. (1950). *The biology of human starvation, Vol. 1.* Minneapolis: University of Minnesota Press.

Lazarus, R., & Launier, R. (1978). Stress-related transactions between person and environment. In L. Pervin & M. Lewis (Eds.), *Perspectives in interactional psychology* (pp. 287–327). New York: Plenum.

Marlatt, G. A., & Gordon, J. R. (1985). *Relapse prevention: Maintenance strategies in the treatment of addictive behaviors.* New York: Guilford Press.

McKay, M., & Fanning, P. (1987). *Self-Esteem.* Oakland, CA: New Harbinger.

Mitchell, J. E., Peterson, C. B. T., & Agras, W. S. (1999). Cost-effectiveness of psychotherapy for eating disorders. In N. E. Miller & K. M. Magruder (Eds.), *Cost-effectiveness of psychotherapy: A guide for practitioners, researchers, and policymakers* (pp. 270–278). New York: Oxford University Press.

Mitchell, J. E., Pyle, R. L., Pomeroy, C., Zollman, M., Crosby, R., Seim, H., Eckert, E. D., & Zimmerman, R. (1993). Cognitive-behavioral group psychotherapy of bulimia nervosa: Importance of logistical variables. *International Journal of Eating Disorders, 14,* 277–287.

Mitchell, J. E., Raymond, N., & Specker, S. (1993). A review of the controlled trials of pharmacotherapy and psychotherapy in the treatment of bulimia nervosa. *International Journal of Eating Disorders, 14,* 277–287.

Mussell, M. P., Peterson, C. B. T., Weller, C. L., Crosby, R. D., de Zwaan, M., & Mitchell, J. E. (1996). Differences in body image and depression among obese women with and without binge eating disorder. *Obesity Research, 4,* 431–439.

Peterson, C. B. (1993). *Body perception and other psychological variables as predictors of treatment outcome in bulimia nervosa.* Unpublished doctoral dissertation. University of Minnesota, Minneapolis.

Peterson, C. B., & Mitchell, J. E. (1999). Psychosocial and pharmacological treatment of eating disorders: A review of research findings. *Journal of Clinical Psychology/In Session: Psychotherapy in Practice, 55,* 685–697.

Polivy, J., & Herman, C. P. (1985). Dieting and bingeing: A causal analysis. *American Psychologist, 40,* 193–201.

Powers, P., Schulman, R. G., Gleghorn, A. A., & Prange, M. E. (1987). Perceptual and cognitive abnormalities in bulimia. *American Journal of Psychiatry, 144,* 1456–1460.

Rodin J. (1992). *Body Traps.* New York: Quill.

Rosen, J. C., & Leitenberg, H. (1985). Exposure plus response prevention treatment of bulimia nervosa. In D. M. Garner & P. E. Garfinkel (Eds.), *Handbook of psychotherapy for anorexia nervosa and bulimia* (pp. 193–212). New York: Guilford Press.

Schroeder, H. E., & Black, M. J. (1985). Unassertiveness. In H. Hersen & A. S. Bellack (Eds.), *Handbook of clinical behavior therapy with adults* (pp. 509–530). New York: Plenum Press.

Slade, P. D., & Russell, G. F. M. (1973). Awareness of body dimensions in anorexia nervosa: Cross-sectional and longitudinal studies. *Psychological Medicine, 3,* 188–199.

Sunday, S. R., Halmi, K. A., Werdann, L., & Levey, C. (1992). Comparison of body size estimation and Eating Disorder Inventory scores in anorexia and bulimic patients with obese, and restrained and unrestrained controls. *International Journal of Eating Disorders, 11,* 133–149.

Wilfley, D. E., Agras, W. S., Telch, C. F., Rossiter, E. M., Schneider, J. A., Cole, A. G., Sifford, L., & Raeburn, S. (1993). Group cognitive behavioral therapy for the nonpurging bulimic: A controlled comparison. *Journal of Consulting and Clinical Psychology, 61,* 296–305.

Wilson, G. T., Fairburn, C. G., & Agras, W. S. (1997). Cognitive-behavioral therapy for bulimia nervosa. In D. M. Garner & P. E. Garfinkel (Eds.), *Handbook of psychotherapy for anorexia nervosa and bulimia* (pp. 67–93). New York: Guilford Press.

Wolf, N. (1991). *The beauty myth: How images of beauty are used against women.* New York: Doubleday.

Yalom, I. D. (1985). *The theory and practice of group psychotherapy* (3d ed.). New York: Basic Books.

# Chapter 7

# Pharmacotherapy

*Scott Crow and James E. Mitchell*

This chapter offers concrete specific recommendations regarding the pharmacotherapy of patients with eating disorders. Although the controlled treatment database in this area has grown considerably in the past decade, many important questions remain unanswered, and thus good clinical judgment and a careful assessment of the individual patient and his or her needs are indicated. Some general guidelines can be offered, although they will require modifications in certain situations.

### Anorexia Nervosa

Anorexia nervosa is unlike many other psychiatric disorders, in that pharmacotherapy is seen as adjunctive and should only be instituted in certain cases. Many patients with anorexia nervosa will respond to outpatient treatment without pharmacotherapy, or in the case of those who are critically low in weight or particularly resistant to outpatient psychotherapy interventions, to inpatient or day hospital treatment. Medications may be considered in certain situations, however, and the following general guidelines can be offered:

1. When individuals with anorexia nervosa are quite low in weight, and early in the course of refeeding, it is probably best to avoid pharmacotherapy, for several reasons. First, it is very difficult to assess the affective state of critically low-weight anorexia nervosa patients because of the effects of starvation. It has also been noted clinically that modest amounts of weight gain during refeeding will result in dramatic changes in the affective state of anorectics. Because of these changes, it is best to reassess mood variables after the initial weight gain. Second,

because of medical issues, it is often wise not to complicate the clinical picture by adding medication unless necessary so that the assessment of any medical symptoms that develop is not confounded by the possibility of medication side effects. This caveat has been somewhat obviated by the introduction of newer antidepressant drugs with more favorable side-effect profiles, but nonetheless it is usually preferable to avoid pharmacotherapy early in the course of refeeding when possible. We also have evidence that the selective serotonin reuptake inhibitors (SSRIs), the safest agents, are probably ineffective in anorexia nervosa patients at low weight (see chapter 1).

2. In situations where certain symptoms persist beyond initial refeeding or when refeeding becomes extremely problematic because of these other symptoms, pharmacotherapy targeting depression, obsessive/compulsive features, and/or cognitive symptoms may be undertaken. Not uncommonly, what will be encountered is a combination of symptoms in an individual, who is depressed, very obsessional and ruminative, and preoccupied with body image disturbance that seems to be of delusional magnitude. In this situation, the usual pharmacotherapeutic approach is to use less anticholinergic antidepressant drugs, such as the SSRIs. The agent probably most commonly employed is fluoxetine hydrochloride, although this drug is only now being empirically studied in this clinical situation. The target symptoms in this situation are both the depression and the obsessive/compulsive symptoms, and for these symptoms, fluoxetine is often used aggressively, usually starting at 10 to 20 mg but at times increasing the dose to 40 to 60 mg if necessary. Alternative SSRIs can be considered as well. Tricyclics are much less valuable in this situation, particularly the highly anticholinergic tricyclic clomipramine, which might have much to offer in terms of its anti-obsessional characteristics but is generally not tolerated by this group of patients because of its side effects.

An alternative to be considered in treatment-resistant patients is low-dose neuroleptic therapy, particularly among those who are extremely obsessional and ruminative regarding the body image disturbance with a symptom picture that is suggestive of psychosis (although not truly psychotic). Risperidone and olanzapine or other "atypicals" appear to be preferable and should be initiated at very low dosage. Whether the effect is on the abnormal cognitions per se, on levels of anxiety, or other target variables is unclear, but such medications can be quite useful with some highly selected, treatment-resistant patients.

3. The main role for pharmacotherapy in anorexia nervosa treatment is treating obsessional and/or depressive symptoms that persist beyond refeeding and may lead to relapse. As outlined in chapter 1, the empirical literature regarding the use of maintenance antidepressants is at this point limited, with one randomized trial suggesting clear efficacy. However, clinical practice at this point suggests that strong consideration be given to using a maintenance antidepressant, such as an SSRI, in patients with anorexia nervosa, particularly in those who have persistent depressive and obsessional symptoms. The SSRI commonly employed has been fluoxetine, with aggressive dosing of 20 to 60 mg per day.

## Bulimia Nervosa

Drug therapy appears to play a more important role in bulimia nervosa than in anorexia nervosa, as outlined in chapter 2. A strong case can be made for combining antidepressant therapy with cognitive-behavioral therapy (CBT) in the treatment of bulimia nervosa when both treatments are available. An alternative approach is to initiate treatment with CBT, adding pharmacotherapy if the patient has a suboptimal response, or if depressive symptoms persist.

The only FDA-approved medication for bulimia nervosa is fluoxetine hydrochloride at a dosage of 60 mg per day. However, most antidepressants have been used in experimental trials, and most seem to be effective, with the possible exception of fluvoxamine in two multicenter unpublished trials from Europe. Also, buproprion, while effective, is usually contraindicated because of the unexplained but clearly elevated seizure risk. Desipramine has been clearly established as effective and may be the second choice after the SSRIs. Based on this discussion and the previous observations, the following recommendations can be made:

1. In situations where both treatments are clinically available and third-party reimbursement is not a significant deterrent for the patient, a combination of CBT, either group or individual, and treatment with fluoxetine hydrochloride, initiating therapy at

60 mg per day and titrating down if necessary for side effects, is the treatment of choice. An alternative is to initiate therapy with CBT and then add fluoxetine therapy in certain situations: (a) if the patient does not have a prompt response to CBT; and (b) if depressive symptoms persist despite CBT, whether or not it is effective for the eating symptoms. Drug therapy probably should be given concomitantly with CBT to individuals for whom there is clear evidence of an active affective disorder before the onset of the eating disorder and/or a strong family history of an affective disorder diathesis and current depressive symptoms.

2. Fluoxetine hydrochloride at a dose of 60 mg per day is probably the drug of choice. If this medication has been ineffective, a reasonable alternative is to switch to an alternative SSRI (sertraline, paroxetine, or citalopram), or to desipramine hydrochloride, with aggressive dosing targeting serum levels comparable to those obtained in depression treatment. Because fluoxetine will increase the desipramine level, and because fluoxetine has a long half-life, considerable care must be exercised in the transition from the SSRI to the tricyclic, and serum levels should be monitored with gradual upward dosage adjustments.

Although used rarely, monoamine oxidase inhibitors should be considered in this population, particularly for those who are unresponsive to other therapies and have an atypical depressive presentation with such symptoms as hypersomnia.

**Binge Eating Disorder**

The pharmacotherapy literature on binge eating disorder remains poorly developed at this point, and there is no clear treatment of choice. Treatment considerations with these patients are often confounded by the presence of obesity, and when considering pharmacotherapy, whether weight loss is desired (by the patient, by the doctor, or both) must be considered in making decisions regarding pharmacotherapy. The following general observations can be offered:

1. If the target symptom is the binge eating behavior, medications that have been shown to be effective for bulimia nervosa are probably effective here as well. Those best established at this point include fluvoxamine at usual antidepressant doses, and desipramine.

| Disorder | Characteristics | Recommendations |
|---|---|---|
| Anorexia nervosa | Low weight early in treatment | Avoid pharmacotherapy |
| | Low weight but very resistant to treatment | Consider SSRI (e.g., fluoxetine 10–60 mg) |
| | Marked depression Marked obsession/ compulsion | Consider alternative antidepressant |
| | Treatment-resistant | Consider neuroleptic (e.g., olanzapine, risperidone) |
| | | Consider SSRI (e.g., fluoxetine 10–60 mg) maintenance treatment |
| Bulimia nervosa | Normal weight | SSRI (fluoxetine 60 mg) Other antidepressants |
| Binge eating disorder | For binge eating For weight loss/ binge eating | Consider an SSRI Consider orlistat or sibutramine Consider phentermine and SSRI |

Figure 7.1. Recommended pharmacotherapy treatments for eating disorders.

2. If weight loss is the desired goal of the pharmacotherapy, then a combination of phentermine and an SSRI should be considered. The combination appears to be effective in inducing modest but clinically significant amounts of weight loss.

3. Although not empirically treated yet in binge eating disorder, the lipase inhibitor orlistat, and the mixed serotonin/ norepinephrine reuptake inhibitor sibutramine should also be strongly considered.

Chapter 8

# Treatment Implications of Comorbid Personality Disorders

*David W. Abbott, Stephen A. Wonderlich, and James E. Mitchell*

Clinicians who work with patients with eating disorders have often been puzzled by the fact that although patients at times seem to have similar levels of eating disorder pathology, in terms of frequency of binge eating and vomiting in bulimia nervosa or amount of weight loss in anorexia nervosa, they may experience widely divergent clinical courses and patterns of outcome. One possible explanation for these divergent courses is the presence of certain underlying personality traits and, in some patients, underlying personality disorders. When such an underlying problem is present, it is reasonable to assume that the personality disorder may complicate the course of the eating disorder and at times may preclude complete recovery from the problem. This chapter will focus on the conceptualization of personality disorders in individuals with eating disorders, summarize the research findings, and in particular focus on the implications of this comorbid problem for treatment.

Any discussion of the implications of comorbid personality disorder for the outcome of eating disorders must first consider the substantial problems that exist in the conceptualization and assessment of personality disorders. Although we will summarize some of these issues, for a more complete overview of this topic, interested readers are referred to several recent reviews: Vitousek & Manke, 1994; Wonderlich, 1996; Wonderlich & Mitchell, 1992; Zimmerman, 1994. First, there are important debates concerning the definition of personality disorders. It is not clear whether it is more useful and accurate to conceptualize disordered personality as falling into discrete pathological entities, as done in the DSM system, or to regard the disorders as a complex of normal personality traits that can be measured and described. If such conceptualization is uncertain, then it follows that the clinical assessment of personality disorders will be difficult, and such is indeed the case. Single, cross-sectional assessment using clinical interviews is generally regarded as the least reliable but most commonly used assessment method (Zimmerman, 1994). Self-report measures of personality consistently overestimate rates of personality disorder diagnosis when compared to semistructured interviews (Wonderlich & Mitchell, 1992), and both often result in several personality disorder diagnoses in the same individual (Powers, Coovert, Brightwell, & Stevens, 1988). Use of collateral informants, such as family members and friends, may add to the reliability (Widiger, 1993), but this approach is considerably more demanding and is often impractical. Presently, semistructured interviews, such as the Structured Clinical Interview for DSM-IV Personality Disorder (SCID-IV), the Structured Interview for DSM-III-R-Personality (SIDP-R), or the Personality Disorder Examination (PDE) may offer the best compromise.

Additional difficulties in conceptualization and assessment arise from the common features between eating disorders and personality disorders. In particular the effects of semistarvation and the symptoms of depression may mimic personality problems. Many of the symptoms of personality disorders, including moodiness, irritability, frequent outbursts of anger, apathy, and personal neglect, may be attributable to the effects of semistarvation. These effects can also simulate all three clusters of DSM-IV personality disorders, including the odd behaviors, humorlessness, and social isolation associated with Cluster A (odd-eccentric); the emotional instability and distress, angry outbursts, and erratic behavior associated with Cluster B (dramatic-emotional-erratic); or the social anxiety, avoidance, and inflexibility associated with Cluster C (anxious-fearful). As noted, the symptoms of depression may also accompany eating disorders and may contribute to the apparent presence of a personality disorder.

Other features of eating disorder symptomatology may overlap with personality disorders, including the impulsivity and affective instability criteria of borderline personality disorder that parallel the binge eating and affective shifts associated with bulimia nervosa (Levin & Hyler, 1986; Piran, Lerner, Garfinkel, Kennedy, & Brouillette, 1988; Pope, Frankenburg, Hudson, Jonas, & Yurgelun-Todd, 1987). Additional symptoms such as stealing (Casper, Eckert, Halmi, Goldberg, & Davis, 1980; Garfinkel, Moldofsky, & Garner, 1980; Krahn, Nairn, Gosnell, & Drewnowski, 1991; Pyle, Mitchell, & Eckert, 1981; Weiss & Ebert, 1983) and substance abuse (Bulik, 1987; Garfinkel et al., 1980; Hudson, Pope, Yurgelun-Todd, Jonas, & Frankenburg, 1987; Mitchell, Hatsukami,

Eckert, & Pyle, 1985; Pyle et al., 1981; Weiss & Ebert, 1983), which often accompany bulimia nervosa, also qualify as impulsive behaviors and together with binge eating, easily meet the criteria of at least two areas of potentially self-damaging activity seen in borderline personality disorder. Thus, the symptoms of an eating disorder often result in the fulfillment of particular criteria for borderline personality disorder and may contribute to the appearance of a comorbid relationship, which may be in fact artifactual.

Another problem in assessing personality disorders pertains to the age at which patients present with eating disorders, since the clinical assessment of personality during adolescence is problematic due to the incomplete development of many of the intra- and interpersonal characteristics on which the assessment of personality is based. Generally, personality disorder diagnosis in adolescents who are currently symptomatic should be avoided.

It is apparent from the foregoing discussion that the implications of the relationship between personality disorders and eating disorders are not a simple matter. There are marked concerns about the validity of the conceptualization and reliability of the assessment of personality disorders in general, and these problems are multiplied when one is dealing with the population of individuals with eating disorders.

### Prevalence of Comorbid Personality Disorders

Because of the aforementioned problems associated with self-report measures, we will focus on the results of studies that employed semistructured interviews to estimate the prevalence of eating disorders and personality disorders as comorbid conditions. Rates vary according to inpatient versus outpatient status, albeit most of the investigations have involved outpatients. Overall, estimates of the frequency with which personality disorders accompany an eating disorder range from 27% to 72% (Herzog, Keller, Lavori, Kenny, & Sacks, 1992; Wonderlich, Swift, Slotnick, & Goodman, 1990). Rates for specific eating disorder subtypes range from 23% to 80% for anorexia nervosa, 21% to 77% for bulimia nervosa, and 35% to 70% for anorexia nervosa–bulimic subtype (Herzog et al., 1992; Powers et al., 1988; Wonderlich et al., 1990). One recent semistructured interview study of binge eating disorder reported a rate of 35% (Yanovski, Nelson, Dubbert, & Spitzer, 1993).

The results of studies examining diagnostic rates for specific personality disorders and various eating disorder subtypes suggest that Cluster A diagnoses were made less often than those of Cluster B and C (see Table 8.1). Besides showing a tendency toward a lower frequency of personality disorders overall, patients with anorexia nervosa show more of the Cluster C diagnoses than do patients with bulimia nervosa, who tend to manifest more Cluster B diagnoses. Patients with the binge-purge subtype of anorexia nervosa tend to exhibit more of an admixture of Cluster B and C diagnoses. Two studies that use self-report measures (Raymond, Mussell, Crosby, de Zwaan, & Mitchell, 1995; Specker, de Zwaan, Mitchell, & Raymond, 1992) combined with a study by Yanovski et al. (1993) suggest that binge eating disorder patients also show more of a mixture of personality symptoms from Cluster B and C.

## Clinical Features of Eating Disorders Associated with Personality Disorders

Examinations of the clinical features of eating disordered individuals with any comorbid personality disorder have enlisted predominantly outpatients with bulimia nervosa, mixed, or unspecified eating disorder subtypes (Ames-Frankel et al., 1992; Herzog et al., 1992; Johnson, Tobin, & Dennis, 1990; Johnson, Tobin, & Enright, 1989; Wonderlich & Swift, 1990; Yates, Sieleni, & Bowers, 1989). These studies suggest that patients with comorbid eating and personality disorders may have been ill for a longer period of time prior to seeking treatment than their non–eating disorder counterparts, but in general do not appear to have significant differences in age of onset of binge eating and vomiting or in frequency of pathological eating behaviors such as binge eating, vomiting, or laxative abuse. The group with personality disorder diagnoses generally scored higher on measures of eating-related attitudes and behaviors, however.

Cluster B personality features have been of considerable interest in this population, and several studies have examined the clinical features of eating disorders associated with Cluster B personality disorder diagnoses (Johnson et al., 1989; Johnson et al., 1990; Wonderlich & Swift, 1990). Results indicate that borderline and non–borderline personality disorder groups do not differ in age of onset of the eating disorder, but there is some suggestion in this literature that the duration of the eating disorder at the time of evaluation may be longer for the borderline group. Eating disorder patients with borderline personality disorder scored higher on measures of disturbed eating attitudes, but the non-borderline patients engaged in more controlled dieting. There were no differences in current weight or previous high or low weight, or percentage of normal

Table 8.1. Personality Disorder Diagnosis Frequencies by Eating Disorder Subtype from Studies Using Semistructured Interviews (%)

| | N | Par | Szd | Szl | Ant | Bor | His | Nar | Avo | Dep | Obs | Pas | Any |
|---|---|---|---|---|---|---|---|---|---|---|---|---|---|
| **Anorexia nervosa** | | | | | | | | | | | | | |
| Gartner et al., 1989 | 6 | 17 | 0 | 17 | 0 | 33 | 0 | 17 | 33 | 17 | 17 | 0 | 33 |
| Herzog et al., 1992 | 31 | 3 | 0 | 0 | 0 | 0 | 0 | 0 | 10 | 3 | 10 | 0 | 23 |
| Wonderlich et al., 1990 | 10 | 0 | 0 | 10 | 0 | 20 | 20 | 0 | 20 | 40 | 60 | 0 | 80 |
| **Bulimia nervosa** | | | | | | | | | | | | | |
| Ames-Frankel et al., 1992 | 83 | 4 | 0 | 2 | 0 | 23 | 10 | 7 | 11 | 12 | 4 | 1 | 32 |
| Gartner et al., 1989 | 8 | 0 | 0 | 0 | 0 | 38 | 12 | 12 | 25 | 38 | 0 | 25 | 62 |
| Herzog et al., 1992 | 91 | 2 | 0 | 2 | 0 | 8 | 7 | 1 | 2 | 1 | 3 | 0 | 21 |
| McCann et al., 1991 | 19 | 0 | nr | 0 | 0 | 16 | 16 | 16 | 16 | 16 | 21 | 5 | nr |
| Powers et al., 1988 | 30 | 27 | 7 | nr | 20 | 23 | 53 | 10 | 10 | nr | 333 | 10 | 77 |
| Wonderlich et al., 1990 | 16 | 0 | 0 | 0 | 0 | 19 | 31 | 0 | 19 | 19 | 13 | 13 | 69 |
| Zanarini et al., 1990 | 34 | 12 | 3 | 3 | 3 | 35 | 12 | 3 | 18 | 9 | 9 | 15 | 50 |
| **Anorexia nervosa/bulimia nervosa** | | | | | | | | | | | | | |
| Gartner et al., 1989 | 21 | 0 | 0 | 5 | 0 | 33 | 5 | 10 | 33 | 19 | 38 | 5 | 62 |
| Herzog et al., 1992 | 88 | 2 | 1 | 2 | 2 | 12 | 7 | 0 | 7 | 6 | 4 | 1 | 35 |
| Wonderlich et al., 1990 | 10 | 0 | 0 | 0 | 0 | 20 | 0 | 0 | 60 | 40 | 0 | 0 | 70 |
| **Binge eating disorder** | | | | | | | | | | | | | |
| Yanovski et al., 1993 | 43 | 0 | 0 | 0 | 0 | 14 | 0 | 0 | 9 | 0 | 7 | 0 | 35 |

*Note:* Par = paranoid; Szd = schizoid; Szl = schizotypal; Ant = antisocial; Bor = borderline; His = histrionic; Nar = narcissistic; Avo = avoidant; Dep = dependent; Obs = obsessive-compulsive; Pas = passive-aggressive; Any = any personality disorder diagnosis; nr = not reported.

weight or ideal body weight. Although binge eating frequency did not differ between borderline and non-borderline groups, reports of purging behavior were mixed, with available studies finding either no difference or higher rates of laxative abuse and vomiting in the borderline group.

Outcome studies and treatment response studies suggest that the course of eating disorder symptoms is significantly influenced by the presence of Cluster B personality features or borderline personality disturbance. For example, several studies suggest that the presence of borderline personality disorder predicts negative eating disorder status at two- and five-year outcome (Steiger & Stotland, 1996; Wonderlich, Fullerton, Swift, & Klein, 1994), particularly if the personality disorder is stable over time (Steiger, Stotland, & Houle, 1994). Furthermore, borderline personality disorder not only predicts negative outcome in terms of eating disorder symptoms but also regarding general psychopathology status in eating disordered individuals (Johnson et al., 1990; Steiger & Stotland, 1996; Wonderlich et al., 1994). Supporting these reports, similar findings were found using a different methodology, which assesses borderline-level ego functions rather than the concept of borderline personality disorder (Norring, 1993).

### Implications for Treatment

The results of the studies that have examined the association of personality disorder with treatment outcome give a mixed picture. The initial presence of *any* personality disorder diagnosis does not predict remission in bulimic patients (Zanarini, Frankenburg, Pope, Yurgelun-Todd, & Cicchetti, 1990), and comorbid personality disorder of any type does not predict binge eating and purging frequency at follow-up (Ames-Frankel et al., 1992; Edelstein, Yager, Gitlin, & Landsverk, 1989; Wonderlich et al., 1994). However, when outcome was defined by a combination of eating disorder symptoms and scores on an eating disorder scale, personality disorder patients had fewer good outcomes and more poor outcomes at five-year follow-up than a non–personality disorder group (Wonderlich et al., 1994).

Although investigations of eating disorder outcome associated with DSM-III-R cluster diagnoses are limited, a few studies have examined the effect of Cluster B comorbidity, specifically of borderline personality disorder. In an uncontrolled treatment outcome study, 62% of borderline personality disordered patients still met criteria for bulimia nervosa at one-year follow-up, while this was true of only 21% of the non–borderline personality disordered subjects (Johnson et al., 1990). Other studies suggested that the presence of borderline personality disorder, or any Cluster B personality pathology, predicts a poorer outcome from individual and group therapy (Herzog, Hartmann, Sandholz, & Stammer, 1991), cognitive-behavioral therapy (Rossiter, Agras, Telch, & Schneider, 1993), and pharmacotherapy (Rossiter et al., 1993). Another study of the effectiveness of cognitive-behavioral therapy for bulimia nervosa found that patients with diagnosable borderline personality disorder at both pre- and post-treatment showed less symptomatic improvement in eating disorder symptoms than other subjects (Pyle, Mitchell, & Callies, 1990).

In considering the implications of these data, it may be most useful to discuss personality disorder clusters, since research addressing each of the personality disorders individually is lacking, and since there tends to be a great deal of overlap between the conditions within a cluster.

### Cluster A: Odd-Eccentric

Individuals with prominent Cluster A characteristics (paranoid, schizoid, and schizotypal) tend to be distrustful, guarded, emotionally restricted, interpersonally removed, and odd or eccentric in their ideas, behaviors, and appearance. They have difficulty engaging in a therapeutic alliance, which is often thought necessary for successful psychotherapy. Since they represent a smaller proportion of eating disorder patients than the other two clusters, this group will be dealt with more briefly.

Given the paucity of research in this area, we can speculate that the patients with Cluster A personality disorders may approach treatment in a more guarded fashion. This may present special problems if the approach used relies on self-disclosure. The latter may include many forms of therapy, including cognitive-behavioral, interpersonal, and psychodynamic. Problems with these patients might be particularly manifest in a group therapy setting, where their eccentricity or suspiciousness may set them apart. Theoretically they might benefit more from approaches that rely less on interpersonal process, such as treatments that focus on psychoeducation and nutritional management, which are more instructional and relatively impersonal. The clinician needs to carefully monitor the quality of the therapeutic alliance and discuss openly any problems that arise.

### Cluster B: Dramatic, Emotional, Erratic

It is well known that individuals with Cluster B personality traits or disorders (antisocial, borderline, histrionic, and narcissistic) frequently demand attention by their dramatic presentation and marked difficulties sustaining any kind of stable positive view of themselves, and that they tend to have turbulent relationships. They tend to be very labile, with angry outbursts, and may be impulsive and erratic in their behavior. They also have marked difficulty in establishing a therapeutic alliance. The treatment course for such patients may be marked by unreasonable demands for praise or reassurance, hostile attacks on the therapist, breech of agreed-on norms and limits in the therapeutic process, and frequently late or missed appointments. Therefore, working with these patients requires a great deal of patience on the part of the therapist and at times a firm confrontational approach.

Johnson et al. (1990) found that eating disorder patients with a concurrent borderline personality disorder demonstrated less overall improvement at one-year follow-up compared to non-borderline patients. They also found, however, that improvement in borderline patients was correlated with the frequency of the sessions, in that these patients seem to benefit more from intensive treatment. Another study suggests that borderline personality patients display lower levels of engagement in cognitive-behavioral therapy for bulimia nervosa (Coker, Vize, Wade, & Cooper, 1993).

Dennis and Sansone (1990) have described a psychodynamically oriented treatment of eating disorder patients with borderline features that incorporates both interpersonal and cognitive-behavioral techniques. The approach focuses heavily on the patient's underlying personality disturbance and places minimal emphasis on change of eating behavior until the therapeutic alliance has been established. There is also a significant emphasis on self-destructive behavior. Empirical examination of the effectiveness of this approach has not been published.

New cognitive and interpersonal models of personality disorder (Benjamin, 1993; Linehan, 1993) highlight the role that particular cognitive patterns have in promoting and maintaining the unstable behavior of these patients. In particular, Linehan's emphasis on attempting to integrate cognitive patterns through dialectical reasoning may be helpful with these patients. The strategy centers on the idea that for every topic, opposite statements are possible. Dialectical reasoning encourages a synthesis of such opposite statements. There is also a strong emphasis on explicit identification of affects, cognitive restructuring surrounding affective experiences, and behavioral activities that directly contradict negative affective arousal, such as the use of relaxation techniques. Linehan's work also suggests that individuals with high levels of Cluster B disturbance may benefit from group settings. This observation must be balanced by the fact that the individual with severe borderline type disturbance may be very disruptive to heterogeneous groups of eating disorder patients, most of whom do not have severe personality disturbance.

### Cluster C: Anxious, Fearful

Individuals with Cluster C traits or disorders (avoidant, dependent, or obsessive-compulsive) tend to be very anxious or fearful in a variety of contexts ranging from social interactions, to being alone, to receiving criticism or disapproval. They often procrastinate, avoid tasks that will involve social functions, tend to be passive and perfectionistic, and rely heavily on authority figures and the approval of others.

The consequences of this personality disorder cluster relative to eating disorder treatment have not been systematically studied. However, it is reasonable to assume that amelioration of more severe symptoms may be necessary before the successful treatment of the eating disorder patient may proceed. For example, when highly moralistic forms of obsessive-compulsive personality disorder coexist with anorexia nervosa and result in severe self-criticism and a sense of moral inferiority, some degree of cognitive restructuring may be necessary before patients can allow themselves to proceed in therapy.

In considering different therapies for different patients, it is reasonable to assume that cognitive therapies may be most acceptable for more-obsessional eating disorder patients, while avoidant or dependent patients may do better with a more interpersonal focus. The choice whether to employ group or individual formats may vary. Highly avoidant or interpersonally anxious people may have great difficulty in groups, for example.

### Case Discussion

Kim, a 24-year-old female of Asian background who was adopted, presented to the outpatient clinic with symptoms of bulimia nervosa. At the time of intake she was binge eating and self-inducing vomiting several times a day. She had abused laxatives for weight-control purposes in the past and had intermittently used over-the-counter diet pills. She had experimented with Ipecac® but did not like the effect of the drug. She had previously had a problem with chemical dependency (i.e., alcohol abuse), but this was inactive. She was working part-time as a waitress and going to school part-time.

She had moved out of the family home one year ago, and at that time her eating behavior worsened dramatically. Binge eating episodes usually took place in early morning or evening and lasted from one to two hours. She was very worried about the possibility of gaining weight.

Currently, Kim was experiencing several other problems. She described numerous symptoms of depression, including a sense of sadness, lethargy, lack of energy, and hopelessness about her future. She also had recurrent thoughts of suicide and a history of frequent parasuicidal behaviors in the form of wrist and forearm scratching and cutting.

She described significant problems with her family. Her mother had experienced a significant depression during Kim's adolescence, and during that time, as Kim described it, she "ran the family." The relationship with her father had been very antagonistic. She denied a history of sexual abuse but acknowledged she had been struck by her father on several occasions during arguments. Kim said she had a boyfriend named Bill, but the relationship sounded highly conflictual. She felt that he had coerced her into sexual activity a year ago, and now she was trying to avoid him. She was bitter and angry about the relationship, although she maintained contact with him.

Kim was originally treated with fluoxetine 60 mg per day and individual psychotherapy using a cognitive-behavioral approach. She experienced minimal symptomatic improvement after two months and began to develop a variety of physical complaints including fatigue and gastrointestinal distress. The family brought her to the emergency room one night when she was unable to get out of bed because of her symptoms, but the medical workup was negative. At that point, she was placed in a partial hospital program, but then she began to exhibit more self-destructive behavior in the form of wrist and forearm cutting and increased thoughts of death and suicide. She was briefly admitted to the inpatient unit and after restabilization transferred back to outpatient treatment. At that time she resumed laxative abuse (20 to 30 Ex-lax® per day) and also began using alcohol and marijuana heavily.

Kim was displaying the pervasive instability that one would anticipate in someone with a Cluster B (i.e., borderline) personality disturbance. Effective treatment of her eating disorder symptoms is likely to depend on the ability to provide some structure that will help reduce the multiple areas of instability she exhibits. First, a clear treatment contract should be devised in which certain self-destructive behaviors call for appropriate responses and contingencies. For example, it is important to formulate a contract in which she agrees to cease taking Ipecac® and to stop engaging in any other behaviors that might be lethal. Other behaviors, such as vomiting or superficial wrist cutting, should be discouraged but not prohibited in the contract. Helping Kim to control the most serious behaviors while accepting and tolerating other behaviors is essential. Also, contingencies need to be derived for admission to partial hospital or inpatient treatment. Second, a clear evaluation of her substance use and likely recommendations for chemical dependency treatment should be initiated. It may be difficult for her to make any progress on her bulimic symptomatology as long as she is actively using alcohol and marijuana excessively. Third, psychotherapy for Kim may beneficially focus on her problematic interpersonal relationships and most likely her extreme difficulty being alone. It may be fruitful to examine her relationship to her boyfriend and the interpersonal patterns that have emerged in that relationship. Helping her to develop a more autonomous and assertive interpersonal style may be most beneficial given her tendency to act out conflicts in relationships rather than to discuss them in the context of the relationship. Fourth, a thorough evaluation of her pharmacotherapy should be initiated to determine if particular agents (e.g., low-dose neuroleptics, monoamine oxidase inhibitors, carbamazapine, or adjustments in her fluoxetine protocol) should be introduced. Fifth, regular meetings of her treatment providers may facilitate a cohesive treatment for Kim, which will undoubtedly be strained by her emotional and behavioral instability and acting-out behaviors. It is possible that her treatment will be relatively long-term with marked ups and downs. It will be important to look for signs of increasing levels of self-dysregulation, perhaps in behaviors other than her eating disorder symptoms. Unfortunately, her eating disorder symptoms may be less lethal than other behaviors and consequently may need to be tolerated if she continues to show stability in other areas of her life.

### References

Ames-Frankel, J., Devlin, M. J., Walsh, B. T., Strasser, T. J., Sadick, C., Oldham, J. M., & Roose, S. P. (1992). Personality disorder diagnoses in patients with bulimia nervosa: Clinical correlates and changes with treatment. *Journal of Clinical Psychiatry, 53,* 90–96.

Benjamin, L. S. (1993). *Interpersonal treatment of personality disorders.* New York: Guilford.

Bulik, C. M. (1987). Drug and alcohol abuse by bulimic women and their families. *American Journal of Psychiatry, 144,* 1604–1606.

Casper, R. C., Eckert, E. D., Halmi, K. A., Goldberg, S. C., & Davis, J. M. (1980.) Bulimia: Its incidence and clinical importance in patients with anorexia nervosa. *Archives of General Psychiatry, 37,* 1030–1035.

Coker, S., Vize, C., Wade, T., & Cooper, P. J. (1993). Patients with bulimia nervosa who fail to engage in cognitive behavior therapy. *International Journal of Eating Disorders, 13,* 35–40.

Dennis, A. B., & Sansone, R. A. (1990). The clinical stages of treatment for the eating disorder patient with borderline personality. In C. Johnson (Ed.), *Psychodynamic treatment of anorexia and bulimia nervosa* (pp. 128–164). New York: Guilford Press.

Edelstein, C. K., Yager, J., Gitlin, M., & Landsverk, J. (1989). A clinical study of anti-depressant medications in the treatment of bulimia. *Psychiatric Medicine, 7,* 111–121.

Garfinkel, P. E., Moldofsky, H., & Garner, D. M. (1980). The heterogeneity of anorexia nervosa: Bulimia as a distinct subgroup. *Archives of General Psychiatry, 37,* 1036–1040.

Gartner, A. F., Marcus, R. N., Halmi, K., & Loranger, A. W. (1989). DSM-III-R personality disorders in patients with eating disorders. *American Journal of Psychiatry, 146,* 1585–1591.

Herzog, D. B., Keller, M. B., Lavori, P. W., Kenny, G. M., & Sacks, N. R. (1992). The prevalence of personality disorders in 210 women with eating disorders. *Journal of Clinical Psychiatry, 53,* 147–152.

Herzog, T. A., Hartmann, A., Sandholz, A., & Stammer, H. (1991). Prognostic factors in outpatient psychotherapy of bulimia. *Psychotherapy and Psychosomatics, 56,* 48–55.

Hudson, J. I., Pope, H. G., Yurgelun-Todd, D., Jonas, J. M., & Frankenburg, F. R. (1987). A controlled study of lifetime prevalence of affective and other psychiatric disorders in bulimic outpatients. *American Journal of Psychiatry, 144,* 1283–1287.

Johnson, C., Tobin, D. L., & Dennis, A. (1990). Differences in treatment outcome between borderline and non-borderline bulimics at one-year follow-up. *International Journal of Eating Disorders, 9,* 617–627.

Johnson, C., Tobin, D., & Enright, A. (1989). Prevalence and clinical characteristics of borderline patients in an eating-disordered population. *Journal of Clinical Psychiatry, 50,* 9–15.

Krahn, D. D., Nairn, K., Gosnell, B. A., & Drewnowski, A. (1991). Stealing in eating disordered patients. *Journal of Clinical Psychiatry, 52,* 112–115.

Levin, A. P., & Hyler, S. E. (1986). DSM-III personality diagnosis in bulimia. *Comprehensive Psychiatry, 27,* 47–53.

Linehan, M. M. (1993). *Cognitive behavioral therapy for borderline personality disorder.* New York: Guilford.

McCann, U. D., Rossiter, E. M., King, R. J., & Agras, W. S. (1991). Non-purging bulimia: A distinct subtype of bulimia nervosa. *International Journal of Eating Disorders, 10,* 679–687.

Mitchell, J. E., Hatsukami, D., Eckert, E. D., & Pyle, R. L. (1985). Characteristics of 275 patients with bulimia. *American Journal of Psychiatry, 142,* 482–485.

Norring, C. (1993). Borderline personality organization and prognosis in eating disorders. *Psychoanalytic Psychology, 10,* 551–572.

Piran, N., Lerner, P., Garfinkel, P. E., Kennedy, S. H., & Brouillette, C. (1988). Personality disorders in anorexic patients. *International Journal of Eating Disorders, 7,* 589–599.

Pope, H. G., Frankenburg, F. R., Hudson, J. I., Jonas, J. M., & Yurgelun-Todd, D. (1987). Is bulimia associated with borderline personality disorder? A controlled study. *Journal of Clinical Psychiatry, 48,* 181–184.

Powers, P. S., Coovert, D. L., Brightwell, D. R., & Stevens, B. A. (1988). Other psychiatric disorders among bulimic patients. *Comprehensive Psychiatry, 29,* 503–508.

Pyle, R. L., Mitchell, J. E., & Callies, A. (1990, May). *Bulimia nervosa treatment and borderline personality symptoms.* Paper presented at the 143d Annual Meeting of the American Psychiatric Association, New York.

Pyle, R. L., Mitchell, J. E., & Eckert, E. D. (1981). Bulimia: A report of 34 cases. *Journal of Clinical Psychiatry, 42,* 60–64.

Raymond, N., Mussell, M., Crosby, R., de Zwaan, M., & Mitchell, J. E. (1995). *Comparison of personality characteristics and psychopathology in patients with binge eating disorder and bulimia nervosa.* Unpublished manuscript.

Rossiter, E. M., Agras, W. S., Telch, C. F., & Schneider, J. A. (1993). Cluster B personality disorder characteristics predict outcome in treatment of bulimia nervosa. *International Journal of Eating Disorders, 13,* 349–357.

Specker, S., de Zwaan, M., Mitchell, J. E., & Raymond, N. (1992, April). *Psychopathology in obese women with binge eating disorder.* Paper presented at the 5th International Conference on Eating Disorders, New York.

Spitzer, R. L., Williams, J. B. W., Gibbon, M., & First, M. B. (1988). *The Structured Clinical Interview for DSM–III–R.* New York: New York State Psychiatric Institute.

Steiger, H., & Stotland, S. (1996). Prospective study of outcome in bulimics as a function of Axis-II comorbidity: Long-term responses on eating and psychiatric symptoms. *International Journal of Eating Disorders, 20,* 149–161.

Steiger, H., Stotland, S., & Houle, L. (1994). Prognostic implication of "stable" versus "transient" borderline features in bulimic patients. *Journal of Clinical Psychiatry, 55,* 206–214.

Vitousek, K., & Manke, F. (1994). Personality variables and disorders in AN and BN. *Journal of Abnormal Psychology, 103,* 137–147.

Weiss, S. R., & Ebert, M. H. (1983). Psychological and behavioral characteristics of normal-weight bulimics and normal-weight controls.
*Psychosomatic Medicine, 45,* 293–303.

Widiger, T. A. (1993). Personality and depression: Assessment issues. In
M. H. Klein, D. J. Kupfer, & M. T. Shea (Eds.), *Personality and depression:
A current view* (pp. 77–133). New York: Guilford Press.

Wonderlich, S. A. (1996). Personality and eating disorders. In K. D. Brownell
& C. Fairburn (Eds.), *Comprehensive textbook of eating disorders and
obesity.* New York: Guilford Press.

Wonderlich, S. A., Fullerton, D., Swift, W. J., & Klein, M. H. (1994). Five-
year outcome from eating disorders: The relevance of personality
disorders. *International Journal of Eating Disorders, 15,* 233–243.

Wonderlich, S. A., & Mitchell, J. E. (1992). Eating disorders and personality
disorders. In J. Yager, H. E. Gwirtsman, & C. K. Edelstein (Eds.), *Special
problems in managing eating disorders* (pp. 51–86). Washington, DC:
American Psychiatric Press.

Wonderlich, S. A., & Swift, W. J. (1990). Borderline versus other personality
disorders in the eating disorders: Clinical description. *International
Journal of Eating Disorders, 9,* 629–638.

Wonderlich, S. A., Swift, W. J., Slotnick, H. B., & Goodman, S. (1990).
DSM-III-R personality disorders in eating-disorder subtypes.
*International Journal of Eating Disorders, 9,* 607–616.

Yanovski, S. Z., Nelson, J. E., Dubbert, B. K., & Spitzer, R. L. (1993).
Association of binge eating disorder and psychiatric comorbidity in obese
subjects. *American Journal of Psychiatry, 150,* 1472–1479.

Yates, W. R., Sieleni, B., & Bowers, W. A. (1989). Clinical correlates of
personality disorder in bulimia nervosa. *International Journal of Eating
Disorders, 8,* 473–477.

Zanarini, M. C., Frankenburg, F. R., Pope, H. G., Hudson, J. I., Yurgelun-
Todd, D., & Cicchetti, C. J. (1990). Axis II comorbidity of normal-
weight bulimia. *Comprehensive Psychiatry, 30,* 20–24.

Zimmerman, M. (1994). Diagnosing personality disorders. *Archives of
General Psychiatry, 51,* 225–245.

Chapter 9

# Working with Families

*Susan Jack*

"She is living on lettuce and popcorn. How can we get her to eat?"

"I know that she is vomiting and using laxatives. Should I say anything?"

"When we try to tempt her with her favorite foods, she cries and gets mad."

"I know it is crazy, but the only way to keep food in the house is to lock the refrigerator and cupboards."

"He says he wants me to stop him from overeating, but then I find him sneaking food!"

An individual's eating disorder affects many other people. Therapists and dietitians working with patients with anorexia nervosa, bulimia nervosa, and binge eating disorder are frequently contacted by family members who express concern, ask for help and guidance in dealing with the problem, and directly or indirectly seek support for themselves. Even when they do not initiate the contact, they usually welcome an opportunity to be involved in the treatment process. Family involvement ranges from receiving information about the eating disorder to participating in formal family therapy.

In addition to providing general information about working with the families of individuals with anorexia nervosa, bulimia nervosa, and binge eating disorder, this chapter will focus on how professionals can help families respond to the "practical" problems they encounter as they deal with the peculiar cognitions and confusing behaviors commonly manifested by individuals with eating disorders. When possible, theory underlying the conceptualization of a problem and intervention will be identified and briefly discussed; however, it is beyond the scope of this chapter to present a comprehensive review of the literature currently available on the theories and techniques of working with "eating disorder families." The reader is referred to the reference list and other resources for further information about theory and research findings.

## Family Assessment and Interventions

### Assessment

According to Bologna (1983), the family therapist's assessment should include both a clinical understanding of the patient and an evaluation of the characteristics and functioning of the family. It is necessary to know the age of the patient (both chronological and functional), the type of eating disorder, the duration of the problem, and the severity of the illness. Because an estimated 20% to 50% of eating disorder patients have experienced some kind of sexual abuse (Pope & Hudson, 1992), it is also important to include questions about abuse history in the individual assessment.

Andersen's (1985) criteria for assessment of the family are (1) interactional patterns, (2) flexibility, (3) sensitivity, (4) family supports and stresses, (5) performance of stage-appropriate tasks, and (6) family knowledge of the illness. To assess interactional patterns, the therapist examines the affective climate of the family, the degree of parental agreement on parenting issues, and alliances within the family. Flexibility is evaluated by the ease with which members move in and out of roles, change plans when necessary, and modify their communication patterns to fit the needs of the family. Sensitivity is measured by how well the family balances concern and support with approval of age-appropriate independence. An assessment of family supports and stresses includes evaluation of the family's work and financial situations, other health concerns, availability of supportive friends and relatives, and so on. One of the most important areas of assessment is evaluation of the performance of developmentally appropriate tasks, that is, the age and stage appropriateness of rights and responsibilities in the family. Assessment of the family's interpretation of the patient's behavior and knowledge about eating disorders helps the therapist to know what education is needed.

### Education

Education about eating disorders serves to reduce anxiety about and reactivity to unpredictable and frustrating eating disorder behaviors. The

| Family characteristic | Assessed through evaluation of: |
|---|---|
| Interactional patterns | Affective climate of the family |
| | Degree of parental agreement on parenting issues |
| | Alliances within the family |
| Flexibility | Ease of role transition |
| | Ability to change plans |
| | Ability to modify communication patterns |
| Sensitivity | Balance of concern/support and age-appropriate independence |
| Supports and stresses | Work and financial situations |
| | Other health concerns |
| | Availability of supportive friends and relatives |
| Performance of developmentally appropriate tasks | Age- and stage-appropriateness of rights |
| | Age- and stage-appropriateness of responsibilities |
| Family knowledge of illness | Family's interpretation of patient's behavior |
| | Families knowledge about eating disorders |

Figure 9.1. Anderson's criteria for family assessment.

more families understand about the etiology, prognosis, physiological and psychological symptoms, treatment process, and expectations of the family during treatment, the more helpful they will be. Family education can be provided in a group setting as a component of a multimodal treatment program, offered to an individual's family as an adjunct to the patient's individual or group treatment, or incorporated into ongoing family therapy (Slagerman & Yager, 1989).

Often, family members have already gathered information from books and television, received advice (both solicited and unwelcome) from relatives and friends, and developed their own theories and plans about how to manage the eating disorder behavior. It is important to ask what family members already know and believe about the eating disorder so that the therapist can understand the context in which they have been making decisions, assess roles in the family and identify important figures such as an influential grandparent or friend, make a general assessment of cognitive functioning, and begin to correct misinformation and "fill in" information gaps.

Families need information about the physiological side effects of eating disorders that result from significant weight loss or the particular method(s) of weight control (Anderson et al., 1992; Mitchell, Specker, & de Zwaan, 1991; Yates, 1989). The medical complications of anorexia nervosa include amenorrhea (absence of menstrual cycle), osteopenia (weakening of bones), slowed heart rate and other cardiac problems, decreased body temperature and blood pressure, hair loss, dry skin, lanugo (fine hair growth on the body), and sensitivity to cold. The most serious and life-threatening side effects are generally related to impaired cardiac functioning. Bulimia nervosa causes the effects of malnutrition as well as swelling of the parotid glands and erosion of tooth enamel, and it can cause gastric and esophageal bleeding and electrolyte imbalance. The risk of serious physiological problems increases dramatically with use of laxatives and Ipecac®, an over-the-counter emetic. The physiological problems associated with binge eating disorder are those of obesity and its complications.

There is controversy about whether eating disorder patients have predictable premorbid personality characteristics. There is agreement, however, that the individual undergoes dramatic changes in personality and behavior as the disorder progresses (Dennis & Sansone, 1994; Fairburn, 1993; Kinoy, 1984). Families must often confront provocative behavior they have never experienced before. In addition to radical changes in the patient's thinking and behavior, family members are expected to change their own eating habits, daily routines, and vacation plans to accommodate the "needs" of the person with the eating disorder (Levine, 1996).

The psychological effects of anorexia nervosa include impaired concentration, decision making, and judgment; mood changes including irritability, depression, and anxiety; apathy, reclusiveness, and social isolation; an increase in perfectionism and neatness; and secretiveness and dishonesty (Byrne, 1987; Jablow, 1992). In addition to all of these problems, patients who binge and vomit may also experience rapid mood swings and exhibit problems of poor impulse control such as chemical abuse, shoplifting, and sexual promiscuity (Fairburn, 1993; Pope & Hudson, 1984). The binge eating disorder patient is particularly prone to social isolation, secretiveness, and the problems associated with the social stigma of being overweight (Jablow, 1992).

Many of the psychological effects of eating disorders *result* from starvation and malnutrition and are corrected as eating and weight are normalized (Keys, Brozek, Henschel, Mickelsen, & Taylor, 1950). Families usually express relief when they learn that much of the anorectic patient's compulsive and ritualistic behavior is directly related to the starvation process, that behaviors such as hoarding food tend to reverse with refeeding, and that much evening binge eating is caused by the physiological effects of food deprivation during the day. When given information about the importance and rationale for corrective nutritional interventions, such as meal planning, families almost always support the individual's efforts to use these tools to reestablish normalized eating patterns.

When the psychological problems do not resolve with improvement in nutritional status, the patient may be suffering a comorbid psychiatric disorder, such as major depression, obsessive-compulsive disorder, an anxiety disorder, bipolar illness, and/or personality disorder (Anderson et al., 1992; Pope & Hudson, 1984). These comorbid illnesses often need to be treated with psychotropic medications and/or psychotherapy. Because there is a higher incidence of affective disorders and chemical dependency in the families of patients with eating disorders, the therapist should also be alert for undiagnosed problems in family members (Anderson et al., 1992).

It is important that the family be educated about the therapist's understanding of the origin and meaning of the eating disorder behavior. One approach is to explain that although eating disorders are a result of a complex interaction of physiological, psychological, familial, and societal factors, families usually find it most helpful to focus on the functional aspects of the behavior. Family members can help their loved ones to find more positive and healthy problem-solving methods to replace the eating disorder, which has been the individual's attempt to solve problems (Byrne, 1987; Jablow, 1992).

### Family Therapy

Andersen (1985), Eisler (1996), Levine (1996), and Vandereycken (1987) caution therapists to not assume there is pathology in all "eating disorder families." They point out that *cause* and *effect* are not clear; the dysfunction and crises seen in the families in which a member is starving or binge eating may be a result rather than the cause of the eating disorder. Family therapy may be recommended not because the family *caused* the disorder, but because they have become intertwined with the problem.

When family therapy is undertaken, parents, siblings, spouse or partner, children, and others are involved in the patient's treatment in an ongoing, intensive, interactive process. Education is just one component of family therapy. The additional goals and interventions of family therapy depend on an assessment of the particular patient and family and the therapist's theoretical beliefs and understandings of the development and maintenance of the eating disorder.

Table 9.1. Family Therapy Models Used in Treatment of Eating Disorders

| Model | Theorist(s) | Therapy goals | Role of symptoms | Role of therapist |
|---|---|---|---|---|
| Structural | Minuchin | Change structure and interactional patterns that differ from normative model<br>"Free" family members to develop normally<br>Enact change within sessions | Treatment does not end with change in symptoms—need structural change in family | Directive and active<br>Practical and positive |
| Strategic | Selvini Palazzoli (Milan group) | Change dysfunctional patterns of communication and interaction so symptoms not necessary or functional | Symptoms protect family and solve problems<br>Symptoms are means of communication<br>Circular questioning used to generate hypotheses and introduce possibility of change | Therapists function as team<br>Introduce new ways of interacting |
| | Haley | Address problems in communication, structure, coalitions, and hierarchies<br>Make explicit the covert family rules | Symptoms are metaphorical and communicative<br>Symptoms are efforts to control | Problem solver |

| | | | | |
|---|---|---|---|---|
| Behavioral/ Cognitive-behavioral | No eating disorder family therapy theorist identified | Reduce or manage negative behaviors<br>Increase positive behaviors incompatible with problematic ones<br>Identify and challenge irrational cognitions that support problem | Focus on symptom reduction | Active and directive |
| Narrative | M. White & D. Epston | Help family "reauthor" stories they learned from dominant culture to explain symptoms<br>Consider past and present influence of larger culture | Externalize the symptoms<br>Create alternative stories | Collaborative |
| Solution-focused | S. de Shazer & I. Berg | Focus on solutions rather than problems | Focus on resources and alternatives to symptoms | Activator of client abilities |

*Note:* Feminist family therapy has not been included because it is more of a perspective that can be applied to all family therapy models rather than a separate model of family therapy.

Until 1980, most family therapy with eating disorders was *structural* or *strategic.* Since that time, *behavioral/cognitive-behavioral, feminist, narrative,* and *solution-focused* family therapies have added important theoretical perspectives and practical innovations to the treatment of eating disorders (Nichols & Schwartz, 1995). Although most therapists now use an eclectic or multitheory approach, it is still important that they understand the theory underlying a particular intervention they are implementing.

*Structural Therapy*

Structural therapy is based on a theoretical model of "normal family structure." According to Schwartz, Barrett, and Saba (1985) and others, the goal of structural therapy is to change structure and interactional patterns within the eating disorder family system that differ from the normative model, with the underlying assumption that when the problematic structure is modified, all family members will be free to develop in a healthy manner. Structural therapists are active and directive, and they work with the symptomatic behaviors. Successful treatment requires that the family *enact* change within the sessions.

In structural therapy, parents of a young anorectic patient are supported in setting limits on the eating disorder behavior. By establishing that they will no longer stay out of the kitchen at certain times or arrange family vacations to accommodate the patient's food-related demands, they reinforce the authority and effectiveness of the parental coalition and provide the patient with security that they are wise and strong enough to care for the family. In the situation in which the patient is an adult, structural therapy focuses on getting the spouse *out* of involvement in food and weight issues, thus reestablishing their relationship as peers.

There is much controversy about whether there are predictable "anorectic" or "bulimic" family patterns of structure and interaction. Although empirical studies have not supported the presence of such patterns uniformly, they can be helpful if they are used as a guide in the assessment process rather than as an assumption of specific pathology. According to Minuchin, Rosman, and Baker (1978), pioneers in the use of structural therapy with anorexia nervosa, "anorectic families" have a predictable structure of "over-organized subsystems," "lack of leadership," and "cross-generational coalitions." They have the "psychosomatic family" patterns of interaction that include enmeshment (overinvolvement and lack of individuation), overprotection, conflict-avoidance, rigidity, and involvement of the child in parental conflict (triangulation and detouring). Root, Fallon, and Fredrich (1986), McNamara and Loveman (1990), and Humphrey (1988) suggest that "bulimic families" have predictable structure and interactional patterns that are more chaotic, disengaged, and overtly conflicted and critical. To our knowledge, there is no information available about the typical binge eating disorder family.

*Systemic-Strategic Therapy*

The Milan group's systemic-strategic model of family therapy is based on a belief that the family is engaged in metaphorical, circular, systemic interactions in which the symptoms play an important function (Selvini Palazzoli, 1988). The symptoms protect the family; they can serve to decrease the threat of the patient's emerging sexuality, reunite the family, and/or avoid other conflicts that have even greater potential for disruption. The symptoms are a means of communication, and they develop as a way to solve an "impasse" in the family.

The systemic-strategic therapists use "circular questioning" to determine the awareness and accuracy with which family members view each other. They identify the family member who has the "strategic advantage," that is, usually the one who displays the most self-sacrifice (Stierlin & Weber, 1989). The family's ambivalence about change is addressed through the use of indirect, sometimes paradoxical, interventions, such as restraining progress, prescribing the symptoms, prescribing a relapse, or assigning ambiguous tasks. Systemic-strategic therapists also reframe the symptom in a positive manner and present their systemic understanding of the meaning of the symptoms to the family. They help the family change dysfunctional patterns of interaction so that the symptom is no longer necessary or functional (Schwartz et al., 1985).

*Behavioral and Cognitive-Behavioral Therapies*

Behavioral and cognitive-behavioral therapies are usually short-term, structured, symptom-focused therapies based on the belief that historical perspective and insight are not necessary to change thinking and behavior (Robin, Moye, & Siegal, 1993). In behavioral therapy, the individual and/or family use contingency management techniques such as positive reinforcement (i.e., praise) and negative reinforcement (i.e., restricting privileges) to reduce or manage disruptive behaviors and increase positive behaviors that are incompatible with the problematic ones. In my clinical experience, families have used everything from permission to participate in basketball or dance line to being excused from our sessions as reinforcement for desired behavior. Behavioral techniques are most commonly used in the beginning stages of treatment, in inpatient treatment, and/or when the patient is in a life-threatening situation.

In cognitive-behavioral therapy, maladaptive and inaccurate cognitions are identified and restructured. Chapter 6 details common patterns of irrational thinking including dichotomous thinking, overgeneralization, minimization, emotional reasoning, catastrophizing, mind reading, and fortune telling. Family members learn to identify and challenge their individual beliefs (e.g., "I already blew it, so I might as well continue," and "If it's done secretly, it 'doesn't count'"). The family is given permission to challenge the inaccurate cognitions of the eating disorder patient, who has often become the family's nutrition and diet "expert."

Implicit and rigid family beliefs that idealize and demand harmony, suppress or prevent resolution of conflict, and deny passion and other "dangerous" emotions are common. It is important that the family identify and challenge maladaptive family beliefs, especially those related to loyalty, sacrifice, specific role prescriptions, and "insightfulness" into others' feelings and thinking (White, 1983).

Behavioral contracts that are developed and implemented either by or with the cooperation of the patient are more effective than those imposed by others. However, whenever behavioral interventions are used by the family, it is important that they be well informed and consider the consequences of any limit they set. (It is equally important that the therapist follow through on any limit or consequence; many families arrive at our clinic angry and distrustful because past therapists did not hospitalize a patient as promised.) Hospitalization, participation in school activities and sports, money for college, needing to leave the home, and other consequences need to be thoroughly discussed and considered before they are used. These contracts can be useful and effective, but they must be used cautiously. All possible consequences, including the common fears of "making him worse" or "pushing her to suicide," should be discussed, and the limits set only when all family members are willing to follow through with the consequences, if necessary.

*Feminist Family Therapy*

This therapy, based on feminist theory first developed in the 1970s, is less of a separate model of family therapy than a lens through which therapists can view the importance of the power imbalance between genders in families (Luepnitz, 1988). Feminist therapy values insight, requires a historical perspective, and emphasizes the importance of the relationship between society and the family.

Feminist therapists have raised questions about the relationship between the dominant, patriarchal society and development of eating disorders in women. Attractiveness and self-worth have been closely linked to thinness. Feminists propose that one reason women develop eating disorders is that they are coping with an impossible "double bind"; they are now expected to be self-reliant and ambitious without giving up the "femininity" that Western society, primarily through the media, defines in terms of dependency, passivity, and thinness. Feminist therapists have also strongly challenged "mother bashing," that is, not considering the needs and best interests of the mother when setting the standard for "healthy" and "normal" family functioning and holding mothers exclusively responsible for the emotional health of the family (Boskind-White & White, 1983; Orbach, 1978).

## Solution-Focused and Narrative Therapies

These therapies are competency-based models of family therapy. Solution-based work is positive and optimistic, here and now rather than historical, and focused on solutions rather than problems (de Shazer, 1985). The goal of narrative therapy is to help people "reauthor" the oppressive stories they have learned from the dominant culture to describe their problems. They are helped to "challenge the constraining influence of their beliefs." The therapist and family "cocreate" narratives that increase the family's sense of competency, separate them from the problem, and increase the family's range of alternative ways of problem solving and interacting (White, 1983).

By referring to the eating disorder as a separate entity outside the individual/family, the narrative therapist externalizes the anorexia nervosa, bulimia nervosa, or binge eating disorder. When the therapist and family explore ways in which the eating disorder problem (not the individual) has controlled the family, they make beliefs explicit and unite the family members in the fight against this enemy. By helping the family to recognize the "exceptions" and "unique outcomes," the ways in which the family has already successfully dealt with the eating disorder, narrative therapy increases the family's confidence that they can manage or overcome the problem.

## Goals for Intervention with Families

### Priority of Medical Stability and Safety

Whether educational, supportive, or therapeutic, the first goal of any family intervention must be medical stability and personal safety. Because medical stability and safety are the priorities, initial interventions may need to be more behavioral, focused on the symptomatic behaviors, and more directive than they will be later in treatment.

It is imperative that eating disorder patients work closely with medical professionals who can monitor their medical status. It is unethical and dangerous for therapists to work with eating disorder patients or their families when the individual is unwilling to be seen regularly by a physician or designated health care professional.

### Structural and Interactional Goals

Only when the person with the eating disorder is not in medical danger and the patient or family members not actively suicidal can the goals for family work be expanded. As soon as possible, the focus should shift from immediate safety to the nutritional goals of returning to normal weight (for an anorectic patient) and resuming normal eating patterns and attaining a healthy nutritional status (for all eating disorder patients). Because there is some evidence that parents, particularly mothers, of patients with eating disorders have more problems with eating disorders themselves and are more dissatisfied with their daughter's appearance than parents of girls who do not have eating disorders (Pike & Rodin, 1991), the family members' attitudes toward the weight, shape, and eating behavior of other members may need to be addressed.

Midstage therapy focuses much less on eating symptoms and more on everyday problems of living in the family. Therapy goals include helping the patient take age-appropriate responsibility for self, encouraging family members to return to or start their own developmentally appropriate tasks, increasing appropriate generational boundaries and adult coalitions, and improving verbal communication, ability to express affect, and conflict resolution within the family. Even when the basic structure and alliances in the family do not change (i.e., certain dyads are still "closer" than others), the family structure and interactional patterns become more flexible, and the family "finds new ways of solving old problems" (Eisler, 1996).

### Termination Goals

In the final stage of therapy, the goals are consolidation of change (Schwartz et al., 1985) and planning for the future. The families learn to live with the changes they have made, some of which they perceive as positive (i.e., improvement in eating disorder symptoms and improvement in family communication) and others they may view more negatively (i.e., increased assertiveness and expression of anger). They demonstrate an increased awareness of the family interactional patterns that are related to the eating disorder, solidify the new image and identity of the former "patient," and accept that the agency for change is within themselves and not with the therapist (Palmer, 1989). "What if" questions should be addressed at the end of therapy; although often reluctant, the family needs to directly confront the issue of relapse, accept that lapses are a normal and expected part of recovery, and plan how any reoccurrence could be handled.

## Considerations in Treatment

### Therapist Role(s)

There is some debate about whether a therapist can or should function as both individual and family therapist with a particular eating disorder client. Eisler (1996) and Fishman (1996) believe that it is helpful for the same person to see both the individual and family as needed. When functioning in both roles, the clinician is forced to maintain a neutral stance without aligning with either the individual or family, and the understanding of each can be applied to the other. The roles of individual and family therapist are most often separated when the individual therapist has a psychodynamic approach, the clinic or treatment center is organized in a way that automatically separates individual and family therapies, or the therapist has concerns about boundary conflicts.

### Whom to Involve

There are many complex issues involved in deciding who should participate in family treatment. The age of the patient, type of eating disorder, configuration of the family, availability and willingness of family members to attend, willingness of the patient to include the family, and theoretical background of the therapist all affect this decision (Root et al., 1986).

### Age of Patient

Age is a critical factor in decisions about intervention. Family therapy is almost always a primary treatment for children and younger adolescents. The eating disorder has developed within the context of the family, and whether or not the therapist attributes the *cause* of the eating disorder to the dynamics within the family, the family's involvement in the illness and recovery process of a child or young adolescent is obvious.

There is some debate about the use of family therapy with adult patients. Dare et al. (1995), LeGrange (1993), and Russell, Szmukler, Dare,
& Eisler (1987) recommend family therapy for the treatment of anorectic patients who had early onset of the disorder regardless of the age of
the patient at the time of treatment. In practice, when the identified patient is over 18 years old, she is more likely to be living away from the
family of origin, and the therapist is less likely to include the family in
therapy (Schwartz, 1988).

## Gender of Patient

Although the estimates vary, there are significantly more females than
males diagnosed with anorexia nervosa, bulimia nervosa, and binge eating
disorder. Yates (1989) maintains that the family dynamics of male and
female eating disorder patients are "remarkably similar." More female
patients are married, and more male patients report that they are bisex-
ual or homosexual (Root, 1995).

## Type of Eating Disorder

The type of eating disorder also affects the choice of treatment. Family
therapy is often a primary treatment for anorexia nervosa. Fairburn (1993)
and Garner, Garfinkel, and Bemis (1982) recommend that bulimia nervosa be treated with a "stepped care" approach in which simple interventions are offered first and more complex combinations of treatments
(including family therapy) are offered only if indicated. There is no information available on the use of family therapy with binge eating disorder.

In the treatment of anorexia nervosa, it is important to differentiate
between *restricting* and binge/purging subtypes because there is mount-
ing evidence that those with anorexia nervosa who binge and purge are
more similar to normal-weight bulimia nervosa patients than they are to
those with anorexia nervosa who only restrict (Byrne, 1987; Yates, 1989).
Dare and colleagues (1995) believe that this distinction also has a significant effect on family therapy.

Therapists are more likely to recommend individual or group therapy than family therapy for bulimia nervosa because there are more data
supporting the efficacy of individual and group CBT treatments with
bulimia nervosa, the bulimic patient is more likely to be living away
from home and the families are therefore less available, and/or the therapist may be making a structural intervention aimed at encouraging
separation and individuation (Fairburn, Agras, & Wilson, 1992). However, in my experience excluding any or all family members to empha-

size the need for an adult patient to increase independence from the family often backfires. When excluded, the families tend to feel indirectly blamed, frustrated by the lack of information and assistance, and resentful, which may lead them to undermine the relationship between the patient and therapist. Even when they are being asked to disengage from the patient, they need help knowing what that is and how to do it.

## Configuration of the Family

When the individual with the eating disorder is a minor living at home with a traditional family, it is relatively easy to know who should be included in family therapy. However, when the patient is living away from home, is an adult still living at home, is in a nontraditional or blended family, or is married or in a primary relationship, it is less obvious. Although there are always exceptions, some general guidelines are helpful. The focus of the work with a patient who is in a committed relationship should be with the patient and spouse or partner. Children living with a parent with an eating disorder usually need to be involved. Sessions with the family of origin should also include the patient's significant other. The family of origin should be included if the adult child lives at home or has significant contact with family. If the patient's parents are divorced, both should be involved in treatment regardless of custody and current visitation arrangements. The two families are almost always seen separately; in my experience, the only exceptions have been joint custody situations in which all parents and stepparents have a long and well-established history working together to parent the child. Gay and lesbian partners or family members should always be included in family therapy sessions; the therapist needs to be willing to explore any issues related to sexual preference without assuming pathology related to it.

Although the family therapy usually starts with all available members of the patient's "current family," it is common to meet with various subsystems at different times throughout treatment (Jablow, 1992). Examples of subsystems include the patient and siblings, the patient and one parent, and the parents alone when the focus is their marital relationship.

Siblings are a powerful but often neglected part of family dynamics (Kinoy, 1984; Vandereycken & Vandereycken, 1993). They are an important source of information about the family. Some siblings appear unaffected and disinterested because they are coping with the eating disorder and disruption in the family by distancing from both. Others become involved in actively supporting one or both parents. Occasionally, siblings are able to express their anger and fears at the time the eating disorder is most active; however, it is more common for siblings to express anger or act out after the patient has started to recover.

Root (1995) refers to the couple as the "overlooked subsystem." According to her, treatment with the "eating disorder couple" does not differ significantly from that with other distressed couples. Common treatment issues include identity, communication, power/status balance, and intimacy. The National Anorexic Aid Society (Dennis & Sansone, 1994) recommends couples treatment when the couple is in overt conflict. However, Fishman (1996) and others maintain that there is a significant correlation between frequency and severity of eating disorder symptoms and the couple's difficulty expressing and resolving conflict, which leads to a recommendation for couples therapy when there is a *lack* of conflict reported.

### Prior Experience with Therapy

It is imperative that the therapist ask about prior therapy experiences because the individual's and family's experiences with earlier treatments will significantly influence their willingness to participate in family therapy. Negative experiences, usually those in which the family feels blamed or discounted, often result in increasing the individual's loyalty to the family and the family's resistance to further involvement. Positive experiences with other therapy or support programs, such as Alcoholics Anonymous, also affect the family's expectations of and participation in the current work.

Timing and/or "pacing" may have been problems in previous therapies. The stage of the eating disorder as well as the style of the particular family must be considered in deciding how and when to make particular interventions.

### Duration of Eating Disorder

Family dynamics tend to vary greatly depending on the duration of the eating disorder. I have found that families often go through predictable stages of denial, fear, self-blame, anger, despair, and finally, in the case of chronic problems, a detachment or acceptance that the individual will continue to engage in self-starvation or binge eating.

When the patient has had the eating disorder for many years, the family members may resist involvement because they have had bad experiences with therapy; feel weary, hopeless, and self-protective; have "heard it all"; and/or have already negotiated some tolerable ways of coexisting with the disorder. Even when some family members are reluctant or unwilling to be involved, the therapist should meet with whoever is available and willing. Unless there is clearly demonstrated and repeated evidence to the contrary, the therapist should assume that all family members are well intentioned, tired, motivated by fear and/or concern, and doing the best they can (Andersen, 1985).

When the family is engaged in what seem to be extreme and pathological behaviors (two examples from my clinical experience are a father sleeping on the kitchen floor so that his bulimic daughter would have to trip over him to get to the refrigerator, and a mother taking her anorectic son to four- and five-star restaurants every night because he refused to eat dinner anywhere else), it is important to remember that these responses developed gradually, are motivated by fear and concern, and are already a source of embarrassment to family members, who do not know how to get out of such "crazy behavior." As extreme as the family behaviors may seem, they have worked to achieve some kind of balance in the system, and changing them can be a risk (Eisler, 1996).

*Language*

Language is powerful. The way in which families "name" what is happening to them provides the therapist with information about their beliefs and feelings about the disorder (e.g., "His whole personality has changed since he *got sick*," "She's just looking for attention.") The professional can ask the family to define their words (e.g., "What do you mean by 'close'?") The therapist can use reframing and relabeling to modify the structure of the system and introduce new ways of viewing the problem.

Many families report that they have become chronically anxious as they attempt to "say the right thing, or at least avoid saying the wrong thing." A common example of this is the patient misinterpreting any comment about improved appearance as, "You're saying I'm fat!" It is helpful for family members to understand this common misperception and try to avoid comments about body shape and weight, but it is also important that everyone accept that despite their best intentions, such misunderstandings happen during this difficult time.

There is some evidence that parental criticism of the identified patient is associated with poor outcome (Dare et al., 1995; Slagerman & Yager, 1989). Feelings of guilt and frustration underlying the criticism need to be addressed in the family. The therapist can use psychoeducational methods to teach more positive ways of speaking.

Although it is helpful to provide families with an understanding of phrases commonly used in treatment (e.g., "goal range," "high-risk situations," etc.), in general, "plain language" is more appropriate for discussions within the family. After all, the goal is to help the family develop or return to a life in which food, weight, and treatment are not the "language" of the family's interactions.

## Discussion of Symptoms

Many family therapists struggle with the issue of how much to focus on, or allow the family to focus on, the symptomatic behaviors. The answer to this question is largely determined by the theoretical beliefs of the therapist and the goals for the therapy. However, even when the theoretical understanding of the problem dictates that the goal of therapy is to change family structure or interactions rather than the eating behavior, I have found that it is still helpful and necessary to deal directly with the eating behaviors, especially at the beginning of treatment. The family needs to talk about the specific behaviors so they can decide how to manage and respond to them. They will probably feel frustrated and not listened to if the therapist dismisses questions and concerns about the eating behaviors as "not the real problem." In an effort to cooperate, they may try to refrain from discussing the symptomatic behavior during sessions and/or attempt to ignore it at home, but unless they have a firm belief that what they are doing will result in changes in the behavior (after all, their primary goals are that the patient not die, and stop starving, vomiting, or binge eating), they are unlikely to really "let go" of their focus on symptoms. Their anxiety and focus on the symptoms will likely remain, but they will be "underground" and not available for discussion and intervention. When the eating disorder behaviors are being discussed in therapy—when past attempts at intervention, the impact of this behavior on the family, or the planning of how to manage this in the future are included in the *content* of the session—the therapist can gather information, make and modify hypotheses about the family, and introduce structural, systemic, cognitive-behavioral, and other changes into the family.

## Coordination of Treatments

Anorexia nervosa, bulimia nervosa, and binge eating disorder are complex problems that usually require a multidimensional treatment approach and a significant amount of communication among treatment providers. It is vital that all of the treatment programs and professionals hold compatible views about the origin and treatment of these disorders so that the patient and family are not "caught in the crossfire" of conflicting advice and direction (Fishman, 1996). When several providers *are* in conflict about the goals of treatment or the techniques of intervention, it is the responsibility of the professionals to negotiate these differences.

## Common Issues in Family Sessions

### Blame/Responsibility

"What caused this eating disorder?" "What did I (we) do wrong?" Questions of blame and responsibility are almost always raised, directly or indirectly, by the family early in treatment. It is not helpful (or accurate) to directly or indirectly blame the family for creating and perpetuating the disorder; this "patient as victim of the family" view not only implies malicious intent and increases guilt and alienation, but also puts the locus of control and power to change outside the individual with the eating disorder (Bruch, 1978). I have found it helpful to use language such as "refusing to eat" rather than "suffering from anorexia" to emphasize the active role of the patient who is engaging in these behaviors.

It is equally ineffective to dismiss or minimize the role that family relationships play in the development and maintenance of eating disorders. When the eating disorder is framed exclusively as an intrapsychic or biochemical problem, the patient and family lose the chance to understand the function that the eating disorder behavior is playing in the patient's relationships with family and how it is being used to manage family-related stresses.

It is critical that the therapist be clear about his or her own theoretical understanding about the development and maintenance of eating disorders. These beliefs will dictate the kind of therapy undertaken, the information given, the responses to questions about blame and responsibility, and, perhaps most importantly, the general attitude of the therapist.

### Control

The most common explanation that patients give for the function of their eating disorder is that it is a way to exercise control in their lives. Biologically, adolescents undergo tremendous hormonal and bodily changes, and the eating disorder is a way to try to gain control over this seemingly chaotic process. With the peer group, weight reduction or ability to deny oneself food are initially reinforced very strongly. Psychologically, the starving, binge eating, and/or purging provide a means to overcome a pervasive sense of ineffectiveness, to control anger, to soothe discomfort, to subvert sexuality, to create a special identity, and/or to deal with boredom and loneliness. In the family, the eating disorder can function as a more acceptable way for a teenager to engage in normal adolescent rebellion, or for an adult who feels otherwise powerless to exercise some control in a marriage (Schwartz et al., 1985). The eating disorder can also be a means of diverting family attention and controlling whether the parents will focus on marital problems, or a way for a child who has functioned as a "pseudo-adult" to elicit more nurturance.

It is important that the family understand how much the patient fears losing control (Palmer, 1989). Because of these fears, the patient is encouraged to follow a meal plan, eat on a regular schedule, and, initially, limit access to high-risk binge foods. The family can support (not control) the individual's treatment by establishing set mealtimes, planning meals ahead, cooperating in limiting the availability of high-risk foods, being willing to spend time together after meals, and not encouraging the intake of foods not on the meal plan (Fairburn, 1993).

Palmer (1989) suggests that family members recognize the "battle within the person" and be allies of the part that is struggling for health. External control may be necessary during times of crises, but whenever possible, it is more effective to encourage the individual to use internal controls.

In family therapy, it is important to clarify exactly what a family member is referring to when *control* is mentioned. By helping the person to identify and be more specific about what has been out of control, and by realizing that it is both normal and positive to try to control that which seems chaotic, the family can learn more about how to tolerate uncertainty, develop alternative ways to manage the discomfort, and/or work to change what has been "out of control."

### Closeness and Dependence/Independence

According to Eisler (1996), eating disorder symptoms are a "distance regulator" that serve the dual purpose of eliciting nurturance and maintaining distance within the family. This "double bind" is often effective in regulating emotional distance, but it results in relationships that are "stuck" and ultimately very dissatisfying.

When family members describe certain dyads in the family as "close," they may mean that these two seem to feel, think, and behave in the same way, value loyalty and togetherness above all else, have an exclusive relationship, or have no overt conflict (Slagerman & Yager, 1989). One of the primary goals of treatment is to help the family redefine "closeness" to mean what Stierlin and Weber (1989) call "related individuation." In a truly "close" family, members are generally warm and supportive but do not "feel each other's feelings" or deny permission for outside relationships. They allow members to do whatever they are capable of doing for themselves, and they openly confront and resolve conflict. In these families, an adolescent is free to develop peer relationships and become more independent, and an adult can be involved in satisfying adult relationships without needing to sacrifice his or her "sense of self."

### Communication

The eating disorder symptoms can be conceptualized as a means of communication. The therapist can assess the behavior in terms of "what is being said to whom," and with assistance, the family members can begin to communicate verbally and directly. They can learn to identify and change negative communication styles, such as double messages, double binds, hostile criticism, blame, and interruption, and increase their use of direct communication that is more positive and focused on problem solving (Slagerman & Yager, 1989).

### Family Rules

Family rules, especially those related to loyalty, sacrifice, safety, and expression of affect, are usually implicit and have developed over many generations. It is important that the therapist respect that these "rules" were likely learned in childhood by the parents, have value and meaning to the family, contribute to individuals' underlying beliefs, and are difficult to challenge and change.

### Case Studies

The following case studies illustrate the way in which families can be involved in the treatment of anorexia, bulimia, and binge eating. Although these case studies are composites and not actual patients or families, the details of the problems and descriptions of treatment are representative of those individuals and families seen in our clinic. The case studies will highlight different stages in the work with these families.

### Inpatient Therapy with a Patient with Anorexia Nervosa

Jody, a 16-year-old white, high school sophomore honor student, was admitted to the hospital for treatment of anorexia. Her parents (Howard, age 46, a sales representative, and Mary, age 44, an office manager) initiated hospitalization against her wishes at the urging of their pediatrician, who was concerned about her inability or unwillingness to gain weight in outpatient treatment. The family therapist asked to meet with all family members living in the home (in this case, the parents, Jody, her 14-year-old sister, Melissa, and her 18-year-old brother, Mark) on the day of admission to allay their fears and anxieties about hospitalization, describe the treatment program, outline the expectations of the family during the hospitalization, answer questions they had about the disorder and treatment, and begin an assessment of the family dynamics. The family did not bring Melissa and Mark to the session, because "they didn't want to come," and "they have gone through enough already." The therapist encouraged the parents to expect both children to attend all sessions. It was explained that the siblings are an integral part of the family; they are valuable to the treatment program, and despite their inclination to avoid the sessions, they will benefit from being part of the process.

The family therapist tried to "head off" common problems encountered in inpatient treatment by providing as much information as possible and being clear with the family about who they could contact with questions and concerns throughout the hospitalization. The therapist anticipated that Jody might complain bitterly to them about such apparently irrational rules as being required to eat foods she has never liked or needing to gain a certain amount of weight to obtain privileges on the unit. Giving the parents the rationale for these requirements ahead of time decreased the likelihood that they would overreact to her complaints and inadvertently undermine treatment. The therapist explained that the treatment in the hospital would initially focus on weight gain rather than individual insight or family issues because Jody was suffering from physiological and psychological effects of starvation that make such treatment ineffective. All family members were given time to talk about their experiences leading up to the hospitalization; in this situation, both parents expressed distrust of psychiatry because of problems they experienced when trying to commit Mary's alcoholic father for treatment, and Jody made a plea to the parents to allow her "one more try" at outpatient therapy.

During the family meetings that were held while Jody was in the hospital, the family worked to support her treatment both in and out of the hospital. They acknowledged their ambivalence about the success that Jody was having in the hospital after their efforts to help her gain weight had failed, but they gave her "permission" to engage with and trust the inpatient staff. Weekend passes home were planned and processed. The family assisted Jody in her treatment by providing her with information about meals and eating at regular times, but they did not "police" what she ate. They let her know that they would no longer cook separate meals, eat only low-fat "diet" foods, or eat elaborate desserts that she baked but would not share. They practiced responding to her repeated questions about her weight and body. The parents engaged in more "couple" activities, encouraged Jody to have contact with her friends from school, and worked to reestablish relationships with the siblings that were not focused on Jody or the eating disorder. The siblings attended the sessions and gradually became more open in expressing their opinions and feelings.

The family expressed a great deal of anxiety as the time for discharge from the hospital approached. A discharge contract was negotiated to clarify who would be involved in her care, who would monitor her weight, the consequences of weight loss or failure to continue to gain, and the family's involvement in future treatment. In this case, they decided to have the physician monitor her weight, a specific weight was determined to be the "readmission weight," and the family agreed to not ask about or be involved in monitoring Jody's weight unless they were notified by the physician or therapist that she had lost more than two pounds in one week or a total of five pounds. The family decided to continue with regular family therapy sessions on an outpatient basis so that they could address the non–food related family issues that had been identified during the inpatient treatment.

### Midstage Therapy with a Patient with Bulimia Nervosa

Kim is a 24-year-old single female of Korean background who was adopted at age 3 by John and Linda, upper-middle-class white Americans who were already the biological parents of twin boys, age 5. They adopted Kim because Linda desired a daughter. The parents separated when Kim was 9 and the brothers were 11, and they divorced 3 years later after a bitter custody fight. Linda was granted custody of all three children, but at age 16 the boys chose to live with their father permanently because of conflict with their new stepfather, Bill. Kim stayed with her mother, gradually decreasing and then ending her involvement with her father and brothers.

Kim described a "close" relationship with her mother, a "distant" relationship with her stepfather, and a "nonexistent" one with her father. She reported that her mother and stepfather have always had a tumultuous relationship and that she has always been her mother's confidante and "best friend."

Kim's bulimia nervosa began when she was 13 years old and continued without the family's knowledge until she was 20, when she told

them that she was leaving college and moving home because she had bulimia nervosa that was "out of control." Six months of outpatient individual therapy resulted in temporary cessation of all binge-vomiting and
laxative use. Kim returned to a local college part-time and continued to
live at home.

Linda suspected that Kim was vomiting, but she did not raise the
issue again after Kim vehemently denied that she was engaging in any
bulimic behavior. Kim's boyfriend, Eric, also suspected that she was actively bulimic, but he did not question her about it because of his belief
that talking about it would upset her.

Four years after the first treatment, Kim lost her waitress job because of coworkers' complaints that she was binge eating at work and
her employer's suspicion that she was stealing money from the restaurant.
She confessed to her mother that the bulimia nervosa was active again,
and she desperately wanted treatment. Her mother was shocked to learn
that Kim had been lying and stealing, because she considered these actions to be very uncharacteristic of Kim.

Kim entered an outpatient group therapy program with a CBT focus.
Her mother, stepfather, and boyfriend attended weekly informational
and support meetings provided by the treatment program. Kim's mother
initiated a request for the family to participate in the family therapy
that was offered as an adjunct to the group treatment. Kim agreed, and
meetings were held with Kim, her mother, and her stepfather; Kim and
her boyfriend; the mother and stepfather alone; Kim and her brothers;
and Kim and her biological father and brothers.

Because Kim was medically stable and the management of her eating disorder symptoms was not an issue for the family, they were able to
focus on relationship and other non-food issues. The family therapist
used an eclectic model of therapy including structural, strategic, CBT,
feminist, narrative, and solution-focused therapies. The structural interventions were aimed at strengthening the coalition between the mother
and stepfather, increasing the ability of the biological parents to have a
civil, working relationship in matters related to their adult children, and
reinforcing more appropriate boundaries between the adults and Kim.
The strategic interventions reframed the bulimia nervosa as a functional
behavior that served the purposes of soothing Kim and keeping her dis-
abled enough to need to stay at home, where she could protect her mother.
The strategic therapy also acknowledged the family's ambivalence about
the changes that might occur in all family relationships if Kim and her
mother became more individuated. The cognitive-behavioral therapy

model was used to explore the thoughts that all family members had about loyalty and loss (i.e., "There is no middle ground; you are either loyal and connected or cut off and completely forgotten," and "You can't love two people"). The feminist perspective was applied when the therapist expanded the work to include discussion of Kim's multiple losses; by focusing on both the trauma of the adoption process and the compounding losses of her father and brothers, it was communicated to the family that the mother was not the "villain" or the only one responsible for Kim's emotional health. The narrative approach was used when the family articulated and then "rewrote" the family story that it is necessary for a daughter to sacrifice her own life to take care of her mother (and that it is necessary for a mother to *have* such a daughter either through birth or adoption). The solution-focused model helped the family recognize and increase the use of many positive skills they already had.

The family struggled with issues of blame and responsibility. Because Kim's mother felt overly responsible for the problem, she was encouraged to develop a loving but more "objective distance" from both Kim and the bulimia nervosa. When Kim told her biological father about the hurt and anger she felt when he "gave her up without a fight," he began to understand the profound effect that his separation from Kim had had on her. The family explored the ways in which the bulimia nervosa functioned as a control for Kim internally and in her relationships with her boyfriend and family. Kim and her mother redefined "closeness" in a way that kept the loving aspects of the relationship but allowed both to engage in other relationships. All family members worked on increasing positive communication and conflict resolution skills.

### Termination of Therapy with a Patient with Binge Eating Disorder

Martin, age 48, had a long history of binge eating disorder, which contributed to and complicated management of his diabetes, high blood pressure, and high cholesterol. Following successful completion of a behaviorally focused individual therapy program, he and his wife were seen for marital therapy to address relationship issues that supported the maintenance of his eating disorder.

The final phase of couples therapy with Martin and Beth focused on consolidation of the changes they had made in their relationship during the therapy and discussion of "relapse prevention." They reviewed the progress they had made in decreasing Beth's attempts to monitor and control Martin's eating behavior and medical conditions and his direct and indirect solicitations of this controlling behavior. Both acknowledged ambivalence about the changes. Although grateful that she now had a "husband rather than another child," Beth expressed some regret at losing the control of parenting and financial matters that she had enjoyed while Martin was in a more dependent role. Martin expressed increased self-esteem and relief that he was now taking charge of his health, but he also stated that he now had to address his own fears about his health rather than allowing Beth to carry and manage that fear. They reviewed the revisions they had made to the "family story" that Beth had actually been effective in controlling Martin's binge eating and that he was incapable of monitoring it himself.

Martin and Beth discussed how they would handle problems that were likely to arise. They developed a specific plan about how and at what point Beth would address concerns about Martin's eating or health. They imagined scenarios in which each of them was angry or in need of affection, and how they might communicate directly and verbally rather than through the use of old patterns of behavior. Beth discussed her fear of abandonment (by his death if he did not choose to care for himself or leaving her if he did not need her anymore), and Martin expressed concerns about the loss of the nurturance he had always associated with her "nagging." They concluded therapy with an invitation to return at any time that either of them believed that it was indicated.

## Conclusions

Families profoundly affect and are affected by a family member's eating disorder. Education and/or family therapy can be offered as primary or adjunctive therapy depending on such factors as the age of the patient, the severity and stage of the illness, and the family's availability and willingness to participate. The goals of family therapy and techniques of intervention depend largely on the model of family therapy being used and the therapist's theoretical understanding of the relationship between the family's dynamics and the eating disorder symptoms. The issues of blame and responsibility, control, closeness and dependence/independence, communication, and family rules need to be addressed in therapy with families in which a member has an eating disorder.

## References

Anderson, A. E. (1985). Family therapy and marital therapy of anorexia nervosa and bulimia. In A. E. Anderson (Ed.), *Practical comprehensive treatment of anorexia and bulimia* (pp. 135–148). Baltimore: Johns Hopkins University Press.

Anderson, A. E., Devlin, M., Mitchell, J., Powers, P., Yates, A., & Yager, J. (1992). *American Psychiatric Association practice guidelines for eating disorders.* Washington, DC: American Psychiatric Association.

Bologna, N. (1983). Therapeutic approaches: Family therapy. In P. A. Neuman & P. A. Halvorson (Eds.), *Anorexia and bulimia: A handbook for counselors and therapists* (pp. 146–148). New York: Van Nostrand Reinhold.

Boskind-White, M., & White, W. C. (1983). *Bulimarexia: The binge/purge cycle.* New York: Norton.

Bruch, H. (1978). *The golden cage: The enigma of anorexia nervosa.* London: Open Books.

Byrne, K. (1987). *Parent's guide to anorexia and bulimia: Understanding and helping self-starvers and binge/purgers.* New York: Henry Holt & Co.

Dare, C., Eisler, I., Colahan, M., Crowther, C., Senior, R., & Asen, E. (1995). Listening heart and chi square: Clinical and empirical perceptions in the family therapy of anorexia nervosa. *Journal of Family Therapy, 17,* 31–57.

Dennis, A. B., & Sansone, R. (1994). Overview of eating disorders. In *National Anorexic Aid Society Overview.* Tulsa, OK: National Eating Disorders Organization.

de Shazer, S. (1985). *Keys to solution in brief therapy.* New York: W. W. Norton.

de Shazer, S., Berg, I. K., Lipchik, E., Nunnally, E., Molnar, A., Gingerich, W., & Weiner-Davis, M. (1986). Brief therapy: Focused solution development. *Family Process, 25,* 207–221.

Eisler, I. (1996). Combining individual and family therapy in adolescent anorexia nervosa: A family systems approach. In J. Werne (Ed.), *Treating eating disorders* (pp. 217–257). San Francisco: Jossey-Bass.

Fairburn, C. G. (1993). *Binge-eating problems: A guide to recovery.* New York: Guilford Press.

Fairburn, C. G., Agras, W. S., & Wilson, G. T. (1992). Research on the treatment of bulimia nervosa: Practical and theoretical implications. In G. H. Anderson & S. H. Kennedy (Eds.), *Biology of feast and famine.* San Diego: Academic Press.

Fishman, H. C. (1996). Structural family therapy. In J. Werne (Ed.), *Treating eating disorders* (pp. 187–215). San Francisco: Jossey-Bass.

Garner, D. M., Garfinkel, P. E., & Bemis, K. M. (1982). A multidimensional psychotherapy for anorexia nervosa. *International Journal of Eating Disorders, 1,* 3–46.

Haley, J. (1976). *Problem-solving therapy.* San Francisco: Jossey-Bass.

Humphrey, L. L. (1988). Relationships within subtypes of anorexic, bulimic and normal families. *Journal of American Academy of Child and Adolescent Psychiatry,* 27: 544–551.

Jablow, M. M. (1992). *A parent's guide to eating disorders and obesity.* New York: Dell Books.

Keys, A., Brozek, J., Henschel, A., Mickelsen, O., & Taylor, H. L. (1950). *The biology of human starvation.* Minneapolis: University of Minnesota Press.

Kinoy, B. P. (1984). *When will we laugh again? Living and dealing with anorexia nervosa and bulimia.* New York: Columbia University Press.

LeGrange, D. (1993). Family therapy outcome in adolescent anorexia nervosa. *South Africa Tydskr, Sielk, 23,* 174–179.

Levine, P. (1996). Eating disorders and their impact on family systems. In F. W. Kaslaw (Ed.), *Handbook of relational diagnoses and dysfunctional family patterns* (pp. 463–476). New York: John Wiley & Sons.

Luepnitz, D. A. (1988). *The family interpreted: Psychoanalysis, feminism and family therapy.* New York: Basic Books.

McNamara, K., & Loveman, C. (1990). Differences in family functioning among bulimics, repeat dieters and non-dieters. *Journal of Clinical Psychiatry, 46,* 518–523.

Minuchin, S., Rosman, D. L., & Baker, L. (1978). *Psychosomatic families: Anorexia nervosa in context.* Cambridge: Harvard University Press.

Mitchell, J. E., Specker, S. M., & de Zwaan, M. (1991). Comorbidity and medical complications of bulimia nervosa. *Journal of Clinical Psychiatry, 52,* 13–20.

Nichols, M. P., & Schwartz, R. C. (1995). *Family therapy: Concepts and methods.* Boston: Allyn & Bacon.

Orbach, S. (1978). *Fat is a feminist issue.* New York: Paddington Press.

Palmer, R. L. (1989). *Anorexia nervosa: A guide for sufferers and their families.* London: Penguin Books.

Pike, K. M., & Rodin, J. (1991). Mothers, daughters and disordered eating. *Journal of Abnormal Psychology, 100,* 198–204.

Pope, H. G., & Hudson, J. I. (1984). *New hope for binge-eaters.* New York: Harper & Row.

Pope, H. G., & Hudson, J. I. (1992). Is childhood sexual abuse a risk factor for bulimia nervosa? *American Journal of Psychiatry, 149,* 455–463.

Robin, A. L., Moye, A., & Siegal, P. (1993). *Family versus individual therapy for anorexia.* Paper presented at NAAS (National Anorexic Aid Society) Conference, Columbus, OH.

Root, M. P. (1995). Conceptualization and treatment of eating disorders in couples. In N. S. Jacobson & A. S. Gurman (Eds.), *Clinical handbook of couple therapy* (pp. 437–457). New York: Guilford Press.

Root, M. P., Fallon, M., & Fredrich, W. N. (1986). *Bulimia: A systems approach to treatment.* New York: Norton.

Russell, G. F. M., Szmukler, G. I., Dare, C., & Eisler, I. (1987). An evaluation of family therapy in anorexia nervosa and bulimia nervosa. *Archives of General Psychiatry, 44,* 1047–1056.

Schwartz, R. C. (1988). Families and eating disorders. In F. Walsh & C. Anderson (Eds.), *Chronic disorders and the family* (pp. 87–103). New York: Haworth Press.

Schwartz, R. C., Barrett, M. J., & Saba, G. (1985). Family therapy for bulimia. In D. M. Garner & P. E. Garfinkel (Eds.), *Handbook of psychotherapy for anorexia nervosa and bulimia* (pp. 280–307). New York: Guilford Press.

Selvini Palazzoli, M. (1988). *The work of Mara Selvini Palazzoli.* Northvale, NJ: Jason Arsonson.

Slagerman, M., & Yager, G. (1989). Multiple family group treatment for eating disorders: A short-term program. *Psychiatric Medicine, 7,* 269–283.

Stierlin, H., & Weber, G. (1989). *Unlocking the family door: A systemic approach to understanding and treatment of anorexia nervosa.* New York: Brunner/Mazel.

Vandereycken, W. (1987). The constructive family approach to eating disorders: Critical remarks on the use of family therapy in anorexia and bulimia. *International Journal of Eating Disorders, 6,* 455–467.

Vandereycken, W., & Vandereycken, E. (1993). Roles of siblings in treatment of eating disorders. *National Anorexic Aid Society Newsletter, 16,* 1–8.

White, M. (1983). Anorexia nervosa: A transgenerational system perspective. *Family Process, 22,* 255–273.

White, M., & Epston, D. (1990). *Narrative means to therapeutic ends.* New York: Norton.

Yates, A. (1989). Current perspectives of eating disorders: History, psychological and biological aspects. *Journal of the American Academy of Child and Adolescent Psychiatry, 28,* 813–823.

Chapter 10

# An Overview of Nutrition

*Carol Brunzell and Mary Hendrickson-Nelson*

Most people desire good health, and a balanced diet is an important factor in the maintenance of good health. Surprisingly, healthful eating is
confusing and difficult to achieve for many people. Fast-paced lifestyles,
disappearance of family meals, and the proliferation of convenience foods
and take-out meals make healthful eating increasingly challenging. Even
though many people desire to improve the quality of their diets, national
food consumption surveys indicate otherwise. For example, on an average day only 23% of Americans consume the recommended five servings or more of fruits and vegetables (Subar et al., 1995). Daily calcium
intakes also fall below recommendations: women on average consume
only about half the recommended dietary allowance (U.S. Department
of Agriculture [USDA], 1997). Also, the typical American diet consists
of approximately 34% of calories from fat, exceeding the recommended
30% for prevention of cardiovascular disease, cancer, obesity, and other
diseases (USDA, 1997). However, despite popular prejudices, fat *is* an
essential nutrient and *is* an important part of a well-balanced diet. We
live in a fat-phobic society that has a love-hate relationship with food.
This has resulted in a good-food/bad-food mentality in which people
associate pleasurable eating with guilt, and this mentality is reinforced
by mixed messages from the media, wherein sound bites of nutrition,
health, and disease information are dispensed injudiciously, before tentative research conclusions are substantiated and confirmed. To compound the problem, the proliferation of low-fat, fat-free, fake-fat, and
sugar-substitute products is overwhelming the marketplace, further reinforcing people's apprehension that enjoyable foods are "not good
for us."

Despite the popularity of dieting in the pursuit of "thinness" (at any given time 50% of women and 25% of men are dieting), 95% of diets fail, and the prevalence of eating disorders is increasing. The risk of developing an eating disorder increases with earlier onset of dieting behaviors (Patton, Seizer, Coffey, Carlin, & Wolfe, 1999). Nutrition messages focused on reducing fat and calories, intended to improve the quality of the diet, are overinterpreted by patients with eating disorders, reinforcing their eating disorder behaviors, with very serious consequences (Berg, 1995). To begin to understand what healthful eating means, it is helpful to look at a "definition of normal eating." Satter (1987) gives an insightful description:

> Normal eating is being able to eat when you are hungry and continue eating until you are satisfied. It is being able to choose food you like and eat it and truly get enough of it, not just stop eating because you think you should.
>
> Normal eating is being able to use some moderate restraint in your normal food selection to get the right food, but not being so restrictive that you miss out on eating pleasurable foods.
>
> Normal eating is three meals a day, most of the time, but it can also be choosing to munch along. It is leaving some cookies on the plate because you know you can have some again tomorrow, or it is eating more now because they taste so wonderful when they are fresh.
>
> In other words normal eating is flexible.

Disordered eating behaviors fall on a continuum with extremes being anorexia nervosa and bulimia nervosa (Beals & Manroe, 1999; Fries, 1974; Neumark-Stainer, 1995; Thompson & Sherman, 1993). Along the continuum of disordered eating, characteristics can include obsessive thoughts of food and weight leading to erratic food intake, rigid dieting with or without episodes of unrestrained eating, unusual or ritualistic eating behavior, and highly restrictive and/or extreme food preferences. These behaviors subsequently impair nutritional status, cognitive and emotional functions, and, ultimately, quality of life (Polivy, 1996).

Whether a person has anorexia nervosa, bulimia nervosa, binge eating disorder, or eating disorder not otherwise specified (EDNOS), the goal of treatment from a nutritional standpoint is to attain medical stability, to normalize eating behaviors and weight, and to reestablish a healthy relationship with food. This chapter will include overviews of general nutrition and metabolism. Case studies will demonstrate application of this information in treating patients with eating disorders.

## General Nutrition

Food supplies nutrients for the body. A nutrient is a substance that serves one or more of the following functions:

1. Provides energy
2. Provides materials for building and maintaining tissue
3. Provides substances for regulation of body processes

Six basic nutrients are essential for optimal health: carbohydrates, protein, fat, vitamins, minerals, and water. "Good nutrition" means providing a balanced intake of these six nutrients to meet metabolic needs. No single food contains all these essential nutrients. Consuming a *variety* of foods *in moderation* is necessary to meet these nutritional goals.

People with eating disorders typically become very rigid with their food selections and engage in dichotomous thinking about food. Consequently, they inappropriately limit their intake to a handful of supposedly "safe" foods, which unfortunately cannot meet their nutritional requirements. People who binge eat also tend to have rigid food beliefs.

### Energy Nutrients

There are three nutrients that provide energy (calories): carbohydrates, protein, and fat.

### Carbohydrates

Carbohydrates are the body's preferred source of fuel; 50% to 65% of total calories should come from foods that are rich in carbohydrates. Carbohydrates are metabolized into blood glucose, which is then utilized by every cell as a primary source of energy. Approximately 1,800 calories of carbohydrates (in the form of glycogen) can be stored in the liver and muscle tissue of an average adult woman (Brown, 1991).

When the diet does not contain an adequate amount of carbohydrates, glycogen stores in liver and muscle are utilized for energy. Conversely, excess intake of carbohydrates coupled with excess total caloric intake results in conversion of carbohydrates to fat for storage.

There are two types of carbohydrates in foods: simple and complex. Simple carbohydrates are found in foods such as sugar, syrup, honey, juice, and sweetened desserts and candies. Complex carbohydrates consist of starch and fibers. Grains, cereals, legumes, and breads are examples of complex carbohydrates. Fruits, vegetables, yogurt, and milk also contain carbohydrates.

Complex carbohydrates contain fiber, which is an important part of a healthy diet. There are two types of dietary fiber: soluble and insoluble. Neither type is digested or absorbed by the body. Fiber adds bulk and roughage to the diet and helps regulate digestion. It is recommended that adults consume between 20 to 35 grams of fiber a day (National Research Council, 1989). Studies show that consuming a diet with adequate amounts of fiber from fruits, vegetables, and whole grains may help to reduce the incidence of certain cancers, heart disease, hypertension, and diabetes.

Fiber is often misused by patients with eating disorders for its laxative effects. Too much fiber in the diet can lead to gas, bloating, and diarrhea. It also can impair absorption of some nutrients, such as calcium, iron, and zinc. Commonly abused high-fiber foods are bran products, prunes, apples, corn, and peas.

A variety of foods consumed from all food groups is recommended for a well-balanced diet. An adequate amount of fiber can be obtained by following the recommendations in the U.S. Department of Agriculture's Food Pyramid. Consuming at least five servings of fruits and vegetables, and at least three servings of whole grains per day is recommended.

## Protein

Protein serves many important functions in the body: it is used in the maintenance and repair of tissue and in the regulation of water balance and immune functions, and is a structural component of all internal organs, muscle, skin, hair, and nails. Protein is also an essential building block for antibodies, enzymes, and hormones. Ideally, 10% to 20% of total calories should be comprised of protein. The recommended dietary allowance (RDA) for protein is 0.8 grams per kilogram per day, or 45 to 65 grams of protein per day. To meet protein requirements, 4 to 6 ounces of meat or meat substitutes and two to three servings of dairy products are recommended per day. Competitive athletes need up to twice the RDA.

Proteins are made up of 20 different amino acids. There are 9 amino acids ("essential amino acids") that the human body cannot manufacture, and, therefore, they must be obtained by eating protein-rich foods. The remaining 11 amino acids ("nonessential amino acids") can be synthesized in the body. Foods rich in protein include meat, eggs, poultry, fish, dairy products, legumes, soy products, nuts, and seeds. Dietary proteins are either *complete* or *incomplete*, depending on the array of amino acids found in the food item. Complete proteins contain all the essential amino acids and are found only in animal sources, such as meat, poultry, fish, eggs, and dairy products. Plant proteins (legumes, nuts, grains, and seeds) contain an incomplete array of amino acids. Consuming the recommended number of servings from the USDA's Food Pyramid will ensure an adequate protein intake.

Many patients with eating disorders omit protein-containing foods from their diets in order to restrict fat and calories, thereby increasing their risk for malnutrition. During starvation, body proteins are used for energy, because energy needs take priority over tissue building. This is an inefficient use of protein. With prolonged starvation, muscle mass and vital organ tissues are broken down for energy, jeopardizing overall health. Loss of lean body tissue reduces metabolic rate, since muscle requires more energy to maintain than does fat tissue. In other situations, as in some athletic settings such as body building, athletes attempt to build muscle by eating excess protein. Excess protein is used for energy or converted to fat for storage. Protein-loading with protein supplements or by consumption of large quantities of meat does *not* help to build muscle, but rather increases fluid requirements, and can lead to dehydration and other serious medical consequences. In addition, high-protein fad diets for weight-loss are popular once again. These practices can be harmful to health and lack scientific evidence to support the claims. Weight loss that occurs with high-protein diets initially comes from loss of water and muscle tissue, but in reality ongoing weight loss from these diets is due primarily to the low-calorie eating plans (Larosa, Fry, Muesing, & Rosing, 1980).

*Fat*

Fat is a secondary energy source, as a stored fuel. It contains 9 calories per gram, which is more than twice as many calories as protein and carbohydrate provide. Dietary fat serves many other vital functions. It is the carrier of the fat-soluble vitamins, A, D, E, and K. It provides essential fatty acids (EFAs), linoleic, and linolenic acid. These EFAs are not synthesized in the body but must be obtained by dietary fat. EFAs are necessary for normal functioning of tissues because they help to maintain the integrity of cell membranes and also function as precursors for hormone synthesis and production. An inadequate intake of EFAs can lead to impaired growth, infertility, scaly skin, and dry brittle hair.

A common misconception is that dietary fat turns directly into body fat. In reality, excess calorie intake (carbohydrate *or* protein *or* fat *or* alcohol) will be converted into fat for storage. A calorie is a calorie is a calorie. When eaten in reasonable amounts, dietary fat is not "fattening" (Golay et al., 1996).

Dietary fat should comprise 20% to 30% of total energy needs. Therefore, the fat content of a typical 2,000-calorie diet should be about 44 to 67 grams per day. This fat-content recommendation does *not* apply to individual food items but rather to the daily intake as a whole: a variety of fat-containing foods can be incorporated into a healthy diet. There are three classifications of dietary fat: saturated, polyunsaturated (PUFA), and monounsaturated (MUFA). To protect against heart disease, no more than 10% of calories should come from saturated fat. Foods that are high in saturated fat are fatty meats, whole milk dairy products, butter, coconut, and palm and palm-kernel oils. MUFAs and PUFAs have been found to be protective against heart disease. The recommended daily intake of MUFAs is 10% to 15%, and of PUFAs, no more than 10% of daily calories (Twin Cities District Dietetic Association, 1999, p. 254). Excellent sources of unsaturated fat include nuts and nut butters, vegetable oils, avocados, salad dressings, and spreads. These foods are also high in vitamin E, a powerful antioxidant that has been shown to help provide protection against cardiovascular disease. Cholesterol is found in animal products, especially organ meats, high-fat dairy products, and eggs. Daily intake of less than 300 mg of cholesterol is recommended (Twin Cities District Dietetic Association, 1999, p. 254). Cholesterol functions as a precursor of steroid hormones and is a major component of cell membranes, myelin, and bile acids (NRC, 1989).

Every healthy body is comprised of fat tissue, which serves many important functions. Body fat provides insulation, helps to regulate body temperature, and cushions internal organs (e.g., kidneys). Brain and nerve tissues are sheathed in fatty tissue (myelin). Fat is vital for proper growth and development in infants and children. Women need a higher percentage of body fat than men for proper functioning of the reproductive system. Estrogen levels depend on adequate body fat stores and can fall to dangerously low levels with a decline in body fat. Low levels of estrogen seriously compromise a woman's reproductive capacity and bone density.

Finally, fat provides flavor, texture, and aroma to foods and gives a feeling of satisfaction (satiety) after meals. In the process of digestion, nutrients leave the stomach roughly in the following order: carbohydrates, protein, and then fat. Meals consisting primarily of carbohydrates (e.g., bagels, fruit, juice) are readily digested and do not have "staying power." Hunger shortly after a meal may be due to lack of fat in the meal. People with eating disorders often lose the ability to detect normal hunger and satiety cues. By introducing a well-balanced meal plan that includes adequate amounts of protein, carbohydrates, and fat at meals, patients eventually rediscover their own hunger and satiety cues, essential to reestablishing normal eating patterns.

*Water*

Water is an important nutrient that is often overlooked. Approximately two-thirds of body weight is water. Water is a medium for chemical reactions, transports nutrients to cells, and carries away waste products from cells. Water lubricates joints and aids in digestion by facilitating movement through the digestive tract. It also helps to regulate body temperature and maintain proper fluid balance. An inadequate intake of fluids results in constipation, dehydration, and alteration in blood pressure with concomitant dizziness. Chronic fluid restriction, coupled with vomiting, diuretic, and laxative abuse, can result in severe dehydration, alteration in electrolytes, renal and cardiac complications, and in extreme cases death. Six to 10 cups daily of noncaffeinated, nonalcoholic beverages are required to maintain fluid balance. Exercise increases fluid requirements. During exercise, 6 to 8 ounces of fluids should be consumed every 15 minutes. Following exercise, each pound of weight lost needs to be replaced with an additional 2 cups of fluid to ensure adequate hydration.

*Vitamins*

The function of vitamins is commonly misunderstood. It is widely believed that vitamins "increase energy." The truth is that vitamins do not provide energy but rather assist in the utilization of energy from the metabolism of carbohydrate, protein, and fat. There are two classes of vitamins: fat-soluble (A, D, E, and K) and water-soluble (B vitamins and C). The body is not capable of storing large amounts of most water-soluble vitamins, and excess amounts are excreted in urine. Fat-soluble vitamins can be stored in liver and fat tissue. Thus, when fat-soluble vitamins are consumed in amounts far exceeding the RDA, toxicity can result. For example, fat-soluble vitamins A and D can be fatal in large amounts. Four times the RDA of vitamin A when taken by pregnant women has been shown to cause birth defects. Oversupplementation can also alter the normal absorption of other vitamins and minerals and alter the therapeutic effects of certain medications. However, supplementation *is* necessary in some situations, such as pregnancy, certain forms of anemia, vegetarian diets, and certain disease states. For example, adequate folic acid intake (a B vitamin) prior to and during the first few months of pregnancy has been shown to prevent defects of the spine and brain in the fetus. The recommended dose is 0.6 mg of folic acid per day. Nevertheless, for most people, a well-balanced diet does provide all the daily requirements of vitamins and minerals, with no need of supplements (NRC, 1989).

Overt vitamin deficiencies are rare in people with eating disorders; however, restrictive food choices can lead to an inadequate intake of vitamins. Vitamins of particular concern for patients with eating disorders are riboflavin, thiamin, folate, B6, and B12 (Rock & Vasantharajan, 1995). Patients with both an eating disorder and alcohol dependency are at increased risk for thiamin and folate deficiency. Consequences of inadequate intake of B vitamins include anemia, neurological changes, and birth defects.

A multivitamin and mineral supplement that provides 100% of the RDA is advisable and is reasonable to prescribe to patients with eating disorders who are having difficulty eating a balanced diet. Generally there are no differences between natural and synthetic versions of vitamins, and "generic" synthetic formulations are entirely acceptable (NRC, 1989).

## Minerals

Minerals of particular concern for the patients with eating disorders are calcium, zinc, and iron. Calcium-rich foods (milk, yogurt, cheese), iron-rich foods (meat, fish, poultry), and zinc-rich foods (meat, fish, poultry, and dairy) are typically avoided because of fears of fat and calories (see Tables 10.1–10.4). Inadequate intakes of calcium, coupled with amenorrhea, predispose anorectic and bulimic patients to osteoporosis. Three to four servings of dairy products are needed daily to meet calcium requirements. Iron deficiencies can result in anemia and fatigue. Animal sources of iron (heme iron) are better absorbed than plant sources (nonheme iron). Vitamin C, found in citrus, berries, and tomatoes, enhances iron absorption when consumed with iron-rich foods. Poor zinc status can result in taste changes, loss of appetite, growth failure, impaired wound-healing, and inability to synthesize body proteins (Birmingham, Goldner, & Bakan, 1994). Fiber-rich foods contain phytates and oxalates, which bind to calcium, iron, and zinc, thereby inhibiting absorption of these minerals (NRC, 1989).

### Table 10.1. Recommended Dietary Allowances (RDAs)

| | |
|---|---|
| Calcium | |
| Age 4–8 | 800 mg/day |
| Age 9–18 | 1,300 mg/day |
| Age 19–51 | 1,000 mg/day |
| Age 50+ | 1,200 mg/day |
| Iron | |
| Women age 11–50 | 15 mg/day |
| Women age 51+ | 10 mg/day |
| Pregnant women | 30 mg/day |
| Men age 11–18 | 12 mg/day |
| Men age 19+ | 10 mg/day |
| Zinc | |
| Women age 11–51+ | 12 mg/day |
| Men age 11–51+ | 15 mg/day |
| Potassium (estimate of requirements) | 1,600–2,000 mg/day |

Potassium regulates electrical processes of the heart and muscles, and transmission of nerve impulses, and assists (along with sodium) in the regulation of fluid balance. Patients with eating disorders compromise their potassium status through vomiting and abusing laxatives and diuretics. Serum potassium levels can become critically low, placing the patient at risk for muscle weakness, confusion, and arrhythmias and heart attack. Foods rich in potassium include citrus fruits, melons, tomatoes, potatoes, bananas, and milk (see Table 10.5). It is helpful to encourage patients to eat high-potassium foods when they are actively engaging in negative, compensatory eating disorder behaviors (Powers, Tyson, Stevens, & Heal, 1995).

### Metabolism

Metabolic rate is influenced by a number of factors, including weight, height, age, caloric intake, and activity level. Metabolic rate reaches its peak during growth spurts in childhood and adolescence, and then gradually decreases after the age of 30 by 2% to 3% per decade. Basal metabolic rate (BMR) is defined as the number of calories required at rest to perform basic life functions such as breathing, organ function, and cellular metabolism. The average female requires about 1,100 to 1,500 calories

Table 10.2. Examples of Calcium Sources

| Food | Portion size | Calcium (mg) |
| --- | --- | --- |
| Milk (low fat) | 1 cup | 300 |
| Chocolate milk (1%) | 1 cup | 285 |
| Fortified soy milk | 1 cup | 200–300 |
| Fortified rice milk | 1 cup | 300 |
| Calcium-fortified orange juice | 1 cup | 250–300 |
| Kemps Yo-J™ | 1 cup | 100 |
| Yogurt, plain low-fat | 1 cup | 415 |
| Yogurt, fruit low-fat | 1 cup | 345 |
| Cheese (various types) | 1 oz | 175–275 |
| Cottage cheese | ½ cup | 70 |
| Tofu | ½ cup | 130 |
| Salmon, red baked | 3 oz | 140 |
| Sardines, canned in oil, bones | 3 oz. | 371 |
| Ice cream | 1 cup | 176 |
| Frozen yogurt | 1 cup | 110–130 |
| Almonds | 1 oz | 75 |
| Broccoli, cooked | ½ cup | 47 |
| Collard greens, cooked | ½ cup | 179 |
| Ensure™ | 1 cup | 125 |
| Boost™ | 1 cup | 300 |
| Carnation Instant Breakfast™ | 1 packet | 150 |
| Nutrigrain Bar™ | 1 bar | 200 |
| Kudos Bar™ | 1 bar | 200 |

*Source:* Pennington et al. (1994); reprinted by permission of Lippincott Williams & Wilkins.

per day at rest, and the average male requires about 1,400 to 2,000 calories. To support additional activity, digestion of food, anabolism, pregnancy, and lactation, additional calories are necessary. In general, women need about 1,800 to 2,500 calories depending on age and activity level, and men need from 2,000 to 3,000. Athletes involved in rigorous training schedules need even more calories to support their increased energy expenditures. See Figure 10.1 for formulas to estimate calorie needs (NRC, 1989).

In a state of semistarvation, such as that induced by chronic dieting, metabolic rate decreases due to restricted caloric intake and decline in total tissue mass (Elliot, Goldberg, Kuehl, & Bennet, 1989). This decline in metabolic rate is a protective mechanism evolved over time to conserve energy stores during periods of famine. Metabolic deficits of 23% to

## Table 10.3. Examples of Iron Sources

| Food | Portion size | Iron (mg) |
|------|-------------|-----------|
| Heme sources | | |
| Beef, cooked | 3 oz | 2.2 |
| Liver, beef, cooked | 3 oz | 7.2 |
| Liver, chicken, cooked | 3 oz | 5.7 |
| Venison, rabbit, elk, cooked | 3 oz | 6.6 |
| Tuna, canned | 3 oz | 2.7 |
| Salmon, canned | ½ cup | 2.1 |
| Chicken, cooked | 3 oz | 1.5 |
| Egg | 1 large | 1.0 |
| Non-heme sources | | |
| Dried beans, cooked | ½ cup | 2.4 |
| Almonds | ½ cup | 2.6 |
| Cereals, fortified with 100% USRDA for iron | 1 oz | 18.0 |
| Bran flakes, dry | ½ cup | 5.5 |
| Cream of Wheat | ½ cup | 5.0 |
| Spinach, raw | 1 cup | 1.5 |
| Swiss chard, cooked | ½ cup | 1.9 |
| Raisins | ¼ cup | 0.8 |

*Source:* Pennington et al. (1994); reprinted by permission of Lippincott Williams & Wilkins.

30% have been reported in patients with anorexia nervosa. Decreases of 10% to 15% have been reported in patients with bulimia nervosa (Gwirtsman, Kaye, Obarzanek, & George, 1989). In the infamous Keys starvation study (Keys, Brozek, Henschel, Mickelsen, & Taylor, 1950), the metabolic rates of the male subjects decreased by as much as 40% by the end of six months of starvation. Vigorous feeding of patients with anorexia nervosa can result in the refeeding syndrome, which includes congestive heart failure and dangerously low serum levels of potassium, phosphorus, and magnesium. To avoid such hazards, a gradual increase in calories is extremely important during the initial refeeding phase, and careful attention to laboratory parameters and vital signs is warranted (Solomon & Kirby, 1990).

### Nutrition Assessment

To accurately evaluate an individual's nutritional status, the following information is needed: anthropometric data (weight, height, recent weight

Table 10.4. Examples of Zinc Sources

| Food | Portion size | Zinc (mg) |
|------|--------------|-----------|
| Beef, lean, cooked | 3 oz. | 5.7 |
| Beef, sirloin, broiled | 3 oz | 5.3 |
| Lamb, cooked | 3 oz | 3.9 |
| Turkey, dark, cooked | 3 oz | 3.9 |
| Ham, roasted | 3 oz | 2.5 |
| Pork, lean, braised | 3 oz | 4.3 |
| Ground beef, 85% lean, broiled | 3 oz. | 4.0 |
| Tuna, canned | 3 oz | 1.3 |
| Cheddar cheese | 3 oz | 2.7 |
| Milk, low-fat | 1 cup | 1.0 |
| Oyster stew | 1 cup | 10.3 |
| Raisin bran, enriched | 1 oz | 3.8 |

*Source:* Pennington et al. (1994); reprinted by permission of Lippincott Williams & Wilkins.

changes), biochemical indices, medical history, diet history, and report of eating disorder behaviors. Most of these data can be collected during a patient interview and from reviewing the patient's medical record. This information is then used to develop a treatment plan for ongoing nutrition counseling in corroboration with the patient.

### Patient Interview

Obtaining an accurate diet and weight history is essential but can be challenging because of the patient's level of denial and the mistrust with which health care professionals are sometimes viewed. Therefore, establishing a trusting and nonjudgmental rapport is crucial in maintaining optimal communication between the dietitian and the patient. The patient interview should address questions related to dieting and weight history, eating behaviors, and food recall (see Figure 10.2). Information on irrational beliefs about food, weight, and exercise should also be explored. The patient's short- and long-term goals for nutrition counseling should also be elicited to help the dietitian and patient negotiate a plan of action.

### Assessment of Nutrient Intake

When attempting to analyze the nutrient composition of an individual's diet, it is important to keep in mind specific differences between patients with anorexia nervosa, patients with bulimia nervosa, and patients with

## Table 10.5. Examples of Potassium Sources

| Food | Portion size | Potassium (mg) |
| --- | --- | --- |
| Milk, skim | 1 cup | 407 |
| All-Bran™, Bran Buds™ | ½ cup | 613 |
| Potatoes (various preparations) | ½ cup | 245–483 |
| Sweet potatoes, yams | ½ cup | 313–468 |
| Dried beans, cooked | ½ cup | 334–374 |
| Spinach, cooked | ½ cup | 419 |
| Winter squash, cooked | ½ cup | 445 |
| Tomatoes, cooked | ½ cup | 312 |
| Banana | 1 | 451 |
| Apricots | 3 medium | 313 |
| Honeydew melon | ⅒ | 340 |
| Cantaloupe | ⅙ | 275 |
| Prunes, dried, cooked | ⅓ cup | 363 |
| Beef, ham, lamb, pork | 3 oz | 369 |
| Fish, white | 3 oz | 300–450 |
| Nuts, mixed | ½ cup | 412 |
| Orange juice | 1 cup | 474 |
| Tomato juice | 1 cup | 536 |
| Vegetable juice | 1 cup | 468 |
| Eggnog | 1 cup | 429 |
| Gatorade™, Powerade™, Exceed™ | 1 cup | 30–45 |

*Source:* Pennington et al. (1994); reprinted by permission of Lippincott Williams & Wilkins.

## Table 10.6. Energy Balance

| Energy out | Energy in |
| --- | --- |
| Resting energy expenditure (REE)<br>  Involuntary muscular activity<br>  Homeostasis<br>Physical activity<br>Digestion and absorption of food<br>Growth/anabolism/pregnancy/lactation | Food (carbohydrates, protein, fat) |

*Source:* Satter, 1987, p. 344; NRC, 1989; Copyright 1989 National Academy of Sciences; reprinted by permission of National Academy Press.

1. RDA:

   Women: Age 11 to 51 = 2,200 kcal

           Age 51+     = 1,900 kcal

           Pregnancy  = +300

           Lactation   = +500 kcal

   Men:    Age 11 to 14 = 2,500 kcal

           Age 15 to 18 = 3,000 kcal

           Age 19 to 50 = 2,900 kcal

           Age 51+     = 2,300 kcal

2. Calories per pound:

   Children age 11–15: gradual decline from 36 to 20 calories per pound

   Young women age 15–20: 15 calories per pound

   Young men age 15–20: inactive: 15 calories per pound

   Moderately active: 18 calories per pound

   Very active: 20–22 calories per pound

   Adults: overweight or inactive women: 10 calories per pound

   Most women: 13 calories per pound

   Sedentary men: 13 calories per pound

   Moderately active men and women: 15 calories per pound

   Very active women: 18–20 calories per pound

   Very active men: 20–25 calories per pound

3. Harris Benedict Equation: a measure of resting energy expenditure

   Women: REE = 655 + (9.6 × weight in kg) + (1.8 × height in cm) – (4.7 × age in yr)

   Men: REE = 660 + (13.7 × weight in kg) + (5.0 × height in cm) – (6.8 × age in yr)

   Multiply by 1.2 to 1.3 for average requirements for activity factor

4. Indirect calorimetry (for measurement of REE)

NRC, 1989; copyright 1989 National Academy of Sciences; reprinted by permission of National Academy Press; and Twin Cities District Dietetic Association, 1994, p. 169.

Figure 10.1. Estimating kcal needs.

binge eating disorder. Patients with anorexia nervosa tend to overestimate portion sizes, rigidly monitor their food intake, severely limit the variety of foods consumed, and underestimate exercise level. Actual calorie intake for patients who binge and purge is difficult to quantify. The average binge varies from 1,200 to 11,500 calories. It has been estimated that approximately 1,100 calories are retained following both large and small binges (Kaye, Weltzin, Hsu, McConaha, & Bolton, 1993), thus explaining the tendency for patients who binge and purge to have more

1. Weight history
   a. Highest and lowest weights
   b. Patient's "desirable" body weight
   c. Recent weight changes
2. Eating disorder behaviors
   a. Restricting
   b. Binge/purge history and frequency
      • Description of a typical binge
      • Binge triggers
      • Timing (including day and night)
   c. Laxative, diuretic, diet pill use
   d. Exercise and motivation for exercising
   e. Food rituals, food and weight myths
   f. "Safe" versus "high-risk" foods
3. Diet history
   a. Amount of food eaten at each meal
   b. Fluid intake
   c. Caffeine intake
   d. Cooking and grocery shopping skills and eating disorder–related behaviors
   e. Alcohol intake
   f. Intake of vitamin and mineral supplements, salt, seasonings
   g. Use of herbal remedies (especially diet and laxative teas, ephedra, etc.)
   h. Use of gum, hard candy, etc.
   i. Ability to recognize internal hunger and fullness cues

Figure 10.2. Patient interview and nutrition assessment.

normal body weight. Between binges, patients can severely restrict their intake and/or excessively exercise, so that the actual average intake may be inadequate. Patients with binge eating disorder tend to consume smaller portions of food than bulimic patients during binges but greater amounts of food than people without eating disorders (Mitchell & Mussel, 1996).

Careful questioning is essential for evaluation of a patient's binge and purge patterns, feared foods, and food myths and rituals. This information is needed for the nutritional counseling and educational component of therapy, where irrational beliefs about food and weight are analyzed and challenged.

For the professional who is not a nutrition specialist, a simple tool to determine nutrient intake is the USDA Food Pyramid (see Figure 10.3). The minimum number of servings for each food group are required to

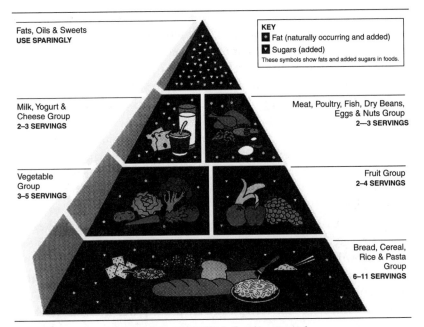

**KEY**
◆ Fat (naturally occurring and added)
▼ Sugars (added)
These symbols show fats and added sugars in foods.

Fats, Oils & Sweets
USE SPARINGLY

Milk, Yogurt &
Cheese Group
2–3 SERVINGS

Meat, Poultry, Fish, Dry Beans,
Eggs & Nuts Group
2—3 SERVINGS

Vegetable
Group
3–5 SERVINGS

Fruit Group
2–4 SERVINGS

Bread, Cereal,
Rice & Pasta
Group
6–11 SERVINGS

Figure 10.3. USDA food pyramid.

meet the minimum average daily requirement for vitamins and minerals. This is a simple way to address omission of common food groups in the diets of patients with eating disorders. Very often these patients omit dairy products, meats/meat-substitutes, and fat groups from their diets; as a result calcium, iron, zinc, and vitamin B12 are the micronutrients that are most commonly deficient in the diets of patients with eating disorders. Macronutrient intake varies with the individual. High-fat and high-carbohydrate foods are typical binge foods: ice cream, desserts, chocolates, fast-foods, and snack foods fall into this category.

### Anthropometrics

Obtaining an accurate weight and height measurement is important in the determination of acute management goals and long-term weight goals. These patients are excessively weight focused, and great care needs to be taken with the method and frequency of weight checks. Therefore, a plan for weight checks should be agreed to beforehand by the patient and his or her treatment team. Manipulation of weight by patients with anorexia nervosa or bulimia nervosa is common. Weights can be readily altered by fluid loading, by hiding objects under clothing, by wearing several layers of clothing, or by wearing bulky clothes. The frequency of checking weight depends on the client setting (inpatient versus outpatient) and on individual patient needs based on the severity of the eating disordered behaviors. In general, low-weight patients need closer monitoring of weight to prevent medical instability. Height should also be periodically reassessed in children and adolescents with anorexia nervosa to reevaluate growth and weight goals.

There are many reference sources for determination of appropriate body weight. A quick way to determine ideal body weight (IBW) is by using the "rule of thumb" (see Figure 10.4). Other commonly used sources are the 1959 and 1983 Metropolitan Life Insurance tables and the Body Mass Index (BMI). For adults, healthy weight ranges are 90% to 120% of IBW, or a BMI between 19 and 24.9 kg/m$^2$. For children, healthy weight ranges are determined by using National Center for Health Statistics growth charts. It is important to remember that individual variations occur. Weight can be influenced by factors not readily apparent in these tables, such as muscle mass, adiposity, frame size, fluid status, and genetics (Volpe, 1999). Generically, a "healthy weight" is a weight at which female patients menstruate and that can be maintained by normal eating and exercise patterns without obsessive thinking about food and weight. When working with patients with binge eating disorder or bulimia, a healthy weight at times translates into a weight of greater than 120% IBW, but one that is healthy for the individual.

Weight gain toward an IBW (at least 90% IBW or a BMI of 19 kg/m$^2$) is a primary goal of nutrition therapy for patients with anorexia nervosa. A weight range of about 10 pounds allows for normal fluctuations in body weight. For patients with bulimia nervosa and binge eating disorder, the primary goal for nutrition therapy is normalization of eating patterns and cessation and/or reduction of dieting and binge eating behaviors. Weight stabilization in the early phases of treatment is desirable. Once eating patterns have normalized, if necessary, gradual weight loss at the rate of ½ pound per week is recommended in these patients. Close monitoring is needed to prevent relapse of binge eating and purging behaviors. Realistic weight goals are crucial, along with gradual incorporation of regular exercise, balanced eating patterns, and behavior changes to maintain a natural body weight. Using weight tables exclusively to determine healthy weights may be detrimental, especially in this population, where focus on a "number" becomes an obsession, and any means to attain the number may be utilized, despite contraindications to health. The ultimate goal is to return to normal eating patterns

Calculations:

Rule-of-thumb for **ideal body weight:**

Females: 100 lbs for 5 ft + 5 lbs per inch over 5 ft

Males:    106 lbs for 5 ft + 6 lbs per inch over 5 ft

**Percent ideal body weight** = $\dfrac{100 \times \text{actual body weight}}{\text{ideal body weight}}$

healthy range 90–120%

**Percent usual body weight** = $\dfrac{100 \times \text{actual body weight}}{\text{usual body weight}}$

Body Mass Index = $\dfrac{\text{weight in kg}}{(\text{height in meters})^2}$

healthy range 19–25%

(< 17 underweight, > 27 obesity)

Waist circumference

Women: > 35 inches*

Men:    > 40 inches*

*Note:* *denotes increased risk for heart disease and diabetes.

Figure 10.4.  Ideal body weight, percent ideal body weight, and percent usual body weight.

without focusing on weight, particularly for the patient with bulimia or binge eating disorder. Continual striving for weight loss often perpetuates eating disorder behaviors.

The use of body fat composition testing has become more popular recently because of increased interest in health and fitness. There are several methods for determining body fat composition, such as underwater weighing, bioelectrical impedance, skin-fold testing, and body circumference measurements. However, there is no absolute "gold standard." There is potentially a great deal of error in these individual measurements: accuracy depends on the skill of the technician and can vary from one technician to another. Variation in an individual's hydration also affects the results. Furthermore, results do not take into account such issues as genetic variations in body composition, or even sports-specific variations (e.g., runners versus swimmers). Because of the great potential for problems in interpretation and errors in measurement, we do not recommend body fat measurements as a reliable or useful indicator. However, if the practitioner chooses to use such measurements, we recommend that the results obtained are used to determine an individual's trends rather than for comparison to statistical norms. Caution and sensitivity must be used when establishing "goals" for individuals, since genetics and many other factors cannot be controlled. Although we recommend *against* use of these data, some guidelines suggest a body fat composition for men from 12% to 20%, and for women from 20% to 30% (Wilmore, 1996). Obesity is defined as a body fat percentage greater than 25% for males, and 30% for females (Twin Cities District Dietetic Association, 1999, p. 117).

### Biochemical Indices

Certain behaviors exhibited by patients with eating disorders can have an immediate effect on their medical stability and can be detected by laboratory analysis. Electrolytes can be altered by laxative and diuretic abuse and by purging. Metabolic alkalosis and low potassium levels occur in cases of frequent purging. Hydration status can be monitored to some extent by fluctuations in serum blood urea nitrogen (BUN), a high BUN suggesting dehydration, by fluctuations in serum sodium (a high serum sodium suggesting dehydration), and by urine specific-gravity measurements (elevation again suggesting dehydration). Chronic laxative abuse results in metabolic acidosis and hypokalemia due to a loss of potassium and bicarbonate (Luder & Schedenbach, 1993). Phenolphthalein in urine can be used to detect some types of laxative abuse. Serum albumin and transferrin are indicators of visceral protein stores and overall nutritional status. Depressed values are seen with malnutrition. However, low serum albumin and transferrin values are rarely observed in patients with anorexia nervosa, because of a gradual adaptation to starvation, resulting in a marasmic profile of malnutrition (loss of adipose and muscle tissue and generalized weight loss, while maintaining relatively normal albumin and transferrin levels).

Micronutrient deficiencies can be assessed with biochemical analyses of blood and/or urine. Overt vitamin and mineral deficiencies are rare. Subclinical deficiencies resolve with normalization of eating behaviors and weight. Macro- and microcytic anemias can occur due to inadequate intakes of iron, folate, and/or B12 but are reversible with supplementation and normal eating (Rock & Vasantharajan, 1995). Serum zinc level should be assessed in patients with anorexia nervosa, especially children and adults. Low zinc levels can also be corrected with supplementation and incorporation of zinc-rich foods into the diet (Birmingham et al., 1994).

To determine the risk of osteoporosis in patients with chronic amenorrhea and with eating disorders, bone mineral density can be checked using photon absorption scanning techniques. The extent to which bone loss is reversible with normalization of weight and eating behaviors is unclear. Weight gain through improved nutritional intake and supplementation of calcium (up to 1,500 mg) and vitamin D3 (up to 800 IU per day) may help stabilize bone demineralization, as may working with the patient's physician to evaluate hormonal therapy and use of biphosphonates (Mehler, 1999).

**Special Considerations:**

In cases of medical instability, patients may require aggressive nutrition support via tube feeding or, very rarely, total parenteral nutrition (TPN). Aggressive nutrition support can be a complex issue, both medically and legally, and requires a multidisciplinary approach in addition to family involvement. Assessment and recommendation of the type of feeding, initiation, and monitoring parameters by a registered dietitian are crucial, since these patients are at risk for refeeding syndrome and delayed gastric emptying. Other medical situations that necessitate dietitian intervention include diabetes mellitus, renal impairment, cystic fibrosis, and other disease states requiring a specialized diet. As always, flexibility on the part of the dietitian and medical team is crucial.

**Case Studies**

*Jody*

Jody is a 16-year-old female admitted with anorexia nervosa to a hospital inpatient program. Jody reported eating half a bagel and an apple at breakfast. Her parents pack her lunch, but Jody throws it away at school. Jody eats dinner with her parents, which includes 1 to 2 ounces of chicken or fish, ½ to 1 cup vegetables, ½ cup skim milk, and a plain baked potato or rice. Jody reluctantly admitted to purging (by vomiting) dinner three to four times each week. Her fluid intake includes 4 to 6 cups of mainly noncaloric and noncaffeinated beverages per day. Her goal is to eat less than 500 calories and less than 5 grams of fat per day. She kept detailed food and calorie records. She exercised for 2 to 4 hours per day (running, basketball, weightlifting, and stair-stepping) with the goal of burning more calories than she consumed, until one month ago, when her parents restricted her exercise. Eventually, Jody admitted to surreptitiously exercising during the past month for about 1 hour per day in her room, doing sit-ups, leg-lifts, and push-ups, and running in place.

Height: 5'5"
Ideal body weight (IBW) 125 lbs ("rule of thumb")
Usual body weight (UBW): 120 lbs
Weight: 85 lbs
  % IBW: 68%
  % UBW: 71%
BMI: 14 kg/m$^2$

Labs:
  albumin: 3.6 mg/dl
  potassium: 3.0 mEq/L (low)
  chloride: 98 mEq/L (low)
  transferrin: 175 mg/dl (mildly low)
  $HCO_3$: 33 mm/L (high)
  Other labs and electrolytes normal

Estimated calorie needs:
  REE: 1,246 kcal $\times$ 1.2 – 1.3 = 1,620 kcal + 1,750 kcal for weight gain of
  ½ lb/d = 3,370 kcal
  Indirect calorimetry: REE = 1,105 kcal per day, on admission

Goal weight: 112 to 122 lbs (based on 90% of weight indicated in 1959
Metropolitan Life Tables, or BMI of 19 kg/m$^2$)

Figure 10.5. Anthropometric and biochemical data for patient
with anorexia nervosa.

Jody's diet recall showed that she consumes less than 500 calories,
10 to 20 grams of protein, and less than 5 grams of fat per day, and her
intake of all macro- and micronutrients is inadequate. Jody's high-risk
foods include red meat, fats, desserts, snacks, and dairy products. "Safe"
foods include fruits, vegetables, and bagels. She is obsessed with reading
labels. Her food rituals include cutting food into tiny pieces, heavily
seasoning her food, and chewing each bite 20 times.

To prevent refeeding syndrome (low serum magnesium, phosphorus,
potassium, and possible heart failure), in the hospital Jody was started
on 1,200 calories (divided into three meals and two snacks), which included a variety of foods negotiated with the patient under the guidance
of the staff dietitian. Jody initially refused to eat meals and was resistant
to treatment due to her level of starvation but did replace meals with a
nutritional supplement (360 ml of Ensure™ at meals and 120 ml for
snacks). After a few days, Jody began to eat but needed close monitoring

by staff and support from peers to decrease her urges to hide and restrict food and to purge after meals. Calories were gradually increased, and serum magnesium, potassium, and phosphorus were monitored to prevent refeeding syndrome until she was medically stable. Weight-gain goals were set at ½ pound per day during her hospital course, with rewards (increased freedom on the unit) for achieving goals. Calories were gradually increased through negotiation with the dietitian to 3,500 kcal (including nutritional supplements) to maintain expected weight gain. Jody frequently met with the dietitian to help her begin to gradually incorporate high-risk foods and to learn meal planning and other pertinent nutrition information (see chapter 11).

### Kim

Kim is a 24-year-old woman who was seen in an outpatient setting by the dietitian. She has been binge eating and vomiting one to three times per day, usually in the late afternoon and evening. Her binges typically include fast-food, ice cream, and cookies. She was fired from her restaurant job for binge eating at work. She formerly induced vomiting with Ipecac®, but now uses her fingers or toothbrush and excess fluids. She binges and purges when she is alone. Kim's triggers include hunger, boredom, loneliness, depression, and anger.

She skips breakfast and lunch and attempts to eat a normal dinner, but the latter often ends in a binge. When she does allow herself to eat a meal, her food selection is limited to vegetarian, low-fat, or nonfat foods, with a daily average intake of about 1,000 calories. She believes that laxatives help her lose weight and takes 20 to 30 pills (Ex-lax®) three to four times per week, usually after large binges. She desperately wants to reduce her weight to 110 pounds but has been unable to lose any weight. After large binges, Kim exercises compulsively for up to 2 hours.

Kim was instructed on the Healthy Eating Guidelines meal planning system, Level 1A (1,800 kcal). She was encouraged to increase her fiber intake to minimize the effects of laxative withdrawal. She set her own goals to gradually work toward eating three meals a day to minimize urges to binge and vomit (see chapter 11).

### Martin

Martin is a 45-year-old male who was treated on an outpatient basis for binge eating disorder. He works as a computer programmer and is married and has two teenagers. His job is sedentary, and he does not engage

Height: 5'5"
Ideal body weight (IBW): 125 lbs ("rule of thumb")
Usual body weight (UBW): 130 lbs
Weight: 130–135 lbs
  % IBW: 108%
  % UBW: 100%
BMI: 21.5 kg/m$^2$

Labs:
  albumin: 4.0 mg/dl
  potassium: 2.8 mEq/L (low)
  chloride: 95 mEq/L (low)
  transferrin: 250 mg/dl (mildly low)
  HCO$_3$: 33 mm/L (high)
  Other labs and electrolytes normal

Weight goal: stabilization
Estimated calorie needs:
  REE: 1,395 kcal $\times$ 1.3 = 1,814 kcal or 13–15 calories per lb. =
  1,690–1,950 kcal

Figure 10.6.  Anthropometric and biochemical data for patient
with bulimia nervosa.

in any form of exercise. Recently, Martin was diagnosed with hyperlipidemia, hypertension, Type II diabetes mellitus, and binge eating disorder. Martin was referred to an outpatient therapist and dietitian.

During the interview, Martin voiced his frustrations with previous weight-loss attempts and his skepticism about "starting another new diet." His diet history indicates that he would normally skip breakfast and eat a sub sandwich and chips and soda, or a hot take-out entrée for lunch. Martin eats dinner with his family but complains that these meals are very stressful. Martin has great difficulty controlling his eating, and he reports significant hunger at lunch and dinner. After dinner, Martin feels out of control with his eating and frequently binges on ice cream, cookies, and chips and dip while working on his computer and/or in front of the TV. Martin consumes about 1,000 calories between lunch and dinner, and 1,000 to 2,000 calories after dinner, and his diet is very high in fat and cholesterol. He does not eat adequate amounts of fruits, vegetables, or whole grains. Martin complained that his wife was trying to manage his eating, and his binges became very secretive. Martin has

Height: 5'8"
Ideal body weight (IBW): 154 lbs ± 10 lbs ("rule of thumb")
Usual body weight (UBW): 250 lbs (increased 30 lbs last year)
Weight: 280 lbs
  % IBW: 182%
  % UBW: 112%
BMI: 42.7 kg/m²

Labs:
  FBG: 150 mg/dl (slightly high)
  total cholesterol 272 mg/dl (high)
  blood pressure 160/90 (high)
  Desired body weight: 200 lbs

Estimated calorie needs:
  (10–13 calories per lb) × (desired body weight) = 2,000–2,600 kcal

Figure 10.7. Anthropometric and biochemical data for patient
with binge eating disorder.

begun to identify his triggers for binge eating as feeling anger and resentment toward his wife and feeling stressed. The family therapist was contacted, and these issues were addressed in therapy. It was agreed that Martin and his wife would meet with the dietitian to review general meal-planning guidelines and nutrition goals, but that Martin was responsible for regulating his eating (see chapter 11).

### References

Beals, K., & Manroe, M. (1999). Subclinical eating disorders in physically active women. *Topics in Clinical Nutrition, 14,* 14–29.

Berg, F. (1995). Health risks of weight loss. *Healthy Weight Journal,* Hettinger ND, 7–8.

Birmingham, C., Goldner, E., & Bakan, R. (1994). Controlled trial of zinc supplementation in anorexia nervosa. *International Journal of Eating Disorders, 15,* 251–255 .

Brown J. (1991). *Every woman's guide to nutrition.* Minneapolis: University of Minnesota Press.

Elliot, D., Goldberg, L., Kuehl, K., & Bennet, W. (1989). Sustained depression of the resting metabolic rate after massive weight loss. *American Journal of Clinical Nutrition, 49,* 93–96.

Fries, H. (1974). Secondary amenorrhea, self-induced weight reduction, and anorexia nervosa. *Acta Psychiatrica Scandinavica (Suppl.)*, *248*, 1–70.

Golay, A., Allaz, A-F., Morel, Y., de Tonnac, N., Tankova, S., & Reaven, G. (1996). Similar weight loss with low- or high-carbohydrate diets. *American Journal of Clinical Nutrition, 63*, 174–178.

Gwirtsman, H., Kaye, W., Obarzanek, E., & George, D. ( 1989). Decreased caloric intake in normal-weight patients with bulimia nervosa: Comparison with female volunteers. *American Journal of Clinical Nutrition, 49*, 86–92.

Kaye, W. Weltzin, T., Hsu, G., McConaha, C., & Bolton, B. (1993). Amount of calories retained after binge eating and vomiting, *American Journal of Psychiatry, 150*: 969–971.

Keys, A., Brozek, J., Henschel, A., Mickelsen, O., & Taylor, H. L. (1950). *The biology of human starvation*. Minneapolis: University of Minnesota Press.

Larosa, J. C., Fry, A. G., Muesing, R., & Rosing, D. (1980). Effects of high-protein, low-carbohydrate dieting on plasma lipoproteins and body weight. *Journal of the American Dietetic Association, 77*, 264–270.

Luder, E., & Schedenbach, J. (1993). Nutrition management of eating disorders. *Topics of Clinical Nutrition, 8*, 48–63.

Mehler, P. (1999). Anorexia and osteoporosis. *Eating Disorders, 7*, 143–147.

Mitchell, J., & Mussel, M. (1996). Binge-eating disorder: An update. *Eating Disorders Review, 7*, 1–2.

National Center for Health Statistics. (1994). Third national health and nutrition examination survey, phase 1, 1988–91. Advanced Data no. 255, Oct. 24.

National Research Council. (1989). *Recommended dietary allowances,* 10th ed. Washington, DC: National Academy Press.

Neumark-Stainer, D. (1995). Excessive weight preoccupation: Normative but not harmless. *Nutrition Today, 30*, 68–74.

Patton, G., Seizer, R., Coffey, C., Carlin, J., & Wolfe, R. (1999). Onset of adolescent eating disorders: Population based cohort study over three years. *British Medical Journal, 3*, 765–768.

Pennington, J. A. T., Bowes, A., & Church, H. (1994). *Bowes and Church's food values of portions commonly used.* Baltimore: Lippincott Williams & Wilkins.

Polivy, J., (1996). Psychological consequences of food restriction. *Journal of the American Dietetic Association, 96*, 589–592.

Powers, P., Tyson, I., Stevens, B., & Heal, A. (1995). Total body potassium and serum potassium among eating disorder patients. *International Journal of Eating Disorders, 18*, 269–276.

Rock, C., & Vasantharajan, S. (1995). Vitamin status of eating disorder patients: Relationship to clinical indices and effect of treatment. *International Journal of Eating Disorders, 18,* 257–262.

Satter, E. (Ed.). (1987). *How to get your kid to eat . . . but not too much.* Palo Alto, CA: Bell Publishing Co.

Siemers, B., Chakmakjian, Z., & Gench, B. (1996). Bone density patterns in women with anorexia nervosa. *International Journal of Eating Disorders, 19,* 179–186.

Solomon, S., & Kirby, D. (1990). The refeeding syndrome: A review. *Journal of Parenteral and Enteral Nutrition, 14,* 90–97.

Subar, A., Heimendinger, J., Patterson, B., Krebs-Smith, S., Pivonka, E., & Kessler, R. (1995). Fruit and vegetable intake in the United States: The baseline survey of the five-a-day for better health program. *American Journal of Health Promotion, 9,* 352–360.

Thompson, R., & Sherman, R. (1993). *Helping athletes with eating disorders.* Champaign, IL: Human Kinetics Publishers.

Twin Cities District Dietetic Association. (1999). *Manual of clinical nutrition* (5th ed.). St. Paul: Author.

U.S. Department of Agriculture, Food Surveys Research Group. (1997). Results from the 1994–96 Continuing Survey of Food Intakes by Individuals and 1994–96 diet and health knowledge survey. Riverdale, MD: USDA, Food Surveys Research Group, Beltsville Human Nutrition Research Center, Agricultural Research Service.

Volpe, S. (1999). Calcium, zinc, iron and exercise in women. *Topics in Clinical Nutrition, 14,* 43–52.

Wilmore, J. (1996). Increasing physical activity: Alterations in body mass and composition. *American Journal of Clinical Nutrition, 63,* 456S-60S.

Yates, A., Schlicker, S., & Suitor, C. (1998). Dietary Reference Intakes: The new basis for recommendations for calcium and related nutrients, vitamins and choline. *Journal of the American Dietetic Association, 98,* 699–706.

Chapter 11

# Nutrition Counseling

*Carol Brunzell and Mary Hendrickson-Nelson*

Counseling patients with eating disorders is a challenging and rewarding field for dietitians. It is also a relatively new field, where dietitians often find themselves with little formal training. The purpose of this chapter is to help the dietitian become aware of strategies to use when counseling patients, and to identify professional and patient resources. One area of this field that is different from the traditional clinical dietitian practice is the emphasis on counseling instead of nutrition education. It is imperative that dietitians work in supervision with a therapist/treatment team for the best management of these patients, and also to improve their own counseling skills. Issues that do not relate to food or weight should be referred to the therapist. It is very important to establish appropriate boundaries with patients and to not deal with issues for which dietitians are not properly trained. The dietitian-therapist team works best when these boundaries are respected, regular communication is fostered, and neither one is dealing with issues out of his or her area of expertise. We recommend that all patients who seek nutrition counseling also work with a therapist in the eating disorder field for the best outcome.

Establishing a therapeutic relationship is of the utmost importance when counseling people with eating disorders. A nonjudgmental supportive environment is essential for the patient to be honest and open about pertinent issues regarding food and weight. For example, people who binge eat are often ashamed of their behavior and need to be able to discuss openly the food beliefs and environmental triggers that lead to their binge eating. Rigid beliefs about "good food" and "bad food" and other kinds of all-or-nothing thinking create a system that perpetuates the eating disorder. In this context, food is used as a source of comfort and punishment, and as a way of coping with stress and emotions. Helping the patient to see food as a *neutral* entity gives control back to the patient.

Many patients feel they need to make changes in a perfect, linear fashion, and then perfection itself becomes the goal again. Helping patients understand that change is gradual and that they may either improve or get worse from time to time is a normal progression toward recovery. Helping patients to accept that mistakes are inevitable and that they in fact can learn from them helps reduce the power of the eating disorder and helps to minimize self-defeating talk. Setting up food-related "experiments" as a way to deal with high-risk foods or high-risk eating situations gives the patient an opportunity to challenge eating disorder patterns. It is helpful to place emphasis on the outcome of the "experiment" as a learning experience and on the insights that were gained rather than view the experiment as strictly a success or failure.

The goals of nutrition counseling are to help guide the patient toward normalization of his or her eating patterns, behaviors, and attitudes about food, weight, and exercise. Nutrition education is also an integral part of counseling, whereby food and weight myths and other misperceptions are addressed and tested on an ongoing basis, and guidance is given to challenge rigid eating patterns, thoughts, and behaviors.

Encouraging patients to learn to trust their own physiological signals that communicate hunger and fullness is an important step in this process. The long-term goal of nutrition counseling is to help the patient let go of chronic dieting patterns and weight obsession and develop a healthy, pleasurable relationship with food.

The hunger and fullness scale is a useful tool for helping patients learn to reconnect with their natural physiological signals to know when to eat and when to stop eating. It is also used to help patients distinguish between emotional eating and true physiological hunger. By having patients eat smaller, more frequent meals (every three to four hours), patients gradually learn where they can be safe using this scale. For example, instead of letting themselves get so hungry, to level 1, and then binge eating to level 10, they find through the use of experimentation with this scale that they feel best when they eat more frequently and stay between level 3 and 7 on the scale.

Once patients begin to recognize that they may be eating to satisfy emotional needs rather than physical needs, it is helpful to have them develop coping strategies to use during high-risk times. Developing a list of alternative activities, such as calling a friend, listening to music,

| 1 | 3 | 5 | 7 | 10 |
|---|---|---|---|---|
| starved | hunger pangs | neutral | comfortably full | over- stuffed |

Figure 11.1. Hunger and fullness scale.

taking a leisurely walk, playing with a pet, reading a book, is a common strategy.

When appropriate, using a meal plan for a limited time period to provide guidance with eating that incorporates moderation, flexibility, and variety can be helpful. Patients with eating disorders are often unable to recognize hunger and satiety. Denial of normal cues, along with starvation and chronic dieting, alters the patient's ability to feel hunger. Patients with eating disorders also select foods based on calorie and fat content rather than choosing foods based on taste preferences (Stoner, Fedoroff, Anderson, & Rolls, 1996). Therefore, the first goal in meal planning is to guide the patient toward eating three meals and snacks per day. To add structure around eating, it is helpful to have the patient define particular eating times for meals and snacks. In general, a simplified meal planning guideline is to have the patient incorporate at least three food groups for a meal; for example, protein, starch, and dairy (turkey sandwich and milk for lunch) and protein, starch, and fruit (peanut butter on toast and juice for breakfast). This structure will gradually help the patient rediscover her natural hunger and fullness cues.

Patients are often afraid of these otherwise normal sensations, equating "feeling full" with "feeling fat." Some patients, especially those whose weight is very low, may have delayed gastric emptying and can experience genuine early satiety. As they establish healthier eating patterns, their gastric emptying rate eventually normalizes. Including nutrient-dense food items (rich in nutrients per calories provided) in their meal plan and dividing food into meals and snacks throughout the day is helpful during the refeeding process. Patients with bulimia nervosa may also benefit from spreading food throughout the day (three meals, three snacks) to avoid feelings of extreme fullness, which might be a trigger for a binge-purge episode.

A review of general nutrition was covered in the preceding chapter. The "Healthy Eating Guidelines," at the end of this chapter, are based on the U.S. Department of Agriculture's Food Pyramid, which recommends 50% to 60% carbohydrate, 10% to 20% protein, and 20% to 30% fat. With this meal planning system, it is strongly emphasized that there are no good or bad foods: all foods are "legal." Nutrient balance is achieved by eating a wide variety of foods from all food groups. There are other approaches available to help structure eating, depending on the cognitive ability and motivation of the patient. It is crucial when working with these patients, that goals be realistic and flexible. Some patients come to nutrition counseling sessions with particular food beliefs that may or may not impede their treatment. It is important to deal with these beliefs in a respectful manner that will enable the patient to make informed decisions about what she eats. The patient ultimately chooses how she will decide to nourish her body. Each patient is unique and presents unique issues, and the goals must be individualized.

Different strategies are necessary when working with patients in inpatient versus outpatient settings. An inpatient approach is more structured: the inpatients have 24-hour supervision, and all meals are monitored. It is typically the case that the patient absolutely must eat to survive because of medical instability. The milieu of an eating-disorder inpatient program assists the patients in eating and in modifying their behaviors with the support of peers and staff. In this setting, a structured meal plan is essential for the refeeding process and attainment of medical stability. Teaching survival skills such as meal planning for home use, grocery shopping tips, strategies for eating out, and tips for managing urges to restrict, binge, or purge are helpful. Prior to discharge, it is also essential to arrange communication with an outpatient dietitian to establish consistency of care. Including the family or other support persons during discharge planning is helpful. Transition from inpatient setting to outpatient setting is stressful, and patients can easily relapse into old behaviors.

By contrast, when working in an outpatient setting, strategies vary depending on the individual patient's motivation, level of starvation, and learning style. It is important for dietitians to be flexible and work closely with outpatients. Having the patient examine the pros and cons of continuing her eating disorder behaviors is a useful tool in assessing readiness to change. Another tool to assess readiness to change is the Prochaska transtheoretical model (Greene et al., 1999; Kristal, Glanz, Curry, & Patterson, 1999; Prochaska, Norcross, & Diclemente, 1994). Other interventions, such as encouraging patients to read eating disorder self-help books, to build support systems, and to examine the consequences of continuing their current eating-disordered behaviors, are also useful during the recovery process.

Frequency of visits will depend on the severity of the eating disorder (usually anywhere from two visits per week to six-week intervals). It is not uncommon to work with patients for several months to a year or more during recovery. Working with the patient to help her set realistic goals is imperative to progress toward normal eating. Progress can be measured by use of meal planning, food and/or hunger and fullness records, and periodic weight checks (primarily for underweight patients). Other tools also can be used to track eating disorder–related behaviors, such as urges to restrict, binge, and purge or exercising to excess. Hunger and fullness scales are useful to assist patients toward normal eating and separation of normal hunger from emotion-generated "hunger" (Kratina, King, & Hayes, 1996; Roth, 1989; Tribole & Rusch, 1995). Since denial of eating disorder thoughts and behaviors is such an integral part of the eating disorder itself, it is sometimes useful in counseling to help patients separate, identify, and isolate the "eating disorder voice" when discussing pertinent issues regarding food and weight.

Guilt from eating "forbidden" foods is common. Discussing this guilt and guiding patients toward acceptance of all foods as neutral and "legal" entities eliminate any need to feel guilty. Being deprived of favorite foods leads to binge eating, guilt, and chronic preoccupation with food. Encouraging the patient to experiment with "forbidden" foods, in a therapeutic setting, helps the patient move away from eating disorder behaviors. Having the patient bring snacks to eat during nutrition counseling sessions is one way to do this.

One meal planning option is the "Healthy Eating Guidelines." This meal planning system lists foods in *single* categories, in contrast to the exchange-based system, for example, which gives *multiple* classifications for some foods. Multiple classification is confusing to many patients. For example, attention to fat content of individual foods can be a major stumbling block in moving toward normal eating. We have found that the "Healthy Eating Guidelines" help patients incorporate commonly feared combination foods such as pizza, casseroles, and desserts in their meal plans without focusing exclusively on fat content.

The quality of the calories during the refeeding period is not always a priority (Twin Cities District Dietetic Association, 1999). Incorporating supplements into the patient's meal plan is helpful for patients with anorexia nervosa who need higher calorie levels during the refeeding process. The meal planning system can easily be adjusted to include nutritional supplements, such as Ensure™, Carnation Instant Breakfast™, and Boost™, as snack exchanges. Snacks and desserts and other nutrient-dense high-calorie foods help patients obtain needed calories without substantially increasing the volume of food.

## The Eating Environment

For many people with eating disorders, mealtimes are extremely stressful. This issue is complex, involving many family-of-origin issues and relationship issues. Just sitting down to a meal is a high-risk event. Creating pleasurable mealtimes is an important part of recovery. Creating a positive environment at mealtimes where family communication and relaxation are fostered reduces stress, tension, and distraction. This involves making mealtimes a priority and adjusting schedules accordingly.

Contributors to an unpleasant eating environment include eating while standing, eating alone, eating while the meal is being prepared, eating "on the run" or in the car, tolerating dining tables full of clutter, having a radio or television on during eating, having telephone interruptions, arguing or discussing stressful topics, and participating in eating-disordered food rituals (breaking food into tiny pieces, inappropriate use of utensils, heavily seasoning foods, eating rapidly, excess chewing of food, playing with food, and counting calories and fat grams). Mealtimes can be made more pleasurable by having a designated place to eat (kitchen or dining room), setting the table attractively, avoiding distractions from TV, radio, phone, and reading materials, socializing, and sharing experiences of the day. A pleasurable eating environment helps to manage eating disorder behaviors and aids in the recognition of hunger and fullness cues (Satter, 1991). An important concept that must not be overlooked is that food is an integral part of day-to-day living and is meant to be enjoyed, savored, and treated with respect.

Strategies to help patients with anorexia nervosa minimize urges to restrict and incorporate meal plan exchanges include identifying a "buddy," such as a peer or a family member, to offer support during the meal, discussing boundaries between being supportive and being "food police" with family and friends, using the meal plan and planning ahead, being flexible when changes in schedule occur, including two to three snacks per day when at higher calorie levels, and selecting nutrient-dense foods (such as nutritional supplements) for meals and snacks.

Strategies for managing the eating environment for patients who binge eat include eating while sitting down, planning meals in advance, slowing down when eating to help improve recognition of hunger and fullness cues, and including some protein and fat at meals and snacks to help reduce preoccupation with food and to improve satisfaction after meals.

Also helpful is the gradual reintroduction of binge foods as eating patterns normalize but using reasonable portion sizes. Using preportioned food items, especially for binge foods, helps maintain control (Patterson, Whelan, Rock, & Lyon, 1989).

Dealing with eating disordered behaviors in people who live alone is particularly challenging. Just being at home alone is a trigger. Some tips to help manage the eating environment for these patients include eating structured meals and snacks throughout the day (emphasizing not coming home from work or school famished), preplanning meals and snacks, grocery shopping on a regular basis with a list, preparing foods in quantities that are safe, and cooking easy recipes or using prepackaged foods to help make mealtime less stressful. Having the patient identify a family member or friend to dine with occasionally is also helpful. Working in conjunction with a therapist to help the patient deal with emotional cues for disordered eating patterns is imperative.

Dining in restaurants, holiday meals, and special occasions are often particularly stressful. These normally pleasurable events can trigger multitudes of disordered eating behaviors. It is helpful to plan coping strategies prior to these events. Utilizing a team approach is helpful: the dietitian's role is to help the patient to develop a realistic meal plan and to work on effective strategies for managing the eating environment. The following sections provide strategies for managing the eating environment.

### Strategies for Social Eating Situations

- Plan ahead: know your meal plan.
- Make decisions about food selections before going. If the menu is known, then plan for specific items. If not, decide on the type of entrée: sandwich, hot entrée, entrée salad, and so on.
- Be flexible: have a backup plan.
- Limit time for making menu selections to 10 minutes.
- Portion sizes are larger in restaurants, so additional grain and fat exchanges must be anticipated.
- When in doubt, clarify portion sizes with family or peers.
- Order the menu items as listed on the menu ("no substitutions").
- Eat with *supportive* family and friends.
- Pay attention to intuitive hunger and satiety cues.
- Aim to enjoy and celebrate the occasion.

### Strategies to Control Binge Eating/Vomiting Urges

- Try to eat on schedule, do not skip meals, do not go to restaurants overly hungry.

- Avoid buffets if possible during the initial recovery phase. If this is not possible, scan available food items before making decisions about what to eat, and go through the buffet line only one time.
- If portion sizes are large, consider splitting the main course with a friend.
- Discuss urges to vomit with a supportive peer and plan an activity after the meal.
- Order "safe" foods initially, working up to "higher-risk" foods over time.
- Give yourself credit for gradual changes and accomplishments.
- Listen to your body: stop eating when you are full.

*Strategies to Control Urges to Restrict*

- Order "safe" foods initially, working up to "higher-risk" foods over time.
- Plan ahead and use peer support.
- Make up missed exchanges at other meals or snacks.
- Give yourself credit for gradual changes and accomplishments.
- Use supportive family or peers to suppress urges to exercise after a meal.

## Nutrition Education

Providing accurate nutrition education for patients with eating disorders is important to their recovery. Nutrition education can be provided to individual patients one-to-one and in groups. Education provided in a group will often allow more opportunities for peer interaction and group discussion. As always, a nonjudgmental approach is desirable to facilitate patients' free expression of fears regarding food and weight. Refer to the following list for examples of topics appropriate for nutrition education classes. In addition, try to make the groups as interactive as possible. There are a variety of professional resources containing ideas for facilitating groups for people with disordered eating behaviors.

- Overview of anorexia nervosa
- Overview of bulimia nervosa
- Overview of binge eating disorder
- Effects of weight loss and starvation
- Medical complications of eating disorders
- Changes associated with weight gain toward a healthy body weight
- Laxative and diuretic abuse

- Human physical development
- Guidelines for good nutrition
- Food myths
- Understanding portion sizes
- Enjoyable physical activities
- Hunger and fullness
- Letting go of numbers, understanding healthy body weight
- Osteoporosis
- Managing your eating environment
- Challenging ritualistic eating behaviors
- Grocery shopping
- Strategies for coping with social eating situations

Nutrition education should incorporate basic nutrition guidelines that are easy to understand and applicable to daily meals. An assessment of an individual's cooking and grocery shopping skills and ability to estimate portion sizes is important. Often patients with eating disorders intellectually understand these basic principles but are unable to apply them day to day. Many patients are not skilled at judging portion sizes, and the use of food models gives a tangible demonstration of appropriate portion sizes. Assisting patients in planning weekly menus and grocery lists is essential and should not be overlooked. Patients may have great difficulty in carrying out these seemingly straightforward tasks. Assistance here may be crucial to success. Providing sample grocery lists to patients is a good way to get started.

### Sample Grocery List

Calcium-rich:

- milk
- yogurt
- Carnation Instant Breakfast™

Grains:

- hot or cold cereal
- bread/bagels
- muffin mix
- pasta
- potatoes
- rice
- tortillas
- crackers/snack chips

Fruits:

- fresh or canned fruit
- fruit juice

Vegetables:

- frozen, fresh, or canned vegetables
- soup
- tomato or V8™ juice

Meats/meat substitutes:

- deli meat
- ground beef or turkey
- chicken/turkey
- beef/pork
- cheese/legumes
- canned tuna
- fish
- eggs

Entrée ideas:

- macaroni and cheese
- chili
- spaghetti or other pasta entrées
- pizza
- baked potatoes with chicken, cheese, vegetables
- stir-fry
- frozen entrées

Desserts:

- brownies
- cookies
- cake
- ice cream or ice milk
- frozen yogurt
- pudding

Fats

- peanut butter
- margarine
- nuts

- cream cheese
- salad dressing
- mayonnaise

## Three Case Studies Continued

### Jody

During the first week-and-a-half of treatment, the main focus was refeeding toward weight normalization. Jody was too malnourished to actively participate in groups or to select appropriate foods. Each meal was a challenge, and Jody needed reminders that she would need to drink Ensure™ if she did not finish her meal within 30 minutes. As she began to gain weight and became medically stable, she was rewarded with short walks and, eventually, with therapeutic passes for having maintained a weight gain rate of half a pound per day. After she was instructed on how to use the "Healthy Eating Guidelines," she was required to outline a strategy for gradual incorporation of high-risk foods. She found peer support at mealtimes and in groups helpful. When she was caught hiding food at meals (hiding butter in a napkin and under tables and chairs), she was confronted by her peers in a supportive manner. Jody then verbalized a plan to help her eat everything at meals. Individual sessions and group classes with the dietitian focused on Jody's specific cognitive distortions concerning food and weight. She found it helpful to write affirmation cards dispelling some of her fears concerning fat and to bring them to meals. She had tremendous anxiety about reaching 100 pounds ("triple digits") and needed extra support from the treatment team to reaffirm the health benefits of reaching a healthy body weight. Jody was afraid to eat in public. Eating out with peers and staff (and eventually with family) was achieved by gradually progressing through a *high-risk hierarchy*; each event was processed with peers and staff after completion. The dietitian was helpful in these situations by assisting her in developing strategies for eating out and making menu selections based on the "Healthy Eating Guidelines." Jody was eventually discharged to an outpatient program at a weight of 102 pounds. In her discharge contract she agreed to gain 1 to 2 pounds per week, and to meet regularly with a dietitian until she reached her goal weight. Jody was reassured that her calories would be readjusted for weight maintenance once her weight stabilized in her goal range. The meal planning system was reviewed with her parents prior to discharge. With the assistance of her therapist,

Table 11.1. Targeted Behaviors for Anorexia Nervosa and
Treatment Strategies

| Targeted behaviors for anorexia nervosa | Treatment strategies |
| --- | --- |
| Rigid behaviors about calories and fat intake | Assess patient's current beliefs. Nutrition education to encourage changes as the patient is able. Challenge food beliefs and gradually incorporate high-risk foods. |
| Compulsive exercise | Cessation of exercise until patient is medically stable and until approved by treatment team. Nutrition education regarding energy balance. |
| Food rituals | Peer confrontation, group discussion, and role modeling by treatment staff. |
| Distorted beliefs about weight | Assess patient's current beliefs. Nutrition education and body image therapy. |

specific guidelines were developed to help normalize mealtimes at home, and to create a supportive eating environment.

### Kim

Kim's eating was out of control; therefore, the focus was to have her eat three meals plus snacks to provide more structure for her eating. It took weeks for her to trust her meal plan and to incorporate all the foods into her meals and snacks. Eventually, she completed meal plans on a daily basis. She was able to make a grocery list for the week's meals and go to the grocery store. At first, Kim was encouraged to avoid high-risk foods, until her eating habits stabilized. As her eating normalized, she gradually reincorporated "forbidden" foods, in a progression from least-feared to most-feared. Kim tried to keep food records, which she shared with the dietitian, to facilitate open discussion of food and weight issues. Restaurant eating was a high-risk activity for Kim. When she was ready, her dietitian worked with her to develop coping strategies for restaurant dining. Kim learned about variety and portion sizes by using the meal planning system. Eventually she was ready to discontinue meal planning, as she found that she was becoming increasingly preoccupied with food and preplanning meals. The use of a less structured, self-regulating approach was initiated, with the primary focus on hunger and fullness recognition. Kim was eventually able to regulate her weight and her food intake by listening to her internal hunger and fullness cues. Kim was also en-

## Table 11.2. Targeted Behaviors for Bulimia Nervosa and Treatment Strategies

| Targeted behaviors for bulimia nervosa | Treatment strategies |
| --- | --- |
| Irrational beliefs about weight control | Assess patient's current beliefs. Nutrition education about laxatives, binge eating, vomiting, exercise, desirable body weight. No dieting. Body image therapy. |
| Rigid beliefs about "good" and "bad" foods | Have patient observe effects of increased variety in diet in relation to weight status to dispel food and weight myths and to "neutralize" foods. |
| Emotional hunger versus physiological hunger | Develop hunger and fullness recognition by use of fullness scales. Referral to therapist. |

couraged to attend a support group facilitated by a therapist and a dietitian, which she found valuable.

### Martin

Martin was encouraged to eat breakfast. Eating at regular time intervals, approximately every three to four hours was encouraged, and actual eating times were identified by Martin. He was provided with simplified nutrition education, using the food pyramid, with emphasis on portion size. He was encouraged to eat balanced meals and spread carbohydrate-containing foods throughout the day. Initially, the primary focus was on normalizing eating patterns, rather than on weight loss. Martin was provided with a reading list and eating disorder references to help him gain insight into his eating disorder. He was encouraged to incorporate fruits and vegetables with his meals to help provide a sense of fullness. Martin kept hunger and fullness/food logs to help him gain insight into his eating patterns. Nutrition goals were identified by Martin, and he gradually incorporated more fruits and vegetables, lower-fat foods, and decreased portion sizes of entrées. These changes gradually helped Martin to decrease his binge eating episodes. He was encouraged to select only one area of the house to eat in even if this meant that for a time he would binge at a table instead in front of the computer. Martin gradually began to realize that healthy eating is flexible, and he was able to incorporate some of his favorite foods. In conjunction with his therapist, Martin was able to identify triggers for binge eating and began to feel

Table 11.3. Targeted Behaviors for Binge Eating Disorder and
Treatment Strategies

| Targeted behaviors for binge eating disorder | Treatment strategies |
| --- | --- |
| Rigid beliefs about healthful eating | Assess patient's current beliefs. Nutrition education to encourage changes as the patient is able. |
| Skipping meals helps control weight | Nutrition education: metabolism, meal plan guidance, structured eating times. |
| Exercise is work | Assist patient's identification of *enjoyable* activities and gradually improve physical fitness by increased activities, pros and cons list. |
| Black-and-white thinking about food and weight loss | Assist patient in setting short-term goals to make gradual changes. Use of experimentation to challenge beliefs. |
| Secretive eating behavior | Use of hunger and fullness scales. Eating at a table with others or with the idea that others may be present. |

more empowered about making decisions about food to nourish his body and to find coping strategies to prevent binges.

Martin was encouraged to gradually incorporate more physical activity throughout the day by using the stairs and by parking his car at the far end of the lot. Using a list of pros and cons to examine reasons to change or not to change was helpful to motivate him to incorporate more physical activity into his daily lifestyle. As his motivation and fitness level gradually improved, he started walking on a regular basis over his lunch hour. His glycemic control, blood pressure, and blood lipids also improved over a period of time with a modest amount of weight loss, physical activity, and appropriate medications.

## HEALTHY EATING GUIDELINES

What does "healthy eating" mean to you? We define it as:

1. Choosing and consuming foods primarily for the purpose of nourishing the body.
2. Being in touch with and responding appropriately to hunger and fullness cues.
3. Eating a wide variety of foods. There are no "good" or "bad" foods. All foods are "allowed" and may be eaten in moderation.

We recognize that although these guidelines may sound simple, for people who struggle with eating disorders they may be extremely difficult. The following meal planning guidelines were developed to help you achieve "healthy eating" habits.

1. Try to eat three fairly equal sized meals daily as specified by your meal pattern. Snacks are necessary at higher levels, but may also be used at lower levels as indicated by your individual needs. Spreading food throughout the day into three meals and one to two snacks may help minimize urges to binge, purge, or restrict.

2. Try to use *regular* foods only, this will help to stop the dieting cycle. Avoid foods labeled "diet" or "lite," for example, diet pop, sugarless gum, sugar substitute, low-fat salad dressings, fat-free or low-fat foods.

3. Choose foods and fluids that count as food units. Limit your intake of noncaloric fluids (coffee, tea, water, and broth) and low-calorie foods (lettuce, raw vegetables, diet foods, etc.) both at meals and in between meals. This prevents feeling overly full or bloated after meals. We recommend that you drink 6 to 8 cups of fluid each day. Limit caffeinated beverages to 2 cups per day. (These do not count toward the total fluid allowance because caffeine is a diuretic.)

4. Limit bran products, such as bran muffins and bran cereals, to two to three servings daily. Excess fiber can cause bloating and gas, and impair absorption of some vitamins and minerals.

5. Try to avoid reading food labels and counting calories or fat grams. Learn to trust that this meal planning system will work for you. You may weigh and measure portion sizes initially. The long-term goal is to trust your visual determination of portion sizes.

6. *This meal planning system is not designed as a precise caloric regimen, but one that provides approximate equivalencies and encourages variety. Remember that healthy eating is flexible.*

7. Please consult with your Registered Dietitian for further information about the "Healthy Eating Guidelines," and for additional support during your recovery.

8. Gradually incorporate higher-risk foods into your meal plan with the support of your dietitian.

Table 11.4. Meal Patterns

| Calories* | Level | Breakfast entrée | Lunch & dinner entrée | Grain | Fat | Fruit | Milk | Dessert | Snack |
|---|---|---|---|---|---|---|---|---|---|
| 1,500 | I | 0 | 2 | 3 | 3 | 3 | 2 | 3/wk | 0 |
| 1,800 | IA | 0 | 2 | 4 | 4 | 4 | 3 | 3/wk | 0 |
| 2,000 | IB | 0 | 2 | 5 | 5 | 5 | 3 | 1 | 0 |
| 2,200 | IC | 0 | 2 | 5 | 5 | 5 | 3 | 1 | 1 |
| 2,500 | II | 0 | 2 | 6 | 6 | 6 | 3 | 1 | 1 |
| 3,000 | III | 0 | 2 | 6 | 7 | 6 | 3 | 2 | 2 |
| 3,500 | IV | 1 | 2 | 6 | 7 | 6 | 3 (2%) | 2 | 3 |
| 4,000 | V | 1 | 2 | 6 | 7 | 6 | 3 (whole) | 2 | 4 |

*For professional use only

## Breakfast Entrées (Levels IV and V)

Egg (1) and 1 slice bacon and toast
Eggs (2) and 1 slice toast
Egg omelet (2 eggs) with 1 ounce cheese or meat
French toast (2 slices)
French toast (1 slice) and ham (2 ounces)
Fruit yogurt (1 cup)
Milk (1 cup) with Carnation Instant Breakfast™ (1 package)
Muffin (1 medium)
Nutrigrain Bar™ and milk (1 cup)
Pancakes (2 pancakes, 4 inches across)
Pancake (1 pancake, 4 inches across) and 1 egg or 1 ounce of ham
  or bacon (2 slices)
Poptart™ (1 pastry)
Supplements: (1 can) Boost™, Ensure™, or generic equivalent.

*Note:* People who are not required to have a breakfast entrée may choose an egg or a breakfast meat as an "extra," and subtract it from lunch and dinner protein portions.

## Lunch and Dinner Entrées

Lunch and dinner entrées consist of 2 to 3 ounces of protein (meat, fish, poultry or meat substitute), plus 1 to 2 grains, plus 1 vegetable, plus 1 fat. An entrée is the "main course." Add other exchanges to your meal to complement the entrée.

*Example 1:* small chicken breast (3 ounces cooked), baked potato, ½ cup green beans, 1 teaspoon butter or margarine

*Example 2:* sandwich: 2 slices bread, 2 ounces turkey, 1 ounce cheese, 1 teaspoon mayonnaise, ½ cup soup

## General Portion Guidelines for Entrées

### Protein Portions

3 ounces of cooked meat, poultry, or fish (equal to the size of a deck of cards). (*Note:* meat loses 25% of its weight with cooking.)

The following items are equal to 1 ounce of protein and may be combined to meet the 2 to 3 ounces of protein needed for an entrée (choose 2 to 3 ounces per entrée):

¼ cup ground meat or tuna fish
1 ounce of deli meat or cooked fish, poultry, beef, pork, etc.
1 ounce of cheese or ¼ cup grated cheese
¼ cup cottage cheese or ricotta cheese
1 egg
⅓ cup tofu or dried beans
¼ cup hummus

### Vegetable Portions

Try to incorporate one deep green or dark orange vegetable each day to meet vitamin A requirements. One vegetable serving equals:

½ cup cooked or 1 cup raw vegetable
½ cup soup
6 ounces vegetable juice
1 cup salad

### Grains

See grain list.

### Fat

See fat list.

## General Portion Guidelines for Casseroles

*Casserole or mixed dish* that includes 2 to 3 ounces of protein (meat, fish, or poultry), plus rice, noodles, or potato and a vegetable (1 ½ cups total).

*Example:* 1 ½ cups casserole, such as tuna noodle casserole. (Add vegetable if casserole does not contain a vegetable.)

## Examples of Entrées

### Asian/Indian Entrées

Egg rolls: 2 rolls, add 1 grain
Indian curry: 1 cup curry, ½ cup rice
Oriental soups with vegetables, noodles, meat (2 cups)
Stir fry or chow mein: 1 cup rice, 1 cup stir fry (includes vegetable, oil, protein)
Thai curry: 1 cup curry, ½ cup rice

### Brunch Entrées

Crepes: 2 filled crepes with sauce
Egg strata: 3-inch square
Omelet: 2 eggs and 1 ounce cheese or meat, add 1 vegetable and 1 grain
Pancakes (2 small or 1 large) with 2 eggs or 2 ounces ham or sausage, and 1 tablespoon syrup
Quiche: 1/6 of pie, add 1 vegetable

### Fast-Food/Sandwiches

Sandwich: 2 to 3 ounces meat or meat substitute, 2 slices bread, 1 fat, and 1 vegetable
BLT: 3 slices bacon, 2 slices bread, 1 tablespoon Miracle Whip, lettuce and tomato
BBQ beef (or pork or chicken) sandwich, add 1 vegetable
Breaded chicken or fish patty sandwich: equals 1 entrée plus 1 fat
Chicken breast sandwich (grilled) on a bun, add 1 fat and 1 vegetable
Chicken strips (2 to 3 depending on size) or Chicken nuggets (5 to 6), add 1 grain and 1 vegetable
Egg McMuffin™, add 1 vegetable or 1 fruit
Fried chicken: 1 piece of chicken, add 1 grain and 1 vegetable
Grilled cheese sandwich, add 1 vegetable
Hamburger or cheeseburger, add 1 vegetable
Hot dog or bratwurst or Polish sausage on a bun, add 1 vegetable
Pita sandwich, falafel, or gyro (includes protein, fat, grain, and vegetable)
Ribs: 3 ribs, add 1 grain and 1 vegetable

Roast beef sandwich, add 1 vegetable
Submarine sandwich: 6-inch sandwich
Tuna (or egg, ham or chicken) salad: ½ cup tuna salad, 2 slices
bread, add 1 vegetable

### Frozen Dinners

Frozen entrée (net weight of 10 to 12 ounces) (1)
Frozen entrée (net weight 8 to 9 ounces): add 1 grain
Chicken or beef pot pie (1)
Hot pockets (1)
Frozen pizza: 2 small slices (¼ of thin-crust frozen pizza)
1 French bread pizza
Pan pizza (⅕ of pizza)
Personal-size pizza

### Italian Entrées

In general use the guidelines for mixed dishes for Italian entrées, where
the portion size equals 1½ cups.

Calzone: 1 small or ½ large, add tomato sauce
Cannelloni: 2 stuffed noodles
Lasagna: 3-inch square
Manicotti: 2 stuffed shells
Pizza: 1 large slice or 2 small slices
Polenta: 3-inch square (include protein and sauce)
Spaghetti: 1 cup noodles, ½ cup meat sauce

### Meatless Entrées

Bean and cheese burrito: 1 large
Hummus bagel sandwich, add 1 vegetable
Peanut butter and jelly sandwich: 2 tablespoons peanut butter, 1
tablespoon jelly, 2 slices bread, add 1 vegetable
Tofu stir fry: 1 cup stir fry, 1 cup rice
Tofu hot dog on a bun, add 1 vegetable
Tempeh burger on a bun, add 1 vegetable
Vegetarian burger on a bun, add 1 fat and 1 vegetable
Vegetarian chili: 2 cups
Spaghetti with marinara sauce: 1 cup noodles, 2 ounces protein,
½ cup sauce

## Mexican Entrées

Burrito: 1 large or 2 small

Chili rellenos: 1

Enchiladas: 2

Fajitas: 1 large tortilla filled with 2 to 3 ounces meat, cheese and/
or beans, and vegetables

Nachos: 2 ounces chips, 2 to 3 ounces meat, beans and/or cheese,
and salsa

Quesadillas: 1 large tortilla filled with 2 to 3 ounces meat, cheese,
and/or beans, and vegetables

Tacos: 2 tacos filled with meat, cheese, and vegetables

Tamales: 1 large or 2 small filled with cornmeal, meat, and sauce

## Salad Entrées

Bread bowl salad and 1 tablespoon dressing: equals 1 entrée plus
1 grain

Chef salad: 2 to 3 ounces meat/cheese/egg, vegetables, 1
tablespoon salad dressing, add 1 grain

Cottage cheese and fruit plate: ½ cup cottage cheese, 1 cup fresh
fruit, add 1 medium muffin

Pasta salad: 1½ cups (includes protein, pasta, dressing, and
vegetables)

Taco salad: ½ cup taco meat/cheese, salad, taco shell: equals 1
entrée plus 1 grain

## Grains and Energy-Rich Vegetables

*All equal 1 grain unless noted.* General serving sizes: 1 slice of bread; 1
ounce of ready-to-eat cereal or snack cracker products; or ½ cup cooked
grain, pasta, rice, hot cereal, or starchy vegetable.

## Breakfast Ideas

Cold cereal (1 ounce):

¾ cup flaked cereals

⅓ cup granola

¼ cup Grapenuts

1½ cups puffed rice or wheat cereals

Hot cereal (½ cup cooked)

Bagel (whole equals 2 grains, half equals 1 grain)

Donut (2 grains)
English muffin (whole equals 2 grains, half equals 1 grain)
French toast (1 slice)
Muffin (small equals 1 grain, medium equals 2 grains, large equals 3 grains)
Nutrigrain bar™ (1)
Pancake (4 inches across)
Poptart™ (1 pastry equals 2 grains)
Toast (1 slice)
Toaster pastry (1 pastry equals 2 grains)
Sweet roll (2 grains)
Waffle (1 square)
Waffle: Belgian (3 grains)

### Lunch or Dinner Ideas

*Breads*

Bagel (whole equals 2 grains, half equals 1 grain)
Banana bread or other specialty bread (1/16 loaf equals 2 grains)
Bread (1 slice)
Biscuit (2½ inches across equals 1 grain) (fast-food biscuit equals 2 grains)
Cornbread (1 small muffin or 2½-inch square)
Croutons (½ cup)
Croissant (small equals 1 grain, large equals 2 grains)
Dinner roll (1)
Hamburger or hot dog bun (whole equals 2 grains, half equals 1 grain)
Muffin (small equals 1 grain, medium equals 2 grains, large equals 3 grains)
Pita or pocket bread (1 large equals 2 grains, 1 small equals 1 grain)
Tortilla or taco shell (6 inches across equals 1 grain, 1 large tortilla equals 2 grains)

*Side Dishes/Pastas*

Bread stuffing (½ cup)
Cream soups or noodle soups (1 cup)
Dehydrated soups in individual containers (2 grains)
Four bean salad (½ cup)
French fries (½ cup) (McDonald's small fries equals 2 grains)

Onion rings: 6 to 7 equals 3 grains
Pasta, couscous, or other cooked grain or noodle (½ cup)
Pasta salad (½ cup)
Potato salad (½ cup)
Rice: any variety (½ cup)

*Snack Foods*

Angel food cake (1-inch slice)
Animal Crackers™ (8 cookies)
Chex™ mix (1 ounce equals ⅔ cup)
Chips: potato, corn, or flavored (1 ounce: about a handful)
Gingersnaps (3 cookies)
Grahams (3 squares, 2 ½ inches across)
French fries (½ cup)
Party mix (½ cup)
Popcorn (3 cups unbuttered, 1 ½ cups buttered)
Pretzels (1 ounce: about a handful)
Hot baked pretzel (one small equals 2 grains, one large equals
    3 grains)
Rice cakes (2 large equals 1 grain or 8 to 9 small equals 1 grain)
Rye Crisps™ (4 crackers)
Saltines™ (6 squares)
Snack crackers (1 ounce serving, about 5 to 6 crackers)
Waffle cone (1 large)
Vanilla Wafers™ (6 cookies)

*Starchy Vegetables/Dried Beans and Peas:*

Baked beans (½ cup)
Corn (½ cup)
Dried beans/peas (⅓ cup cooked)
Peas (½ cup)
Potatoes: baked potato (1 medium); hash browns (½ cup), french
    fries (½ cup), mashed or scalloped potatoes (½ cup), tator tots (6)
Sweet potato or yams (½ cup)
Winter squash (1 cup)

## Fruits

*All equal 1 fruit unless noted.* Choose at least 3 of your fruit servings as
fruits or juices. Try to incorporate 1 citrus fruit each day to meet Vitamin
C requirements.

Canned fruit or fruit sauce (½ cup or 2 halves pears or peaches)
Dried fruit (¼ cup).
Fresh fruit (1 piece or 1 cup pieces or chunks)
Fruit juice (½ cup)
Grapefruit sections (½ cup or ½ grapefruit)
Raisins (2 tablespoons)
Banana (whole banana equals 2 fruits, half equals 1 fruit)
Cranberry sauce (2 tablespoons)
Chutney (2 tablespoons)

The following items are high in simple sugars and can be incorporated in moderation into meal plans:

Gatorade™ or other sports drinks (1 cup)
Hi-C™, Koolaid™, Tang™, lemonade (½ cup)
Instant package of hot chocolate or other instant sugared beverage package made with water
Sodas: regular, not diet (½ can equals 1 fruit, 1 can equals 2 fruits)
Carmel or chocolate syrup (1 tablespoon)
Fruit Rollups™ or Fruit by the Foot™ (1 packet)
Honey (1 tablespoon)
Jelly or preserves (1 tablespoon)
Sugar (4 teaspoons or 4 packets)
Syrup (1 tablespoon)

## Calcium-Rich Foods

*All equal 1 calcium-rich*

Milk, any type (1 cup)
Hot chocolate made with milk (1 cup)
Fruit yogurt (6 ounces)
Plain or vanilla yogurt (1 cup)
Calcium fortified orange juice (1 cup)
Calcium fortified soy or rice beverage (1 cup)
Kefir™ or Yo J™ (1 cup)

## Fat

*All equal 1 fat unless noted.*

### Spreads/Dips/Dressings

Butter or margarine (1 teaspoon)
Cheese sauce (1 tablespoon)

Cream cheese (1 tablespoon)
Fruit dip (1 tablespoon)
Gravy (¼ cup)
Guacamole (2 tablespoons)
Mayonnaise (1 teaspoon)
Miracle Whip™ (1 tablespoon)
Oil (1 teaspoon)
Peanut butter or other nut butters (1 tablespoon equals 2 fats)
Salad dressing (1 tablespoon)
Salad dressing dip or mayonnaise-based dip (1 tablespoon)
Sour cream (2 tablespoons)
Sour cream dip (2 tablespoons)

### Nuts and Seeds and Miscellaneous

Avocado (⅛ medium)
Bacon (1 slice)
Cashews and almonds (6 nuts)
Coconut, shredded (2 tablespoons)
Olives (¼ cup sliced or 10 small olives or 5 large olives)
Peanuts (⅛ cup or ½ ounce, about 20 nuts)
Pumpkin seeds (3 tablespoons in shell, 1 tablespoon unshelled)
Sunflower seeds (2 tablespoons in shell, 1 tablespoon unshelled)
Walnuts and pecans (2 whole)
Other nuts and seeds (1 tablespoon without shells)
Creamer: half and half or nondairy creamer (2 tablespoons)
Coffee whitener (1 tablespoon powder)
Heavy whipping cream (1 tablespoon)
Cool Whip™ or Reddi Whip™ (4 tablespoons)

### Desserts

*All equal 1 dessert*

Angel food cake (1/12 of cake)
Candy bar (1 bar or 2 small snack size bars)
Cookie (3 inches across or 3 small holiday cookies)
Fruit Newtons™ (3 cookies)
Gingersnaps (6 cookies)
Granola bar (1 package)
Sandwich cookie (3 cookies)
Vanilla Wafers™ (12 cookies)
Bars or brownies (2½-inch square)

Cake with frosting (2-inch square)
Cheesecake (1-inch sliver)
Cream puff or cannoli (1)
Cupcake (1)
Fruit or cream pie (⅛ of pie)
Flavored yogurt (1 cup)
Frozen yogurt (¾ cup)
Fruit ice (1 cup)
Ice cream (½ cup)
Ice milk (¾ cup)
Ice cream sandwich (1) or ice cream bar (1)
Ice cream cone (1 single dip and cone)
Pudding (½ cup)
Sherbet (¾ cup)
Sundae (½ cup ice milk with 2 tablespoons chocolate or
    butterscotch syrup)
Eggnog (½ cup)

## Snack Ideas

*All equal 1 snack exchange.*

Bagel (whole) and cream cheese (2 tablespoons) or other fat
    (2 exchanges)
Candy bar (1.7 ounce) and juice (4 ounces) or regular soda
    (6 ounces)
Carmel corn (2 cups)
Cheese (2 ounces) and snack crackers (1 ounce)
Cookies (2 cookies, 3-inch diameter, or 6 sandwich cookies)
Cottage cheese (½ cup) and canned or fresh fruit (½ cup) and
    graham squares (3)
Crackers and cheese or crackers and peanut butter snack package
    and juice (4 ounces)
Donut and juice or milk (4 ounces)
English muffin (whole) and peanut butter (1 tablespoon)
Fresh fruit (2 cups) and fruit dip (3 tablespoons)
Frozen yogurt (1 ½ cups)
Granola bar (1 individual package) and juice (8 ounces)
Ice cream (1 cup)
Ice cream (½ cup) and vanilla wafers (10)

Ice milk (1½ cups)

Microwave popcorn (½ bag) and regular soda (6 ounces)

Muffin (medium) and juice (4 ounces)

Peanuts (¼ cup) and raisins (2 tablespoons) and plain M & M's (¼ cup)

Pudding (½ cup) and graham crackers (6 squares)

Sandwich cookies (3) or fruit newtons (3) and milk (8 ounces)

Sherbet (1 ½ cups)

Snack crackers or chips or pretzels (1 ounce) and regular soda (1 can) or juice (12 ounces)

Sweet roll and juice or milk (4 ounces)

Tortilla (large) with cheese (1 ounce) and salsa

Trail mix (½ cup) and juice (4 ounces)

### Supplements

1 can Boost™, Ensure™, or generic equivalent

Carnation Instant Breakfast™ (1 packet) with 2% milk (8 ounces)

Carnation Instant Breakfast™ (1 packet) with skim milk (8 ounces) and 1 fruit or 1 grain exchange

### Restaurant Snack Exchanges

Breeze™ (1 small)

Decaffeinated or regular café latté and small muffin or biscotti (1 large or 2 small)

French fries (small order) and regular soda (8 ounces)

Hot baked pretzel (1 large) and regular soda (8 ounces)

Milkshake (1 small)

Sundae (regular)

### Snack Equivalents

1 snack equals:

2 desserts

2 grains and 1 calcium-rich

2 grains and 2 fruits

2 grains and 2 fats

1 grain, 2 ounces protein, and 1 fat

1 grain, 2 ounces protein, 1 fruit

1 grain, 3 fruits

| Food item | Amount | Hot entrée | Other entrée | Grain | Fat | Fruits | Calcium | Dessert |
|---|---|---|---|---|---|---|---|---|
| **Breakfast 8 AM** | | | | | | | | |
| waffles | 2 squares | | | 2 | | | | |
| margarine | 2 tsp | | | | 2 | | | |
| maple syrup | 2 tbsp | | | | | 2 | | |
| strawberries | 1 cup | | | | | 1 | | |
| skim milk | 1 cup | | | | | | 1 | |
| **Lunch 12 noon** | | | | | | | | |
| McDonald's® hamburger with side salad | 1 order | 1 | | | | | | |
| french fries | small order | | | 2 | | | | |
| salad dressing | 2 tbsp | | | | 2 | | | |
| juice | ½ cup | | | | | 1 | | |
| frozen yogurt cone | small | | | | | | | 1 |
| **Snack 3 PM** | | | | | | | | |
| pear | 1 medium | | | | | 1 | | |
| **Dinner 6 PM** | | | | | | | | |
| Vegetable and chicken stir-fry/rice | 2 cups | | 1 | | | | | |
| rice | ½ cup | | | 1 | | | | |
| cashews (on stir-fry) | 6 | | | | 1 | | | |
| skim milk | 1 cup | | | | | | 1 | |
| **Snack 9 PM** | | | | | | | | |
| Fruit yogurt | 6 ounces | | | | | | 1 | |
| Total food units above | | 1 | 1 | 5 | 5 | 5 | 3 | 1 |
| Individualized meal pattern ("Goal for the day") | | 1 | 1 | 5 | 5 | 5 | 3 | 1 |

Figure 11.2. Meal plan worksheet.

### Becoming Aware of Common Eating and Exercise Myths

During individual and/or group sessions, the discussion may need to be directed so as to challenge irrational food and weight myths. Reputable nutrition references and education materials are essential to help patients challenge cognitive distortions. The following section gives a sample exercise concerning food and exercise myths.

#### A Sample Exercise for Patients

One strategy for changing unhealthy habits is to identify, evaluate, and change faulty beliefs. The following exercise is intended to help patients become aware of some of their beliefs about eating and exercise that accompany unhealthy behaviors.

#### Identifying the Problem

On the following pages are lists of words and a rating scale for each word. Think about what each word means to you. How would you rate each word on a "positive-negative" scale? Mark your response by placing an "X" anywhere along the scale. See the example below.

Night

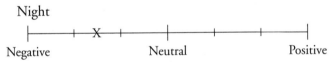

Negative                    Neutral                    Positive

For this person, night is negative. While night is thought of as a time for sleep and rest, it means something different for this person. It may signify a time when the person is alone. This person may not like to be alone. Please keep in mind that you are completing this worksheet for yourself. How you use the words positive or negative is entirely up to you. Feel free to write notes to yourself as you go through the worksheet.

1. Fat

Negative                    Neutral                    Positive

2. Dairy Products

Negative                    Neutral                    Positive

3. Carbohydrates

Negative                    Neutral                    Positive

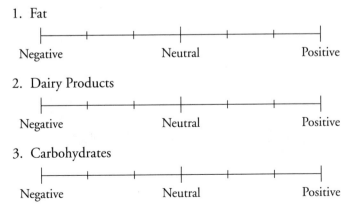

4. Protein

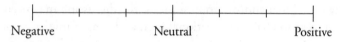

Negative                        Neutral                        Positive

5. Apples (fruit)

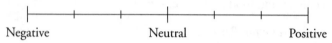

Negative                        Neutral                        Positive

6. Eating after 8:00 P.M.

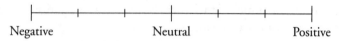

Negative                        Neutral                        Positive

7. Fiber

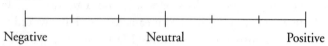

Negative                        Neutral                        Positive

8. Regular meals

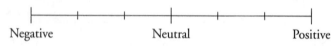

Negative                        Neutral                        Positive

9. Water

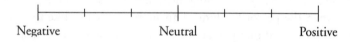

Negative                        Neutral                        Positive

10. Desserts

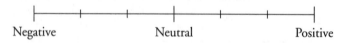

Negative                        Neutral                        Positive

11. Exercise

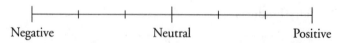

Negative                        Neutral                        Positive

12. Daily caloric requirements are less than 500 per day.

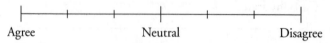

Agree                          Neutral                        Disagree

13. Calories burned must be greater than calories taken in.

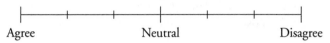

Agree                    Neutral                    Disagree

14. There are "magic" foods that help you lose weight.

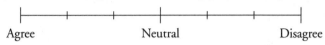

Agree                    Neutral                    Disagree

15. Purging after bingeing prevents calories from being absorbed.

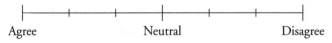

Agree                    Neutral                    Disagree

16. Using laxatives prevents calories from being absorbed.

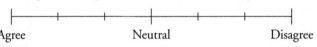

Agree                    Neutral                    Disagree

Have patients try to challenge these myths after being provided with nutrition education.

### Fat

Myth: Fat is bad ("Fat turns directly into body fat." "Fat needs to be avoided for successful weight control").

Fact: Many people believe that "fat" turns directly into body fat and has no other value. The nutrient "fat" (the satiety nutrient contained in food) provides the body with slow releasing energy, and so can be referred to as the satiety factor. When eaten in reasonable amounts, the satiety factor (a) provides the body with a sense of satisfaction after a meal, (b) helps to control obsessive thoughts of food and eating, and (c) helps to reduce the tendency to feel overly hungry and to overeat at the next meal. Also, a pound or two gained does not necessarily indicate body fat gained but indicates shifts in many minerals, fluid, and lean tissue such as muscles.

Myth: "I can eat as much as I want as long as it is fat-free, and I won't gain weight."

Fact: A calorie is a calorie. Eating fat-free foods in abundance will cause weight gain. Despite the great variety of fat-free foods at the supermarket, people continue to gain weight. In fact, in America calorie intakes have actually increased because people tend to overeat fat-free foods. Energy balance (calories in versus calories out), not energy composition, determines weight loss or gain.

### Dairy Products

Myth: Dairy products are "fattening" or "of little nutritional value other than calories."

Fact: Milk (along with yogurt, cheese, custard, and other calcium-rich foods) is a good source of carbohydrates and protein. More importantly, these foods provide calcium, which is an essential nutrient for blood clotting, muscle contraction, and maintenance of strong bones and teeth. An inadequate intake of calcium prior to age 35 may lead to poor bone formation, which cannot be completely corrected later in life. Milk and other calcium-rich foods are essential to healthy eating. Three to four servings from the calcium-rich group are needed to meet daily requirements for calcium.

### Carbohydrates

Myth: Carbohydrates are "fattening," and "to be avoided."

Fact: Carbohydrates, including pasta, bread and other grains, fruits, and desserts, are a primary source of energy for the body. Avoiding carbohydrates deprives one's body of essential nutrients and energy. Complex carbohydrates are excellent sources of fiber and B vitamins, essential for health and well-being. Spreading carbohydrates throughout the day will help stabilize mood, maximize energy and concentration levels, and decrease urges to binge.

### Protein

Myth: Protein often gets mixed ratings: Some see it as overly positive (to build muscles), while others think of it negatively (as a fattening food).

Fact: Protein is the major building block of all cells. It is found in muscles, tendons, and connective tissue throughout the body. Hormones that regulate body processes, such as the menstrual cycle and energy metabolism, contain protein. Enzymes that either initiate or promote the breakdown of food in the body also contain protein. Some proteins in the blood (antibodies) help fight infection. Others help prevent abnormal amounts of fluid in the blood from passing into extracellular tissue, which can cause edema (swelling of body tissue). Some people may associate protein with red meat, and red meat is often thought of negatively. However, red meat is not only a very important source of protein but is also a good source of iron and zinc. Diets that are extremely high in protein and low in carbohydrates are unhealthy and result mostly in the loss of body water. Diets that are extremely low in protein can lead to malnutrition. Protein needs can be met by eating 4 to 6 ounces of meats/meat substitutes and 2 to 3 servings of dairy products each day.

### Apples/Fruits

Myth: Apples (or other fruits) are great: since "an apple a day keeps the doctor away, then lots of apples a day is even better."

Fact: An apple (or any other variety of fruit) is a good source of simple sugar (carbohydrate), vitamins, minerals, and fiber. Many people with eating problems believe that the sugar in fruit is substantially different and "healthier" than the sugar in a candy bar, cookie, or piece of cake. As far as metabolism is concerned, the primary carbohydrate in all of these food items is a simple sugar. Overeating apples or any other fruit leads to poor nutrition in the same way as overeating any single food item leads to poor nutrition. In fact, eating an occasional candy bar, cookie, or piece of cake may be more satisfying than eating lots of apples. The key to balanced, healthy eating is to include moderation and variety in food choices. There is no perfect fruit. Eating a variety of fruits with the goal of 3 to 5 servings per day will help meet daily nutrient requirements. One should try to eat at least one vitamin C–rich (e.g., citrus), and one vitamin A–rich (e.g., deep orange–colored fruit) each day.

### Time of eating

Myth: Eating after 8:00 p.m. causes weight gain.

Fact: The time you eat does not influence weight gain provided that:
  (a) you eat the recommended amount of food on your individualized meal pattern;
  (b) the amount of food on your meal pattern is distributed evenly across at least three meals. Distributing food equally over at least three meals prevents a person from becoming overly hungry. Overeating in the evening is often related to inadequate food intake earlier in the day.

## Fiber

Myth: Eating lots of fiber prevents calorie absorption.

Fact:   Some fibers may speed up the transit time of food through the intestine while others may delay it. However, fiber does not alter the absorption of calories, and too much of it can lead to bloating and flatulence (gas) and affect how certain minerals are absorbed. The recommended dietary allowance for fiber is 20 to 35 grams per day, which can easily be met by consuming whole grain products and 5 servings of whole fruits and vegetables each day.

## Regular meals

Myth: Eating one meal a day is the best way to stay thin.

Fact:   Irregular eating patterns can affect hunger sensations to the point that one does not know when or what to eat. It is important to eat at least three meals a day. In addition, planned snacks are a helpful option to ensure a well-balanced diet. Eating just one meal a day slows down one's metabolism, most likely will not contain the adequate nutrients and calories needed daily, and may lead to binge eating. Eat when you are hungry, stop when you are full (once you learn to experience and recognize hunger and fullness signals). Many people find that eating every 3 to 4 hours helps them to stay in touch with their hunger and fullness cues, along with feeling more energized.

## Fluid

Myth: Fluid intake results in weight gain.

Fact:   Second to oxygen, water is the most vital substance for survival; one could live only a few days without it. Water is the medium in which all metabolic processes take place. About 60% of body weight is water. Since water is lost from the body daily, it must be replaced. The daily water requirement is about 2 to 3 quarts a day, or 8 to 12 cups; however, this amount need not exclusively come from drinking water but can come from foods and beverages as well. Caloric fluids are incorporated into the meal plan in the calcium-rich group and in the fruit group. An otherwise well-balanced diet requires only about 6 to 8 cups of fluid per day. Since water has no calories, it cannot result in weight gain.

## Desserts

Myth: Desserts (or any other "feared food") "turn immediately into fat" and are not part of a "healthy diet."

Fact: Desserts such as brownies, cakes, ice cream, and pie are often viewed as high-risk foods. However, it is important to remember that they can contain some essential nutrients, and that eating a high-risk food (such as a chocolate brownie) will not "cause you to gain 10 pounds." The following are examples to show just how many nutrients desserts can contribute to the diet.

ICE CREAM: Ice cream is a good source of carbohydrate, protein, satiety factor, and calcium.

CHOCOLATE BROWNIE: A chocolate brownie is a good source of carbohydrate and satiety factor.

FRUIT PIE: Pie is a good source of carbohydrate, satiety factor, and fruit (all of which contain important vitamins and minerals).

Desserts are part of a healthy diet, when consumed in moderation with attention to portion size.

## Exercise

Myth: The more exercise the better.

Fact: Most people really need only 20 to 30 minutes of exercise 3 to 5 times per week. Most women who exercise strenuously cease to menstruate. These women have lower than normal estrogen levels, a hormone that is essential for maintaining the integrity of bones. With low estrogen levels, bones are gradually demineralized and become weakened. Women who have amenorrhea (absence of menstruation) are at risk for stress fractures and osteoporosis. A diet low in calories coupled with low body fat stores and strenuous exercise sets the stage for amenorrhea and sports injuries to develop. Overtraining does not "help you get into better shape."

## Daily caloric requirements are less than 500 calories per day

Myth: Women need only about 500 calories per day.

Fact: It is impossible to achieve an adequate intake with only 500 calories per day. Prolonged intake of less than 500 calories per day will result in malnutrition, nutrient deficiency, loss of lean body mass, and profound weight loss. To meet daily requirements for all vitamins and minerals, women need approximately 1,500 calories per day, and men need approximately 1,800 calories. To maintain normal body weight and to support activity, most women need about 1,800 to 2,500 calories, and men about 2,000 to 3,000 calories daily. The higher the activity level, the more calories needed.

## Calories burned must be greater than calories taken in

Myth: If I eat 200 calories, then I must exercise until I burn 200 calories or more.

Fact: Two major contributors to energy expenditure are metabolic processes and voluntary activities such as standing, exercise, or eating. Metabolic energy expenditure accounts for at least two-thirds of the energy spent to maintain heartbeat, lung function, cellular activity, and nerve function. This is referred as *basal energy expenditure,* and is typically 1,200 to 1,500 calories for women and 1,500 to 2,000 calories for men daily. These are just the calories necessary to maintain weight while lying in bed all day without moving. However, most of us do not spend our days in bed: we are up and active. This is *voluntary activity.* Voluntary activities must be added in to the basal energy expenditure to correctly calculate daily energy needs: once again, *the higher the activity level, the more calories needed.*

## Magic foods

Myth: There are some foods that have negative calories or cause weight loss.

Fact: There are no known foods that help assist in weight loss. Some common myths are that celery has negative calories because it is so hard to digest, that a "grapefruit diet" will help you lose weight, and that eating "the cabbage soup diet" will cause a rapid weight loss. Even though there are many so-called magic foods out there, there is no scientific evidence to support claims that they aid in weight loss. Keep in mind that there are many people trying to make money selling weight-loss books and products without a college degree in nutrition or medicine.

## Vomiting prevents weight gain

Myth: Vomiting after binge eating prevents calories from being absorbed.

Fact:   Binge eating episodes are difficult to define. Typically, people eat very large amounts of food during a binge, at times 3,500 calories or more. Vomiting is not an effective way to lose weight nor to maintain weight. If anything, individuals with bulimia nervosa will eventually begin to gain weight, as it has been demonstrated that calories are absorbed with each binge eating episode, and the larger the eating binge, the more calories absorbed.

## Laxatives prevent weight gain

Myth:   Using laxatives prevents calories from being absorbed.

Fact:   Inducing diarrhea by laxatives does not significantly change the absorption of food in the body. Consequently, laxatives do not significantly prevent weight gain. What appears to be weight loss is actually dehydration. Laxatives work near the end of the bowel, in the colon, where they primarily affect the absorption of water and electrolytes (like sodium and potassium), after most of the energy nutrients from the food have already been absorbed into the body.

## References

### Literature Cited

Greene, G., Rossi S., Rossi, J., Velicer, W., Fava, J., & Prochaska, J. (1999). Dietary applications of the Stages of Change Model. *Journal of the American Dietetic Association, 99*, 673–678.

Kratina, K., King, N., & Hayes, D. (1996). *Moving away from diets.* Lake Dallas, TX: Helm Seminars Publishing.

Kristal, A., Glanz, K., Curry, S., & Patterson, R. (1999). How can stages of change be best used in dietary interventions? *Journal of the American Dietetic Association, 99*, 679–684.

Patterson, C., Whelan, D., Rock, C., & Lyon, T. (1989). *Nutrition and eating disorders: Guidelines for the patient with anorexia nervosa and bulimia nervosa.* Van Nuys, CA: PM Inc.

Prochaska, J., Norcross, J., & Diclemente, C. (1994). *Changing for good: The revolutionary program that explains the six stages of change and teaches you how to free yourself from bad habits.* New York: William Morrow.

Roth, G. (1989). *Why weight? A guide to ending compulsive eating.* New York: Penguin.

Satter, E. (1991). *Child of mine: Feeding with love and good sense.* Palo Alto, CA: Bull Publishing.

Stoner, S., Fedoroff, I., Anderson, A., & Rolls, B. (1996). Food preferences and desire to eat in anorexia nervosa and bulimia nervosa. *International Journal of Eating Disorders, 19,* 13–22.

Tribole, E., & Rusch, E. (1995). *Intuitive eating: A revolutionary program that works.* New York: St. Martin's Press.

Twin Cities District Dietetic Association. (1999). *Manual of clinical nutrition* (5th ed.). St. Paul, MN: Author.

### Suggested Reading (Professional References)

Fairburn, C. G., & Wilson, G. T. (Eds.). (1993). *Binge eating: Nature, assessment, and treatment.* New York: Guilford Press.

Kratina, K., King, N., & Hayes, D. (1996). *Moving away from diets.* Lake Dallas, TX: Helm Seminars Publishing.

Reiff, D., & Reiff, K. (1992). *Eating disorders: Nutrition therapy in the recovery process.* Gaithersburg, MD: Aspen Publishers.

Thompson, R., & Sherman, R. (1993). *Helping athletes with eating disorders.* Champaign, IL: Human Kinetics Publishers.

### Patient Self-Help Books

Fairburn, C. G. (1995). *Overcoming binge eating.* New York: Guilford Press.

Hirschmann, J., & Munter, C. (1995). *When women stop hating their bodies: Freeing yourself from food and weight obsession.* New York: Fawcett Columbine.

Johnson, C. (1995). *Self-esteem comes in all sizes: How to be happy and healthy at your natural weight.* New York: Doubleday.

Kano, S. (1989). *Making peace with food: Freeing yourself from the diet-weight obsession.* New York: Harper and Row.

McKay, M., & Fanning, P. (1992). *Self-Esteem.* Oakland, CA: New Harbinger Publications.

Roth, G. (1989). *Why weight? A guide to ending compulsive eating.* New York: Penguin.

Tribole, E., & Rusch, E. (1995). *Intuitive eating: A revolutionary program that works.* New York: St. Martin's Press.

Chapter 12

# Exercise in the Treatment of Eating Disorders

*LeAnn Snow*

The topic of exercise in the treatment of eating disorders is only in the early stages of scientific study. The issue is complex, being influenced by the numerous medical complications of eating disorders as well as by the presence of compulsive exercising in some of these patients. Few firm conclusions can currently be drawn from the literature as to specific exercise prescriptions for eating disorder patients. The information in this chapter will include basic principles of exercise science and musculoskeletal medicine that can reasonably be applied to this patient population. Wherever possible, specific information regarding exercise in the eating disorders context will be included. The reader should be aware that information on this topic is sparse, and the current suggestions may need modification as further studies yield new data.

Two important principles concerning the use of exercise in the therapy of eating disorders are (1) that its use should be a part of a comprehensive treatment plan for the patient as formulated by the entire treatment team, and (2) that the patient needs to be sufficiently medically stable to begin an exercise program and should be at a point in the psychiatric and nutritional therapy program where exercise use is permissible.

The following observations and techniques can guide the clinician who works with eating disorders patients. Ideally, the team responsible for treatment planning should have the assistance of a person or persons specifically trained in exercise science and/or therapeutic exercise. Such professionals include physical therapists, occupational therapists, exercise physiologists, and physicians specializing in physical medicine and rehabilitation, and may also include some family practitioners, cardiologists, and orthopedic surgeons with a special interest in exercise.

## Types of Exercise

We begin with some definitions and other background material.

### Flexibility

The term *flexibility* applies to the range of motion available at a joint in its normal motion planes (Knapik, Jones, Bauman, & Harris, 1992). This range of motion involves the bones of the joint itself as well as the muscle, tendons, and other connective tissues that support the joint. Range of motion can be evaluated with the patient actively participating (active range of motion, active assistive range of motion) or by the evaluator alone (passive range of motion). For optimal performance of daily living tasks, full joint range of motion is ideal. Limitations in joint range of motion may require alterations in the way a limb is used, and this alteration may consequently result in undue muscular fatigue or injury.

Flexibility limitations have numerous etiologies. Impairments may be congenital or secondary to injury or disease. When evaluation reveals decreased flexibility, the reason should be determined as accurately as possible so that a decision can be made as to the prognosis for correction of the deficit. If there is bony ankylosis or fusion such as in osteoarthritis when the changes are actually in the bone, the potential for improvement of joint range of motion is poor, and compensatory techniques need to be addressed. Alternatively, if the flexibility problem is related to soft tissue tightness or contracture, prognosis for improvement is better, and appropriate restorative therapy should be instituted.

Evaluation of flexibility and joint range of motion is important prior to the institution of an exercise program. Poor flexibility or imbalances of flexibility between agonist/antagonist muscle groups (flexors/extensors, abductors/adductors, etc.) or between right and left sides may predispose a person to injury (Knapik et al., 1992). In instances of hyperflexibility, risk of injury may also be increased. Flexibility deficits may indicate sites of prior injury that were not adequately rehabilitated and that may predispose the participant to future injury.

Joint range of motion and flexibility are easily evaluated by physical therapists, occupational therapists, or physicians with specialization in musculoskeletal medicine. If abnormalities are found, further evaluation and treatment are merited. Treatment may involve specific stretching exercises and therefore could be included in an individualized exercise program for the patient.

General principles of performing stretching exercises include avoidance of pain, and avoidance of bouncing or ballistic movements. It has been determined that of the stretching techniques available, ballistic stretching provides less satisfactory results in safe flexibility attainment; in theory, this type of stretching activates receptors that may enhance muscle contraction rather than relaxation and stretch. When performing static stretching exercises, it is recommended that each position be held for at least 30 seconds at a time (Shellock & Prentice, 1985). The participant may have a sense of muscle stretch or tightness, but no actual pain should occur if the exercise is done properly. Sometimes better results are obtained if an isometric muscle contraction of the muscle to be stretched is done prior to the actual stretch itself (Sady, Wortman, & Blanke, 1982; Wallin, Ekblom, Grahn, & Nordenborg, 1985). Most often a physical therapist assists in deciding which specific technique to use.

If normal joint range of motion or flexibility is present, the merit of a generalized stretching program is controversial. At this time experimental evidence is lacking to show that stretching prevents injury in persons with normal range of motion (Knapik et al., 1982; Pope, Herbert, Kirwan, & Graham, 2000; Wilmore & Costill, 1994). However, if the demands of a particular activity require increased flexibility, specific areas may be targeted. If rehabilitation after an injury is an issue, then flexibility programs should be applied to the body part with deficit to allow attainment of symmetric flexibility from right to left.

## Strength

*Muscle strength* is defined as the maximal force exerted by a contracting muscle (DeLateur & Lehmann, 1990). Strength is proportional to the muscle's cross-sectional area and is influenced by the speed of contraction. Static, or isometric, contractions are those in which the contractile units of the muscle shorten but there is no joint motion. Static contractions are used by the body to stabilize body limbs or trunk during activity. Dynamic contractions are those in which the muscle either shortens (concentric) or lengthens (eccentric) while effecting bone or joint movement. Such contractions either initiate and accelerate limb movement (concentric) or decelerate limb motion (eccentric). The measurement of strength can be accomplished using various means depending on the type of muscle contraction being measured.

Static contraction strength is quantified in the laboratory by measuring muscle tension with a strain gauge. However, in practical application, static strength is exemplified by the ability of a muscle group to exert and maintain a maximal contraction against an immovable object. Dynamic muscle strength is quantified by a combination of the applied resistance or weight lifted, and the number of repetitions performed. Re-sistance can include the weight of the limb to be moved, free weights, or weight machine plates.

As the trained muscle group gains in strength, the amount of resis-tance or number of repetitions is increased. The type of specific strength-training program instituted depends on the goals of the trainee since mus-cle tissue is very specific in its adaptations to demands applied (Frontera, 2000; Hoffman, Sheldahl, & Kraemer, 1998). The demands applied to the muscle must also be greater than those of daily activity for strength to improve (overload principle).

As with flexibility, deficits in muscle strength can have many etiolo-gies. In addition to weakness from specific muscular or nervous system diseases, weakness can result from injury to muscle or bone or nerve; weakness can also result from simple disuse. Weakness from disuse was probably a common problem several decades ago when a common prac-tice in some treatment programs was to confine anorexia nervosa patients to bed rest. Prolonged immobilization alone can decrease muscle strength at a rate of up to 3% to 5% per day (Appell, 1986; Joynt, 1988). Under-standing the etiology of existing muscle weakness allows for the most ac-curate application of a strength-training program. Needs for strengthen-ing can be as basic as to allow a person to get out of bed, to dress, or to walk. Alternatively, strength can be used for body building or for specific training to meet demands of a sport.

Detailed muscle strength evaluation is easily performed by physical therapists, occupational therapists, or physicians with specialized train-ing in neuromusculoskeletal medicine. When deficits are found on eval-uation, further searching may be required to elucidate the etiology. In the majority of cases of weakness, strengthening exercise is in order. Specific components of a program depend on the individual's needs, baseline mus-cle strength, and cause for the weakness.

Components of strengthening programs include the identification of the muscles to be trained, the type of contractions to be used, the amount of resistance to be used, the number of repetitions to be done, and the frequency of training sessions. Depending on the goal of the pro-gram, rate of repetition performance may also be specified. An example of a dynamic strengthening exercise program in a healthy person who desires non–sport specific strengthening is as follows: The biceps and tri-ceps, knee flexors and extensors, and ankle plantarflexors and dorsiflex-ors are targeted. Concentric and eccentric contractions are performed, and resistance of 60% to 80% of the one repetition maximum is used initially. Three sets of 5 to 10 repetitions each are performed. Rest between sets is 2 to 3 minutes. The program could be done three times a week, every other day. Reevaluation of muscle strength can be done in two to four weeks to determine whether resistances need to be increased.

Effects of muscle strengthening programs are multiple. Obviously, the primary gain is that of strength. Within the first several weeks after institution of a strengthening program, muscle strength is usually increased but not yet accompanied by muscle enlargement, or hypertrophy. This strength change is thought to be due to neurologic factors (Moritani, 1992; Sale, 1988, 1992). The muscular hypertrophy that results from strength training usually occurs after the first several weeks of a program. The extent of hypertrophy is quite variable and depends on the specific design of the program in addition to individual differences. The amount of hypertrophy development differs between males and females. Actual muscle tissue characteristics are identical between men and women; however, it is thought that men tend to develop greater strength and hypertrophy than women because the male hormone testosterone contributes to muscle growth (Fleck & Kraemer, 1987; Miller, MacDougall, Tarnopolsky, & Sale, 1993). Women, having much lower levels of testosterone, do not respond to strength training with the degree of muscle hypertrophy seen in men and therefore should not be hesitant to undertake strength training because of the risk of "bulking up." Strength training programs can also be tailored to de-emphasize muscle hypertrophy if desired.

Along with muscle hypertrophy, an increase in lean body mass is seen with strength training (Fleck & Kraemer, 1987). Due to the increase in lean body mass, body weight may increase, but the percentage of body fat actually decreases. This result is not seen in every person and tends to be seen with longer and more strenuous programs. In addition, strength training results in increasing bone density of the exercised limbs (Chilibeck, Digby, Sale, & Webber, 1995; Eickhoff, Molczyk, Gallagher, & De Jong, 1993; Heinonen, Oja, Kannus, & Sieranen, 1993; Heinrich et al., 1990; Stone, 1992) and also appears to increase strength of the tendons attached to the exercising muscles (Stone, 1992).

Although there are variations across programs, strength training in general is an anaerobic activity (Skinner, 1987) and does not result in cardiovascular conditioning (Fleck, 1992). Likewise, fewer calories are usually expended during strength training programs than during cardiovascular endurance training programs. Therefore, strength programs alone are not generally recommended for weight loss. Lastly, "spot reducing" is not possible with strength training techniques (Wilmore & Costill, 1994).

## Aerobic

Aerobic exercise is designed to improve the function of the heart and lungs. Therefore, it can also be also termed cardiopulmonary exercise. Such programs usually involve frequent and repetitive motions of large muscle groups with low resistances, as opposed to the fewer repetitions with high resistances seen in strength training. For adequate cardiopulmonary conditioning to occur, the activities are performed three to five times a week for a long enough time to maintain a designated target heart rate for approximately 20 to 30 minutes (American College of Sports Medicine, 1998; Wilmore & Costill, 1994). The target heart rate is defined as the desired heart rate to be maintained during cardiovascular exercise and is designated as a percentage of the maximal heart rate or peak heart rate. Aerobic activities may include running, biking, walking, hiking, swimming, and various aerobic workouts associated with health club programs. Some aerobic activities involve weight bearing (running, walking, hiking), and some aerobic activities are considered non–weight bearing (biking and swimming).

Evaluation of a person's baseline cardiovascular fitness can be performed in a number of ways. The most accurate and sophisticated method involves a graded aerobic exercise test with simultaneous measurement of oxygen consumption, heart rate, and blood pressure, and an electrocardiogram. In these tests, the difficulty of the aerobic task is gradually increased, and the parameters are monitored over time. At the conclusion of the test, a peak exercise heart rate is known, as are a peak oxygen consumption rate and a peak blood pressure response. With this information, an exercise program is constructed that assists the patient to exercise at a designated percentage of their peak values for heart rate or oxygen consumption. Given that this testing is sophisticated and requires special personnel and equipment, it is not always available, affordable, or practical, and in considering exercise recommendations for eating disorder patients, such an evaluation is rarely indicated. However, it is important that such testing be performed in persons with known heart or lung disease prior to institution of an exercise program. Testing is also merited in persons who are at high risk for developing heart disease. Risk factors include high blood lipids, smoking, hypertension, diabetes mellitus, abnormal EKG, and positive family history. Sedentary lifestyle is also a risk factor (Fleck & Kraemer, 1987; Hoffman et al., 1998; Skinner, 1987). Such issues are usually not relevant for eating disorder patients with anorexia nervosa or bulimia nervosa but may be of great importance in working with individuals who have binge eating disorder.

In persons with low risk of heart disease, simpler methods for target heart rate estimation are available. The easiest method is to use the following formula (Fleck & Kraemer, 1987; Skinner, 1987):

220 − age in years = heart rate maximal, or HR max.
(Maximal heart rate) × (___%) = target heart rate.

The percentage figure to be used in this formula depends on the person's baseline level of cardiovascular conditioning and can be set anywhere from 50% to 80%. The more sedentary an individual has been, the lower the percentage number that should be used in the target heart rate formula.

*Example:* A 50-year-old woman with binge eating disorder but no other risk factors for heart disease except lifestyle has been advised to begin an aerobic exercise program. She has been sedentary for 10 years. Maximal heart rate is determined by using the formula; maximal heart rate = 220 − 50 = 170.

Since she has been sedentary, the intensity of exercise should be somewhat low to begin with, so 60% of maximal can be used as the starting figure.

Exercise heart rate (target heart rate) is determined by using the formula:

Target heart rate = (60%)(170) = 102.

Another formula that can be used is the heart rate reserve formula (Fleck & Kraemer, 1987; Skinner, 1987; Wilmore & Costill, 1994):

(___%) (HR max − HR rest) + HR rest = target heart rate.

This formula is used to more closely approximate heart rate values to the actual oxygen consumption.

*Example:* For the 50-year-old woman in the example above at an exercise intensity of 60%, and with a resting heart rate of 70 beats/minute, target heart rate is determined from the formula:

(60%) [170 − 70] + 70 = (.60)(100) + 70 = 60 + 70 = 130.

Since the values obtained from use of these formulas are estimates, a small amount of variability is acceptable in their application.

Once a baseline level of fitness (sedentary, moderately active, etc.) and a target heart rate are determined, the exercise prescription is written with the individual's activity interests in mind. The principle of overload applies with aerobic exercise as well as with strength training. The intensity of aerobic exercise must be greater than that of daily activity to result in fitness improvement. A suggested starting target heart rate for previously inactive individuals with low cardiac disease risk is 60% to 65% of heart rate maximal. For persons of lower fitness level, aerobic benefit can occur at levels of 50% of maximal (Skinner, 1987). As the level of cardiovascular conditioning improves, there are several ways to adjust the exercise program to advance the level of training. The percentage of maximal heart rate that can be tolerated usually increases. For example, a person who started an exercise program at 60% of maximal intensity may later exercise at 70% to 80% of heart rate maximal with no increase in discomfort. As a frame of reference, persons in excellent aerobic condition may regularly exercise at 80% to 90% of their peak heart rate (Fleck & Kraemer, 1987). Another way of advancing the program is to prolong the duration of exercise time without changing the target heart rate.

Performance of an aerobic exercise program is recommended for a minimum of three times a week. In healthy adults, exercise frequency of greater than five times a week may promote injuries from bone and tendon overuse and hence is not strongly recommended (Wilmore & Costill, 1994). This precaution becomes even more important for the compulsively exercising eating-disorder patient because of the increased risk to bone associated with amenorrhea and low bone mineral density (Joyce, Warren, Humphries, Smith, & Coon, 1990).

Evaluation of aerobic parameters may be performed by various exercise professionals depending on the measures required. Evaluation of pulse at rest and after exercise can be done by nurses, physical therapists, and occupational therapists. As part of their exercise program, patients should be taught to take their own pulse. Conducting an exercise stress test or a maximal oxygen consumption evaluation requires the expertise of physicians (often internal medicine specialists or cardiologists) and exercise physiologists.

Effects of regularly maintained cardiovascular exercise include a lowering of resting pulse and a lowering of pulse rise for a given amount of exercise work (Skinner, 1987). Also, the amount of blood per beat that the heart can pump is increased both at rest and during exercise. Blood pressure at rest and during exercise tends to decrease, both systolic and diastolic. In addition, the ability of the body to deliver oxygen to the muscles during exercise is enhanced, and the ability of the body to extract the oxygen from the blood is also improved (Frontera, 2000). Muscle enzymes for aerobic metabolism increase, but there is little to no change in muscle strength or muscle hypertrophy as a result of aerobic training. This result is another example of the principle of specificity of training.

As may be surmised, aerobic exercise requires oxygen for fuel metabolism by the muscles and other tissues. Main body fuels for aerobic exercise include carbohydrates and fat. The caloric cost of aerobic exercise is usually higher than that of strength training exercise.

Aerobic exercise is important for maintaining overall health and is part of a comprehensive approach to decreasing the risk of heart disease (Hoffman et al., 1998). In persons who have already had a heart attack or who have required heart bypass surgery, as may be the case in obese individuals with binge eating disorder, cardiac rehabilitation is comprised primarily of aerobic exercise. Unfortunately, aerobic types of exercise are often the types overused by compulsive exercisers with eating disorders (Beumont, Brenden, Russell, & Touyz, 1994; Michielli, Dunbar, & Kalinski, 1994).

### Endurance

*Endurance* is defined as the body's ability to continue a task (DeLateur & Lehmann, 1990). In the context of exercise, endurance may be related to cardiovascular fitness or to muscular activity maintenance, or to both. *Cardiovascular endurance* is the ability of the body to continue in aerobic tasks. *Muscular endurance* is the ability of the body's muscles to either hold an isometric contraction for a length of time or to continue a series of contractions at a set level of resistance over many repetitions.

A person with excellent strength will not necessarily have good cardiovascular endurance or muscular endurance. Some studies have noted that subjects who train for both high-level strength and high-level endurance experience performance compromise in one of the areas, with strength more likely to suffer decreases than endurance (DeLateur & Lehmann, 1990; Joynt, 1988; Kraemer et al., 1995; Nelson, Arnall, Loy, Silvester, & Conlee, 1990). This response of the body is another example of the specificity of training response. A well-designed exercise program should account for the specificity of the body's response to muscular endurance tasks as well as to strength and aerobic tasks.

*Warm-up*

Warm-up exercises are low-intensity activities, such as jogging or calisthenics, that are designed to prepare the body for more intense exercise. Warm-up exercises are designed to increase heart rate, increase respiratory rate, and increase muscle temperature. Warm-up may also be important for injury prevention (Wilmore & Costill, 1994). Warm-up should precede most exercise sessions and should last 10 to 15 minutes. Cool-down exercises should be performed for 5 to 10 minutes after an exercise bout to decrease blood pooling in the extremities and to prevent dizziness or fainting (Wilmore & Costill, 1994). Cool-down activities can include walking or stretching but should not involve sitting.

## Exercise in the Eating Disorders Population: Unique Problems and Precautions

*Medical Complications*

As delineated in other chapters, the eating disorder patient is at risk for a number of medical complications. In patients with anorexia nervosa, these complications include electrolyte abnormalities, hypoglycemia, cardiac abnormalities, myopathy, neuropathy, temperature regulation changes, osteoporosis, and overall weakness. In the bulimia patient, medical conditions include both skeletal and cardiac myopathies, electrolyte abnormalities, reflex constipation, and peripheral neuropathy. The cardiac and skeletal muscle myopathies result from Ipecac® toxicity. The electrolyte abnormalities often result from purging with laxatives or diuretics. In the binge eater who is overweight, medical conditions relate primarily to increased body weight and include osteoarthritis, hypertension, and Type II diabetes mellitus.

*Preliminary Evaluation*

A thorough health history and physical examination need to be obtained prior to formulation of the exercise prescription. The history should include information on general health and specifics of the patient's eating disorder and information on medications, cardiac history, and endocrine history. Exercise history should include information on the types, duration, and frequency of exercise that the patient has participated in. The exercise history also needs to include information on how many years the patient has exercised, the occurrence of any exercise-related injuries, as well as subsequent treatment of these injuries and degree of recovery. Of particular concern is a history of stress fractures, which may be related not only to overuse but also to amenorrhea and osteoporosis (American College of Sports Medicine, 1997).

In the physical examination it is important to include body weight, height, vital signs, cardiopulmonary examination, and neurologic examination, with particular attention to cardiac rate and rhythm, muscular weakness, musculoskeletal pain, and sensory or reflex abnormalities. Laboratory examinations should include a complete blood count, serum electrolytes (sodium, potassium, chloride, bicarbonate), serum calcium, fasting glucose, and muscle enzymes (creatine phosphokinase, aldolase, lactate dehydrogenase, and alkaline phosphatase). In addition, an electrocardiogram should be obtained with particular evaluation of rhythm and QT interval (Cooke et al., 1994). An electromyogram may be indicated if proximal muscle weakness exists, or if abnormality presents in the muscle enzyme lab tests. In some patients skeletal X rays may be required, particularly if there has been a history of musculoskeletal pain or injury in the recent past. Depending on the results of the X rays, bone scans or bone density determinations may be needed. Specific criteria for use of bone densitometry have not yet been developed for use in the eating disorder patient. However, good clinical judgment should be used in deciding whether such a study is necessary. As previously mentioned, there is particular concern for bone density in the anorexic patient. Such patients may have bone densities below fracture threshold and are therefore at risk for pathologic fracture with or without activity (Sharp & Freeman, 1993).

If abnormal exam findings exist, use of appropriate consultants and further tests should be made and the conditions treated prior to initiation of an exercise program.

Many of the medical problems will likely have resolved prior to the point at which the patient is ready to begin an exercise program. However, there are some complications that are more prolonged in duration and may affect the parameters established for an exercise regimen. Therefore exercise programs for eating disorder patients need to be individually established in consultation with the treatment team members and in the context of the patient's treatment as a whole.

## Medical Complications in the Context of Exercise

### Electrolyte Abnormalities

A common electrolyte abnormality in anorexia nervosa and bulimia nervosa is decreased potassium from low body weight, from vomiting, or from laxative or diuretic abuse (Alloway, Reynolds, Spargo, & Russell,

1985; Bonne, Bloch, & Berry, 1993; Edwards, 1993; Hartman, 1995; Hofland & Dardis, 1992; McClain, Humphries, Hill, & Nickl, 1993; Mehler, 1996b; Mitchell, Pomeroy, & Huber, 1988; Powers, Tyson, Stevens, & Heal, 1995; Sharp & Freeman, 1993). Low potassium levels may affect contraction of skeletal muscles and of the heart. Muscle weakness, cramps, and heart arrhythmias may result, and the arrhythmias may be life threatening. Given that aerobic exercise increases heart rate, increases stroke volume, and places more demand on the heart, low potassium needs to be corrected prior to initiation of the exercise program.

Low magnesium is another abnormality that can be seen in anorexia and bulimia (Bonne et al., 1993; Hofland & Dardis, 1992). Effects of low magnesium are similar to those of low potassium in terms of cardiac arrhythmias and muscle cramps. Sodium levels may affect the fluid balance in the body and are involved in sweating during exercise. Therefore, the low sodium that is occasionally seen (Mitchell et al., 1988) should be normalized before exercise begins. Calcium is important for muscle contraction, again both in heart and skeletal muscle. Significantly low calcium levels may be related to muscle cramping and pain and therefore should be corrected before exercise is initiated (Hofland & Dardis, 1992).

*Muscle and Nerve Complications*

Overall muscle weakness may result from undernutrition and is certainly seen in severe anorexia nervosa. In addition, however, specific muscle diseases (myopathies) can be seen in bulimia nervosa and anorexia nervosa, especially if purging is involved. The myopathies may result from malnutrition (McLoughlin et al., 1998) or from abuse of Ipecac®, because of accumulation of the myotoxic compound emetine (Brotman, Forbath, Garfinkel, & Humphrey, 1981; Dresser, Massey, Johnson, & Bassen, 1992; Palmer & Guay, 1985; Pomeroy & Mitchell, 1989; Woodruff, Morton, & Russell, 1994). The myopathy presents with proximal muscle weakness in the arms and/or legs. Deep tendon reflexes may be decreased, but sensation is preserved. The weakness may be severe enough to prevent a patient from being able to lift her head, brush her hair, get up from a chair, walk, or climb stairs. With discontinuation of the Ipecac® and treatment of the eating disorder, the weakness tends to gradually resolve over a period of weeks to months. Since a patient may be allowed to add exercise to her program before complete resolution of the myopathy, the exercise prescription needs to include judicious use of strengthening exercises. Care must be taken not to overstress the weak muscles, since injuries may result.

Peripheral neuropathy may be seen in patients with anorexia nervosa and, more rarely, in patients with bulimia nervosa (Patchell, Fellows, & Humphries, 1994). The neuropathy is manifested variously by paresthesias in the hands and feet, decreased deep tendon reflexes, or just nerve conduction changes on EMG (Alloway et al., 1985). Clinically evident motor neuropathies have not yet been reported in eating disorder patients. Sensory deficits must be taken into account during an exercise program because these deficits may affect the stability and coordination of upper extremity and lower extremity motor performance. If the neuropathy is only sensory, strengthening exercises are not usually contraindicated, but caution is advised. If sensory function returns, exercise can be instituted more vigorously.

## Cardiovascular Complications

The usual cardiovascular complications of anorexia center around benign rhythm disturbances such as sinus bradycardia, sinus arrhythmia, orthostatic hypotension, and mild ST depression on EKG (Edwards, 1993; Kreipe & Harris, 1992; Nudel, Gootman, Nussbaum, & Shenker, 1984; Pomeroy & Mitchell, 1989). These changes are related to malnutrition and usually correct with rehydration and refeeding. If heart rate is less than 60 beats per minute, exercise is contraindicated (Kreipe & Harris, 1992). Although less frequent, more serious rhythm disturbances are those of QT interval prolongation, or ventricular dysrhythmias, which may be potentially fatal (Cooke et al., 1994). Their presence contraindicates exercise. The occurrence of these arrhythmias may be exacerbated by or contributed to by use of tricyclic antidepressants because these medications may affect cardiac conduction.

In addition to blood pressure and rhythm changes, cardiomyopathy may be seen in anorexia nervosa and bulimia nervosa and is most often due to Ipecac® toxicity (Mehler, 1996a; Mitchell et al., 1988). Emetine is toxic not only to skeletal muscle but also to heart muscle. In cardiomyopathy, tachycardia may be seen instead of bradycardia. Improvement in the cardiomyopathy is gradual after discontinuation of Ipecac®.

Since aerobic exercise places increased demand on the heart, cardiac health is important to the safety of aerobic exercise. Studies of anorexic women have found decreased exercise capacity compared with controls (Mehler, 1996a). Also, the anorexic women showed blunted blood pressure response to exercise, less rise in heart rate, and a lower maximal oxygen consumption than exercising controls (Nudel et al., 1984). If any question exists as to the safety of an exercise program in the presence of an abnormal exam or abnormal EKG, cardiology consultation should be requested and cardiology clearance should be obtained prior to beginning an exercise program.

In binge eating disorder, obesity is common (de Zwaan & Mitchell, 1992; de Zwaan et al., 1994; Wing & Greeno, 1994), and hypertension is a common complication of obesity (Buskirk, 1987; Sannerstedt, 1987). Since blood pressure increases during performance of both strength and aerobic exercise, awareness of the presence of hypertension is important with regard to exercise recommendations. In general, low- to moderate-intensity aerobic exercise should be acceptable (Hill & Butler, 1991; Skinner, 1987). Due to more pronounced blood pressure rise with isometric contractions (Sannerstedt, 1987), strengthening programs should be avoided or should emphasize dynamic contractions with proper breathing techniques.

*Bone Complications*

Another major medical problem, especially in anorexia nervosa, is osteoporosis associated with low body weight and amenorrhea (LaBan, Wilkins, Sackeyfio, & Taylor, 1995). This osteoporosis may differ in several aspects from post-menopausal osteoporosis because of earlier age of onset, prior to attainment of peak bone mass. For post-menopausal osteoporotic females, it is recommended that weight bearing exercise be an important part of their treatment (Carmichael & Carmichael, 1995; Chilibeck et al., 1995) to maintain bone density. However, in the osteoporosis of anorexia nervosa, it is not clear whether exercise contributes to any improvement in bone mineral density or whether exercise prevents further bone loss (Hay et al., 1992; Rigotti, Neer, Skates, Herzog, & Nussbaum, 1991). In fact, too much exercise may contribute to actual bone mineral loss (Salisbury & Mitchell, 1991). This observation may be of particular relevance to anorexia nervosa patients who compulsively exercise. It is also not clear how much refeeding and body weight recovery contribute to improved bone mineral density (Andersen, Woodward, & LaFrance, 1995; Baum, Kramer, Sanger, & Pena, 1987; Rigotti et al., 1991). It is apparent that if improvements occur, they occur quite slowly over months to years (Kotler, Katz, Anyan, & Comite, 1994). Peak bone mineral density may never be reached (Carmichael & Carmichael, 1995).

Because of the osteoporosis, the eating disorder patient is at risk for fractures, whether stress fractures or pathologic fractures without associated injury (Hartman, 1995; Sharp & Freeman, 1993). In addition to the osteoporosis seen in the anorectic patient, osteoporosis has also been seen in amenorrheic women who participate in frequent, prolonged aerobic exercise such as distance running (Carmichael & Carmichael, 1995; Putukian, 1994). Similar exercise patterns may also be seen in the eating disorder patient who is a compulsive exerciser (Brewerton, Stellefson, Hibbs, Hodges, & Cochrane, 1995). Therefore, the exercise itself, if excessive, becomes an additional potential contributor to the risk for fracture, not only from overuse but also from osteoporosis (Salisbury & Mitchell, 1991). Therefore careful attention needs to be paid to any patient complaints of pain in the extremities, pelvis, back, or ribs, and an evaluation should be done. If fractures are present, exercise should be limited until healing has occurred. If bone density is extremely low, certain types of exercise may need to be avoided. There are currently no clear guidelines as to the role of exercise for the osteoporotic eating disorder patient. However, consideration may be given to specific strengthening of the back extensors and avoidance of trunk flexion during abdominal muscle strengthening (Eickhoff et al., 1993; Sinaki, Wollan, Scott, & Gelczer, 1996). Consultation with an endocrinologist and/or orthopedist is suggested to answer questions when they arise.

In contrast to the osteoporosis seen in low-weight patients, a common problem in obese persons is that of osteoarthritis in the weight-bearing joints due to the additional weight that the joints need to support (Buskirk, 1987). With osteoarthritis, there is inflammation and spurring in the joints with resultant stiffness, pain, and decreased range of motion. In the prescription of an exercise program for a person with osteoarthritis, a balance must be established between maintaining functional joint range of motion and strength and preventing undue joint stress with increased pain and possible progression of the disease. Therefore, a strengthening program in this population may include more isometric contractions or dynamic contractions carried through less than a full active range of motion. Aerobic exercise should be directed toward non–weight bearing types of activities, such as swimming, or weight-bearing activity of less severe joint loading, such as walking instead of running or jumping (Edwards, 1993).

### Endocrine Complications

In anorexia nervosa, low fasting blood sugar is a common finding and is thought to be due to decreased liver glycogen and decreased substrate usable for glucose synthesis (Mehler, 1996a; Sharp & Freeman, 1993). Glucose is the primary substrate for exercise, and intensity of exercise may also influence blood sugar levels. No studies are available regarding the effect of exercise on the low blood sugar in anorexia nervosa. The hypoglycemia may resolve quickly with refeeding; however, serum glucose should be followed during exercise introduction to avoid adverse effects from hypoglycemia.

A common complication of obesity is Type II diabetes mellitus. The patient with diabetes mellitus presents a complex treatment problem that needs to be addressed by multiple team members including physicians, nutritionists, nurses, and educators. Aerobic exercise is an important component of diabetes management, not only in terms of blood sugar control but in terms of cardiovascular health and weight control (Hoffman et al., 1998). The standard recommendations for aerobic exercise should suffice for use in the overweight diabetic patient. Intensity should begin at a relatively low level in order to maximize compliance with a regular exercise program (Buskirk, 1987; Edwards, 1993).

*Other Complications*

Altered thermal regulation is yet another consequence of eating disorders, especially of anorexia nervosa (Hartman, 1995; Howard, Leggat, & Chaudhry, 1992). Patients complain of sensation of coldness and do not respond to changes in environmental temperature with usual amounts of shivering or vasodilatation (Sharp & Freeman, 1993). During mild to moderate exercise, the body generates heat with resultant need for sweating to dissipate this heat. The altered thermoregulatory mechanism in the anorectic patient may affect her response to exercise, but no specific data are available on this topic. Care should be taken to avoid undue heat or cold stress during exercise, however.

Regular exercise has been suggested as an important component of therapy for the reflex constipation seen after laxative discontinuation (Mehler, 1996b). Exercise has also been suggested as an alternative activity to substitute for high-risk situations for the binge eater (Mitchell, Hoberman, & Pyle, 1989).

As stated previously, all patients should be medically stable and cleared for exercise by their treatment team prior to institution of an exercise program. Also, ongoing patient education is an important ingredient of successful treatment and should include instruction in the principles of safe exercise.

*Additional Considerations*

In the anorexia nervosa patient, body mass index values are sometimes used as one parameter in determining permissibility of exercise. Body mass index is defined as (Edwards, 1993):

$$\frac{\text{weight, in kg}}{(\text{height})^2, \text{ in meters}}$$

In the University of Minnesota eating disorders program, attainment of a body mass index of 19 is recommended for low-weight patients prior to the patient being allowed to do any exercise.

There are also estimates of caloric expenditures of specific activities, which have been published (Noble, 1986) (see Table 12.1). This information may be useful to nutritionists, patients, and exercise specialists in planning with regard to the balance between caloric intake, weight goals, and exercise performed. These energy expenditure values are only rough estimates but may serve as a general guide. In addition to being only estimates, the values were obtained by evaluating healthy persons, not patients with eating disorders, and therefore their application needs to be placed in the proper perspective.

## Applications

### General Principles for Exercise by Low-Body-Weight Eating-Disorder Patients

#### Acute Needs

If the patient's condition is severe enough to require hospital admission, the initial care plan will not likely include exercise. The patient may be diffusely weak and unable to walk or to move in bed, but strengthening needs to be preceded by establishment of medical stability, with institution of a sound refeeding program. Exercise is therefore limited to that needed for activities of daily living. Bed rest is recommended for 15 to 30 minutes after meals to avoid worsening of impaired gastric emptying; compulsive exercisers must be closely monitored.

#### Subacute Needs

Once medical stability has been obtained and associated conditions addressed, and once the patient has been approved for exercise by the treatment team, a preliminary exercise prescription can be formulated. The program may include flexibility and posture exercises and could emphasize strengthening exercise more than aerobic exercise (Michielli et al., 1994), although conclusive data are not available to support this assumption. If strength and flexibility are stressed, the caloric expenditure could be less than with aerobic exercise, and this exercise may contribute to increase in bone mass of the exercised limbs as well as to increased

Table 12.1. Energy Expenditure Estimates for Selected Activities

| Activity | Approximate caloric expenditure (kcal/minute) |
|---|---|
| Bicycling | |
| 5.5 mph | 4.5 |
| 9.4 mph | 7.0 |
| Football | 8.9 |
| Golf | 5.0 |
| Running | |
| Short distance | 13.3–16.6 |
| Cross-country | 10.6 |
| Swimming | |
| Backstroke | 11.5 |
| Breaststroke | 11.0 |
| Freestyle/crawl | 14.0 |

Source: From Noble, 1986.

lean body mass and therefore to increase in weight. Use of strength training also de-emphasizes the activities that often are undertaken by the compulsive exerciser. Resistances used for the strength training can be as little as the weight of the limb being moved or as great as barbells or free weights, depending on the patient's pre-exercise status. Care needs to be taken to avoid use of too heavy resistance due to risk of stress fracture (Baum et al., 1987). Aspects of the exercise program should be supervised by a physical therapist or other suitably trained professional to assure that safe techniques are followed and limits are observed. Aerobic activity can be limited to 15 to 20 minutes of leisurely and normal speed (not rapid) walking every day.

Regular updates are needed to make sure that the patient is continuing to meet caloric intake and weight gain goals during this time. If the patient fails to meet goals, revisions in the plan need to be considered by the treatment team, and the exercise prescription may need modification accordingly.

*Chronic Needs*

A foundation needs to be established on which the patient can build a reasonable and safe pattern of activity for health maintenance in the long term. As weight gain goals continue progressively to be met, the amount of aerobic activity in the exercise program can be increased. Individual programs will vary. If the patient has a history of compulsive exercise, it may be that the maximal aerobic exercise suggested should always be limited to three times a week for 20 to 30 minutes each session, and be limited to less stressful forms of activities, such as walking as opposed to running. Supplemental strength training can also be done but again may be limited in intensity and frequency to avoid overindulgence. For maintenance, the patient may have a program designed for use at a health club with use of a swimming pool, walking track, exercise bikes, and free weights or weight machines. For persons without a history of compulsive exercise, aerobic workouts may be more liberal but should always be evaluated within the context of the patient continuing to maintain healthy weight and avoiding injury. Continuation of weight-bearing activity and strength training may also help with bone mass maintenance, but more study is needed of this topic prior to formulation of firm conclusions.

## General Principles for Exercise by Overweight Eating-Disorder Patients

### Initial Needs

The situation of the overweight patient is different from that of the underweight patient in that emphasis for exercise is on weight loss and subsequent weight control. There may also be a component of stress management. Therefore, after the patient has attained medical stability and has been cleared for exercise by the treatment team, an exercise prescription should be formulated to include a greater emphasis on aerobic exercise than on strength training, although both are important. Flexibility and posture exercise may also be included and would be applicable for problems such as decreased joint range of motion in the back, hips, or knees. To begin with, target heart rate may be set at a relatively low percentage of peak heart rate, such as 50% to 60%, and activities may need to be relatively mild if the patient has previously been inactive. Suggested activities include walking, low- or medium-speed stationary bicycling with low pedal resistance, or slow swimming or water aerobics. At the start of the program, the activity should be done three to four times per week. Strengthening exercise may be done, limiting joint range of motion to pain-free ranges. Strengthening can be done two to three times per week. Emphasis should also be put on reasonably reachable goals with minimal to moderate stress or discomfort so as to encourage continuation in the program. Group activities and support may also be helpful (Wing & Greeno, 1994).

*Subacute Needs*

As the treatment program progresses, the patients will ideally be able to tolerate longer bouts of aerobic exercise at gradually higher percentages of their peak heart rate. Therefore, the program can be modified to allow for either longer periods of the preceding exercise or for increased intensity of exercise, such as faster biking with greater pedal resistance. Patients can be taught to monitor their own pulse and to keep track of their target heart rate for the designated times. Strength training can be modified with increasing resistance, and frequency can possibly be decreased to one to two times per week. Flexibility and posture exercises can be continued as needed.

*Chronic Needs*

Ultimately the patient should be educated in ways to maintain an exercise program for overall health. Aerobic exercise should continue at a frequency of three to five times per week with target heart rate individualized, and with activities recommended that the patient enjoys or at least will find acceptable. Strength training may be combined with an aerobic workout in a properly performed circuit training program. The circuit training exercise regimen is one in which multiple repetitions of a resistance exercise are performed rapidly with only short rests between sets, and short rests between muscle group exercises. It is one of the few strengthening programs that results in aerobic benefit as well (Frontera, 2000). Circuit training is a demanding activity and therefore may not be suitable for less than highly motivated persons. If circuit training is not a reasonable option, strength training may be done one to two times per week in addition to the aerobic work. Care needs to be taken to avoid unreasonable time demands that will lessen successful participation. Maintenance of a baseline level of strength and endurance may be obtained by the aerobic exercise and by active participation in the activities of daily living and general activities, such as housework, gardening, stair climbing, lawn care, and walking to work.

*General Principles for Exercise by Normal-Weight Eating-Disorder Patients*

For this group of patients, emphasis needs to be on continuation of normal weight and on achievement of good cardiovascular fitness and reasonable strength. A combination of aerobic, strengthening, and flexibility exercises may be used, with a target heart rate of 50% to 80% of maximal heart rate. Aerobic exercise can be done three to five times per week. Strength training can be done two to three times per week. Monitoring may be needed to assure avoidance of excessive exercise. The goal is maintenance of a regular exercise program in the community, either at a health club or YMCA, or in a home-based, independently performed program.

## Case Studies

### Jody (Anorexia Nervosa)

Several items are noted in Jody's situation. First, her condition is serious enough to require hospitalization. She is also a compulsive exerciser. Although she has experimented with binge eating, a history of regular Ipecac® use is absent in her history. At a height of 5 feet, 5 inches and a weight of 85 pounds, her body mass index is 14.5 kg/m². Therefore, exercise is not indicated at this time. Jody requires close observation for exercise sneaking. Once her weight has reached about 111 pounds, her BMI will be 19, and an exercise program could be considered if her treatment team approves. Guidelines to follow are those for the low-weight patient.

### Kim (Bulimia Nervosa)

In Kim's case, there is a history of laxative abuse and use of diet pills but not a clear history of Ipecac® abuse. The exercise-related concerns that should be evaluated are electrolyte abnormalities and cardiac alterations.

Since Kim's weight is in a normal range and since her condition is satisfactory enough to allow for outpatient therapy, an exercise program could be started once her condition is deemed stable enough to do so by the treatment team. A well-rounded program with aerobic components and flexibility and strength components would be acceptable, with guidelines as presented above. Circuit training could be recommended. Efforts can be coordinated with Kim's psychiatric caregivers and her dietitian so that exercise can be incorporated into her methods for substituting healthy behaviors for binge eating or purging in response to trigger stimuli.

### Martin (Binge Eating Disorder)

Several items in Martin's history deserve comment with regard to use of exercise. First, Martin has several sequelae related to binge eating disorder and increased weight including hypertension, increased cholesterol, and pre-diabetes mellitus. At 285 pounds, he is overweight for his height. His lifestyle is sedentary, both at work and at home. Prior to an exercise program, he needs a complete evaluation of his hypertension, blood glucose, and cholesterol. Appropriate treatment for these problems needs to be instituted, including use of medications, diet modifications, and education. It would be advisable for him to have a graded exercise test or cardiac stress test prior to exercise parameter-setting. Martin should be encouraged to participate in an exercise program that keeps his heart rate at 50% to 60% of his maximal heart rate for 20 to 30 minutes three times per week. He estimates that to walk from the parking lot to his office, rather than taking the shuttle bus, would take him 15 to 20 minutes; this walk is the exercise to choose to begin his program. In addition, it is recommended that Martin climb the flight of stairs to his office instead of taking the elevator. He is also advised to take a short walk or to do stretching exercises during his work breaks rather than going to the vending machine for a snack.

Prior to institution of this program at work, Martin should be observed doing a 30-minute walk several times a week in the presence of a physical therapist, who monitors his pulse and blood pressure prior to beginning, halfway through, and after his exercise, (immediately, 5 minutes after, and 10 minutes after). If his systolic blood pressure does not increase by more that 20 to 30 mm of mercury during the walk, no modifications to the walking pace or duration will be necessary. Martin should learn how to monitor his pulse and be told signs to watch for.

Given his work schedule, he would be unable to incorporate more exercise than his daily walk; therefore, strength training is not added due to concern about a lack of compliance with demands that are too great. Strength training could be added at a later time, however, should the patient so desire.

## References

Alloway, R., Reynolds, E., Spargo, E., & Russell, G. (1985). Neuropathy and myopathy in two patients with anorexia and bulimia nervosa. *Journal of Neurology, Neurosurgery, and Psychiatry, 48*, 1015–1020.

American College of Sports Medicine. (1997). The female athlete triad. *Medicine and Science in Sports and Exercise, 29*, i–ix.

American College of Sports Medicine. (1998). The recommended quantity and quality of exercise for developing and maintaining cardiorespiratory and muscular fitness in healthy adults. *Medicine and Science in Sports and Exercise, 30,* 975–991.

Andersen, A., Woodward, P., & LaFrance, N. (1995). Bone mineral density of eating disorder subgroups. *International Journal of Eating Disorders, 18,* 335–342.

Appell, H. (1986). Skeletal muscle atrophy during immobilization. *International Journal of Sports Medicine, 7,* 1–5.

Baum, M., Kramer, E., Sanger, J., & Pena, A. (1987). Stress fractures and reduced bone mineral density with prior anorexia nervosa. *Journal of Nuclear Medicine, 28,* 1506–1507.

Beumont, P., Brenden, A., Russell, J., & Touyz, S. (1994). Excessive physical activity in dieting disorder patients: Proposals for a supervised exercise program. *International Journal of Eating Disorders, 15,* 21–36.

Bonne, O., Bloch, M., & Berry, E. (1993). Adaptation to severe chronic hypokalemia in anorexia nervosa: A plea for conservative management. *International Journal of Eating Disorders, 13,* 125–128.

Brewerton, T., Stellefson, E., Hibbs, N., Hodges, E., & Cochrane, C. (1995). Comparison of eating disorder patients with and without compulsive exercising. *International Journal of Eating Disorders, 17,* 413–416.

Brotman, M., Forbath, N., Garfinkel, P., & Humphrey, J. (1981). Myopathy due to ipecac syrup poisoning in a patient with anorexia nervosa. *CMA Journal, 125,* 453–454.

Buskirk, E. (1987). Obesity. In J. Skinner (Ed.), *Exercise testing and exercise prescription for special cases.* Philadelphia: Lea & Feiger.

Carmichael, K., & Carmichael, D. (1995). Bone metabolism and osteopenia in eating disorders. *Medicine, 74,* 254–267.

Chilibeck, P., Digby, G., Sale, D., & Webber, C. (1995). Exercise and bone mineral density. *Sports Medicine, 19,* 103–122.

Cooke, R., Chambers, J., Singh, R., Todd, G., Smeton, J., Treasure, J., & Treasure, T. (1994). QT Interval in anorexia nervosa. *British Heart Journal, 72,* 69–73.

DeLateur, B., & Lehmann, J. (1990). Therapeutic exercise to develop strength and endurance. In F. Kottke, K. Stillwell, & J. Lehmann (Eds.), *Krusen's handbook of physical medicine and rehabilitation* (4th ed.). Philadelphia: W. B. Saunders.

de Zwaan, M., & Mitchell, J. (1992). Binge eating in the obese. *Annals of Medicine, 24,* 303–308.

de Zwaan, M., Mitchell, J., Seim, H., Specker, S., Pyle, R., Raymond, N., & Crosby, R. (1994). Eating related and general psychopathology in obese females with binge eating disorder. *International Journal of Eating Disorders, 15,* 43–52.

Dresser, L., Massey, E., Johnson, E., & Bassen, E. (1992). Ipecac myopathy and cardiomyopathy. *Journal of Neurology, Neurosurgery, and Psychiatry, 55,* 560–562.

Edwards, K. (1993). Obesity, anorexia, and bulimia. *Medical Clinics of North America, 77,* 899–909.

Eickhoff, J., Molczyk, L., Gallagher, J., & De Jong, S. (1993). Influence of isotonic, isometric, and isokinetic muscle strength on bone mineral density of the spine and femur in young women. *Bone and Mineral, 20,* 201–209.

Fleck, S. (1992). Cardiovascular response to strength training. In P. Komi (Ed.), *Strength and power in sport.* Oxford: Blackwell Scientific Publications.

Fleck, S., & Kraemer, W. (1987). *Designing resistance training programs.* Champaign, IL: Human Kinetic Books.

Frontera, W. (2000). Exercise in physical medicine and rehabilitation. In M. Grabois (Ed.), *Physical medicine and rehabilitation: The complete approach.* Malden, MA: Blackwell Scientific Publications.

Hartman, D. (1995). Anorexia nervosa: Diagnosis, aetiology, and treatment. *Postgraduate Medicine, 71,* 712–716.

Hay, P., Delahunt, J., Hall, A., Mitchell, A., Harper, G., & Salmond, C. (1992). Predictor of osteopenia in premenopausal women with anorexia nervosa. *Calcified Tissue International, 50,* 498–501.

Heinonen, A., Oja, P., Kannus, P., & Sieranen, H. (1993). Bone mineral density of female athletes in different sports. *Bone & Mineral, 23,* 1–14.

Heinrich, C., Going, S., Pamenter, R., Perry, C., Boyden, T., & Lohman, T. (1990). Bone mineral content of cyclically menstruating female resistance and endurance trained athletes. *Medicine and Science in Sports and Exercise, 22,* 558–563.

Hill, D., & Butler, S. (1991). Haemodynamic responses to weight lifting exercise. *Sports Medicine, 12,* 1–7.

Hoffman, M., Sheldahl, L., & Kraemer, W. (1998). Therapeutic exercise. In J. DeLisa (Ed.), *Rehabilitation medicine: Principles and practice* (3rd ed.). Philadelphia: Lippincott-Raven.

Hofland, S., & Dardis, P. (1992). Bulimia nervosa: Associated physical problems. *Journal of Psychosocial Nursing and Mental Health Services, 30,* 23–27.

Howard, M., Leggat, H., & Chaudhry, S. (1992). Haematological and immunological abnormalities in eating disorders. *British Journal of Hospital Medicine, 48,* 234–239.

Joyce, J., Warren, D., Humphries, L., Smith, A., & Coon, J. (1990). Osteoporosis in women with eating disorders: Comparison of physical parameters, exercise, and menstrual status with SPA and DPA evaluation. *Journal of Nuclear Medicine, 31,* 325–331.

Joynt, R. (1988). Therapeutic exercise. In J. DeLisa (Ed.), *Rehabilitation medicine: Principles and practice.* Philadelphia: J. B. Lippincott.

Knapik, S., Jones, G., Bauman, C., & Harris, J. (1992). Strength, flexibility, and athletic injuries. *Sports Medicine, 14,* 277–288.

Kotler, L., Katz, L., Anyan, W., & Comite, F. (1994). Case study of the effects of prolonged and severe anorexia nervosa on bone mineral density. *International Journal of Eating Disorders, 15,* 395–399.

Kraemer, W., Patton, J., Gordon, S., Harman, E., Deschenes, M., Reynolds, K., Newton, R., Triplett, N., & Dziades, J. (1995). Compatibility of high-intensity strength and endurance training on hormonal and skeletal muscle adaptations. *Journal of Applied Physiology, 78,* 976–989.

Kreipe, R., & Harris, J. (1992). Myocardial impairment resulting from eating disorders. *Pediatric Annals, 21,* 760–768.

LaBan, M., Wilkins, J., Sackeyfio, A., & Taylor, R. (1995). Osteoporotic stress fractures in anorexia nervosa: Etiology, diagnosis, and review of four cases. *Archives of Physical Medicine and Rehabilitation, 76,* 884–887.

McClain, C., Humphries, L., Hill, K., & Nickl, N. (1993). Gastrointestinal and nutritional aspects of eating disorders. *Journal of the American College of Nutrition, 12,* 466–474.

McLoughlin, D., Spargo, E., Wassif, W., Newham, D., Peters, T., Lantos, P., & Russell, G. (1998). Structural and functional changes in skeletal muscle in anorexia nervosa. *Acta Neuropathologica, 95,* 632–640.

Mehler, P. (1996a). Eating disorders: 1. Anorexia nervosa. *Hospital Practice, 31* (1), 109–113, 117.

Mehler, P. (1996b). Eating disorders: 2. Bulimia nervosa. *Hospital Practice, 31* (2), 107–123.

Michielli, D., Dunbar, C., & Kalinski, U. (1994). Is exercise indicated for the patient diagnosed as anorectic? *Journal of Psychosocial Nursing and Mental Health Services, 32,* 33–35.

Miller, A., MacDougall, J., Tarnopolsky, M., & Sale, D. (1993). Gender differences in strength and muscle fiber characteristics. *European Journal of Applied Physiology, 66,* 254–262.

Mitchell, J., Hoberman, H., & Pyle, R. (1989). An overview of the treatment of bulimia nervosa. *Psychiatric Medicine, 7,* 317–332.

Mitchell, J., Pomeroy, C., & Huber, M. (1988). A clinician's guide to the eating disorders medicine cabinet. *International Journal of Eating Disorders, 7,* 211–223.

Moritani, T. (1992). Time course of adaptations during strength and power training. In P. Komi (Ed.), *Strength and power in sport.* Oxford: Blackwell Scientific Publications.

Nelson, A., Arnall, P., Loy, S., Silvester, L., & Conlee, R. K. (1990). Consequences of combining strength and endurance training regimens. *Physical Therapy, 70,* 287–294.

Noble, B. (1986). *Physiology of exercise and sport.* St. Louis: Mosby College Publications.

Nudel, D., Gootman, N., Nussbaum, M., & Shenker, I. (1984). Altered exercise performance and abnormal sympathetic responses to exercise in patients with anorexia nervosa. *Journal of Pediatrics, 105,* 34–37.

Palmer, E., & Guay, A. (1985). Reversible myopathy secondary to abuse of ipecac in patients with major eating disorders. *New England Journal of Medicine, 313,* 1457–1459.

Patchell, R., Fellows, H., & Humphries, L. (1994). Neurologic complications of anorexia nervosa. *Acta Neurologica Scandinavica, 89,* 111–116.

Pomeroy, C., & Mitchell, J. (1989). Medical complications and management of eating disorders. *Psychiatric Annals, 19,* 488–493.

Pope, R., Herbert, R., Kirwan, J., & Graham, B. (2000). A randomized trial of preexercise stretching for prevention of lower-limb injury. *Medicine and Science in Sports and Exercise, 32,* 271–277.

Powers, P., Tyson, I., Stevens, B. A., & Heal, A. (1995). Total body potassium and serum potassium among eating disorder patients. *International Journal of Eating Disorders, 18,* 269–276.

Putukian, M. (1994). The female triad: Eating disorders, amenorrhea, and osteoporosis. *Medical Clinics of North America, 78,* 345–356.

Rigotti, N., Neer, R., Skates, S., Herzog, D., & Nussbaum, S. (1991). The clinical course of osteoporosis in anorexia nervosa: A longitudinal study of cortical bone mass. *Journal of the American Medical Association, 265,* 1133–1138.

Sady, S., Wortman, M., & Blanke, D. (1982). Flexibility training: Ballistic, static, or proprioceptive neuromuscular facilitation? *Archives of Physical Medicine and Rehabilitation, 63,* 261–263.

Sale, D. (1988). Neural adaptation to resistance training. *Medicine and Science in Sports and Exercise, 20,* 5135–5145.

Sale, D. (1992). Neuronal adaptation to strength training. In P. Komi (Ed.), *Strength and power in sport.* Oxford: Blackwell Scientific Publications.

Salisbury, J., & Mitchell, J. (1991). Bone mineral density and anorexia nervosa in women. *American Journal of Psychiatry, 148,* 768–774.

Sannerstedt, R. (1987). Hypertension. In J. Skinner (Ed.), *Exercise testing and exercise prescription for special cases.* Philadelphia: Lea & Feiger.

Sharp, C., & Freeman, C. (1993). The medical complications of anorexia nervosa. *British Journal of Psychiatry, 162,* 452–462.

Shellock, F., & Prentice, W. (1985). Warming-up and stretching for improved physical performance and prevention of sports-related injuries. *Sports Medicine, 2,* 267–278.

Sinaki, M., Wollan, P., Scott, R., & Gelczer, R. (1996). Can strong back extensors prevent vertebral fractures in women with osteoporosis? *Mayo Clinic Proceedings, 71,* 951–956.

Skinner, J. (1987). General principles of exercise prescription. In J. Skinner (Ed.), *Exercise testing and exercise prescription for special cases.* Philadelphia: Lea & Feiger.

Stone, M. (1992). Connective tissue and bone response to strength training. In P. Komi (Ed.), *Strength and power in sport.* Oxford: Blackwell Scientific Publications.

Wallin, D., Ekblom, B., Grahn, R., & Nordenborg, T. (1985). Improvement of muscle flexibility. A comparison between two techniques. *American Journal of Sports Medicine, 13,* 263–268.

Wilmore, J., & Costill, D. (1994). *Physiology of sport and exercise.* Champaign, IL: Human Kinetics Publishers.

Wing, R., & Greeno, C. (1994). Behavioral and psychosocial aspects of obesity and its treatment. *Baillieres Clinical Endocrinology and Metabolism, 8,* 689–703.

Woodruff, P., Morton, J., & Russell, G. (1994). Neuromyopathic complications in a patient with anorexia nervosa and vitamin C deficiency. *International Journal of Eating Disorders, 16,* 205–209.

Chapter 13

# Medical Evaluation and Medical Management

*Claire Pomeroy*

The eating disorders—anorexia nervosa, bulimia nervosa, and binge eating disorder—are associated with serious medical risks (Comerci, 1990; de Zwaan & Mitchell, 1992; Mcgilley & Pryor, 1998; Mehler, Gray, & Schulte, 1997; Mitchell, Seim, Colon, & Pomeroy, 1987; Pomeroy & Mitchell, 1989; Sharp & Freeman, 1993; Wiseman, Harris, & Halmi, 1998). Patients with eating disorders may develop medical complications involving virtually every organ system. A thorough medical evaluation and appropriate follow-up of medical complications are critical to the management and successful treatment of eating disorders (Becker, Grinspoon, Klibanski, & Herzog, 1999; Carney & Andersen, 1996). The medical clinician is an important member of the team providing care to patients with eating disorders (see Figure 13.1).

### Entry into the Health Care Delivery System

Recognition and appropriate diagnosis of eating disorders can be difficult. Too often serious symptoms and signs are ignored by family, friends, and coworkers—or by the patient herself. Unfortunately, physicians and other medical providers at times fail to recognize these serious medical illnesses. Early diagnosis is a critical determinant of prognosis and should be the goal of all health care workers.

The primary care setting is the optimal health care delivery site for recognizing and diagnosing eating disorders. Screening for eating disorders should be considered part of the routine health maintenance examination, particularly in young women in the age groups at highest risk. During health maintenance visits, medical practitioners should provide appropriate counseling regarding the role of good nutrition for all pa-

## Prevention

- Provide appropriate counseling regarding nutrition and health, for all patients during health maintenance exams
- Identify high-risk patients and provide appropriate advice regarding eating habits and weight
- Avoid medical interventions that might precipitate eating disorders in high-risk individuals (for example, low-calorie diets, diuretic/laxative/diet pill prescriptions)

## Identification

- Screen for eating disorders during health maintenance exams
- Identify patients with eating disorders and arrange for appropriate referrals

## Medical Management

- Rule out other medical illnesses that may mimic eating disorders
- Identify acute medical complications at presentation (see text)
- Monitor for potential medical complications during therapy
- Provide long-term monitoring of physical health
- Coordinate subspecialty medical consultations as necessary

## Other

- Facilitate education/involvement of family members/caretakers
- Encourage community awareness (for example, schools, religious organizations, community groups)

Figure 13.1. Role of the medical clinician in care of patients with eating disorders.

tients and should be alert to clues that may identify patients at risk of developing an eating disorder. The routine medical history should include questions about dietary habits and body image. A preoccupation with weight and body image, especially in young women, should prompt further evaluation. For patients judged to be at risk, extra time should be taken to explain the importance of healthy eating habits. In addition, the clinician should be vigilant about avoiding medical interventions that might precipitate eating disorders in susceptible individuals, such as advising low-calorie diets or prescription diuretics, laxatives, or diet pills.

Once the possibility of an eating disorder is suspected, many primary care physicians will elect to refer the patient to an eating disorder specialist or treatment program for further evaluation. Others with appropriate experience and training will feel comfortable initiating treatment of the less seriously ill patients. In either case, it is desirable for the primary care provider to remain involved in the patient's care to coordinate ongoing health care management.

Patients may enter the health care delivery system through other routes. Some patients may seek help directly from a clinic or program specializing in treatment of eating disorders. Such clinics are increasing in number and are present in many larger cities. They are usually staffed by a variety of health care professionals, including psychiatrists, dietitians, and social workers. Other patients may elect to directly consult a psychiatrist or psychologist who is experienced in treating patients with eating disorders. Unfortunately, a few patients are identified only after hospitalization for life-threatening medical complications.

## Symptoms and Signs of Eating Disorders

Most eating disordered patients will not present with symptoms obviously attributable to the eating disorder, and in fact may attempt to conceal evidence of disordered eating from the physician. A history of caloric restriction or bingeing and purging will often not be revealed to the physician. If the patient is presenting for medical evaluation because other family members are concerned that the patient has an eating disorder, the patient may be particularly resistant to discussion.

In anorexia nervosa, the symptoms and signs are usually those that occur secondary to caloric restriction and weight loss (see Table 13.1). Although anorectics will rarely complain about disordered eating, they may be concerned about other symptoms, such as lethargy, abdominal pain, or amenorrhea. On physical examination, evidence of excessive weight loss is usually the most prominent finding. Unfortunately, because of society's emphasis on thinness, both family members and physicians may fail to recognize the seriousness of the patient's condition. Health care workers should not be fooled by attempts to conceal weight loss, such as wearing baggy clothes or artificially inflating weight by hidden objects. Most of the physical manifestations of anorexia nervosa are similar to the complications that are observed in patients with starvation due to other causes. However, there are a few important differences. For example, most starving patients will note lethargy and inability to exercise, whereas anorectics may exercise excessively in attempts to lose weight. Patients with weight loss from other causes will express concern about thinness, while anorectics usually minimize, deny, or take pride in their

Table 13.1. Major Symptoms and Signs in Eating Disorders

| Anorexia nervosa | Bulimia nervosa | Binge eating disorder |
|---|---|---|
| **Symptoms** | | |
| Amenorrhea | Irregular menses | Request for diet advice |
| Agitation (hyperactivity) | Abdominal pain | Eating binges |
| Irritability, withdrawal | Abdominal bloating | Weight concerns |
| Sleep disturbances, lethargy | Lethargy | Abdominal pain, bloating |
| Fatigue, headaches | Fatigue, headaches | Depression |
| Constipation | Constipation | |
| Abdominal pain | Swelling hands/feet | |
| Cold intolerance | Depression | |
| **Signs** | | |
| Inanition | Often appear well | Often overweight |
| Low body temperature | Russell's sign | Otherwise usually appear well |
| Bradycardia, hypotension | Parotid gland swelling | |
| Dry skin, brittle hair, brittle nails | Erosion of dental enamel | |
| "Yellow" skin, especially palms | Periodontal disease | |
| Lanugo hair | Edema | |
| Hair loss on scalp | | |
| Edema | | |

low body weight. Finally, many anorectics will deny feelings of hunger, an unusual finding in other forms of starvation.

In contrast to anorectics, patients with bulimia nervosa or binge eating disorder often appear physically healthy (see Table 13.1). Bulimics and binge eaters may have few symptoms and signs of illness; when present, they are usually attributable to purging or associated behaviors of diet pill, diuretic, or laxative abuse. A subset of these patients are overweight and may present for advice on dieting. Such patients should be carefully interviewed about eating habits. Because binge eating is often done secretively, most patients will not provide this information unless specifically asked. In addition, the associated behaviors of purging and laxative, diet pill, diuretic, or Ipecac® abuse are often concealed from the health care worker. Most often such patients present for medical care with nonspecific complaints of "feeling bloated," "heartburn," constipation, or swelling of the hands and feet. The diagnosis can be easily overlooked if the physician misses these subtle clues.

### Initial Medical Evaluation

After a diagnosis of an eating disorder is made, referral to a medical physician for a complete medical history and physician examination is essential. The importance of evaluating and treating medical complications at the same time that psychotherapy and nutritional counseling are undertaken for all patients with eating disorders has recently been emphasized (Becker et al., 1999). We strongly advise that eating disorder programs include a medical physician—family practitioner, internist, or pediatrician—as a member of the treatment team. Although the psychological aspects of the eating disorder may dominate the presentation, it is critical that assessment of the patient's physical status be incorporated into the treatment program. At the initial medical visit, the physician should complete a careful medical history and physical examination in a nonjudgmental and caring atmosphere (see Figure 13.2).

The medical history should include questions that allow the physician to assess the severity and chronicity of the eating disorder. Inquiries about dietary habits and weight history should be routine. A review of actual body weights from childhood to the present is critical. Since menstrual irregularities are an important clue to the presence of an eating disorder and since prolonged amenorrhea is associated with a high risk of osteoporosis, a careful history regarding menstrual function is important. Given the frequency of comorbid psychiatric conditions, especially depression and chemical dependency, a psychiatric, alcohol, and illicit drug use history is essential. Finally, particular attention should be paid to eliciting any history of use of diuretics, diet pills, or laxatives.

A thorough physical examination should be performed for every patient with a possible eating disorder. The history will provide clues to areas that should be emphasized in the examination. Special attention should be paid to obtaining an accurate height and weight and assessing the degree of inanition or overweight. The state of hydration should be assessed by examination of mucus membranes and skin turgor, and if indicated, by orthostatic blood pressure measurements. In bulimics, a careful dental examination to search for evidence of dental caries and enamel erosion is paramount. Thorough cardiac, lung, and abdominal examinations may reveal important evidence of medical complications in these organ systems. A screening neurologic exam, including visual field

History, with special emphasis on:
- Weight history
- Diet history
- Menstrual history (women)/sexual history
- Psychiatric history
- Chemical abuse/dependency history
- Use of diuretics/laxatives/diet pills/Ipecac®

Physical examination, with special emphasis on:
- Weight, degree of inanition
- State of hydration
- Dental examination
- Cardiac, abdominal, and neurologic examinations
- Gynecologic examination

Figure 13.2. Initial medical evaluation of patients
with eating disorders.

testing, is important to rule out central nervous system lesions, which might mimic eating disorders. A gynecologic examination is appropriate for all women, with attention paid to detecting possible signs of estrogen deficiency.

Choice of laboratory tests at the initial medical evaluation will be guided by the results of the history and physical examination. Most patients with eating disorders should have screening laboratories (see Figure 13.3). A complete blood count with differential, electrolytes, blood urea nitrogen, creatinine, glucose, calcium, and liver enzymes are indicated for most patients. Albumin or transferrin may be measured as an indicator of nutritional status. Since the symptoms and signs of both hyper- and hypothyroidism can mimic eating disorders, thyroid function tests are appropriate. Urinalysis and stool guaiac examinations are also important. An electrocardiogram with rhythm strip is desirable for some patients, especially severely emaciated anorectics and patients who have abused diuretics or Ipecac®. Specific complaints or abnormalities on physical examination may prompt further tests, such as chest or abdominal roentgenograms, electromyography, head CT or MRI scans, or gastrointestinal endoscopy. In anorectic patients, especially those with prolonged amenorrhea, bone densitometry to assess the extent of osteoporosis may be useful. Finally, if diuretic or laxative abuse is suspected but denied by the patient, urine samples to detect the surreptitious use of these agents can be ordered.

---

Complete blood count with differential
Electrolytes, glucose, calcium, magnesium, phosphorus
Liver function tests: SGOT, alkaline phosphatase, bilirubin
Albumin, transferrin
BUN, creatinine
Thyroid function tests: $T_3$, $T_4$, thyroid index, TSH
Urinalysis, stool guaiac
Electrocardiogram
Other laboratory tests as indicated by history and physical, including:
    Chest X ray, abdominal X ray, head CT scan
    Urine drug screen (illicit drugs, diuretics, laxatives)
    Bone densitometry

---

Figure 13.3. Initial screening labs recommended for evaluation of patients with eating disorders.

## Differential Diagnosis of Eating Disorders

Because eating disorders can be mimicked by many other medical conditions, a critical goal of the initial medical evaluation is to rule out other causes of disordered eating (see Figure 13.4). Many of the symptoms and signs of the eating disorders can be caused by a variety of underlying medical conditions—misdiagnosis can be tragic. Other illnesses can result in weight loss and mimic many of the secondary manifestations of anorexia nervosa. A careful history and physical should detect many of these, especially occult malignancies, chronic infections, diabetes, and malabsorption syndromes. Selected laboratory tests can facilitate diagnosis of other illnesses, such as Addison's disease (Blaustein, Golden, & Shenker, 1998), thyrotoxicosis, and renal abnormalities, which may simulate anorexia nervosa.

Similarly, a variety of other medical conditions may present with symptoms that are difficult to distinguish from bulimia nervosa. For example, illnesses such as inflammatory bowel disease and connective tissue syndromes may cause abnormal gastrointestinal motility and result in many of the same symptoms as bulimia nervosa. A careful history to elicit description of self-induced vomiting can avoid protracted, expensive, and uncomfortable evaluations.

Finally, binge eating disorder must be differentiated from several genetic or acquired central nervous system abnormalities that result in comparable disordered eating behaviors. Most of these entities are quite rare, however, and other evidence of pathology often accompanies them. Generally speaking, a thorough medical history and physical examination,

**Anorexia nervosa**

Thyrotoxicosis
Malignancies, especially lymphoma, stomach cancer
Chronic infection, especially tuberculosis, AIDS
Addison's disease
Diabetes mellitus
Hypothalamic lesions or tumors, diencephalic tumors
Undiagnosed cystic fibrosis
Superior mesenteric artery syndrome
Malabsorption syndromes
Inflammatory bowel disease: Crohn's disease, ulcerative colitis
Parasitic intestinal infections, e.g., nematodes, *Giardia*
Simmond's disease (hypophyseal cachexia)
Sheehan's syndrome
Zinc deficiency

**Bulimia nervosa**

Scleroderma or other connective tissue disorders with GI involvement (and
    abnormal gut motility)
Inflammatory bowel disease
Peptic ulcer disease
Parasitic intestinal infections
Pancreatitis
Hypothalamic lesions or tumors

**Binge eating disorder**

Kleine-Levin syndrome
Prader-Willi syndrome
Temporal lobe or limbic seizures
Lesions of the hypothalamus, frontal lobe, or temporal lobe (e.g., bilateral
    temporal lobe ablation of Kluver-Bucy)

Figure 13.4. Other medical conditions that may mimic
eating disorders.

and basic laboratory screening tests are sufficient to make these diagnoses. Complex and expensive workups are rarely indicated.

## Medical Complications

A major role of the medical clinician is to examine the eating disordered patient to detect medical complications of his or her disease and provide ongoing medical management of these complications. The eating disorders can cause serious, at times fatal, medical complications (see Tables 13.2 and 13.3).

Mortality in anorexia nervosa is distressingly high, ranging from 6% to 20% in reported series (Crisp, Callender, Halek, & Hsu, 1992; Patton, 1988; Ratnasuriya, Eisler, Szmukler, & Russell, 1991). Death is usually attributable to inanition, fluid and electrolyte abnormalities, or suicide. Mortality in bulimia nervosa is less well studied, but fatalities clearly do occur. Fatalities are most commonly due to the complications of purging or the associated abuse of laxatives, Ipecac®, diet pills, or diuretics. Although deaths due to binge eating have been described (for example, gastric rupture), fatal outcomes are unusual. Nevertheless, the morbidity, especially the emotional suffering, attributable to these disorders can be devastating.

### Cardiovascular Complications

Cardiac abnormalities are quite frequent in patients with eating disorders (Isner, Roberts, Heymsfield, & Yager, 1985; Kreipe & Harris, 1992), especially in very low-weight anorectics and bulimics with electrolyte abnormalities secondary to purging and diuretics or laxative abuse. In anorectics, starvation may be associated with sinus bradycardia, sinus arrhythmia, or low blood pressure. These abnormalities are generally considered to be a physiologic adaptation to the hypometabolic state of starvation and are usually not life threatening. Both anorexia nervosa and bulimia nervosa may be associated with dehydration, orthostatic blood pressure changes, and hypotension. In anorexia nervosa, these complications are primarily due to restriction of fluid intake, whereas in bulimia, self-induced vomiting and abuse of laxatives and diuretics are usually implicated.

A variety of conduction defects and rhythm disturbances are well described in patients with eating disorders. Indeed, sudden cardiac death is a leading cause of mortality in anorexia nervosa and bulimia nervosa. Electrolyte abnormalities are the major cause of serious rhythm disturbances and cardiac deaths in eating disordered patients. Hypokalemia, and less frequently hypocalcemia, hypophosphatemia, or hypomagnesemia, predispose patients to potentially fatal ventricular arrhythmias.

Other cardiac complications of eating disorders are less common. Refeeding cardiomyopathy may result from overly aggressive caloric replacement in anorexia nervosa. Bulimics who abuse Ipecac® can develop Ipecac®-associated cardiomyopathy (Ho, Dweik, & Cohen, 1998). Because of the long half-life of Ipecac®, the drug can accumulate in cardiac tissue and cause prolonged or even irreversible cardiac dysfunction.

## Table 13.2. Medical Complications of Eating Disorders (by Major Organ System)

| Complication | Related to calorie restriction/ starvation | Related to bingeing/ purging | Related to associated behaviors |
|---|---|---|---|
| **Cardiovascular** | | | |
| Orthostasis/hypotension | X | X | X |
| Bradycardia | X | | |
| Congestive heart failure | X | | X |
| EKG abnormalities | X | X | X |
| Refeeding cardiomyopathy | X | | |
| Refeeding edema | X | | |
| Arrythmias | | | X |
| Sudden cardiac death | X | X | X |
| Ipecac® myocarditis | | | X |
| **Renal/Electrolytes** | | | |
| Dehydration; volume depletion | X | X | X |
| Decreased glomerular filtration rate | X | X | X |
| Abnormal electrolytes | X | X | X |
| Kaliopenic nephropathy | | | X |
| Refeeding edema | X | | |
| Reflex edema (after stopping laxatives, diuretics) | | | X |
| **Endocrine** | | | |
| Growth retardation | X | | |
| Delayed onset of puberty | X | | |
| Abnormal HPG axis, irregular menses, amenorrhea, estrogen deficiency | X | X | |
| Abnormal HPA axis: sustained hypercortisolism | X | | |
| Abnormal thyroid function tests | X | | |
| **Gastrointestinal** | | | |
| Salivary/parotid gland hypertrophy | | X | |
| Hyperamylasemia | | X | |
| Esophageal perforation/esophagitis | | X | |
| Mallory-Weiss tears | | X | |
| Delayed gastric emptying | X | X | X |
| Superior mesentery artery syndrome | X | | |

Table 13.2. *Continued*

| Complication | Related to calorie restriction/ starvation | Related to bingeing/ purging | Related to associated behaviors |
|---|---|---|---|
| **Gastrointestinal** *(continued)* | | | |
| Gastric dilatation/rupture | | X | |
| Refeeding pancreatitis | X | | |
| Constipation | X | X | X |
| Melanosis coli | | | X |
| Steatorrhea/protein-losing gastroenteropathy | | | X |
| Cathartic colon | | | X |
| Hypokalemic ileus | X | X | X |
| **Metabolic** | | | |
| Osteoporosis/osteopenia | X | | |
| Trace mineral deficiencies (e.g., zinc) | X | X | X |
| Vitamin deficiencies (unusual) | X | X | X |
| Hypercholesterolemia | X | | |
| Obesity (see also Figure 13.5) | | X | X |
| **Pulmonary** | | | |
| Subcutaneous emphysema | | X | |
| Pneumomediastinum | | X | |
| Aspiration pneumonitis | | X | X |
| **Dermatologic** | | | |
| Hair loss | X | | |
| Lanugolike hair growth | X | | |
| Dry skin, brittle hair, nails | X | | |
| Petechiae, purpura (secondary to thrombocytopenia) | X | | |
| Russell's sign (finger calluses and abrasions) | | X | |
| **Hematologic/Immunologic** | | | |
| Anemia | X | | |
| Leukopenia with relative lymphocytosis | X | | |
| Thrombocytopenia | X | | |
| ?-Impaired cell-mediated immunity | X | | |
| Abnormal CD4/CD8 counts | X | | |
| Abnormal cytokines | X | | |

Table 13.2. *Continued*

| Complication | Related to calorie restriction/ starvation | Related to bingeing/ purging | Related to associated behaviors |
|---|---|---|---|
| **Neurologic** | | | |
| Enlarged ventricles | X | | |
| ?-Abnormal pituitary gland size | X | | |
| ?-Abnormal EEG/sleep disorders | X | X | |
| Sleep disorders | X | X | |
| Abnormal PET scans | X | X | |
| **Other** | | | |
| Dental complications | | X | |
| Impaired thermoregulation | X | | |
| Vitamin K deficient coagulopathy | | X | X |
| Skeletal muscle myopathy | | | X |

Most patients with eating disorders should receive a baseline electrocardiogram. This is particularly important in low-weight anorectics, bulimics who are actively purging or abusing other medications, and binge eaters with significant obesity. If significant abnormalities, especially conduction defects, rhythm disturbances, or a prolonged QT interval, are identified, frequent evaluation of the electrocardiogram is indicated until weight gain and/or cessation of bulimic behaviors has been achieved. Electrocardiogram abnormalities in eating disordered patients are of major concern; however, the true prevalence is somewhat controversial, ranging from very frequent in some studies to virtually nonexistent in others. However, serious abnormalities, such as prolongation of the QT interval, clearly do occur and predispose patients to potentially life-threatening arrhythmias.

Mitral valve prolapse has been reported to be common in patients with anorexia nervosa. Prolapse results from the decreased left ventricular size that accompanies dramatic weight loss, resulting in disproportion between the ventricle and the mitral valve (Meyers, Starke, Pearson, Wilken, & Ferrell, 1987). This abnormality appears to be reversible with weight gain. The true increase in incidence of mitral valve prolapse is difficult to discern since mitral valve prolapse is quite common in young women in the general population, and well-matched control groups have not been included in many studies. If in fact echocardiographic

Table 13.3. Common Laboratory Abnormalities in Eating Disorders

| Eating disorder | Laboratory test | Abnormalities |
|---|---|---|
| Anorexia nervosa | Complete blood count | Anemia, leukopenia, relative lymphocytosis, thrombocytopenia |
| | Immune function | Depressed granulocyte killing |
| | Complement | Low serum complement, especially C3, alternative pathway components |
| | Electrolytes | Hypokalemia |
| | | Metabolic alkalosis |
| | | Elevated BUN |
| | | Low glucose |
| | Chemistries | Low magnesium, phosphorus, calcium |
| | | Abnormal liver function tests |
| | Endocrine | See Table 13.4 |
| | Other | Increased plasma cholesterol |
| | | Increased plasma carotene |
| | | Hypofibrinogenemia |
| | | Low plasma zinc |
| | | Elevated growth hormone levels |
| | | Decreased antidiuretic hormone secretion |
| Bulimia nervosa | Complete blood count | Iron-deficiency anemia (if GI blood loss) |
| | Electrolytes | Hypokalemia, hyponatremia |
| | | Metabolic alkalosis with hypocholeremia |
| | | Metabolic acidosis (if laxative abuse) |
| | | Elevated BUN |
| | Chemistries | Low magnesium, phosphorus, calcium |
| | | Abnormal liver function tests |
| | Endocrine | See Table 13.4 |
| | Other | Hyperamylasemia |
| | | Protein urea, pyuria, hematuria |
| | | Low vitamin K-dependent coagulation factors |
| Binge eating disorder | | Often normal; comparable to bulimia nervosa if illness includes binge/purge episodes or abuse of laxatives, diuretics, or Ipecac® |

evaluation for evidence of mitral valve prolapse is pursued more aggressively in eating disordered patients, an artificially inflated frequency of diagnoses may result.

## Renal and Electrolyte Complications

Electrolyte abnormalities are a major cause of morbidity and mortality in patients with eating disorders (Mitchell, Hatsukami, et al., 1987; Mitchell, Pyle, Eckert, Hatsukami, & Lentz, 1983), especially anorectics with major weight loss and bulimics engaging in severe purging and laxative or diuretic abuse. Many of the deaths attributable to eating disorders can be linked to hypokalemia. Low serum potassium levels may result from decreased intake and/or increased potassium losses due to self-induced vomiting or laxative or diuretic abuse. Careful monitoring of serum potassium levels in such patients throughout the course of treatment is a major responsibility of the clinician. Unfortunately, correction of hypokalemia can be quite difficult. Diuretic abuse and vomiting result in a hypochloremic contraction alkalosis, which must be corrected before potassium supplements will prove effective. Hypokalemia, if persistent, can directly cause organ dysfunction. Cardiac arrhythmias and decreased cardiac performance are the most obvious consequences, but hypokalemic nephropathy and myopathy are also important. Hypokalemic nephropathy may be associated with elevated blood urea nitrogen and serum creatinine levels, and even chronic renal failure (Abdel-Rahman & Moorthy, 1997).

Elevated blood urea nitrogen and creatinine levels may also reflect fluid depletion, hypovolemia, and decreased glomerular filtration rate (Boag, Weerakoon, Ginsburg, Harvard, & Dandona, 1985). Hypomagnesemia is not uncommon in anorectics and may be associated with persistent hypocalcemia or hypokalemia, which will only resolve if magnesium is replaced simultaneously. Hyperphosphatemia may be present in patients who vomit excessively. Conversely, profound hypophosphatemia can complicate refeeding and result in myocardial dysfunction and neurological complications, especially seizures (Wada, Nagase, Koike, Kugai, & Nagata, 1992).

Prolonged purging and/or diuretic or laxative abuse can result in a hypovolemic state, which stimulates the renin-angiotensin-aldosterone system as the body's homeostatic mechanisms attempt to conserve fluids (Mitchell, Pomeroy, Seppala, & Huber, 1988). When the patient attempts to curtail diuretic or laxative use, persistent hyperaldosteronism results in reflex edema formation. Unfortunately, this often triggers severe anxiety about weight gain and resumption of diuretic or laxative abuse. This self-perpetuating cycle can be extremely difficult to interrupt, and the patient must be reassured that fluid retention is a temporary condition, which will resolve if bulimic behaviors can be avoided.

### Endocrine Complications

A vast array of endocrine abnormalities characterize anorexia nervosa; similar, albeit less severe, perturbations of endocrine function are often observed in bulimic patients (see Table 13.4) (Boyar et al., 1977; Curran-Celentano, Erdman, Nelson, & Grater, 1985; Devlin et al., 1989; Gold et al., 1986; Gwirtsman et al., 1989; Hudson et al., 1983; Kiriike, Nishi-waki, Izumiya, Maeda, & Kawakita, 1987; Laue, Gold, Richmond, & Chrousos, 1991; Levy, Dixon, & Malarkey, 1988; Mortola, Rasmussen, & Yen, 1989; Pirke et al., 1987; Rich, Caine, Findling, & Shaker, 1990; Thomas & Rebar, 1990).

Amenorrhea is frequent in anorectics, although the exact etiology remains incompletely defined. Amenorrhea may result from weight loss per se; cessation of menses is quite predictable in starvation from other causes. However, menstruation has been reported to cease before any weight loss in some patients, and a history of irregular menses precedes the onset of anorexia in one-third of patients. Consequently, some authorities speculate that both amenorrhea and disordered eating may be attributable to a primary hypothalamic abnormality. Severe anorexia is associated with low levels of plasma estradiol, leutenizing hormone (LH), and follicle-stimulating hormone (FSH) levels. An "immature" response (resembling that of premenarchal girls) of LH and FSH to gonadotropin-releasing hormones is observed. Generally speaking, these endocrine abnormalities normalize with successful weight gain, but there may be a significant lag period or persistent irregularities of menstrual function (Golden et al., 1997).

Menstrual abnormalities are also seen in patients with bulimia nervosa (Pirke et al., 1987), although less frequently than in anorexia nervosa. In bulimia, irregular menses is more common than amenorrhea. A decreased number of LH secretory spikes and abnormal LH responses to gonadotropin-releasing hormones have been reported in some bulimic patients.

Thyroid function tests are frequently abnormal in people with anorexia nervosa (Curran-Celentano et al., 1985). The most common finding in anorectics is a normal $T_4$, decreased $T_3$, and normal thyroid stimulating hormone (TSH). The "low $T_3$ syndrome" is due to decreased

Table 13.4. Endocrine Function in Eating Disorders

| | Anorexia nervosa | Bulimia nervosa | Binge eating disorder |
|---|---|---|---|
| Thyroid gland | | | |
| $T_4$ | Normal | Normal | ? |
| $T_3$ | Decreased; preferential deiodination to "reverse $T_3$" | May be decreased | ? |
| Basal metabolic rate | Decreased | Usually normal | ? |
| Adrenal gland | | | |
| Plasma cortisol | Increased loss of normal diurnal variation | Usually normal; may be increased in a subset | ? |
| Dexamethasone suppression test | Nonsuppression | Normal or nonsuppression (multifactoral; see text) | Nonsuppression may occur in obese; consider double dexamethasone dose |
| Gonadotropins | | | |
| Estradiol | Decreased | Normal or decreased | ? |
| LH, FSH | Decreased | Abnormal patterns or decreased | ? |
| Response to gonadotropin-releasing hormone (LHRH) | Decreased | Normal or decreased | ? |
| Growth hormone | Often increased | Usually normal | ? |
| Prolactin | Usually normal or decreased | Usually normal | ? |

peripheral conversion of $T_4$ to $T_3$. There is preferential deiodination to "reverse $T_3$," a less active form of the hormone. The secretion of TSH is normal unless there is simultaneous thyroid gland failure. A delayed but intact response of TSH to exogenous thyroid-releasing hormone (TRH) provocative testing is seen (Levy et al., 1988). Symptoms of cold intolerance, bradycardia, dry skin, and constipation are frequently observed. These symptoms represent a normal adaptation to starvation, and the "hypometabolic" state can be considered a physiologic response to low body weight. The most appropriate treatment for these patients is weight gain; thyroid hormone administration is not appropriate for patients with "low $T_3$ syndrome" and a normal TSH. A few eating disordered patients, however, will have true thyroid dysfunction. Since the symptoms of eating disorders and thyroid dysfunction are often similar, all eating disordered patients should have thyroid function tests checked.

Extensive abnormalities of the hypothalamic-pituitary-adrenal (HPA) system occur in anorexia nervosa. Sustained hypercortisolism is a hallmark characteristic of anorexia (Boyar et al., 1977; Gold et al., 1986; Gwirtsman et al., 1989). Both plasma and cerebrospinal levels of free cortisol are elevated. High cortisol levels have been attributed to both increased production and decreased metabolic clearance. Nonsuppression of cortisol by dexamethasone is common in anorectic patients. Plasma ACTH levels are generally normal, but cerebrospinal fluid ACTH levels have been reported to be low. Most authorities believe that hypercortisolism in anorectics reflects a defect at or above the hypothalamus, perhaps secondary to hypersecretion of corticotropin releasing factor (CRF).

The HPA system has been less extensively evaluated in patients with bulimia nervosa (Laue et al., 1991). Most studies have found that plasma cortisol and ACTH levels in bulimics are similar to those of controls. Others have reported that a subset of bulimic women, including some of normal weight, have elevated plasma cortisol and ACTH levels with blunted responses to CRF (Hudson et al., 1983; Mortola et al., 1989). It is not known if these abnormalities reflect periods of semistarvation, stress, or primary central nervous system dysfunction. Nonsuppression on the dexamethasone test occurs in some bulimic patients (Mitchell, Pyle, Hatsukami, & Boutacoff, 1984). Again, the etiology is unclear. Some abnormal dexamethasone suppression test (DST) results may be due to sustained hypercortisolism while others may be due to erratic absorption of dexamethasone in bulimics with altered gastrointestinal function.

We are unaware of studies of cortisol in patients with binge eating disorder. However, it is known that obese patients, at least some of whom presumably binge eat, have abnormal DST results. This is usually due to inadequate dosage of dexamethasone in obese patients with a large volume of distribution. Repeat testing with 2 mg (instead of 1 mg) of dexamethasone will often result in normal suppression.

Anorexia nervosa is associated with impaired or erratic release of vasopressin. Many patients, therefore, develop partial neurogenic diabetes insipidus, characterized by polyuria and polydipsia. There is often a lag period after weight gain before these abnormalities reverse.

Other endocrine abnormalities in the eating disorders are less well studied. Acute hypoglycemia has been reported anecdotally (Rich et al., 1990). Prolactin levels are generally reported to be normal. One study found elevated prolactin values, while others have found decreased basal prolactin levels in anorectics and some bulimics (Kiriike et al., 1987). In anorexia nervosa, growth hormone may be elevated, as in other forms of starvation. Elevated basal levels of growth hormone probably reflect decreased production of somatomedin C. Some studies have demonstrated pathologic growth hormone responsiveness to provocative stimuli such as TRH or glucose administration, but others have failed to confirm these results. Elevated growth hormone levels, promoting gluconeogenesis and reducing peripheral use of glucose, represent a protective physiologic adaptation to the state of starvation.

### Gastrointestinal Complications

Gastrointestinal complications are a prominent cause of morbidity for persons with eating disorders (Anderson, Shaw, & McCargar, 1997; Cuellar & Van Thiel, 1986). Swelling of the parotid or submandibular glands is a classic finding in bulimia nervosa and is often one of the few physical examination clues to the diagnosis. Parotid hypertrophy may result in macroamylasemia; differentiation of hyperamylasemia secondary to pancreatitis by measuring amylase isoenzymes can be helpful. Parotid hypertrophy has also been described in malnourished anorectics who do not purge (Kinzl, Biebl, & Herold, 1993). Resolution of parotid and salivary gland hypertrophy after successful treatment of the eating disorder is the norm, although this can take several months.

Abnormal gastrointestinal motility is a major problem for many patients with eating disorders (Cuellar & Van Thiel, 1986; Cuellar, Kaye, Hsu, & Van Thiel, 1988; Geliebter et al., 1992; Kamal et al., 1991). Impaired gastric emptying, described in patients with anorexia nervosa or bulimia nervosa, probably contributes to symptoms of "bloating" and early satiety. Abnormal gastrointestinal motility with prolonged whole-gut transit times has been well described and may contribute to abdominal pain, constipation, and ileus. Abnormal gut motility can be exacerbated by hypokalemic ileus or ileus secondary to superimposed pancreatitis. In anorexia nervosa, abdominal pain can also be due to compression of the third portion of the duodenum by the superior mesenteric artery.

Esophageal problems seen with eating disorders are diverse and range from mild esophagitis to esophageal rupture. Esophagitis, erosions, ulcerations, and bleeding are frequently observed in bulimics with recurrent self-induced vomiting. Mallory-Weiss tears may lead to significant gastrointestinal bleeding. Esophageal rupture (Boerhoove's syndrome) is a catastrophic manifestation requiring emergent medical and surgical intervention. Chronic sequelae of recurrent vomiting include the development of esophageal strictures or Barrett's esophagus.

Acute gastric dilatation and rupture have been described in bulimics during bingeing and in anorectics during refeeding (Abdu, Garritano, & Culver, 1987). Rapid onset of nausea, vomiting, and abdominal pain indicate gastric distention and in most cases can be treated conservatively by nasogastric suction and fluid/electrolyte replacement. In extreme cases, gastric rupture can occur, causing dramatic pain and shock and requiring emergent surgical intervention.

Colonic complications, especially constipation and abdominal pain, may be attributable to decreased intake, dehydration, or altered motility. Laxative abuse can cause or exacerbate these symptoms since chronic use of stimulant laxatives may result in loss of normal peristaltic function. Laxative abusers usually complain of periods of diarrhea alternating with episodes of constipation. Cathartic colon can become severe and may even necessitate colonic resection. Chronic, recurrent use of laxatives may result in gastrointestinal bleeding, ranging from occult to frank blood loss. Long-term complications may include malabsorption, steatorrhea, or protein-losing gastroenteropathy. Nonspecific inflammation or melanosis coli may be seen on colonscopic examination. Rectal prolapse has been associated with bulimia nervosa (Malik, Stratton, & Sweeney, 1997).

Acute pancreatitis may develop during bingeing in bulimics and refeeding in anorectics, or because of associated alcohol abuse. Careful monitoring of the abdominal examination is indicated in these patients. If signs or symptoms of pancreatitis, such as abdominal pain, nausea, or vomiting are observed, measurement of serum amylase and isoenzymes will suggest the correct diagnosis. When pancreatitis is diagnosed, treatment with bowel rest, nasogastric suction, and intravenous fluid replacement should be promptly instituted. One study described several patients who relapsed during therapy for hyperlipidemic pancreatitis and were diagnosed with an eating disorder (Gavish et al., 1987).

*Metabolic Complications*

Skeletal abnormalities are serious complications of anorexia nervosa (Biller et al., 1989; Newman & Halmi, 1989; Rigotti, Nussbaum, Herzog, & Neer, 1984; Salisbury & Mitchell, 1991). Delayed bone maturation (chronological age > bone age), decreased bone density (osteoporosis), and pathologic fractures are consistently reported in anorectics. Low body weight, prolonged amenorrhea, adolescent onset of eating disorder, hypercortisolism, relative inactivity, and low calcium intake increase the risk for osteoporosis in anorectics. Extent of bone demineralization has generally been found to correlate with body mass index and duration of illness (Grinspoon et al., 1999). New technologies to quantitate bone loss have allowed investigations that reveal that up to 50% of severe anorectics suffer from significant osteoporosis (Hotta, Shibasaki, Sato, & Demura, 1998).

The mechanism of development of osteoporosis in anorectics is presumed to be multifactorial (Newman & Halmi, 1989). The low estrogen levels in anorectics appear to be a major etiologic factor in the pathogenesis of osteoporosis, akin to the development of decreased bone mineral density in other estrogen-deficient states, such as post-menopausal osteoporosis. This would be consistent with observations that duration of amenorrhea is a significant predictor of the severity of osteoporosis in anorectics. The precise method by which hypogonadism causes bone loss remains to be determined. However, disordered calcium regulation and bone remodeling, possibly mediated by estrogen effects on osteoclasts/osteoblasts or altered interleukin-6 levels, have been implicated. The sustained hypercortisolism observed in anorectics may also play a role in the development of osteoporosis. A significant negative correlation between cortisol excretion and bone density has been reported. Since excess glucocorticoids tend to inhibit osteoblast proliferation and function, these findings are not unexpected. Other factors, such as decreased calcium intake, low vitamin D levels, or excess growth hormone, may play less important roles in osteoporosis in anorexia nervosa. In contrast, the excess exercise pursued by many anorectics may actually have a protective effect. Osteoporosis is not usually seen in bulimics, unless they have a previous history of anorexia nervosa and low weight.

Other metabolic abnormalities have been reported in patients with anorexia nervosa and bulimia nervosa. Hypercholesterolemia is observed in patients with anorexia nervosa, in contrast to other forms of starvation in which low serum cholesterol levels are expected. Elevated serum carotene levels are found in nearly three-fourths of anorectics and may be associated with frank carotenodermia (Gupta, Gupta, & Haberman, 1987). Hypercarotenemia is primarily a result of elevation of vitamin A active carotenoids, especially β-carotene. Recently, the true incidence of these observations has been questioned (Mehler, Lezotte, & Eckel, 1998). Zinc deficiency has been anecdotally reported in some anorectics, and other trace metal and vitamin deficiencies, such as pellagra and scurvy, have on occasion been observed in patients with diet peculiarities.

Recent studies have focused on the possible role of leptin in anorexia nervosa. Leptin is a hormone produced by adipocytes that regulates body weight, appetite, and energy expenditure. Leptin levels are low in anorexia nervosa, as would be expected in low-weight individuals (Eckert et al., 1998; Lear, Pauly, & Birmingham, 1999), but some studies have suggested dysregulation that might contribute to pathogenesis of anorexia nervosa (Eckert et al., 1998).

The major medical complication of binge eating disorder is obesity. Obesity is a common problem in the industrialized world, affecting up to 25% of Americans. Morbid obesity, usually defined as weight greater than 170% of ideal body weight, affects about 3% to 5% of the population. Obesity may be complicated by a variety of medical conditions, with the risk increasing as the degree of overweight increases (Atkinson, 1991).

Cardiovascular complications are a major source of morbidity and mortality in obese individuals. The obese have an increased risk of hypertension and atherosclerotic cardiovascular disease, including myocardial infarction (Alpert & Hashimi, 1993). In addition, the combination of hypertension and obesity may result in ventricular hypertrophy and eventually cardiomyopathy of the obese and heart failure (Benotti, Bistrain, Benotti, Blackburn, & Forse, 1992). Obese patients also have an increased incidence of cerebrovascular accidents.

Obese patients are at increased risk for several endocrine and metabolic conditions. Diabetes mellitus is frequently diagnosed in obese patients. The mechanism remains poorly understood, but it is clear that insulin resistance is critical to the pathogenesis. Metabolic abnormalities in obesity including hyperlipidemia, especially hypertriglyceridemia, undoubtedly contribute to the accelerated development of atherosclerosis in the obese. An increased risk of gout characterizes obese patients.

**Cardiovascular**

- Hypertension
- Atherosclerotic cardiovascular disease, including myocardial infarction
- Ventricular hypertrophy and congestive heart failure
- Cerebrovascular accidents

**Endocrine**

- Diabetes mellitus

**Gastrointestinal**

- Gall bladder disease, secondary to obesity; risk further increased during rapid weight loss
- Fatty liver, portal inflammation, and fibrosis: "nonalcoholic steatohepatitis"

**Metabolic**

- Hyperlipidemia, especially hypertriglyceridemia
- Gout

**Skeletal**

- Degenerative osteoarthritis

**Pulmonary**

- Sleep apnea
- Obesity hypoventilation syndrome (Pickwickian syndrome)

**Other Medical**

- Increased cancer risk, especially breast, uterus, colon, prostate
- Increased surgical risk
- Decreased fertility (men and women)
- Adverse perinatal outcomes
- Early mortality

Figure 13.5.  Medical complications of obesity.

A variety of gastrointestinal illnesses have been described in obese patients. Cholesterol gallstones are a recognized complication both of obesity and, paradoxically, of rapid weight loss (Shiffman, Sugerman, Kellum, Brewer, & Moore, 1991). Gallstone disease occurs in about one-third of morbidly obese patients. Furthermore, gallstone formation has been reported to accompany rapid weight loss due to very low-calorie diets or gastric bypass surgery in up to one-fourth of patients (Worobetz, Inglis, & Shaffer, 1993). Gallstones will resolve spontaneously in about half of these patients, but symptoms will necessitate cholecystectomy in the remainder. Abnormal liver enzymes (especially LDH and serum transaminases) usually reflect fatty infiltration of the liver (Andersen, 1992). Portal inflammation and fibrosis, called "nonalcoholic steatohepatitis," also occurs in many morbidly obese patients.

Obese patients frequently have a variety of musculoskeletal complaints. These probably relate primarily to the high incidence of degenerative osteoarthritis seen in these patients. Wear and tear on joints, such as the knees, is directly attributable to the excess stress placed on weight-bearing joints in the obese.

Obesity causes chronic airflow limitation with decreased lung capacities, even in nonsmokers (Rubinstein, Zamel, DuBarry, & Hoffstein, 1990). In the most severe cases, respiratory insufficiency, commonly known as Pickwickian syndrome, may develop (Sugerman et al., 1992). Obese patients may develop obstructive sleep apnea syndrome or the obesity hypoventilation syndrome. In sleep apnea, the patient experiences intermittent pauses in breathing, especially while sleeping, resulting in hypoxia, disrupted sleep, and daytime somnolence. Excessive snoring is a major clue to sleep apnea. In contrast, obesity hypoventilation syndrome results in hypoxia at any time and is due to decreased lung volumes. Long-term complications of these syndromes include pulmonary hypertension, arrhythmias, and cardiac failure (Rajala et al., 1991). These patients are at high risk of sudden death (Rossner, Lagerstrand, Persson, & Sachs, 1991).

Other medical complications of obesity include an increased risk of cancer, especially of the breast, uterus, colon, or prostate; increased surgical risk, including postoperative pneumonias, wound infections, and deep venous thrombosis; and increased mortality. Decreased fertility is common in the obese, with abnormal menstrual function in women and abnormal sperm production in men. An increased risk of adverse perinatal outcomes has been reported for obese women (Perlow, Morgan, Montgomery, Towers, & Porto, 1992).

### Pulmonary Complications

Bulimics with recurrent vomiting are at risk of developing aspiration pneumonia or chemical pneumonitis secondary to aspiration of gastric acid. In addition, spontaneous pneumothorax, pneumomediastinum, and subcutaneous emphysema can occur in patients with anorexia nervosa or bulimia nervosa (Adson, Crow, & Mitchell, 1998; Hatzitolios et al., 1997). The mechanism is poorly studied, but it seems logical that vomiting could raise intrathoracic pressures and rupture a bleb or other weakened area. However, this complication has been described in anorectics who do not vomit, possibly secondary to poor tissue integrity due to malnutrition. Ventilatory failure, presumably caused by a combination of decreased energy reserves and electrolyte abnormalities, has been reported in severe cases of anorexia nervosa (Ryan, Whittaker, & Road, 1992).

*Dermatologic Complications*

The dermatologic manifestations of eating disorders have been classified into four subgroups:

1. complications associated with starvation and malnutrition,
2. complications of self-induced vomiting,
3. complications of abuse of laxatives/diuretics/Ipecac®, and
4. complications associated with concomitant psychiatric illness (Gupta et al., 1987).

Nearly one-third of patients with anorexia nervosa will develop increased lanugolike hair on the face and other parts of the body. This may be accompanied by loss of scalp hair, emphasizing the presence of facial hair. Dry scaly skin and brittle hair and nails are common in anorexia nervosa. As mentioned earlier, hypercarotenemia and carotenodermia may be present in anorectics, in contradistinction to other forms of starvation. Rare cases of pellagra (niacin deficiency) or scurvy (vitamin C deficiency) may be associated with the skin changes characteristic of these deficiencies. Rarely, petechiae or purpura may be clues to thrombocytopenia resulting from starvation-induced hypoplasia of bone marrow.

Calluses, abrasions, and/or bruising on the dorsum of the hand or thumb, called "Russell's sign," are the classic clue to recurrent self-induced vomiting characteristic of bulimia nervosa. Damage to the skin is caused by rubbing against the teeth during induction of vomiting by manual stimulation of the gag reflex. Transient facial purpura or conjunctival hemorrhage may result from the increased intrathoracic pressures generated during recurrent vomiting.

Fixed drug eruptions secondary to phenolphthalein-containing laxatives and photosensitivity due to thiazide diuretics are dermatologic clues to the abuse of drugs consumed to lose weight. Finally, self-induced dermatoses from repetitive excoriation of the skin, compulsive hand washing, or trichotillomania have been reported in patients with eating disorders and comorbid psychiatric conditions.

## Hematologic/Immunologic Complications

Leukopenia, anemia, and thrombocytopenia have been reported in persons with anorexia nervosa (Howard, Leggat, & Chaudhry, 1992; Saito, Kita, Morioka, & Watanabe, 1999). If starvation is severe, frank marrow necrosis can occur (Smith & Spivak, 1985). Leukopenia usually reflects decreased neutrophil numbers; relative lymphocytosis is the norm, but total lymphocyte counts may be decreased. Low white cell counts do not appear to increase risk of infection, possibly because bone marrow neutrophil reserves are normal (Bowers & Eckert, 1978). Neutrophils may also have disordered functional capacity. Abnormalities of chemotaxis and microbicidal activity have been reported but not in all anorectics or in all studies.

Other abnormalities of immune function have been described in some patients with anorexia nervosa (Howard et al., 1992). Significant reductions in complement, especially components of the alternative pathway, have been reported. These values normalized with refeeding and weight gain (Pomeroy et al., 1997). Immunoglobulin levels have been reported to be low in some anorectics, but other studies have refuted these findings.

Delayed type hypersensitivity skin testing is an excellent screening test for responsivity of the immune system, especially cell-mediated immunity. Failure to respond to skin testing (anergy) is characteristic of anorectics who weigh less than 60% of ideal body weight. Variable responses are obtained in anorectics with less severe weight loss.

Lymphocyte phenotypes in anorectics have been the subject of several studies, with varying results. Some authors report that CD4+ cells are normal, while others have found decreased CD4+ counts, as observed in other forms of starvation. We studied lymphocyte phenotypes in anorectics and found that CD4+ cell counts do not differ significantly from controls; however, CD8+ cell counts were decreased both before and after successful treatment (Fink, Eckert, Mitchell, Crosby, & Pomeroy, 1996). Low CD8+ counts have been reported previously in stress and depression. Our findings of low CD8+ counts may be a manifestation of one of these comorbid conditions.

Recent investigations have focused on a possible role of cytokines in the pathogenesis of anorexia nervosa and/or its associated medical complications (Nakai, Hamagaki, Takagi, Taniguchi, & Kurimoto, 1999; Pomeroy et al., 1994). Cytokines are polypeptides, which act as molecular signals for communications between cells, especially cells of the immune, neurologic, and endocrine systems. Production of some cytokines, such as γ-interferon, may be reduced in anorectics. In contrast, levels of other cytokines, such as tumor necrosis factor-α (TNF-α), interleukin-6, and transforming growth factor-β, are elevated in untreated anorectics (Nagata, Tobitani, Kiriike, Iketani, & Yamagami, 1999; Pomeroy et al., 1994). In some studies, cytokines tend to normalize with refeeding (Pomeroy et al., 1994), but not in others (Nakai et al., 1999). Further studies are needed to determine the pathophysiologic significance of these findings.

Despite suggestions of multiple perturbations of immune function in anorexia nervosa, it appears that these patients remain remarkably free of infections. Exploration of this apparent paradox requires additional investigation.

### Neurologic Complications

Because many of the basic control systems for feeding behavior and neuroendocrine function are located in the central nervous system, examination of the neurological system has been an area of research emphasis in the eating disorders. Sleep studies have yielded conflicting results. Several reports have suggested that patients with anorexia nervosa have fragmentation of sleep continuity and reduction of rapid eye movement sleep, with early morning waking. However, these results have not been consistently replicated in more recent studies.

Pneumoencephalograms and CT scans demonstrate enlarged ventricles and external cerebrospinal fluid spaces in many patients with anorexia nervosa and some bulimics (Krieg, Backmund, & Pirke, 1987; Krieg et al., 1989; Krieg, Pirke, Lauer, & Backmund, 1988). These abnormalities have been termed "pseudoatrophy" of the brain because they generally normalize after weight gain. "Pseudoatrophy" appears to correlate with the severity of endocrine abnormalities. In other studies, cerebral blood flow has been reported to be normal. One report suggests that the pituitary glands of patients with both anorexia nervosa and bulimia nervosa may be significantly smaller than those of controls, as assessed by MRI scanning (Doraiswamy et al., 1991).

Recent investigations have used positron emission tomography (PET) to study brain function. Glucose hypermetabolism was noted in the caudate nuclei of anorectics during starvation (Herholz et al., 1987); this normalized with weight gain. These findings again raise the possibility of primary central nervous system dysfunction in patients with eating disorders, but this remains speculative.

## Dental Complications

Dental abnormalities characterize the subset of patients with eating disorders who engage in repetitive, self-induced vomiting (Milosevic, 1999; Roberts & Li, 1987; Simmons, Grayden, & Mitchell, 1986). Decalcification of the lingual, palatal, and posterior occlusive surfaces of the teeth is referred to as perimylolysis and results from erosive acid coming from the back of the mouth. Because amalgams are resistant to acid, they become much more obvious as enamel erosion progresses. Increased temperature sensitivity and increased incidence of caries have also been reported but not confirmed in all studies. Involvement of a concerned dentist and careful dental examinations are a critical component of treatment for patients with bulimia nervosa and anorexia patients who vomit.

## Temperature Regulation

Disordered thermoregulation is a common complaint of patients with eating disorders. Persons with anorexia nervosa often demonstrate aberrant autonomic responses when exposed to extremes of environmental temperature. In one study, thermal sweating was observed to occur at lower core and skin temperatures in patients with anorexia nervosa than in controls. Some patients with eating disorders also complain of Raynaud's phenomenon in the cold, and easy vasodilatation and swelling of the hands and feet in warm temperatures. It has been proposed that some anorectics have a central thermoregulatory disorder, possibly another manifestation of hypothalamic dysfunction. Symptoms of disordered thermoregulation can be quite distressing to the patient, but no specific therapy is available.

## Abuse of Laxatives, Diuretics, Diet Pills, and Ipecac®

Individuals with eating disorders may misuse a variety of drugs in an attempt to promote weight loss by suppressing appetite, minimizing food absorption, eliminating fluid, or inducing vomiting (Mitchell & Boutacoff, 1986; Mitchell, Hatsukami, Eckert, & Pyle, 1985; Mitchell et al.,

Table 13.5. Over-the-Counter Medications That May Be Abused
by Eating Disordered Patients

| Category | Brand names | Major active ingredient |
|---|---|---|
| Stimulant laxatives | Agoral, Correctol, Dialose Plus, Doxidan Liqui-gels, Ex-Lax®, Feen-A-Mint, Philip's Gelcaps | Phenolphthalein |
| | Dulcolax | Bisacodyl |
| | PeriColace | Casanthranol |
| Diuretics* | Bayer Select Menstrual, Midol, Pamprin, Premsyn-PMS, Odrinal, Diurex-2, Diurex-MPR | Pamabrom |
| Diet pills | Acutrim, Appendrine, Control, Dexatrim, Hungrex, Permathene, Thinz, Super Odrinex | Phenylpropanolamine |
| Ipecac® | Ipecac® | Emetine base |

*Generally marketed as preparations for treatment of premenstrual symptoms.

1987). Bulimics may abuse laxatives, diuretics, diet pills, and/or Ipecac® (see Table 13.5). It is estimated that nearly two-thirds of bulimics use laxatives, and one-third use diuretics in an attempt to augment weight loss.

*Laxatives*

Some bulimics ingest huge amounts of laxative drugs, many times in excess of the amount recommended by the manufacturer. Stimulant-type laxatives are most frequently used and are available in many over-the-counter preparations (see Table 13.5). Abuse of laxatives is not an effective method of weight loss, because weight loss occurs predominantly due to transient loss of fluids or stool rather than prevention of calorie absorption. Furthermore, laxative use precipitates activation of the renin-angiotensin-aldosterone system, and secondary hyperaldosteronism subsequently promotes fluid retention. Chronic use of laxatives can result in serious sequelae, including loss of the normal colonic peristatis (laxative dependency) and cathartic colon (loss of normal colon function). This results in a potentially vicious cycle of further laxative abuse. Most recently, it has been recognized that bulimics may also use enemas in an attempt to lose weight (Mitchell, Pyle, Hatsukami, & Eckert, 1991).

Fleet® enemas or tap water enemas may be used as often as several times a week or daily.

## Diuretics

Diuretics are available in a wide variety of over-the-counter formulations for treatment of premenstrual symptoms and are frequently used in large quantities by bulimics to promote weight loss (Mitchell, Pomeroy, & Huber, 1988; Pomeroy & Mitchell, 1989). Pamabron is the main active ingredient in many of the currently available over-the-counter diuretic preparations. Diuretic use may begin as an attempt to control "edema" and progress to abuse with ingestion of diuretics in progressively larger quantities over time. Indeed, the initial diuretic use may promote secondary hyperaldosteronism and reflex fluid retention when diuretics are discontinued. Instead of allowing the system to readjust and fluid balance to be restored, the patient resumes diuretic use, believing that continued diuretic use is required to control the edema.

Bulimics may also abuse prescription diuretics. This is particularly common among health care workers who have access to such medications. Thiazide diuretics, such as hydrochlorothiazide, loop diuretics, such as furosemide, and potassium-sparing diuretics, such as spironolactone and triameterene, have all been described as drugs of abuse in bulimia nervosa. Physicians should exercise caution in prescribing these medications for at-risk individuals, especially if the reason for the drug request is vague or poorly documented.

## Diet Pills

Although many individuals with eating disorders use diet pills at some point in the course of their illness, long-term, high-dose abuse is uncommon, possibly because of the untoward side effects of these drugs or their relative inefficacy in promoting weight loss. However, cases of abuse of over-the-counter diet pills, either alone or in combination with illicit amphetamines, have been well described. Phenylpropanolamine is the active ingredient in the over-the-counter diet pills. In addition, some patients may abuse thyroid hormone in attempt to induce a hypermetabolic state and weight loss (Wark, Wallace, Wigg, & Tippett 1998). Abuse of any of these agents may result in anxiety and agitation, hypertension, and seizures in some patients, and may even precipitate strokes or intracranial hemorrhage in susceptible individuals. These drugs should never be ingested in amounts in excess of the manufacturers' recommendations, and the patient should have close medical follow-up while these drugs are being used.

## Ipecac®

While Ipecac® has undoubtedly saved lives, it has emerged as a serious drug of abuse in eating disordered patients. Huge quantities of Ipecac® may be repetitively ingested to induce vomiting. The active ingredient, emetine, has a long half-life, resulting in accumulation of large amounts of drug in the body over time. Serious skeletal muscle myopathy and cardiomyopathy can result (Ho et al., 1998; Mitchell, Pomeroy, & Huber, 1988; Palmer & Guay, 1985). Recovery may be prolonged, and fatalities due to Ipecac®-induced cardiomyopathy have been reported.

## Ongoing Medical Management

The medical clinician should have a major role in the ongoing medical management of patients with eating disorders. The physician is responsible for collaborating on treatment decisions, such as prescribing approaches to nutritional therapy, monitoring the patient's physical condition during therapy, and managing medical complications.

The medical clinician should work together with the eating disorder psychiatric specialist to determine if the patient with an eating disorder requires hospitalization. Obviously, medical emergencies such as cardiac arrhythmias, serious electrolyte disturbances, or significant gastrointestinal bleeding require admission and stabilization on a medical ward. Otherwise, the decision to hospitalize a patient for treatment of the eating disorder should be prompted by poor prognostic medical, psychiatric, or social factors. Specifically, hospitalization should be considered if an anorectic has weight loss greater than 25% to 30% of ideal body weight or a rapidly decreasing weight. Patients who are judged to be at significant risk for suicide or who have other serious comorbid psychiatric conditions, such as intractable depression, may also benefit from hospitalization. A poor social situation that will interfere with successful outpatient treatment of the eating disorder may also necessitate hospitalization. Finally, failure of intensive outpatient therapy may appropriately prompt admission to an inpatient facility.

Nutritional management is obviously a critical component of therapy for patients with eating disorders. Inclusion of the medical clinician as part of the team responsible for dietary decision is usually appropriate. Many different regimens for refeeding the anorectic patient have been successfully used. In general, nasogastric tube feeding or hyperalimentation are virtually never required and should be avoided if at all possible. An expected weight gain of 1 to 2 pounds per week is generally considered optimal. More rapid caloric replacement can result in serious medical complications, including pancreatitis, electrolyte abnormalities, and refeeding cardiomyopathy. For bulimics and patients who binge eat, reinforcement of normal eating behaviors is the goal. The medical clinician should be actively involved in reinforcing the medical need for good eating habits.

The best methods for voluntary weight loss and control remain incompletely studied and controversial (NIH Technology Assessment Conference Panel, 1992). Surgical approaches to weight reduction have been associated with significant medical risks. After jejunoileal bypass, up to 6% of patients develop gallstones, and, more importantly, liver injury occurs in about 3% of patients, with a 20% fatality rate (Andersen, 1992). As a result, this procedure has been largely supplanted by gastric bypass or gastroplasty. Liver injury and gallstones are complications of these procedures as well, albeit at a lower rate. Thus, surgical approaches should be limited to those patients with potentially life-threatening complications of obesity (such as sleep apnea) who have failed nonsurgical therapies.

Early use of "liquid protein diets" proved to have a variety of untoward consequences, especially electrolyte disturbances, cardiac arrhythmias, and sudden death. More recent formulations of very-low-calorie diets can be used safely if used as directed and with careful medical supervision (Anderson, Hamilton, & Kaplan-Brinkman, 1992; Pi-Sunyer, 1992). Nevertheless, patients must be closely monitored, especially for complications such as gallstone formation.

For many eating disordered patients, electrolyte abnormalities are the most prominent medical complication. The medical clinician should closely follow these patients to ensure adequate correction of electrolyte values. Asymptomatic hypokalemia should generally be treated with oral potassium supplementation; intravenous replacement should be reserved for hospitalized patients with very low potassium levels or symptoms attributable to hypokalemia. There are no absolute guidelines for when to institute potassium replacement; treatment decisions must be individualized based on severity of electrolyte abnormalities, chronicity, and anticipated compliance. Generally, we recommend starting oral potassium supplements when the serum potassium falls below 3.2 to 3.3 mEq/L (normal range 3.5 to 5.0 mEq/L) and considering hospitalization if potassium levels are below 2.8 to 3.0 mEq/L. It must be emphasized, however, that no level is "safe," and the level of serum potassium cannot be reliably used to predict when complications will occur in an individual patient. Unfortunately, many eating disordered patients are reluctant to comply with oral potassium replacement; careful explanation of the importance of the intervention is critical. The efficacy of potassium supplements is often attenuated by the presence of contraction metabolic alkalosis. The patient must understand that cessation of vomiting is necessary if treatment is to be successful. In the presence of severe electrolyte abnormalities, hospitalization for intravenous fluid and electrolyte management may be lifesaving.

Treatment of hypogonadism and the attendant complications of amenorrhea and osteoporosis has been inadequately studied, and conclusive recommendations cannot be made at this time. Nevertheless, osteoporosis and the risk of pathologic fractures are a major concern in most anorectic and some bulimic patients. Some authors have suggested that cyclic estrogen replacement (with or without progesterone) and/or oral calcium supplementation should be used to maintain or restore bone mineral density (Salisbury & Mitchell, 1991). Until results from controlled trials are available, the clinician will have to individualize this treatment decision. Obviously, these interventions are less desirable than treatment of the eating disorder and normalization of endocrine function by weight gain.

Frequent dental evaluation is strongly recommended for all patients who engage in recurrent vomiting (Milosevic, 1999). The use of bicarbonate rinses after vomiting may curtail enamel erosion. It remains unclear if brushing immediately after vomiting is beneficial or harmful; studies are ongoing. Consideration should be given to recommending that bulimic patients use fluoridated mouth rinses daily, that if they continue to vomit, they rinse their mouths with bicarbonate rinses shortly after vomiting, and that their dentists consider administering topical fluoride treatments. Careful dental evaluation is indicated on a frequent basis for all bulimics who engage in recurrent vomiting.

The importance of counseling patients to cease abuse of laxatives, diuretics, diet pills, and Ipecac® cannot be overemphasized. Attempts to discontinue these associated behaviors may be quite distressful to eating disordered patients, and close follow-up during these periods is important. Patients who stop laxatives after chronic use often suffer from transient constipation. Resumption of stimulant laxatives should be avoided. Use of bulk-type laxatives, increased roughage in the diet, maintenance of normal hydration, and regular exercise can be used to assist with restoration of normal bowel function. Discontinuation of diuretics may also be quite difficult for patients. Because chronic diuretic use results in secondary hyperaldosteronism, patients may develop reflex edema when they attempt to stop taking diuretics. The use of a mild sodium restriction during the first few days following discontinuation of diuretics and reassurance that the fluid balance will soon normalize can be useful.

### Interactions with Other Medical Conditions

Many medical diseases can be exacerbated by an eating disorder. Illnesses that require dietary control, such as hyperlipidemia, pancreatitis, malabsorption, or renal failure, can be very difficult to treat in patients with eating disorders. Supportive nutritional counseling by a nonjudgmental clinician or dietitian is required. The patient needs to understand that calorie restriction, binge eating, or purging behaviors create a variety of nutritional imbalances that may adversely affect the course and outcome of the underlying medical illness.

### *Diabetes Mellitus*

The patient with concurrent diabetes mellitus and an eating disorder presents a serious challenge to the clinician treating either condition (Rodin & Daneman, 1992). Whether a specific association exists between these two disorders remains controversial, but it seems reasonable to speculate that certain aspects of diabetes and its management may trigger the expression of an eating disorder in susceptible individuals. Furthermore, management of diabetes is clearly complicated by the simultaneous presence of an eating disorder.

Control of diabetes obviously requires strict dietary management. The anorectic patient may be unwilling to comply with the specified number of calories required to maintain good nutrition. Bulimic binge-purge behaviors make consistent control of glucose levels extremely difficult. Eating disordered patients may provide inaccurate reports of their dietary intake. Perhaps of most concern, patients may withhold insulin in a deliberate attempt to induce glycosuria and subsequent weight loss. Such behaviors may contribute to impaired metabolic control with the attendant risks of hypoglycemia or diabetic ketoacidosis and may accelerate the development of the long-term microvascular complications of diabetes.

The eating disorder patient with insulin-dependent diabetes requires the consistent support of a physician who understands that difficulties with body image are often exacerbated by concurrent diabetes. Both illnesses often result in a sense of lack of control, especially in adolescent patients. The endocrinologist and the eating disorder specialist must work together to ensure successful treatment for these patients.

## Pregnancy

Infertility may result from an untreated eating disorder (Stewart, 1992). Recent studies have emphasized that eating disorders should be considered as an etiology of infertility and that screening for an eating disorder may obviate the need for expensive and uncomfortable gynecologic evaluations. Bulimics, as well as anorectics, may develop infertility as a complication of their eating disorder.

Pregnancy may be quite problematic for women with eating disorders (Stewart, 1992). Discomfort with body image is often exacerbated by the physiologic changes that occur during pregnancy. This may worsen the severity of the pregnant woman's eating disorder, resulting in enhanced calorie restriction in anorectics and increased binge-purge episodes in bulimics. One study indicated that bulimic symptoms improve throughout pregnancy, but they worsen in the majority of patients after delivery (Morgan, Lacey, & Sedgwick, 1999). Women with eating disorders seem to be at significantly increased risk of developing hyperemesis gravidarium. Maternal weight gain is often inadequate in patients with a simultaneous eating disorder.

Women who have an active eating disorder at the time of conception appear to have smaller babies with lower 5-minute Apgar scores. They may also have more difficulty with breast-feeding after delivery. A variety of other complications have been anecdotally described in eating disordered pregnant women, including difficult labor, increased need for Cesarean section, and increased risk of developing pregnancy-associated hypertension.

Authorities have recommended that a dietary review and a history of eating disorders should be a part of the routine assessment of patients with infertility problems, prenatal patients with hyperemesis gravidarium, and women who fail to gain weight adequately in pregnancy or who have small babies for gestational age. For women with known eating disorders, it may be advisable to postpone pregnancy until the eating disorder is in remission. If an eating disordered woman does become preg-

Table 13.6. Routine Medical Follow-up Evaluation of Patients
with Eating Disorders

|  | Frequency | Comment |
|---|---|---|
| History and physical | 1 month– 1 year | More frequent follow-up visits to briefly assess patient progress may be indicated. |
| CBC with differential | 6 months– 1 year | More often if abnormal or bleeding is suspected |
| Electrolytes, BUN, creatinine, glucose | 3 months– 6 months | Up to weekly if abnormal |
| Thyroid function tests | 1 year | More often if receiving replacement therapy |
| Electrocardiogram | 1 year | More often if abnormal |
| Urinalysis, stool guaiac | 1 year | More often if abnormal |

*Note:* These are suggested guidelines only. Follow-up evaluations should be done more frequently if abnormalities have been identified, the patient's condition has deteriorated, or medical interventions are planned that might affect these parameters.
*Source:* Table adapted from Sharp & Freeman, 1993.

nant, careful collaboration between the obstetrician and the eating disorders specialist is advisable to ensure the best outcome for the patient and her baby.

## Medical Follow-up of Patients with Eating Disorders

Careful ongoing medical management is an essential component of the treatment plan for eating disordered patients. The medical clinician should evaluate patients with eating disorders on a regular basis. Frequency and content of medical follow-up visits must be individualized for each patient, depending on the severity and chronicity of the eating disorder, and the associated medical complications. For medically stable patients, return visits approximately every three months may be appropriate, and should include routine evaluation of history, physical, and laboratory findings (see Table 13.6). Follow-up evaluations should be done more frequently if medical complications have been identified, the patient's condition has deteriorated, or other medical interventions are planned. All health care workers who care for these patients must be aware that eating disorders pose serious medical risks and predispose to development of serious medical complications.

# References

Abdel-Rahman, E. M., & Moorthy, A. V. (1997). End-stage renal disease (ESRD) in patients with eating disorders. *Clinical Nephrology, 47,* 106–111.

Abdu, R. A., Garritano, D., & Culver, O. (1987). Acute gastric necrosis in anorexia nervosa and bulimia. *Archives of Surgery, 122,* 830–832.

Adson, D. E., Crow, S. J., & Mitchell, J. E. (1998). Spontaneous pneumothorax in anorexia nervosa. *Psychosomatics, 39,* 162–164.

Alpert, M. A., & Hashimi, M. W. (1993). Obesity and the heart. *American Journal of the Medical Sciences, 306,* 117–123.

Andersen, T. (1992). Liver and gallbladder disease before and after very-low-calorie diets. *American Journal of Clinical Nutrition, 56,* 235–239.

Anderson, J. W., Hamilton, C. C., & Kaplan-Brinkman, V. (1992). Benefits and risks of an intensive very-low-calorie diet program for severe obesity. *American Journal of Gastroenterology, 87,* 6–15.

Anderson, L., Shaw, J. M., & McCargar, L. (1997). Physiological effects of bulimia nervosa on the gastrointestinal tract. *Canadian Journal of Gastroenterology, 11,* 451–459.

Atkinson, R. L. (1991). Massive obesity: Complications and treatment. *Nutrition Reviews, 49,* 49–53.

Becker, A. E., Grinspoon, S. K., Klibanski, A., & Herzog, D. B. (1999). Eating disorders. *New England Journal of Medicine, 340,* 1092–1098.

Benotti, P. N., Bistrain, B., Benotti, J. R., Blackburn, G., & Forse, R. A. (1992). Heart disease and hypertension in severe obesity: The benefits of weight reduction. *American Journal of Clinical Nutrition, 55 (Suppl. 2),* 586–590.

Biller, B. M., Saxe, V., Herzog, D. B., Rosenthal, D. I., Holzman, S., & Klibanski, A. (1989). Mechanisms of osteoporosis in adult and adolescent women with anorexia nervosa. *Journal of Clinical Endocrinology and Metabolism, 68,* 548–554.

Blaustein, S. A., Golden, N. H., & Shenker, I. R. (1998). Addison's disease mimicking anorexia nervosa. *Clinical Pediatrics, 37,* 631–632.

Boag, F., Weerakoon, J., Ginsburg, J., Harvard, C. W., & Dandona, P. (1985). Diminished creatinine clearance in anorexia nervosa. Reversal with weight gain. *Journal of Clinical Pathology, 38,* 60–63.

Bowers, T. K., & Eckert, E. (1978). Leukopenia in anorexia nervosa: Lack of increased risk of infection. *Archives of Internal Medicine, 138,* 1520–1523.

Boyar, R. M., Hellman, L. D., Roffwarg, H. P., Katz, J., Zumoff, B., O'Connor, J., Bradlow, H. L., & Fukushima, D. K. (1977). Cortisol secretion and metabolism in anorexia nervosa. *New England Journal of Medicine, 296,* 190–193.

Carney, C. P., & Andersen, A. E. (1996). Eating disorders: Guide to medical evaluation and complications. *Psychiatric Clinics of North America, 19,* 657–679.

Comerci, G. (1990). Medical complications of anorexia nervosa and bulimia. *Medical Clinics of North American, 74,* 1293–1310.

Crisp, A. H., Callender, J. S., Halek, C., & Hsu, L. K. (1992). Long-term mortality in anorexia nervosa. *British Journal of Psychiatry, 161,* 104–107.

Cuellar, R. E., Kaye, W. H., Hsu, L. K., & Van Thiel, D. H. (1988). Upper gastrointestinal tract dysfunction in bulimia. *Digestive Diseases and Sciences, 33,* 1549–1553.

Cuellar, R. E., & Van Thiel, D. H. (1986). Gastrointestinal consequences of the eating disorders: Anorexia nervosa and bulimia. *American Journal of Gastroenterology, 81,* 1113–1124.

Curran-Celentano, J., Erdman, J. W., Nelson, R. A., & Grater, S. J. (1985). Alterations in vitamin A and thyroid hormone status in anorexia nervosa and associated disorders. *American Journal of Clinical Nutrition, 42,* 1183–1191.

Devlin, M. J., Walsh, B. T., Katz, J. L., Roose, S. P., Linkie, D. M., Wright, L., Van de Wiele, R., & Glassman, A. H. (1989). Hypothalamic-pituitary-gonadal function in anorexia nervosa and bulimia. *Psychiatric Research, 28,* 11–24.

de Zwaan, M., & Mitchell, J. E. (1992). Binge eating in the obese. *Annals of Medicine, 24,* 303–308.

Doraiswamy, P. M., Krishnan, K. R., Boyko, O. B., Husain, M. M., Figiel, G. S., Palese, V. J., Escalona, P. R., Shah, S. A., McDonald, W. M., Rockwell, W. J. K., & Ellinwood, E. H. (1991). Pituitary abnormalities in eating disorders: Further evidence from MRI studies. *Progress in Neuro-Psychopharmacology and Biological Psychiatry, 15,* 351–356.

Eckert, E. D., Pomeroy, C., Raymond, N., Kohler, P. F., Thuras, P., & Bosers, C. Y. (1998). Leptin in anorexia nervosa. *Journal of Clinical Endocrinology and Metabolism, 83,* 791–795.

Fink, S., Eckert, E., Mitchell, J., Crosby, R., & Pomeroy, C. (1996). T-Lymphocyte subsets in patients with abnormal body weight: Longitudinal studies in anorexia nervosa and obesity. *International Journal of Eating Disorders, 20,* 295–305.

Gavish, D., Eisenberg, S., Berry, E. M., Kleinman, Y., Witztum, E., Norman, J., & Leitersdorf, E. (1987). Bulimia: An underlying behavioral disorder in hyperlipidemic pancreatitis: A prospective multidisciplinary approach. *Archives of Internal Medicine, 147,* 705–708.

Geliebter, A., Melton, P. M., McCray, R. S., Gallagher, D. R., Gage, D., & Hasim, S. A. (1992). Gastric capacity, gastric emptying, and test-meal intake in normal and bulimic women. *American Journal of Clinical Nutrition, 56,* 656–661.

Gold, P. W., Gwirtsman, H., Avgerinos, P. C., Nieman, L. K., Galluci, W. T., Kaye, W., Jimerson, D., Ebert, M., Rittmaster, R., Loriaux, D. L., & Chrousos, G. P. (1986). Abnormal hypothalamic-pituitary-adrenal function in anorexia nervosa. *New England Journal of Medicine, 314,* 1335–1342.

Golden, N. H., Jacobson, M. S., Schebendach, J., Solanto, M. V., Hertz, S. M., & Shenker, I. R. (1997). Resumption of menses in anorexia nervosa. *Archives of Pediatric and Adolescent Medicine, 151,* 16–21.

Grinspoon, S., Miller, K., Coyle, C., Krempin, J., Armstrong, C., Pitts, S., Herzog, D., & Klibanski, A. (1999). Severity of osteopenia in estrogen-deficient women with anorexia nervosa and hypothalamic amenorrhea. *Journal of Clinical Endocrinology and Metabolism, 84,* 2049–2055.

Gupta, M. A., Gupta, A. K., & Haberman, H. F. (1987). Dermatologic signs in anorexia nervosa and bulimia nervosa. *Archives of Dermatology, 123,* 1386–1390.

Gwirtsman, H. E., Kaye, W. H., George, D. T., Jimerson, D. C., Ebert, M. H., & Gold, P. W. (1989). Central and peripheral ACTH and cortisol levels in anorexia nervosa and bulimia. *Archives of General Psychiatry, 46,* 61–69.

Hatzitolios, A. I., Sion, M. L., Kounanis, A. D., Toulis, E. N., Dimitriadis, A., Ioannidis, I., & Ziakas, G. N. (1997). Diffuse soft tissue emphysema as a complication of anorexia nervosa. *Postgraduate Medical Journal, 73,* 662–664.

Herholz, K., Krieg, J. C., Emrich, H. M., Pawlik, G., Beil, C., Pirke, K. M., Pahl, J. J., Wagner, R., Wienhard, K., Ploog, D., & Heiss, W. D. (1987). Regional cerebral glucose metabolism in anorexia nervosa measured by positron emission tomography. *Biological Psychiatry, 22,* 43–51.

Ho, P. C., Dweik, R., & Cohen, M. C. (1998). Rapidly reversible cardiomyopathy associated with chronic Ipecac® ingestion. *Clinical Cardiology, 21,* 780–783.

Hotta, M., Shibasaki, T., Sato, K., & Demura, H. (1998). The importance of body weight history in the occurrence and recovery of osteoporosis in patients with anorexia nervosa: Evaluation by dual X-ray absorptiometry and bone metabolic markers. *European Journal of Endocrinology, 139,* 276–283.

Howard, M. R., Leggat, H. M., & Chaudhry, S. (1992). Haematological and immunological abnormalities in eating disorders. *British Journal of Hospital Medicine, 48,* 234–239.

Hudson, J., Pope, H. G., Jonas, J. M., Laffer, P. S., Hudson, M. S., & Melby, J. C. (1983). Hypothalamic-pituitary-adrenal axis hyperactivity in bulimia. *Psychiatry, 8,* 111–117.

Isner, J. M., Roberts, W. C., Heymsfield, S. B., & Yager, J. (1985). Anorexia nervosa and sudden death. *Annals of Internal Medicine, 102,* 49–52.

Kamal, N., Chami, T., Andersen, A., Rosell, F. A., Schuster, M. M., & Whitehead, W. E. (1991). Delayed gastrointestinal transit times in anorexia nervosa and bulimia nervosa. *Gastroenterology, 101,* 1320–1324.

Kinzl, J., Biebl, W., & Herold, M. (1993). Significance of vomiting for hyperamylasemia and sialadenosis in patients with eating disorders. *International Journal of Eating Disorders, 13,* 117–124.

Kiriike, N., Nishiwaki, S., Izumiya, Y., Maeda, Y., & Kawakita, Y. (1987). Thyrotropin, prolactin, and growth hormone responses to thyrotropin-releasing hormone in anorexia nervosa and bulimia. *Biological Psychiatry, 22,* 167–176.

Kreipe, R. E., & Harris, J. P. (1992). Myocardial impairment resulting from eating disorders. *Pediatric Annals, 21,* 760–768.

Krieg, J. C., Backmund, H., & Pirke, K. M. (1987). Cranial computed tomography findings in bulimia. *Acta Psychiatrica Scandinavica, 75,* 144–149.

Krieg, J. C., Lauer, C., Leinsinger, G., Pahl, J., Schreiber, W., Pirke, K. M., & Moser, E. A. (1989). Brain morphology and regional cerebral blood flow in anorexia nervosa. *Biological Psychiatry, 25,* 1041–1048.

Krieg, J. C., Pirke, K. M., Lauer, C., & Backmund, H. (1988). Endocrine, metabolic and cranial computed tomographic findings in anorexia nervosa. *Biological Psychiatry, 23,* 377–387.

Laue, L., Gold, P. W., Richmond, A., & Chrousos, G. P. (1991). The hypothalamic-pituitary-adrenal axis in anorexia nervosa and bulimia nervosa: Pathophysiologic implications. *Advances in Pediatrics, 38,* 287–316.

Lear, S. A., Pauly, R. P., & Birmingham, C. L. (1999). Body fat, caloric intake, and plasma leptin levels in women with anorexia nervosa. *International Journal of Eating Disorders, 25,* 283–288.

Levy, A. B., Dixon, K. N., & Malarkey, W. B. (1988). Pituitary response to TRH in bulimia. *Biological Psychiatry, 23,* 476–484.

Malik, M., Stratton, J., & Sweeney, W. B. (1997). Rectal prolapse associated with bulimia nervosa: Report of seven cases. *Diseases of the Colon and Rectum, 40,* 1382–1385.

Mcgilley, B. M., & Pryor, T. L. (1998). Assessment and treatment of bulimia nervosa. *American Family Physician, 57,* 2743–2750.

Mehler, P. S., Gray, M. C., & Schulte, M. (1997). Medical complications of anorexia nervosa. *Journal of Women's Health, 6,* 533–541.

Mehler, P. S., Lezotte, D., & Eckel, R. (1998). Lipid levels in anorexia nervosa. *International Journal of Eating Disorders, 24,* 217–221.

Meyers, D. G., Starke, H., Pearson, P. H., Wilken, M. K., & Ferrell, J. R. (1987). Leaflet to left ventricular size disproportion and prolapse of a structurally normal mitral valve in anorexia nervosa. *American Journal of Cardiology, 60,* 911–914.

Milosevic, A. (1999). Eating disorders and the dentist. *British Dental Journal, 186,* 109–113.

Mitchell, J. E., & Boutacoff, L. I. (1986). Laxative abuse complicating bulimia: Medical and treatment implications. *International Journal of Eating Disorders, 5,* 325–334.

Mitchell, J. E., Hatsukami, D., Eckert, E. D., & Pyle, R. L. (1985). Characteristics of 275 patients with bulimia. *American Journal of Psychiatry, 142,* 482–485.

Mitchell, J. E., Hatsukami, D., Pyle, R. L., Eckert, E. D., & Boutacoff, L. I. (1987). Metabolic acidosis as a marker for laxative abuse in patients with bulimia. *International Journal of Eating Disorders, 6,* 557–560.

Mitchell, J. E., Pomeroy, C., & Huber, M. (1988). A clinician's guide to the eating disorders medicine cabinet. *International Journal of Eating Disorders, 7,* 211–223.

Mitchell, J. E., Pomeroy, C., Seppala, M., & Huber, M. (1988). Pseudo-Bartter's syndrome, diuretic abuse, idiopathic edema and eating disorders. *International Journal of Eating Disorders, 7,* 225–237.

Mitchell, J. E., Pyle, R. L., Eckert, E. D., Hatsukami, D., & Lentz, R. (1983). Electrolyte and other physiological abnormalities in patients with bulimia. *Psychological Medicine, 13,* 273–278.

Mitchell, J. E., Pyle, R. L., Hatsukami, D., & Boutacoff, L. I. (1984). The dexamethasone suppression test in patients with bulimia. *Journal of Clinical Psychiatry, 45,* 508–511.

Mitchell, J. E., Pyle, R. L., Hatsukami, D., & Eckert, E. (1991). Enema abuse as a clinical feature of bulimia nervosa. *Psychosomatics, 32,* 102–104.

Mitchell, J. E., Seim, H. C., Colon, E., & Pomeroy, C. (1987). Medical complications and medical management of bulimia. *Annals of Internals Medicine, 107,* 71–77.

Morgan, J. F., Lacey, J. H., & Sedgwick, P. M. (1999). Impact of pregnancy on bulimia nervosa. *British Journal of Psychiatry, 174,* 135–140.

Mortola, J. F., Rasmussen, D. D., & Yen, S. S. C. (1989). Alterations of the adrenocorticotropin-cortisol axis in normal weight bulimic women: Evidence for a central mechanism. *Journal of Clinical Endocrinology and Metabolism, 68*, 517–522.

Nagata, T., Tobitani, W., Kiriike, N., Iketani, T., & Yamagami, S. (1999). Capacity to produce cytokines during weight restoration in patients with anorexia nervosa. *Psychosomatic Medicine, 61*, 371–377.

Nakai, Y., Hamagaki, S., Takagi, R., Taniguchi, A., & Kurimoto, F. (1999). Plasma concentrations of tumor necrosis factor-alpha (TNF-alpha) and soluble TNF receptors in patients with anorexia nervosa. *Journal of Clinical and Endocrinology and Metabolism, 84*, 1226–1228.

Newman, M. M., & Halmi, K. A. (1989). Relationship of bone density to estradiol and cortisol in anorexia nervosa and bulimia. *Psychiatric Research, 29*, 105.

NIH Technology Assessment Conference Panel. (1992). Methods for voluntary weight loss and control. *Annals of Internal Medicine, 116*, 942–949.

Palmer, E. P., & Guay, A. T. (1985). Reversible myopathy secondary to abuse of Ipecac® in patients with major eating disorders. *International Journal of Eating Disorders, 7*, 211–223.

Patton, G. C. (1988). Mortality in eating disorders. *Psychological Medicine, 18*, 947–951.

Perlow, J. H., Morgan, M. A., Montgomery, D., Towers, C. V., & Porto, M. (1992). Perinatal outcome in pregnancy complicated by massive obesity. *American Journal of Obstetrics and Gynecology, 167*, 958–962.

Pirke, K. M., Fichter, M. M., Chlond, C., Schweiger, U., Laessie, R. G., Schwingenschloegel, M., & Hoehl, C. (1987). Disturbances of the menstrual cycle in bulimia nervosa. *Clinical Endocrinology, 27*, 245–251.

Pi-Sunyer, F. X. (1992). The role of very-low-calorie diets in obesity. *American Journal of Clinical Nutrition, 56*, 240–243.

Pomeroy, C., Eckert, E., Hu, S., Eiken, B., Mentink, M., Crosby, R. D., & Chao, C. C. (1994). Role of interleukin-6 and transforming growth factor-β in anorexia nervosa. *Biological Psychiatry, 36*, 836–839.

Pomeroy, C., & Mitchell, J. E. (1989). Medical complications and management of eating disorders. *Psychiatric Annals, 19*, 488–493.

Pomeroy, C., Mitchell, J., Eckert, E., Raymond, N., Crosby, R., & Dalmasso, P. (1997). Effect of body weight and caloric restriction on serum complement proteins, including Factor D/adipsin: Studies in anorexia nervosa and obesity. *Clinical and Experimental Immunology, 108*, 507–515.

Rajala, R., Partinen, M., Sane, T., Pelkonen, R., Huikuri, K., & Seppalainen, A. M. (1991). Obstructive sleep apnea syndrome in morbidly obese patients. *Journal of Internal Medicine, 230,* 125–129.

Ratnasuriya, R. H., Eisler, I., Szmukler, G. I., & Russell, G. F. (1991). Anorexia nervosa: Outcome and prognostic factors after 20 years. *British Journal of Psychiatry, 158,* 495–502.

Rich, L. M., Caine, M. R., Findling, J. W., & Shaker, J. L. (1990). Hypoglycemic coma in anorexia nervosa. *Archives of Internal Medicine, 150,* 894–895.

Rigotti, N. A., Nussbaum, S. R., Herzog, D. B., & Neer, R. M. (1984). Osteoporosis in women with anorexia nervosa. *New England Journal of Medicine, 311,* 1601–1606.

Roberts, M. W., & Li, S. H. (1987). Oral findings in anorexia nervosa and bulimia nervosa: A study of 47 cases. *Journal of the American Dental Association, 115,* 407–410.

Rodin, G. M., & Daneman, D. (1992). Eating disorders and IDDM. *Diabetes Care, 15,* 1402–1412.

Rossner, S., Lagerstrand, L., Persson, H. E., & Sachs, C. (1991). The sleep apnea syndrome in obesity: Risk of sudden death. *Journal of Internal Medicine, 230,* 135–141.

Rubinstein, I., Zamel, N., DuBarry, L., & Hoffstein, V. (1990). Airflow limitation in morbidly obese, nonsmoking men. *Annals of Internal Medicine, 112,* 828–832.

Ryan, C. F., Whittaker, J. S., & Road, J. D. (1992). Ventilatory dysfunction in severe anorexia nervosa. *Chest, 102,* 1286–1288.

Saito, S., Kita, K., Morioka, C. Y., & Watanabe, A. (1999). Rapid recovery from anorexia nervosa after a life-threatening episode with severe thrombocytopenia: Report of three cases. *International Journal of Eating Disorders, 25,* 113–118.

Salisbury, J. J., & Mitchell, J. E. (1991). Bone mineral density and anorexia nervosa in women. *American Journal of Psychiatry, 148,* 768–774.

Sharp, C. W., & Freeman, C. P. L. (1993). The medical complications of anorexia nervosa. *British Journal of Psychiatry, 162,* 452–462.

Shiffman, M. L., Sugerman, H. J., Kellum, J. M., Brewer, W. H., & Moore, E. W. (1991). Gallstone formation after rapid weight loss: A prospective study in patients undergoing gastric bypass surgery for treatment of morbid obesity. *American Journal of Gastroenterology, 86,* 1000–1005.

Simmons, M. S., Grayden, S. K., & Mitchell, J. E. (1986). The need for psychiatric-dental liaison in the treatment of bulimia. *American Journal of Psychiatry, 143,* 783–784.

Smith, R. R. L., & Spivak, J. L. (1985). Marrow cell necrosis in anorexia nervosa and involuntary starvation. *British Journal of Haematology, 60,* 525–530.

Stewart, D. E. (1992). Reproductive functions in eating disorders. *Annals of Medicine, 24,* 287–291.

Sugerman, H. J., Fairman, R. P., Sood, R. K., Engle, K., Wolfe, L., & Kellum, J. M. (1992). Long-term effects of gastric surgery for treating respiratory insufficiency of obesity. *American Journal of Clinical Nutrition, 55 (Suppl. 2),* 597–601.

Thomas, M. A., & Rebar, R. W. (1990). The endocrinology of anorexia nervosa and bulimia nervosa. *Current Opinions in Obstetrics and Gynecology, 2,* 831–836.

Wada, S., Nagase, T., Koike, Y., Kugai, N., & Nagata, N. (1992). A case of anorexia nervosa with acute renal failure induced by rhabdomyolysis: Possible involvement of hypophosphatemia or phosphate depletion. *Internal Medicine, 31,* 478–482.

Wark, H., Wallace, E. M., Wigg, S., & Tippett, C. (1998). Thyroxine abuse: An unusual case of thyrotoxicosis in pregnancy. *Australian and New Zealand Journal of Obstetrics and Gynecology, 38,* 221–223.

Wiseman, C. V., Harris, W. A., & Halmi, K. A. (1998). Eating disorders. *Medical Clinics of North America, 82,* 145–159.

Worobetz, L. J., Inglis, F. G., & Shaffer, E. A. (1993). The effect of ursodeoxycholic acid therapy on gallstone formation in the morbidly obese during rapid weight loss. *American Journal of Gastroenterology, 88,* 1705–1710.

# Contributors

**David W. Abbott,** M.D., is assistant professor and director of the Psychiatry Residency Training Program of the Department of Neuroscience, University of North Dakota School of Medicine and Health Sciences. He received his M.D. degree from Tulane University and completed his psychiatry residency training at Tulane and at the University of Minnesota. He is the former director of the Fargo Clinic/MeritCare Inpatient and Outpatient Eating Disorders Programs, and his clinical practice has focused on eating disorders for more than 12 years.

**Roslyn B. Binford** is a doctoral student in the clinical science and psychopathology research training program at the University of Minnesota and research assistant at the university's Eating Disorders Research Program. She has provided individual and group psychotherapy to patients with eating disorders at an eating disorders treatment facility in St. Paul, Minnesota.

**Carol Brunzell,** R.D., C.D.E., is a certified diabetes educator with 13 years of experience as a clinical dietitian in both inpatient and outpatient settings at Fairview-University Medical Center in Minneapolis. She has authored numerous publications and given many presentations on eating disorders, diabetes, and cystic fibrosis–related diabetes.

**Scott Crow,** M.D., is associate professor of psychiatry at the University of Minnesota. He is director of the Clinical Populations/Assessment Subcore of the Minnesota Obesity Center and president-elect of the Minnesota Psychiatric Society. His research interests include the treatment, course, and complications of obesity and eating disorders.

**Martina de Zwaan,** M.D., is associate professor in the Department of General Psychiatry at the University Hospital of Vienna, Austria, where she works as a psychiatrist and psychotherapist. She is director of the Eating Disorders Clinic there and conducts research on the treatment, neurobiology, and epidemiology of eating disorders. She teaches psychiatry to medical students and is involved in behavior therapy training for psychologists and physicians.

**Mary Hendrickson-Nelson,** M.S., R.D., L.D., received a B.S. in nutrition and dietetics from the University of Minnesota and an M.S. in nutrition science from Colorado State University. She has provided counseling to patients with anorexia nervosa, bulimia nervosa, and binge eating disorders on an inpatient and outpatient basis during the past 10 years. She is currently working with clients with eating disorders individually and in psychoeducational groups at HealthPartners of Minnesota. She is coauthor of *Healthy Eating Manual–2.1.*

**Susan Jack,** Ph.D., is an individual and family therapist in the Adult Psychiatry Clinic at Fairview-University Medical Center in Minneapolis. She has worked as a clinician in the University of Minnesota's Department of Psychiatry for 20 years, and she received her doctorate in family social science from the University of Minnesota in 1999.

**Pamela K. Keel,** Ph.D., is assistant professor in the Department of Psychology at Harvard University. She conducts research on eating disorders and teaches abnormal psychology, professional ethics, and an eating disorders seminar. She also treats patients in the eating disorders unit of Massachusetts General Hospital in Boston. She completed her Ph.D. in clinical psychology at the University of Minnesota and her clinical psychology internship at Duke University Medical Center.

**James E. Mitchell,** M.D., is currently professor and chair of the Department of Neuroscience at the University of North Dakota School of Medicine and Health Sciences, and president of the Neuropsychiatric Research Institute. He is an active clinician and researcher in the area of eating disorders; his work has focused on the development of treatments for various forms of eating disorders. He has published extensively in the scientific literature and is past president of the Eating Disorders Research Society, past president of the Academy of Eating Disorders, and a member of the editorial board of the *International Journal of Eating Disorders* and the *Eating Disorders Newsletter.*

**Melissa Pederson Mussell** is assistant professor at the University of St. Thomas in Minnesota. She received her Ph.D. from the University of Minnesota and has worked for a number of years with the Eating Disorders Research Program at the university. She maintains a private practice specializing in helping individuals overcome eating disorders. She recently received the Young Investigator Award from the Eating Disorders Research Society.

**Carol B. Peterson**, Ph.D., is a senior research scientist in the Eating Disorders Research Program at the University of Minnesota. She also has a part-time private practice. Her research and clinical work have focused on the assessment, diagnosis, and treatment of eating disorders. She received her Ph.D. in clinical psychology from the University of Minnesota.

**Claire Pomeroy,** M.D., is professor and chief of infectious diseases in the Department of Internal Medicine at the University of Kentucky. She also serves as associate dean for research and informatics and associate chief of staff for the College of Medicine. Her research interests have focused on host immune function in infectious and nutritional diseases, including alterations observed in patients with anorexia nervosa. She has published extensively on medical complications due to eating disorders.

**LeAnn Snow** has an M.D. degree from the University of Minnesota with a specialization in physical medicine and rehabilitation. She has taught in the Department of Physical Medicine and Rehabilitation at the University of Minnesota. She is a Ph.D. candidate in exercise physiology and kinesiology at the university and is currently in private practice.

**Stephen A. Wonderlich**, Ph.D., is professor and associate chairman in the Department of Neuroscience at the University of North Dakota School of Medicine and Health Sciences. He is also codirector of the Eating Disorder Institute in Fargo, North Dakota. He has published extensively in the areas of psychiatric comorbidity and eating disorders, the effects of childhood maltreatment on psychopathology, and treatment approaches for personality disorders and eating disorders. He serves on the board of directors of the Eating Disorders Research Society and is a past president of the Academy for Eating Disorders.

# Index

by Celeste Newbrough